Plantations by Land and Sea

Archipelagic Studies

Series Editors

Peter Lang
Oxford · Bern · Berlin · Bruxelles · New York · Wien

Plantations by Land and Sea

North Channel Communities of the Atlantic Archipelago c.1550-1625

Alison Cathcart

Peter Lang
Oxford · Bern · Berlin · Bruxelles · New York · Wien

Bibliographic information published by Die Deutsche Nationalbibliothek
Die Deutsche Nationalbibliothek lists this publication in the Deutsche Nationalbibliografie; detailed bibliographic data is available on the Internet at http://dnb.d-nb.de.

A catalogue record for this book is available from the British Library.

Library of Congress Cataloging-in-Publication Data

Names: Cathcart, Alison, author.
Title: Plantations by land and sea : North Channel communities of the Atlantic Archipelago c.1550-1625 / Alison Cathcart.
Description: Oxford ; New York : Peter Lang, 2022. | Series: Archipelagic studies, 2732-5253 ; Volume 1 | Includes bibliographical references and index.
Identifiers: LCCN 2021028762 (print) | LCCN 2021028763 (ebook) | ISBN 9781789973785 (paperback) | ISBN 9781789973792 (ebook) | ISBN 9781789973808 (epub)
Subjects: LCSH: Plantations--Northern Ireland and Ireland--Ulster--History. | Plantations--Scotland--History. | North Channel (Northern Ireland and Scotland)--History.
Classification: LCC HD1471.I732 U56 2022 (print) | LCC HD1471.I732 (ebook) | DDC 306.3/49--dc23
LC record available at https://lccn.loc.gov/2021028762
LC ebook record available at https://lccn.loc.gov/2021028763

Cover Image: The Plotte of Irelande with the Confines (1610). © The National Archives, MPF1/67.
Cover design by Brian Melville for Peter Lang.

ISSN 2732-5253
ISBN 978-1-78997-378-5 (print)
ISBN 978-1-78997-379-2 (ePDF)
ISBN 978-1-78997-380-8 (ePub)

Published by Peter Lang Ltd, International Academic Publishers,
52 St Giles, Oxford, OX1 3LU, United Kingdom
oxford@peterlang.com, www.peterlang.com

This publication has been peer reviewed.

Contents

Illustrations

Maps

Acknowledgements

Arts and
Humanities
Research Council

Given the length of time it has taken to complete this book, it is perhaps unsurprising that I have accumulated a significant debt of gratitude to various individuals, institutions and funding bodies. The majority of this research was facilitated by an AHRC Research Grant (Early Career) Scheme AH/H009043/1: 2010–12, 'Living on the Edge?: plantation and politics in the north Atlantic archipelago, 1493–1637' and my sincere thanks to the AHRC for this funding. Without it, the collaboration between myself and my former post-doctoral fellow, Dr Aonghas MacCoinnich (now at the University of Glasgow), would not have come to fruition, and I am enormously grateful to Aonghas for his detailed knowledge of archives and libraries, an endless supply of references, constant conversations about research, his encouragement of my efforts to grapple with Gaelic and his companionship on this project. His own monograph resulting from this project came out a number of years ago (*Plantation and Civility in the North Atlantic World. The Case of the Northern Hebrides, 1570–1639* (Brill, Leiden, 2015)) and I hope this book, my own contribution, can somehow begin to measure to up to his scholarship. Above all, I am grateful for the years of research collaboration and personal friendship. As well as UKRI I want to acknowledge the financial support provided by the Carnegie Trust for the Universities of Scotland. In 2008 their funding facilitated research into the Campbells and enabled me to spend time in Inveraray Castle Archives and Argyll and Bute Council archives in Lochgilphead; this was supplemented by additional financial assistance from the Society of Antiquaries of Scotland. I was aided in this by Linda Fryer and am grateful to her for many conversations about the Campbells. A fellowship at the Huntington Library and Art Gallery, San Marino, California, enabled me to devote time to consulting the Hastings Papers and the fabulous Ellesmere Bridgewater Collection and also to spend time in an environment that encourages research, reflection and thinking. I well remember a quiet Saturday morning in the Ahmanson reading room that fundamentally changed the direction of my research and shaped my thinking. I am grateful also for the friendship and collegiality of staff and other fellows who were always ready to discuss research (and music). Another fellowship at the Huntington in 2016, along with a Carnegie Trust Research Incentive Grant that allowed me to spend three weeks in the archives Manx National Heritage, Douglas, Isle of Man, provided the foundation of my next monograph, but this research has offered further context for these North Channel communities. The time I was able to spend in these archives was facilitated by periods of leave supported by the School of Humanities, University of Strathclyde, who also financially supported other smaller research trips. In addition, I am most grateful to the Curran Library at Strathclyde for their acquisition of various collections, but especially parts I and II of State Papers Online, published by Gale: Cengage Company. This resource has been invaluable for my work and I am also grateful to the National Library of Scotland for enabling readers to access parts I to IV via their reading rooms both at George IV bridge and Kelvin Hall. I am grateful too to the Strathmartine Trust who generously funded the illustrations for this book, but previously supported publication of an edited volume, a special volume of *Journal of the North Atlantic*, which was also an outcome of the AHRC project. All of this funding has enabled me to spend considerable time in various archives and libraries both across the archipelago and elsewhere. My thanks especially to the patience and advice of staff at Argyll and Bute Council Archives, British Library, Dumfries and Galloway Archives, National Library of Ireland, National Library of Scotland, National Maritime Museum, National Records of Scotland, Public Records of Northern Ireland, The National Archives and the archives at Trinity College Dublin. My thanks especially to the Factor and staff at Inveraray Castle Archives who allowed me access to the material before an archivist was appointed; and also to Wendy Thirkettle at Manx National Heritage for allowing me to rely so much on her knowledge of the fantastic material there. Thanks to Mary Robertson and Vanessa Wilkie, respectively former and current William A. Moffat Curator of Medieval Manuscripts and British History at the Huntington, for their generous assistance with the collections there.

I am also indebted to the professional scholarship and personal friendship of many in the fields of Scottish, Irish and British history and archaeology many of whom I am fortunate enough to consider friends and whose work has been invaluable for my own. Indeed, I am fully aware that I stand, albeit rather shakily, on the shoulders of giants and recognise the benefit of a wider collegial network of scholars without which the process of researching and writing this book would have been much less enjoyable, while the book itself much less rich. It would take far too long to list them but I am grateful to them all for their time and sharing ideas so willingly. It would be wrong of me, however, not to mention Aonghas MacConnich, Allan Macinnes, Martin MacGregor, David Caldwell, Roger Mason, Catriona MacDonald and Michael Brown. I have had the joy of teaching the plantations to a number of fourth year special subject students, both at the University of Strathclyde and now also at the University of Stirling, and I have appreciated their engagement with and response to the material and questions I posed. Most especially I must mention Alan Kelly, Lauren McDougall and Vivien Wilsdon, members of my 2016–17 cohort, who pushed me on terminology and forced me to define more clearly what I meant. Above all, I have been privileged to supervise a number of PhD and Masters students. Conversations about and engagement with their research over the years has been a constant stimulation. My own ideas have been shaped by them and I am grateful to them all, past and current: Elizabeth Koprowski, James Mitchell, Charles Haggerty, Peter Jones, Philip Braat, David Wilson, Lesley Riddoch, Laura Moffat, Rowena Hutton, Lauren McDougall, Ian MacLellan and Scott Carballo. Thanks also to Neil McIntyre, while I did not supervise his work, he formed a core part of a postgraduate community at Strathclyde and it has been a pleasure to work with him on another project. I owe David Wilson so much, not just for producing the maps for this book, but for conversations about piracy and customary law of the sea, for covering my teaching while I was swamped with administrative matters (and thus learning more about Ireland than he ever cared too), and for any number of conversations about music. Of my former colleagues at Strathclyde I am grateful to the wonderful CST especially Mo McDonald, Ann Bartlett and Mark Law (now at University of Glasgow); meanwhile the friendship of Churnjeet Mahn and David Wilson has made my life all the richer. My new colleagues in the Division of History, Heritage and Politics at Stirling have been so welcoming and a joy to work with. I am incredibly fortunate to have joined them and I am most grateful these past eighteen months for their support and encouragement. I am also thankful for the assistance of Phil Dunshea and especially Lucy Melville at Peter Lang for her patience in seeing this through to the very end. The input of all these individuals has enriched my own work, while any remaining errors and weaknesses, and I am sure there are many, are my own.

The process of researching and writing this book was impacted by a period of significant mental and physical ill-health. I am grateful to UKRI for their understanding and patience regarding the delay but also to a number of colleagues who supported me during this time. Aonghas MacCoinnich stepped in to cover my teaching at the time while no doubt all of my colleagues in History at Strathclyde carried some of the burden. Above all, I am forever indebted to the then Head of School, Dr David Goldie, English Studies, who regularly took time to encourage me, refused to accept any attempt on my part to resign and supported me through a particularly grim period as I transitioned back to full-time work. The ongoing support and friendship of Catriona MacDonald, Allan Macinnes and Roger Mason during this time was also fundamental to my recovery. Without them, I would not have stayed in academia and this book would not have been written. Outside of academia and funding bodies, I am continually upheld by my own wider kin network on either side of the Channel who put up with prolonged absences and silences yet always have a bed ready or a back door open. In particular, my thanks to Dave McCarthy who, I do not know how, tolerates this extreme introvert and my constant need for solitude, while sustaining and encouraging me even through the very darkest of days.

Abbreviations

APS	*Acts of the Parliament of Scotland,* eds, T. Thomson and C. Innes, 12 vols (Edinburgh, 1814–75)
BL	British Library
CCM	*Calendar of the Carew Manuscripts, preserved in the Archiepiscopal Library at Lambeth, 1515–1624,* eds, J. S. Brewer and William Bullen, 6 vols (London, 1867–73)
CSP Ireland	*Calendar of State Papers Relating to Ireland of the Reigns of Henry VIII, Edward VI, Mary and Elizabeth,* eds, H. C. Hamilton et al., 11 vols (London, 1860–1912)
CSP Scotland	*Calendar of State Papers Relating to Scotland and Mary, Queen of Scots, 1547–1603*, eds, J. Bain et al., 13 vols (Edinburgh, 1898–1969)
ER	*The Exchequer Rolls of Scotland 1264–1600: Rotuli Scaccarii Regum Scotorum 1264–1600*, eds, George Burnett and John Stuart, 23 vols (Edinburgh, 1878–1908)
HL	Huntington Library
ICA	Inveraray Castle Archives
L&P Henry VIII	*Letters and Papers, Foreign and Domestic, of the Reign of Henry VIII,* eds, J. S. Brewer et al., 21 vols (London, 1862–1910, 1929–32)
LPL	Lambeth Palace Library
MNH	Manx National Heritage
NLI	National Library of Ireland
NLS	National Library of Scotland

NMM	National Maritime Museum
ODNB	*Oxford Dictionary of National Biography* (Oxford, 2004; online edition 2008–14), <www.oxforddnb.com/>
PRONI	Public Record Office of Northern Ireland
RMS	*Registrum Magni Sigilli Regum Scotorum / The Register of the Great Seal of Scotland, A.D. 1306–1688,* eds, J. M. Thomson et al., 11 vols (Edinburgh, 1882–1914)
RPCS	*Register of the Privy Council of Scotland, 1545–1625*, eds, R. K. Hannay and John Hill Burton, 14 vols (1877–98)
RPS	K. M. Brown et al., eds, *Records of the Parliament of Scotland to 1707* (St Andrews, 2007–09), <www.rps.ac.uk>
RSS	*Registrum Secreti Sigilli Regum Scotorum / The Register of the Privy Seal of Scotland, 1488–1580*, eds, M. Livingstone et al., 8 vols (Edinburgh, 1908–66)
SP	State Papers Online, 1509–1714: Part II: The Tudors: Henry VIII to Elizabeth I, 1509–1603: State Papers Foreign: Ireland, Scotland, Borders and Registers of the Privy Council. The National Archives of the UK from *State Papers Online* available via Gale: A Cengage Company
TA	*Accounts of the Lord High Treasurer of Scotland, 1473–1580: Compota Thesaurariorum Regus Scotorum*, eds, T. Dickson, J. B. Paul, and C. T. Innes, 13 vols (Edinburgh, 1877–1978)
TCD	Trinity College Dublin
TNA	The National Archives

CHAPTER 1

Setting the scene

Introduction

On 27 May 1597 a case came before the Privy Council in Edinburgh concerning an incident which had taken place over a decade earlier in September 1584. Gilbert Thomson, a burgess of Ayr, along with his nephew David Reid and 'ane gentilman of Irland' had 'ladened a boat of his with wines, salt and other merchandise, at the haven of Air intending to transport the same to the Isle of Lochfeule in Irland, and there to sell the same'. The journey did not go as planned. According to Thomson, 'a grite storme and tempest' arose whereby they were 'drevin in to the ile of Rachrie, pertening to Angus McConeill of Dunnyveg'. Upon their arrival 'ane grite noumer of people within that cuntrey, being all men and servandis to the said Angus ... patt violent hands' on Thomson and his party. The 'gentilman of Irland, quha ... sould have bene his convoy to the said Ile in Irland', and Thomson's nephew Reid, were stripped and 'cruellie and barbarouslie slew', with Thomson himself only saved from the same fate by 'ane gentilman of that cuntrey, quha knew him, [and] relevit him'. While they spared his life, the islanders 'violentlie intromettit' with the boat and its merchandise, leaving Thomson 'destitute'. Bereft of clothes and money Thomson 'repaired to the residence of the said Angus and complained to him of the said slaughter and spuilyie committed by his men'. In response, Angus promised to make restitution of Thomson's boat and goods, and to punish any of his own servants that had been involved in this crime. MacDonald, however, failed to follow through with these assurances and, some thirteen years later, Thomson was forced to take alternative measures in order to gain compensation. In his statement to the Privy Council he argued that by these 'oppressionis and wrangis' he was 'ulluterlie wrackit and herreit, having nothing now quhairupoun to sustene him' and, 'being past the age of lxxx yeiris, unable to travel for his leving'. The Privy Council called both parties to appear to hear the case in full and allow MacDonald the opportunity to answer the allegations made against him. While Thomson appeared in person, MacDonald failed to do likewise and was 'denounced rebel'.[1]

At first glance there seems little that is remarkable or notable about this attack by the inhabitants of Rathlin Island on a ship with a full cargo and its crew. The Privy Council of Scotland had every right to hear and deal with the case; it was a domestic issue involving two subjects of the Scottish crown.[2] The defendant, Angus MacDonald of Dunivaig, was an important Highland clan chief whose estate lay primarily in Islay and Kintyre in the southwest of Scotland; while the complainant was Gilbert Thomson, burgess of the thriving burgh of Ayr, one of the main ports on the southwest coast of Scotland. This was but one of a number of similar cases brought before the Privy Council relating to attacks on shipping, the theft of cargo and the injury, if not murder, of crew-members. Such incidents of maritime violence were common in the waters off the west coast of Scotland where island and coastal communities existed, survived and thrived on account of their maritime strength. This was especially true of the waters of the North Channel which saw frequent traffic between Scotland and Ireland. While little else is known about Thomson, we do know much more

1 For all quotations in this paragraph see *RPCS*, V, 393.

2 Cases involving parties from different countries were more complicated and protracted affairs. See, for example, the case concerning William Ocarmyke and William Arnold, both Scots, and their ship 'callyd the goddes gr[ac]e if the Towne of Ayre' carrying a cargo of 'xiiii tonnes and on[e] hogeshedd of Rochell wyne fyve tonnes of yron and other gooddes and m[er]chantdice to the value of' £600 sterling in late January 1563. They were attacked in 'the haven of Carlingford' by 'Fferdoro[u]gh McGynysse and his men under the rule of Oneill'. Shane O'Neill refused to make restitution until he was compensated for the losses he claimed he had sustained at the hands of James MacDonald but was unable to present his case to Mary, Queen of Scots, because his letters were intercepted by the English, obviously fearful of O'Neill's activities (see below pp. 76–9, 101–8). Carmyke and Arnold and their 'pore wyves and childern', unable to get redress, were 'dryven utt[er]ly to begge'. SP 63/10, fols 72, 74, 147; *CSP Ireland*, I, 236, no.66.

about Angus MacDonald of Dunivaig, and this opportunistic attack, despite resulting in the death of the Irish pilot as well as loss of goods, could easily be dismissed as a piratical endeavour by the lawless and disobedient MacDonalds.[3] Although it had clear ramifications for both individuals (loss of livelihood for Thomson and MacDonald put to the horn) in the bigger picture this event is barely a footnote in history. However, a closer consideration raises a number of questions, interpretations and historiographical issues that this book seeks to explore.

At the time of the attack, Gilbert Thomson from Ayr had been taking his cargo to Derry, the 'isle of Lochfeule' [Lough Foyle], to sell.[4] Thomson was one of a growing number of Lowland Scots including fishermen and merchants who operated in the waters between Ireland and Scotland. While it is difficult to ascertain the intensity of fishing in this region during the sixteenth century, evidence from the late seventeenth century gives a strong indication of the number of boats involved and the distances they travelled to both fish and trade.[5] The scale of activity would have been increasing

3 Pilots were often hired to guide merchants to the Isles or to Ireland. In this case Thomson was using an Irish pilot to navigate the voyage to Lough Foyle. For further examples of the hiring of pilots to navigate the waters of the Western Isles see *Kirkcudbright Town Council Records 1576–1604*, trans., M. B. Johnston and C. M. Armet at the instance of John, Marquis of Bute (Edinburgh, 1939), 116, 118. For more on the relationship of the MacDonalds with crown and government at this time, see pp. 232–5 below.

4 Before land reclamation efforts that came later Derry was virtually surrounded by water and often referred to at this time as an island.

5 This was the focus of a short-term 'Bridging the Gap' collaborative research project 'What's the catch? The environmental history of the north Minch fishery' involving Dr Aonghas MacCoinnich, now University of Glasgow, and Dr Dougie C. Speirs and Professor Mike Heath from the Department of Mathematics and Statistics at the University of Strathclyde. I am grateful to the University of Strathclyde for funding this study. See also Colin Breen, 'Marine Fisheries and Society in Medieval Ireland', in J. H. Barrett and D. C. Oton, eds, *Cod and Herring. The Archaeology and History of Medieval Sea Fishing* (Oxford, 2016), 91–8; Martin Rourke, 'The Scottish Herring Trade, 1470–1600', *Scottish Historical Review*, 84 (2005), 149–65; Aonghas MacCoinnich, 'The Maritime Dimension to Scotland's 'Highland Problem', ca.1540–1630', *Maritime Communities of the North Atlantic Arc in the Early Modern Period: Journal of the North Atlantic*, ed., Alison Cathcart, special volume 12 (2019), 44–72.

due to developing markets in Ireland despite the possibility of opportunistic attacks on ships laden with cargo, common on account of the wider unrest in the region.[6] The surviving port books from Ireland exist only for a few years in the early seventeenth century and give no indication of the level of trade across the North Channel during the latter decades of the sixteenth century (see Map 1). Nonetheless, burgh records from towns like Ayr, Wigton and Kirkcudbright on the southwest coast of Scotland highlight the activity of individuals trading with Ireland, the western Isles and the Isle of Man alongside occasional reference to journeys further south to Wexford, Waterford and Brittany.[7] This is supported by rental and custom accounts from the Isle of Man which suggest something of the activity of Scots who regularly traded there.[8]

6 J. C. Appleby, 'A Nursery of Pirates: The English Pirate Community in Ireland in the Early Seventeenth Century', *International Journal of Maritime History* II/1 (1990), 1–27; J. C. Appleby, 'The Problem of Piracy in Ireland, 1570–1630', in Claire Jowitt, ed., *Pirates? The Politics of Plunder 1550–1650* (Basingstoke, 2007), 41–55; David Ditchburn, 'Piracy and War at Sea in Late Medieval Scotland', in T. C. Smout, ed., *Scotland and the Sea* (Edinburgh, 1992), 35–58; Timothy O'Neill, *Merchants and Mariners in Medieval Ireland* (Dublin, 1987), 119–29; Keith Pluymers, "Pirates' and the Problems of Plantation in Seventeenth-Century Ireland', in Peter C. Mancall and Carole Shammas, eds, *Governing the Sea in the Early Modern Era: Essays in Honor of Robert C. Ritchie* (San Marino, 2015), 79–108. For a broader overview of the development of piracy within the waters around the archipelago see N. A. M. Rodger, *The Safeguard of the Sea. A Naval History of Britain, 660–1649* (London, 2004), 149–50, 179, 188, 190–203.

7 *Kirkcudbright Town Council Records*, 1, 118, 155–7, 167, 311, 339, 341, 371, 375, 380, 389, 410; Ross MacKenzie, *Ayr's Export Trade at the End of the 16th Century* (Ayrshire Archaeological and Natural History Society, 1988).

8 For some indication of the extent of trading activity, albeit small scale, occurring during the late sixteenth century see MNH, MS 10058; Accounts of the Water Bailiff, Ingates and Outgates 1579–1610 where there is a wealth of evidence regarding trade with the Isle of Man. The Custom Books point to the number of Scots and Irishmen who appear regularly in the Manx records engaged in trade mostly in oats, wheat and barley, hides, lamb fells, herring, household stuff and agricultural tools. The presence of Scots in the Isle of Man in the late sixteenth and early seventeenth centuries is corroborated by the regular mention of Scotsmen in court records also: see MNH MS 10071: Judicial records. See also *Kirkcudbright Town Council Records*, 371, 375, 380; *Kirkcudbright Town Council Records 1606–1658*, vol.

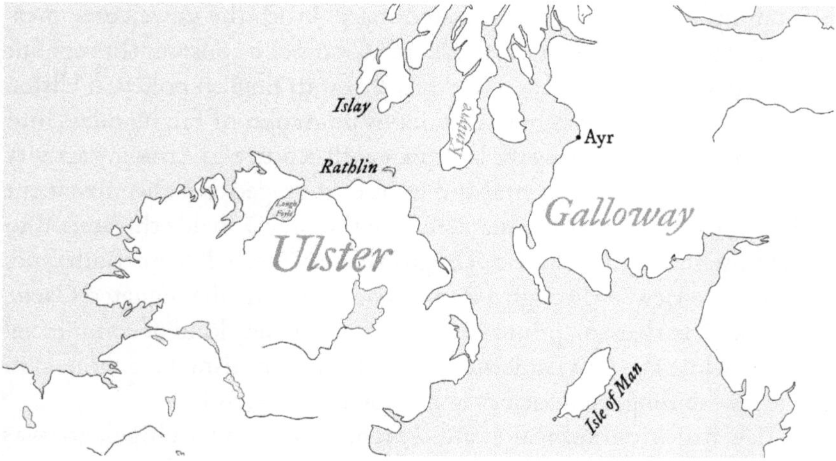

Map 1. North Channel region

This trade between Ireland and Scotland on the part of men like Thomson was crucial for the survival of the English forces in Ireland. Throughout the sixteenth century, the English faced a constant pressure to provide victuals for its forces in Ireland and, more specifically in relation to Ulster, for its garrisons at Carrickfergus and, from the turn of the seventeenth century, also at Derry. While ships regularly brought supplies from London, Chester, or Liverpool, often they were delayed or, at times, ruined by the time they reached their destination.[9] Scottish merchants who traded across the North Channel found ready markets for the raw materials Scots exported. These merchants were the acceptable type of Scot, Lowlanders engaged in commercial activity whose endeavours facilitated and supported the English forces in Ireland and, later in the sixteenth century, who afforded a lifeline to the English garrison at Derry and the developing

I, trans., John, IV Marquis of Bute and C. M. Armet (Edinburgh and London, 1958), xvi, 83.

9 For further development of the obstacles the English faced in supplying their forces in Ireland see ch.5 and Alison Cathcart, 'The Maritime Dimension to Plantation in Ulster, *c.*1550–*c.*1600', *Maritime Communities of the North Atlantic,* ed., Cathcart, 95–111.

plantations in Ulster. This contrasted sharply with the unwelcome presence of the Highland Scots in the North Channel, a constant throughout the century and regarded as a very real threat to English policy in Ulster, especially the temporary but continuous migration of Highlanders into Ulster to fight there during the later sixteenth century. The trading activity of men like Thomson was vital and to be encouraged, but the movement and military activity of Highlanders like the MacDonalds threatened to de-stabilise and ultimately de-rail English endeavours in Ireland. Both types of Scot were viewed through a Renaissance lens, one that equated Gaelic society with barbarism, primitivism, and without any kind of commercial activity; while the Lowlanders engaged in mercantilism were more akin to the law-abiding, civil society of Elizabethan England.

This historiographical trend which, within the archipelago, was clearly articulated by Giraldus Cambrensis in the twelfth century, was sustained with Renaissance ideals of civil society, and further perpetuated by a Whiggish reading of the past by historians such as Patrick Fraser Tytler.[10] Consequently, Gaelic society in Ireland and Scotland during the late medieval and early modern period often has been regarded as a sideshow to mainstream political development.[11] This is a rather short-sighted perspective.[12] Time and again, events and developments in the west have

10 There is a significant body of literature on concepts of civility and 'wild' or barbarous peoples. Such ideas can be traced back to Aristotle, Plato, Hippocrates, Galen and Ptolomy.

11 P. F. Tytler, *History of Scotland*, 9 vols (Edinburgh, 1828–43). For a broader historiographical overview see Alison Cathcart, *Kinship and Clientage: Highland Clanship 1451–1609* (Leiden, 2006), 1–7; Richard D. Oram, 'A Celtic Dirk at Scotland's Back? The Lordship of the Isles in Mainstream Scottish Historiography since 1828', in Richard D. Oram, ed., *The Lordship of the Isles* (Leiden, 2014), 1–39.

12 Ciaran Brady, 'East Ulster, the MacDonalds and the Provincial Strategies of Hugh O'Neill, Earl of Tyrone, 1585–1603', in William P. Kelly and John R. Young, eds, *Scotland and the Ulster Plantations. Explorations in the British Settlements of Stuart Ireland* (Dublin, 2009), 45; see also the concluding arguments of Jane H. Ohlmeyer, *Civil War and Restoration in the Three Stuart Kingdoms. The Career of Randal MacDonnell, Marquis of Antrim* (Cambridge, 1993; reprinted Dublin, 2001), 278–89 and especially 289 where she argues that 'historians ignore men from the periphery at their peril'.

forced monarchs at both Edinburgh and London to pay attention to its outlying, 'peripheral' regions.[13] During the period under discussion, both Tudor and Stuart monarchies preferred to focus on continental affairs and Anglo-Scottish relations, but repeatedly it was demanded of them that they consider the place of their respective Gaelic subjects. For both royal houses, however, the 'periphery' of the Gaelic north and west fell far down the agenda further compounding their inability to effectively counter the Highlanders' cross-(North) channel activity. In part a result of their reluctance to acknowledge the maritime superiority of the Highland Scots, the English struggled to command the waters of the North Channel because of the ever-changing and increasingly complex political situation in the communities that existed around the edges of those waters. Indeed, because Ireland and Gaelic Scotland were viewed as 'peripheral', the English failed to realise the centrality of the North Channel, a body of water where territorial, political, economic, social, cultural, linguistic and confessional boundaries met, crossed and conflicted, and its place at the very apex of the British and Irish archipelago.

The North Channel forms part of a waterway that stretches from Scandinavia to the continent. From the ninth to the eleventh centuries the Vikings had dominated these waters and the Irish Sea had been central to the establishment and maintenance of Norse power in the western Isles, Ireland and Man.[14] From the late eleventh through to the mid-thirteenth century Man and the Isles had been a separate kingdom ruled by successive Manx kings.[15] It was a kingdom connected by the sea, not just to its immediate neighbours of Scotland and Ireland, but also to Orkney,

13 This has been argued for the fourteenth and fifteenth centuries also by Simon Egan, 'The Resurgence of Gaelic Power in Ireland and Scotland and Its Wider Impact, *c.*1350–1513' (University College Cork, PhD, 2016).

14 The Viking Age is commonly regarded as roughly 800–1079. See A. D. M. Forte, Richard D. Oram and Frederik Pedersen, *Viking Empires* (Cambridge, 2005). It ought to be acknowledged that the important history of the Irish Sea dates much earlier than the Viking period.

15 Although often referred to as Scandinavian or Viking, these are rather unhelpful designations when considering the other external influences Man was open to, including Gaelic and European. See R. Andrew McDonald, 'The Manx Sea Kings and the Western Ocean: The Late Norse Isle of Man in Its North Atlantic Context,

Shetland, and Norway to the north and Cumberland, Solway, Wales and Brittany to the south.[16] Following the formal secession from Norwegian jurisdiction to that of the Scottish crown in the 1267 Treaty of Perth, the western Isles underwent something of a reorientation and, rather than continue to look exclusively westwards to a maritime sea world of which the Isles formed a fundamental part, increasingly also they looked east to the Scottish kingdom of which the Isles were now a part. This resulted in the gradual but deliberate integration of the indigenous elite of the Isles into the Scottish political community.[17] Nonetheless, a Norse maritime influence remained strong in the region.

In earlier centuries the waters of the west coast of Scotland may well have been a Viking sea-road and the means by which the kingdom of Man and the Isles was governed, but by the turn of the sixteenth century, these waters were less well known to the political rulers of the insular world. The main arena for English and Scottish maritime activity lay in the east, through the North Sea and the Narrow Seas (now known as the English Channel).[18] This was the result of a number of factors. For some time the

---

1079–1265', in Benjamin Hudson, ed., *Studies in the Medieval Atlantic* (New York, 2012), 149, 151.

16 McDonald, 'The Manx Sea Kings', 145–6; E. G. Bowen, 'Britain and the British Seas', in D. Moore, ed., *The Irish Sea Province in Archaeology and History* (Cardiff, 1970), 24–8; E. G. Bowen, *Saints Seaways and Settlements in the Celtic Lands* (Cardiff, 1977), 7–8. This maritime highway carried the Vikings as far south as Normandy, see: Élisabeth Ridel, 'From Scotland to Normandy: The Celtic Sea Route of the Vikings', in Beverley Ballin Smith, Simon Taylor and Gareth Williams, eds, *West over Sea: Studies in Scandinavian Sea-Borne Expansion and Settlement before 1300: A Festschrift in Honour of Dr Barbara E. Crawford* (Leiden, 2007), 81–94.

17 R. Andrew McDonald, 'Matrimonial Politics and Core-Periphery Interactions in the Twelfth- and Early Thirteenth-Century Scotland', *Journal of Medieval History* 21/3 (1995), 227–47; Richard D. Oram and W. Paul Adderley, 'Innse Gall: Culture and Environment on a Norse Frontier in the Scottish Western Isles', in Steinar Imsen, ed., *The Norwegian Domination and the Norse World, c.1100–c.1400* (Trondheim, 2010), 125–49. Nonetheless, this was a slow process as the Scottish monarchy was rather inconsistent in its efforts to integrate the region into the Scottish kingdom. My thanks to Dr David Caldwell for discussing this point with me at length.

18 See also the perspective in Steve Murdoch, *Terror of the Seas?: Scottish Maritime Warfare, 1513–1713* (Leiden, 2010).

maritime and trading activity of the Scots had maintained an eastward perspective. The royal burghs that engaged in international trade were situated on its eastern coastline, especially around the Firths of Forth and Tay alongside Aberdeen further north.[19] Scotland's main trading partners were Scandinavia, the Baltic States and, when international diplomacy allowed, France. England too sought to trade with European states and both had to deal with the Hansa, a loose confederation of German-speaking ports that, by the mid-fifteenth century, largely dominated the export of salt from near La Rochelle, the trade in Bordeaux wine, and grain and fish from the Baltic.[20] On account of this eastward focus, the main area of shipbuilding activity lay in the Firth of Forth, situated at Leith and other smaller locations along the Forth.[21] For England, the main areas of shipbuilding, such as Chatham, Woolich and Deptford, were located around the Thames estuary while many of its key ports lay along its southern coast and the Cinque Ports, whose loyalty to the crown was expected in return for certain privileges, were located in the south east. Indeed, the strategic location of the Cinque Ports across the Narrow Seas from Flanders may indicate the real value in their loyalty to the crown.[22] Alongside these dominant mercantile factors were climatic and environmental reasons which shaped much earlier trading patterns. Prevailing winds and tidal currents meant that the journey from Scotland to France via the east coast was faster than a journey through the Irish Sea.[23] It was also safer.

The reign of Henry V had shown that with regular and sustained efforts at scouting and patrolling, the English could 'dominate confined sea

19 Scotland also had key political allies to the east, such as Denmark-Norway, allied through the marriage of James III and Margaret, daughter of Christian I, in 1468 which also saw Orkney and Shetland pledged to the Scottish crown. Meanwhile England looked south across the Narrow Seas to Flanders, France and beyond.

20 Rodgers, *Safeguard of the Sea*, 150.

21 Frederic Hendry, 'James IV and the Scottish Navy', *Aberdeen University Review* (1920), 46–8.

22 Rodgers, *Safeguard of the Sea*, 126.

23 For an analysis of the importance of wind and tidal currents see Alfred W. Crosby, *Ecological Imperialism: The Biological Expansion of Europe, 900–1900* (Cambridge, 1986, 2nd edn 2004), 104–31.

areas' for a period of time but this was never put into effect in the Irish Sea.[24] The neglect of English shipping following Henry's death meant that piracy flourished during the fifteenth century with the most successful pirates, from the West Country, able to prey on Breton trade. Throughout the fifteenth century England was embroiled in civil war, but it retained overseas possessions, notably Calais and Ireland. The garrison at Calais was a key concern, the only remnant of a once-mighty cross-(English) channel empire but, while there was frequent traffic between England and Ireland, little attention was paid to the Irish Sea. By the mid-sixteenth century, however, it had become evident to both Tudor and Stewart monarchs that more detailed knowledge of the maritime context of the archipelago was essential.

At the turn of the century, developments in the field of navigation and maritime mapping had largely been adopted from the continent.[25] Portolan charts, maritime maps giving compass directions, coastal observations and estimated distances were first produced by the Italians in the thirteenth century. The Mediterranean Sea favoured the development of more advanced navigation and astronomical observation, and by the late fifteenth century the Italians had been joined by the Portuguese and the Spanish in making much more accurate navigational aids, vital during the age of discovery. Mariners and pilots had learned to use a quadrant, astrolabe, or cross-staff to ascertain latitude and point to their position on a chart by observing the Pole Star at night or the sun's altitude at noon.[26] This, as well as experience and understanding of the Atlantic and Pacific wind patterns, allowed them to venture further afield.[27] In contrast, expertise in navigation within the archipelago was not particularly well-advanced by the early sixteenth century, nor was there sufficient knowledge of its coastline. Although the Italians, who were trading with the Low Countries

24 Rodgers, *Safeguard of the Sea*, 145.

25 For a brief overview see O'Neill, *Merchants and Mariners*, 113–19.

26 Alexander Lindsay, *A Rutter of the Scottish Seas (ca. 1540)*, I. H. Adams and G. Fortune, eds (Greenwich: National Maritime Museum, 1980), 5.

27 Crosby, *Ecological Imperialism*, 104–31; J. H. Elliott, *Empires of the Atlantic World. Britain and Spain in America 1492–1850* (New Haven and London, 2006), 108–9, 111–12.

and England, had extended their portolan charts to include the western coasts of Europe and parts of the Atlantic archipelago, the tidal conditions, shallow seabeds and variable winds of the archipelago prevented further developments.[28] In more northern regions, and especially so around the coastline of Scotland and Ireland, pilots navigated by setting a course from one headland to the next while contending with tidal streams and hidden rocks. Such coastal navigation required less sophisticated equipment such as a magnetic compass, a sand-glass, lead and line, and a rutter, a set of sailing directions used by a pilot in coastal navigation.[29] As a result, before the mid-sixteenth century most of England's navigational tracts were translations of continental manuscripts while the majority of maps were also of foreign origin.[30] Indeed *The Rutter of the Sea*, published in England in 1528 was a translation from an earlier French work.[31]

In the early sixteenth century, therefore, neither England nor Scotland were dominant maritime powers.[32] Perhaps on account of the efforts of Lambert Simmel and Perkin Warbeck, both of whom sought support elsewhere (Ireland and Scotland respectively) for a rebellion against Henry Tudor, and on account of the internal unrest following the final forfeiture

28 How detailed these were for the British Isles and Ireland is questionable and it is doubtful they would have been of much use for navigation close to the coastline.

29 *A Rutter of the Scottish Seas*, 5, 20–2; Colin Martin, 'A Maritime Dominion – Sea-Power and the Lordship', in Oram, ed., *The Lordship of the Isles*, 176–99, especially 176–9. Possibly a traverse-board was also used.

30 E. G. R. Taylor, *Tudor Geography, 1485–1583* (London, 1930), 4; Susan Rose, 'Mathematics and the Art of Navigation: The Advance of Scientific Seamanship in Elizabethan England', *Transactions of the Royal Historical Society*, sixth series (2004), 175–84 especially 175–7. For knowledge and mapping of the waters around Ireland see Mark Gardiner and T. E. McNeill, 'Seaborne trade and the commercialisation of fifteenth- and sixteenth-century Gaelic Ulster', *Proceedings of the Royal Irish Academy. Section C: Archaeology, Celtic Studies, History, Linguistics, Literature* (2016), 1–34, especially 11–18.

31 It has been suggested this was Pierre Garcie's *La Routier de la Mer* (Rouen, 1502–10) but see W. Senior, 'The Rutter of the Sea', *The Mariner's Mirror* 6/8 (1920), 243–6; Taylor, *Tudor Geography*, 13.

32 J. J. Scarisbrick, *Henry VIII* (New Haven and London, 1987), 21, 499–501; Rodger, *Safeguard of the Sea*, 165, 172–5.

of the Lordship of the Isles, monarchs of both realms were aware of the need for greater security around the western coasts. In the winter of 1494–5 James IV commenced with a programme of shipbuilding and repair work at Dumbarton, while in subsequent years he established royal garrisons and fortifications around the coast and the Clyde.[33] While working to strengthen the security of the western coast, James was involved in something of a naval battle with the new king of England, Henry VIII. Henry's predecessor and father, Henry VII, had not paid much attention to naval matters, but when Henry VIII saw the Scottish king building an impressive new fleet of ships (albeit paid for by the French king Louis XII), he realised he needed to keep pace. On the eve of the Battle of Flodden in 1513 Scotland had the more impressive fleet, with the *Michael* of significant size and stature.[34] Despite this advantage, the naval force played little part in the Anglo-Scottish engagement. It sailed around the north of Scotland, made a detour to Carrickfergus on the east Antrim coast, before arriving, rather too late, at Brest in early September.[35] After the defeat at Flodden *Michael* was sold to France, while the rest of the fleet returned to Scotland.[36]

33 Norman Macdougall, *James IV* (Edinburgh, 1997), 104–5, 115–16; Martin, 'A Maritime Dominion', 194–5. In 1494 James placed a royal garrison in Dunaverty Castle, on the southern tip of Kintyre, while in 1495 construction of a castle at Loch Kilkerran, near Campbeltown, commenced. During his three naval expeditions of 1498 James visited his fortresses of Kilkerran and Tarbert, at the mouth of the Clyde. Parliament recommended that a castle be built at Inverlochy on Loch Linnhe and that Stornoway, Dunaverty and Cairn-na-Burgh be reinforced. The construction of Saddell Castle in Kintyre and the proposal to transfer the see of Argyll from Lismore to Saddell Abbey in 1512 was part of this same strategy to fortify the west; see Iain G. MacDonald, *Clerics and Clansmen: The Diocese of Argyll between the Twelfth and Sixteenth Centuries* (Leiden, 2013), 77–8.

34 For some of the English ships built at this time see R. C. Anderson, 'Henry VIII's "Great Galley"', *The Mariner's Mirror* 6/9 (1920), 274–81; Rodger, *Safeguard of the Sea*, 164–75.

35 MacDougall, *James IV*, 268–9. Although MacDougall argues it was the weather, more than any other factor, that prevented the Scottish fleet making any meaningful impact during this campaign.

36 Rodger, *Safeguard of the Sea*, 167–72.

Unlike his father who tried to contain the maritime potential of the western Highlands and Isles, James V followed in the path of previous Scottish monarchs and attempted to harness it for the benefit of the crown in a cross-channel context.[37] James' decision to work with his Highland elite capitalised on the position Alexander MacDonald of Dunivaig and the Glens had in Ireland at the time, exploiting the opportunity to cause trouble for James' uncle, Henry VIII. But James also wanted to gain some leverage over the military trade that was ongoing between the west of Scotland and the north of Ireland, potentially using this military and maritime force for his own ambitions in the wider archipelagic context. This was not to be and by the end of the 1530s the context had changed dramatically. Further rebellion in the Isles resulted in James embarking on an expedition to the Isles in June 1540 that would have wider repercussions for the region.[38] Considerable energy and expense was invested in fitting out the fleet that departed from Leith and sailed around the north of the kingdom before it arrived in the Isles calling at various locations between Lewis and Dumbarton. This was to reinforce defences and either gain the submission of, or apprehend, a number of Hebridean lords, such as Hector MacLean of Duart in Mull and James MacDonald of Dunivaig and the Glens in Islay. The real significance

37 Steve Boardman, 'The Campbells and Charter Lordship in Medieval Argyll', in Steve Boardman and Alasdair Ross, eds, *The Exercise of Power in Medieval Scotland, c.1200–1500* (Dublin, 2003), 113–14. Boardman has shown, 'galley service as a feudal due in charter form was especially noticeable in the reign of Robert I' both to secure the western coastline from attack by exiled Highland lords and to provide transportation for the Bruce invasion of Ireland in 1315.

38 Jamie Cameron, *James V: The Personal Rule, 1528–1542* (East Linton, 1998), 239, 245–8; Roger A. Mason, 'This Realm of Scotland Is an Empire? Imperial Ideas and Iconography in Early Renaissance Scotland', in B. E. Crawford, ed., *Church, Chronicle and Learning in Medieval and Early Renaissance Scotland* (Edinburgh, 1999), 81 argues that the expedition was show of royal authority aimed at 'daunting the iles'; hence the 'circumnavigation' of the kingdom.

of the expedition, however, lay in the extensive survey of the land and its rentals.[39]

Often overlooked is the fact that this expedition followed the sailing instructions provided by Alexander Lindsay's *Rutter of the Scottish Seas*.[40] It is suggested that Lindsay's rutter was compiled partly from earlier Scottish material dating back to the fifteenth century, as well as a rutter for the north of England.[41] New knowledge of the maritime region of the west may have been gathered on an earlier, abortive attempt by the king to go to France in 1536. On this occasion, having departed from Fife the king sailed north with a fleet of five or six ships before putting in at the Isle of Whithorn on account of bad weather.[42] Regardless of the outcome, this voyage afforded invaluable information for the completion of Linday's *Rutter*. There may well have

39 Cameron, *James V*, 228–54; Alison Cathcart, 'The Forgotten '45: Donald Dubh's Rebellion in an Archipelagic Context', *Scottish Historical Review*, XCI:2/232 (2012), 239–41, 252. A royal garrison was established at Dunivaig and troops and canon were left on Islay. Meanwhile the chiefs arrested by the king were taken back to Edinburgh and warded in various locations.

40 Lindsay, *A Rutter of the Scottish Seas*; Andrea Thomas, *Princelie Majestie: The Court of James V of Scotland, 1528–1542* (Edinburgh, 2005), 162–3.

41 Lindsay, *A Rutter of the Scottish Seas*, 23, 28. Indeed, on account of the accuracy of the information contained in the rutter, it is likely to have been compiled over some time and utilised numerous 'sub-rutters' written by a variety of pilots with detailed local knowledge. For further discussion of the problems of navigation in the waters around Scotland see A. D. M. Forte, ' "Kenning be Kenning and Course be Course", Alexander Linsday's Rutter and the Problematics of Navigation in Fifteenth and Sixteenth Century Scotland', *Review of Scottish Culture* 11 (1998–99), 32–45.

42 Cameron, *James V*, 239 argues that the 'embarrassment … this caused James meant that the whole affair was hushed up'. Margaret Tudor, James' mother, and Eustace Chapuys, the Spanish ambassador, had different theories. However, it is likely that James intended to travel to France unnoticed by English observers, the queen mother and Chapuys. There were further rumours of the king intending for either France or Ireland in 1540 also, aided by the fact that James was not particularly forthcoming regarding his whereabouts; see Amy L. Blakeway, 'The Privy Council of James V of Scotland, 1528–1542', *The Historical Journal* 59/1 (2016), 23–44.

been a need for more detailed sailing instructions around the coast of Scotland in general but, for a journey around the north and through the western Isles, additional information was vital. It is possible the king already had requested a comprehensive rutter and the work produced by Lindsay offered invaluable guidance for navigating the north and west coasts of Scotland.[43] Further evidence that James had done so is found within the rutter itself. The sailing instructions take a course from Leith, anti-clockwise around the north of Scotland, through the Isles to Kintyre and on to the Solway Firth. Rather than end there, the rutter continues on to provide more general information concerning passage to the Isle of Man.[44] In the light of the Highlanders activities in the Irish Sea earlier in the 1530s James may have sought information on voyaging to this particular island, formerly part of the kingdom of Man and the Isles.[45]

43 *TA,* VIII, 159. In 1538 18s. 6d. was used to purchase 'foure horologis and ane compas' for the royal flagship the *Salamander.*

44 Lindsay, *Rutter of the Scottish Seas*, 53.

45 The expedition was also concerned with increasing crown revenue from the lands in the Isles following the annexation of the lordship of the Isles to the crown in December 1540 thus assigning the designation of Prince or Lord of the Isles to the crown: see *RMS*, III, no. 2233; *APS*, II, 360–1, 404–5; *RPS*, 1540/12/26, accessed 30 June 2012. The Act of Annexation extended to the 'landis and lordschipis of all his [the king's] Ilis, south and north; the tua Kintyris, with the castellis partening tharto and thare pertinentis; the landis and lordschip of Orknay and Yetland and the ilis pertening thereto and thare pertinentis'. The following year, in 1541, James undertook a survey of the rental value of these recently acquired lands, 'because the patrimonie of his croune and revenois therof being augmentit is the grett weill and proffitt baith to the kingis grace and all his liegis': see *RPS*, 1540/12/26, accessed 30 June 2012. The sailing instructions to the Isle of Man may have been part of lingering claims to the island by the Stewart monarchs; see Alison Cathcart, 'Island Empire: James VI and I and the Isle of Man', in Neil McIntyre and Alison Cathcart, eds, *Scotland and the Wider World* (Woodbridge, forthcoming).

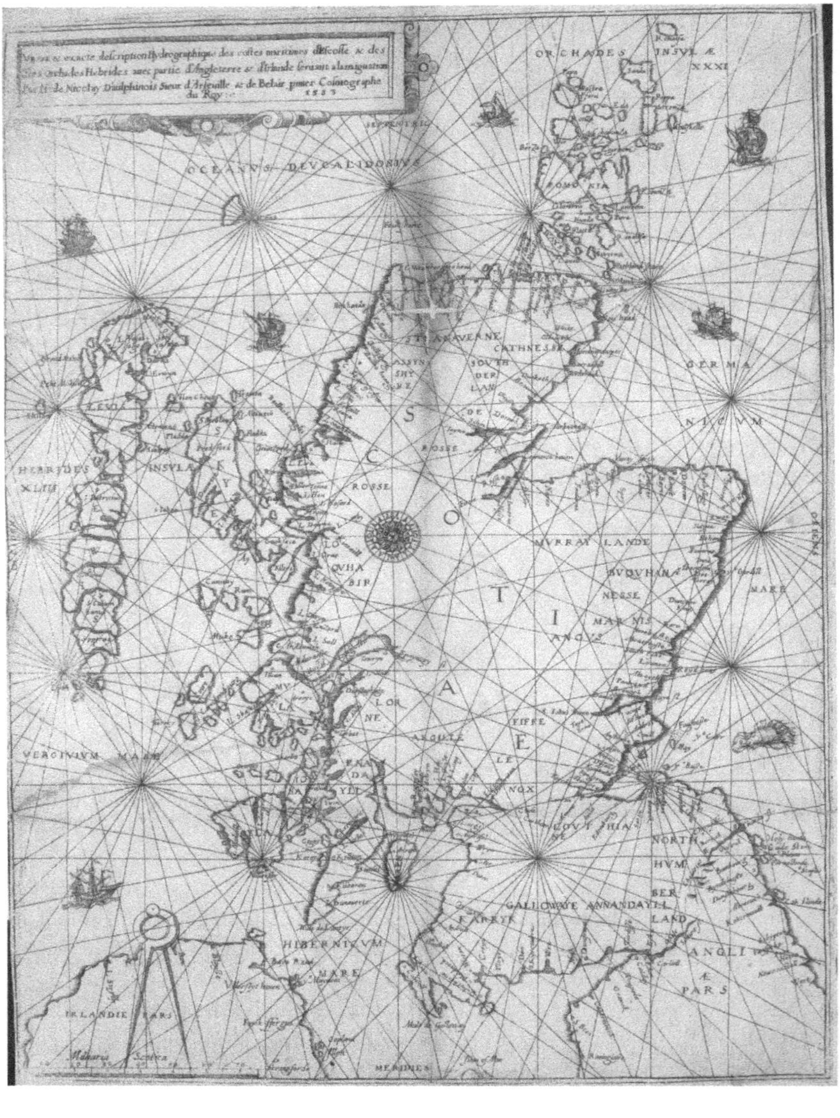

Vraye & exacte description Hydrographique des costes maritimes d'Escosse & des Isles Orchades Hebrides avec partie d'Angleterre & d'Irlande servant a la navigation, Par N. de Nicolay D'auphinois Sieur d'Arfeville & de Belair … (ID 1374). Reproduced with the permission of the National Library of Scotland.

The rutter was translated into French and published, along with this map, in 1583 by Nicholas de Nicolay, sieur d'Arfeville, chief cosmographer royal at the French court.

By 1540 the Scottish king had acquired detailed navigational knowledge of the waters around his kingdom. Henry VIII had been doing much the same. Competition between European powers within the Atlantic combined with increasing international tension arising from Henry's break with Rome in the 1530s, meant it was no longer enough to rely on the transmission and translation of European knowledge to the archipelago.[46] Specific information concerning the 'sea coasts, roads, creeks, and other places' around England was necessary for reasons of strategic security and advice was to be taken concerning the 'fortification of places where there is danger of invasion'.[47] Indeed, the 'Defence of the Coast' of 1539 highlighted Henry's concern to secure strategic fortifications and ensure they were well supplied with ordnance and powder. As well as enquiring about military preparedness Henry also ordered all beacons to be repaired and wanted to 'know the number and quantity of ships in the realm, their portage and burden, ordnance and artillery, and the number of mariners in every port'.[48] These were accompanied by 'plats' that identified the various locations in need of reinforcement in an effort to protect his southern coastline.[49] In the early 1540s, embarking on an invasion of Scotland, Henry was keen to acquire geographical and maritime knowledge about the more northern parts of the archipelago. He benefitted from the arrival in England of Protestant cosmographers and navigators seeking refuge during a time of religious persecution in France. Although the best map-makers of the time were Flemish, many of these French exiles found employment at Henry's court where their knowledge was readily exploited. By the end of his reign, as many as sixty French mariners and pilots were in Henry's service.[50] Nonetheless, the king still sought to utilise local knowledge,

46 Rodger, *Safeguard of the Sea*, 178–9.

47 *L&P Henry VIII*, XIV (I), nos 399, 400 (153).

48 *L&P Henry VIII*, XIV (I), nos 398, 400 (153).

49 BL Cotton Ms. Augustus I: Maps and Plans, i, 35, 36, 38, 39; see also the British Library online gallery at: <http://www.bl.uk/onlinegallery/onlineex/henryviii/militmap/coastdef/index.html>, accessed 30 July 2018; E. Ives, 'Henry VIII (1491–1547), king of England and Ireland', *ODNB*, accessed 30 July 2018.

50 Taylor, *Tudor Geography*, 4, 13, 15–16, 35–6. The numerous restrictions Francis I of France had placed on overseas endeavours meant that many Frenchmen sought

exploiting the 'assured lords' of the southwest of Scotland and making alliance with the chiefs of the western Highlands and Isles in an effort to open a second front in his war on Scotland in 1545.[51]

Sir Ralph Sadler regarded Dumbarton and the Firth of Clyde as the 'kaye of the North' at the time of the 1545 rebellion, but he was not the first to recognise the importance of the west.[52] Arguably Henry was copying what his nephew, James V, had attempted in seeking to harness the maritime power of the lords of the west and the Islesmen. Both monarchs failed to do so and both failed to gain leverage over the ongoing movement of Highlanders across the North Channel. The activity of the Scottish Highlanders in Ireland was more of a problem for Henry, but he had looked to James to assist in efforts to curtail the traffic. Repeated requests from English ambassadors for the Scottish monarch to prevent his subjects travelling to Ireland met with little response. Indeed, when James V was asked to forbid Scots to travel to Ireland he refused, arguing that 'the prohibition would rather provoke them to go thither than otherwise'.[53] In 1567 Elizabeth I expressed her 'intent[i]on to wryte to the Q[ueen] of Scotes, to p[ro]hibit the frequentation and passage of her people into that our Realm'.[54] Later in the sixteenth century Elizabeth looked to James VI for assistance in 'the staying of ... any subiectes of yo[u]rs, who usuallie frequent the companie and actions of diverse barbarous rebelles in the

to develop their knowledge and expertise in England where, during the reigns of Henry and Edward VI, French Hugenots also found religious toleration. For the 'rough wooing' see Marcus Merriman, *The Rough Wooings: Mary Queen of Scots, 1542–1551* (East Linton, 2000).

51 For the 'assured lords' see Marcus Merriman, 'The Assured Scots: Scottish Collaborators with England during the Rough Wooing', *Scottish Historical Review*, XLVII:1/147 (1968), 10–34.

52 Joseph Bain, ed., *The Hamilton Papers: Letters and Papers Illustrating the Political Relations of England and Scotland in the Sixteenth Century*, 2 vols (Edinburgh, 1890–92), II, no.4 (7). For more on this and the role of the Scot, John Elder, in providing Henry with useful information, including a map, see Cathcart, 'Forgotten '45', 239–64.

53 *L&P Henry VIII*, VIII, no.429.

54 SP 63/20, fol.20v.

northren provinces of that o[u]r kingdome' of Ireland.[55] In reality, even if he wanted to, James could do little to prevent them; passing legislation in Edinburgh was relatively straightforward, but putting it into effect on the ground in Kintyre or the Isles was another matter altogether. Either way, legislation would not easily solve a problem that was, in many respects, a maritime one.

The 1540s saw the beginnings of a change in ship design and naval tactics alongside developments in gunfounding.[56] As these took some time to be fully realised, in the mid-sixteenth century ships remained large and relatively slow, designed to transport an armed force, while fighting at sea consisted of grappling and boarding.[57] At the same time, the English fleet was concentrated in the Narrow Seas and around the south and east coasts of the kingdom. This was due to the ongoing English presence in Calais, the remnant of a former significant overseas empire that had once incorporated Normandy and Gascony, and the protection of outlying English territories, primarily the Channel Islands.[58] It was also a result of Henry VIII's renewal and continuation of warfare with France. While the Auld Alliance ensured this meant some attention had to be paid to Scotland, continental affairs always loomed larger than matters elsewhere in the archipelago.

The English may have prioritised naval matters of the Narrow Seas over the Irish Sea but, due to the situation in Ireland, there was constant traffic between England and Ireland. Throughout the sixteenth century, and especially so after Henry VIII's break with Rome, there was an increased desire on the part of the English to reform Ireland and extend English law, custom and religion as a means of securing England's borders. This involved

55 SP 52/52, fol.19, 4 January 1593–4.

56 Rodger, *Safeguard of the Sea*, 204–20.

57 Scarisbrick, *Henry VIII*, 29 n.3, 500; Rodger, *Safeguard of the Sea*, 205–6; David B. Quinn & A. N. Ryan, *England's Sea Empire, 1550–1642* (London, 1983), 49–51.

58 French victory at the Battle of Castillon in 1453, which brought an end to the Hundred Years War, reduced the England's territories in France to Calais. It was lost in 1558. The Channel Islands had passed to the English crown along with the duchy of Normandy in 1066 and, despite occasional French efforts, to reclaim the islands, they remained territories of the English crown. The dominions and territories of the English crown also including the Isle of Man. These outlying dominions are the focus of my current research.

a commitment in terms of men, money and munitions. Although there was never a large army in Ireland until the end of the century, on account of death, desertion and sporadic hostings by the Lord Deputy, reinforcements of men and munitions had to be sent regularly from England. Shipments departed mainly from London, Bristol or Chester, depending on where the regiments or victuals had been raised.[59] Some convoys rendezvoused at the Isle of Man before making the onward journey to Ireland, either to Dublin or Carrickfergus in Ulster.[60] This need to constantly replenish the army in terms of both manpower and victuals demanded much of the English. A regular supply of shipping was required to make the journey between Ireland and England, while officials, Lord Deputies and their communications also needed to be carried through the Irish Sea.[61]

The increased efforts on the part of the Tudor monarchy to realise reform in Ireland ensured constant traffic between England and Ireland but, from the perspective of Edinburgh or London, the Irish Sea was of little real significance.[62] It was traversed only when necessary and tidal conditions were more challenging. The lack of frequent or regular patrols, even in times of war, meant it was used by those wishing to avoid detection.[63] The west and its waterways became significant for Henry VIII when he was able to contemplate opening a second front in his war against Scotland in the

59 At times it was difficult to purchase victuals in England to be sent to Ireland: SP 63/38, fol.121; SP 63/52, fol.64; SP 63/59, fol.118. See also SP 63/44, fol.168; SP 63/68, fols 41, 43; and pp. 185–96 below.

60 Later in the sixteenth century, after a garrison had been firmly established, shipments proceeded on to Derry on Lough Foyle.

61 Victualling remained a problem throughout the century, see Rodgers, *Safeguard of the Sea*, 234–6, 337, 339, 408–9.

62 When travelling from Scotland to the continent the preference was for the east coast due to prevailing winds, tidal currents and regular patrols, as well as the location of Scotland's prominent burghs on the east side of the kingdom.

63 When Francis I of France sent munitions and money to Scotland to support Matthew Stewart, Earl of Lennox, and the Franco-Catholic faction in Scotland in 1543, they sailed undetected through the Irish Sea. See '*Discours des affaires du Royaume dEscosse depuys le jour que nous Jacques de le Brousse Seigneur dudict lieu Eschansson de Roy at Jacques Mesnaige Docteur es Droictz Seigneur de Caigny Conseiller dudict seigneur et ses Ambassadeurs audict Royaume sommes arrives a Dombertran jusqua ce jour*', in *Two Missions of Jacques de le Brosse: An Account of*

1540s; but when this came to nothing the west quickly retreated from his view.[64] This was somewhat typical of the perspective of the 'centre', whether London or Edinburgh and, just as English piracy thrived on account of the lack of royal efforts to curtail it, so too was there an increase in piratical activity in the North Channel. In this northern region of the Irish Sea, piracy remained more opportunistic than in the south where notorious pirates operated in the waters of the west coast.[65] Ultimately, however, neither royal authority in Scotland nor in England was able to dominate or effectively police the maritime activity – and violence – of the North Channel, despite the repercussions for each respective realm.

It was exactly this kind of opportunistic piratical attack that Thomson fell victim to in 1584.[66] For men like Thomson, a burgess and inhabitant of Ayr, the waters of the west coast were his livelihood. Throughout the sixteenth century the town of Ayr had grown in population and as a port and burgh.[67] Its location on the west coast with a fine, natural harbour made it a safe location for ships in bad weather and a perfect place for loading and unloading of cargo. Thomson traversed the waters of the Irish Sea and, although he had sought to use the knowledge of an Irish pilot in his journey to Derry in the northwest of Ireland, based on the examples of other

the Affairs of Scotland in the Year 1543 and the Journal of the Siege of Leith, 1560, ed., Gladys Dickinson, series three, vol. XXXVI (Edinburgh: Scottish History Society, 1942), 25; *The Scottish Correspondence of Mary of Lorraine Including Some Three Hundred Letters from 20 February 1542–3 to 15 May 1560,* ed., A. I. Cameron, series three, vol. X (Edinburgh: Scottish History Society, 1927), nos 27–8.

64 Cathcart, 'The Forgotten '45', 230–64, especially 249–50.

65 It is probable this conclusion is about to be significantly revised by forthcoming research; see Scott Carballo, 'Piracy in the Irish Seas: Sovereignty, Economy, and the Scottish Western Burghs, 1560–1630', University of Stirling ESRC-funded PhD (in progress).

66 It is crucial, however, that we move away from such basic, yet prevailing, notions of the Highlander as the perpetrator and the Lowlander as the innocent victim.

67 NLS, Denmilne Adv MSS 33.1.1., vol. III, no.37. In February 1610, before trade was stimulated further on account of the Plantation of Ulster, the Privy Council petitioned the king regarding necessary repairs to the harbour at Ayr. The council argued that without vital improvements the whole trade of the west coast would flounder, while the town also afforded immediate access into the 'north pairtis' of Ireland, 'whair the seid of all the rebellioun of that kingdome tooke roote'.

captains and merchants it is likely he traded with nearby Carrickfergus, the western Isles, the Isle of Man and further afield in Ireland, possibly Dublin or Wexford. As navigational aids were limited within the context of the North Channel, knowledge of winds, tidal currents and the weather was of more importance; '[f]inding land was less of a problem than coming safely to it.'[68] It is probable that Thomson had a wealth of experience gained at sea but the fact he had hired a pilot for this voyage suggests a level of unfamiliarity with the tidal currents off the north coast of Ireland. Indeed, for mariners and merchants who operated in these waters, familiarity with the currents and coasts of Scotland and Ireland was an undoubted advantage. It was this intimate, sustained experience of the waters that gave both the Highlanders and men from the southwest the upper hand in this maritime region.[69]

For Thomson and his attacker, MacDonald, the waters of the North Channel were a core part of their livelihood. The two men represent the wider Lowland and Highland Scottish communities that traded and interacted with both the Irish and English in Ulster. For some Scots, both Highland and Lowland, the North Channel, 'anciently known as … *Sruthar-na-Mailé Chinntiré*, 'the Current of the Mull of Cantire'', was a bridge, a means of communication and contact with others, whether family, allies, or trading partners.[70] In contrast, for the English the North Channel represented a barrier, a frontier between peoples, mentalities and communities that were separated by religion, nationality, language or culture. This study aims to examine the communities brought together by the waters of the North Channel, the reasons for their activity in the channel, and evaluate the extent to which their efforts were successful. The incident between Thomson and MacDonald helps to open up many of the themes this study will address: the presence of Highland Scots in the northeast of Ulster and their maintenance of a maritime estate straddling the North Channel; the efforts of the English in Ireland to expel these Highland Scots, identified as the main obstacle to the progress of English policy in

68 Denis Rixon, *The West Highland Galley* (Edinburgh, 1998), 174.

69 For more discussion of the maritime context see pp. 69–74, 196–215 below.

70 George Hill, *An Historical Account of the Macdonnells of Antrim: Including Notices of Some Other Septs, Irish and Scottish* (Belfast, 1873), 4.

the north of Ireland, and the means by which they sought to achieve this which, ultimately, resulted in the development of a policy of plantation. Plantation was also attempted on the other side of the North Channel as James VI took steps to 'civilise' his Gaelic subjects but, following the regnal union of 1603 and events in Ireland in the early years of the seventeenth century, the situation in the insular world changed considerably. James VI of Scotland became James I of England and Ireland and thereby eliminated some of the previous tensions caused by conflicting political and territorial jurisdictions. The ending of Tyrone's rebellion, following his submission to Lord Deputy Mountjoy in 1603, allowed a different outcome for the Irish under a different monarch, but the unexpected course of events that unfolded in 1607 and 1608 paved the way for plantation on an unprecedented scale. The result was the subsequent arrival of men predominantly from the southwest of Scotland and their participation in a British, Protestant project for plantation in Ulster.

Throughout the period under study, therefore, Scottish (Highland and Lowland), English and Irish communities and individuals were interacting, allying, opposing and conflicting with each other across and around the waters of the North Channel. Nonetheless, it was in the north of Ireland that these communities primarily interacted, integrated and conflicted but what facilitated these processes was the waters of the North Channel. What follows aims to examine the relationships between these communities at this time, communities that existed around, and were brought together by, a body of water that itself continually ebbed and flowed, hindering and enabling the relationships that existed across it. In doing so, the main focus will be the development of plantation, both policy and practice, by land and sea. There have been a number of excellent studies of plantation but these have tended to focus on individual plantations or planters, plantations of a region, or on plantations on one or other side of the Irish Sea, or indeed the Atlantic.[71] Plantation has not always been seen as part of an ongoing

71 Philip Robinson, *The Plantation of Ulster* (Belfast, 1984); Michael MacCarthy-Morrogh, *The Munster Plantation. English Migration to Southern Ireland, 1583–1641* (Oxford, 1986); Nicholas Canny, *Making Ireland British, 1580–1630* (Oxford, 2003); Jonathan Bardon, *The Plantation of Ulster: The British Colonisation of the North of Ireland in the Seventeenth Century* (Dublin, 2011); Colin Breen, *Dunluce Castle: History and Archaeology* (Dublin, 2012); Éamonn Ó Ciardha and Micheál

process, the development of a policy that emerged out of security concerns. It evolved to incorporate other agendas, such as reform and commercial orientation and, following successive failures, resulted in a mix of models utilised by James VI and I, whether private enterprise or state-sponsored, both within the archipelago and in the later seventeenth-century settlements in the Americas. This study aims to trace the development of that policy, and examine both policy and process as implemented on either side of the North Channel, within a wider archipelagic context.

Historiographical context

The approaches that have shaped this study include long-standing schools of thought as well as more recent historiographical developments. The current field of early modern British and Irish history has been in part a response to J. G. A. Pocock's advocacy for a genuinely 'British', or rather archipelagic, approach to the history of the peoples and cultures existing within the islands of Great Britain and Ireland.[72] This nuanced understanding of the 'peoples and nations, ethnic cultures, social structures and locally defined communities' that existed within these islands would

Ó Siochrú, eds, *The Plantation of Ulster: Ideology and Practice* (Manchester, 2012); Colin Breen, 'Randal MacDonnell and Early Seventeenth-Century Settlement in Northeast Ulster, 1603–30', in Éamonn Ó Ciardha and Micheál Ó Siochrú, eds, *The Plantation of Ulster. Ideology and Practice* (Manchester, 2012), 143–57; Audrey Horning, *Ireland in the Virginian Sea. Colonisation in the British Atlantic* (Chapel Hill, 2013); William Roulston, 'Scottish Settlement and Society in Plantation Ulster, 1610–40', in David Edwards with Simon Egan, eds, *The Scots in Early Stuart Ireland. Union and Separation in Two Kingdoms* (Manchester, 2016), 95–115; Aonghas MacCoinnich, *Plantation and Civility in the North Atlantic World: the Case of the Northern Hebrides, 1570–1639* (Leiden, 2015).

72 John G. A. Pocock, 'British History: A Plea for a New Subject', *New Zealand Historical Journal* 8 (1974), 3–12; J. G. A. Pocock, 'British History: A Plea for a New Subject', *Journal of Modern History* 74/4 (1975), 601–21; J. G. A. Pocock, 'The Limits and Divisions of British History: In Search of the Unknown Subject', *American Historical Review* 87/2 (1982), 311–26.

only be achieved by a shift away from traditional national histories that dominate much of the historiography of these islands. Early modern historians have reacted differently to this New British and Irish History. While some responded enthusiastically others found the concept immediately problematic and historians continue to debate the extent to which such history can and has been written.[73] Arguably medieval historians have been most successful in attempting to write British history with R. R. Davies and Robin Frame leading the way in transforming our understanding of the first English empire and relations between England and its neighbours during the medieval era.[74] Similarly, an integrated approach to the seventeenth, eighteenth and nineteenth centuries has produced much scholarship, highlighting the need for a non-anglocentric perspective and a greater understanding of how events in one part of the archipelago influenced the course of development elsewhere.[75] Non-anglocentric British history has produced a flourishing of scholarship focusing on Scotland, Ireland and, albeit to a lesser extent, Wales.

73 Within the plethora of literature debating the history and historiography of the New British History see Steven G. Ellis and Sarah Barber, eds, *Conquest and Union: Fashioning a British State, 1485–1725* (London, 1995); Brendan Bradshaw and John Morrill, eds, *The British Problem, c.1534–1707. State Formation in the Atlantic Archipelago* (Basingstoke, 1996); Brendan Bradshaw and Peter Roberts, eds, *British Consciousness and Identity: The Making of Britain, 1533–1707* (Cambridge, 1998); Glenn Burgess, ed., *The New British History: Founding a Modern State, 1603–1715* (London, 1999); S. J. Connolly, ed., *Kingdoms United? Great Britain and Ireland since 1500: Integration and Diversity* (Dublin, 1999); a number of articles in the AHR forum of the *American Historical Review*, 104:2 (April, 1999); David Armitage, ed., *British Political Thought in History, Literature and Theory 1500–1800* (Cambridge, 2006); Michael J. Braddick and David L. Smith, eds, *The Experience of Revolution in Stuart Britain and Ireland: Essays for John Morrill* (Cambridge, 2011).

74 R. R. Davies, ed., *The British Isles, 1100–1500: Comparisons, Contrasts, Connections* (Edinburgh, 1988); R. R. Davies, *Domination and Conquest: The Experience of Ireland, Scotland, and Wales, 1100–1300* (Cambridge, 1990); Robin Frame, *The Political Development of the British Isles, 1100–1400* (Oxford, 1995); Robin Frame, *Ireland and Britain, 1170–1450* (London, 1998); R. R. Davies, *The First English Empire: Power and Identities in the British Isles 1093–1343* (Oxford, 2002).

75 The most obvious example of this is the civil wars and revolution of the seventeenth century. See, for example, Martyn Bennett, *The Civil Wars in Britain and Ireland, 1638–51* (Oxford, 1997); J. P. Kenyon and Jane Ohlmeyer, eds, *The Civil*

The New British and Irish Histories nonetheless remain problematic.[76] It has been accused of anglocentrism and anti-Europeanism.[77] By prioritising interrelations between the peoples and nations within the insular world such an approach overlooks enduring connections with Europe and imposes a sense of integration and connectedness that may not have existed.[78] By focusing too much on attempts to write a history of the insular world of Britain and Ireland there is a danger of neglecting the importance of European affairs. For example, at certain times in the political development of England, Scotland, or Ireland, relations with France or Spain had as great an, if not a greater, influence as those elsewhere within the archipelago.[79] Despite the work by Harris, Pincus and others, the lack

---

Wars: A Military History of England, Scotland and Ireland (Oxford, 1998); Allan I. Macinnes, *The British Revolution, 1629–1660* (Basingstoke, 2005); Tim Harris, *Revolution: The Great Crisis of the British Monarchy, 1685–1720* (London, 2006). This is also the case for later centuries where historians have more usefully adopted integrated approaches to the histories of England, Ireland and Scotland; see Ian McBride, *Protestantism and National Identity: Britain and Ireland, c.1650–c.1850* (Cambridge, 1998); Keith Robbins, 'Historians and Twentieth-Century British History, 1983–2008', unpublished paper presented at the Conference on Modern British History, University of Strathclyde, 24 June 2008.

76 The term New British History is immediately problematic as it ignores Ireland completely. Although Northern Ireland currently remains part of the United Kingdom of Great Britain and Northern Ireland and some of its inhabitants can speak of a 'British' identity, no part of Ireland is, or indeed ever was, encompassed in the terms Britain or Great Britain. As a result, New British and Irish Histories is more appropriate. Some of these problems are discussed more fully in John Morrill, 'The British Problem, c.1534–1707' in Bradshaw and Morrill, eds, *The British Problem, c.1534–1707*, 1–38.

77 Keith M. Brown, 'Seducing the Scottish Clio: Has Scottish History Anything to Fear from the New British History', in Burgess, ed., *The New British History*, 238–65; Tim Harris, 'Critical Perspectives: The Autonomy of English History?', in Burgess, ed., *The New British History*, 266–86; John Reeve, 'Britain or Europe? The Context of Early Modern English History: Political and Cultural, Economic and Social, Naval and Military', in Burgess, ed., *The New British History*, 287–312.

78 Morrill, 'The wars of the Three Kingdoms', in Burgess, ed., *The New British History*, 79.

79 More recent historiography has sought to redress these issues; see Tim Harris, *The Final Crisis of the Stuart Monarchy: The Revolutions of 1688–91 in the British*

of engagement with both European and Atlantic contexts is not the only failing of this approach. While the aim may have been to move away from models of traditional, national histories, conversely the New British and Irish Histories actually encourage such a mind-set by its use of a three-kingdoms or four-nations framework. Indeed, it has been suggested that what has developed from Pocock's plea is, at best, often little more than 'a more integrated reading of English, Scottish and Irish histories' and, at worst, English history writ large.[80]

Nonetheless, within the insular world framework, comparative approaches to aspects of the history of the islands found favour with medievalists and early modernists who explored the different experiences of and reactions to English efforts at empire, compared political developments such as state formation, or looked at responses to the Reformation.[81] While the framework of the New British and Irish Histories may appear to prioritise 'unity at the expense of diversity', historians are keen to emphasise divergence as much as connection.[82] Within the early modern period, however, the contribution of seventeenth- and eighteenth-century historians stands

Atlantic and European Contexts (Woodbridge, 2015). Steven C. A. Pincus, *1688: The First Modern Revolution* (New Haven, 2009) was able to focus more on the influence of continental factors, and specifically relations with France.

80 Peter Lake, 'Retrospective: Wentworth's Political World in Revisionist and Post-Revisionist Perspective', in J. F. Merritt, ed., *The Political World of Thomas Wentworth, Earl of Strafford, 1621–1641* (Cambridge, 1996), 281 quoted in Jane Ohlmeyer, 'Seventeenth-Century Ireland and the New British and Atlantic Histories', *American Historical Review* 104/2 (April 1999), 446–62, at 448.

81 Davies, *The First English Empire*; Steven Ellis, *Tudor Frontiers and Noble Power: The Making of the British State* (Oxford, 1995); Ciaran Brady, 'Comparable histories?: Tudor reform in Wales and Ireland', in Ellis and Barber, eds, *Conquest and Union*, 64–86; Brendan Bradshaw, 'The Tudor Reformation and the Revolution in Wales and Ireland: The Origins of the British Problem', in Bradshaw and Morrill, eds, *The British Problem*, 39–65; Brendan Bradshaw, 'The English Reformation and Identity Formation in Ireland and Wales', in Bradshaw and Roberts, eds, *British Consciousness and Identity*, 43–111.

82 Quotation from Ó Ciardha and Ó Siochrú, eds, *The Plantation of Ulster*, 4; see also Michael Brown, *Disunited Kingdoms. Peoples and Politics in the British Isles 1280–1460* (Harlow, 2013).

in stark contrast to sixteenth-century historians who, despite notable exceptions, have not placed Scottish history into a wider, nuanced British or archipelagic context. For the most part, comparative studies in the sixteenth century have focused predominantly on the interactions between or comparisons of two of the three kingdoms (or four nations) although, in large part, pre-1600 Scottish history has tended largely to ignore Ireland in preference for studies that focus on either England or France.[83] Comparative analyses have been useful and enlightening, but too often are bound by national, territorial contexts.

While there has been both a positive and negative response to these historiographical developments there is no doubt that the abundance of scholarship which emerged has illuminated aspects of the past that were overlooked as a result of traditional, national history. Despite efforts to write an integrated, nuanced history of the insular world, such national frameworks still tend to dominate the field of early modern British and Irish history. This is partly the result of history. The rise of dominant territorial monarchs increasingly challenged the jurisdiction of the papacy and asserted both spiritual and temporal authority within their realms, thereby emphasising claims to be imperial monarchs, while also pursuing centralising policies. Although national or territorial boundaries may have become more clearly defined in the fifteenth and sixteenth centuries, and while monarchs were increasingly concerned with their ability to convey imperial ideology, the outlook and mentalities of the vast majority of peoples and communities in the archipelago were shaped largely by kinship, locality and

83 Of course there are notable exceptions: Jenny Wormald, 'The Creation of Britain: Multiple Kingdoms or Core and Colonies?', *Transactions of the Royal Historical Society*, 6th series, 2 (1992), 175–94; David Armitage, 'Making the Empire British: Scotland in the Atlantic World, 1542–1707', *Past and Present*, 155 (1997), 34–63; Jane Dawson, *The Politics of Religion in the Age of Mary, Queen of Scots. The Earl of Argyll and the Struggle for Britain and Ireland* (Cambridge, 2002); Steven G. Ellis with Christopher Maginn, *The Making of the British Isles: The state of Britain and Ireland, 1450–1660* (Harlow, 2007); Jenny Wormald, 'James VI, James I and the Identity of Britain', in Bradshaw and Morrill, eds, *The British Problem*, 148–71; Jenny Wormald, 'The 'British' Crown, the Earls and the Planation of Ulster', in Ó Ciardha and Ó Siochrú, eds, *The Plantation of Ulster*, 18–32; Edwards with Egan, eds, *The Scots in early Stuart Ireland*.

geography, factors which bore little relation to national concerns. There is no doubt that identities were articulated by elites, whether that be family name, confessional grouping, or, post-1603, 'Britishness', but these identities were all in play at the same time with each coming to the fore in different circumstances and for different reasons. While there has been a greater attempt to explore local and regional diversity, notwithstanding these developments the state continues to loom large in early modern history.[84]

The dominance of national history and studies that focus on events at the 'centre' are also in part a consequence of the abundance of material for the early modern period. This emanates from the centre in the form of state papers, parliamentary records, exchequer rolls and privy council registers and their availability online has transformed how, where and when historical research can be undertaken. This has given historians unrivalled access to the workings of government, but over-reliance on such evidence tends towards a distorted view of history that priorities the centre at the expense of the locality. The result is a reading of history where decisions are made at the centre and imposed onto the periphery, a perspective that fails to take into account both the extent to which policy was ever followed through in the periphery (because a piece of legislation was passed in London or Edinburgh, does not mean it was either fully implemented or had any impact in Tyrconnell or Kintyre), and the extent to which policy formulated at the centre was a reaction to events in the periphery. The framework of centre and periphery was favoured by economic historians who argued for a core-dependency model in relation to a realm and its dominions and colonies but such theories have been discredited since the 1960s. Yet within much of Scottish, and indeed British, history of the late medieval and early modern period, the core-periphery or centre-locality framework is a constant. Historians might like to think they have moved beyond it, especially as the limits of such an approach have been widely acknowledged, but the language and conceptual framework remains

84 Again, of course, there are notable exceptions. Brendan Smith, *Crisis and Survival in Late Medieval Ireland: The English of Louth and Their Neighbours, 1330–1450* (Oxford, 2013), 1 emphasises the importance of local and regional studies to bring nuance to wider, national narratives, especially so in the case of Ireland; and see p.4 above.

pervasive.[85] At times a centre-periphery framework is appropriate, but too often the result is that governance is conveyed as a one-way process, one that takes place at the 'centre' and is projected onto the 'periphery', rather than a dialogue, with government, state officials, local authorities and individuals each communicating with, responding to and being shaped by the other. The centre-periphery approach is also a significant contributing factor to the trend for studies of state formation.

During the 1970s and 1980s, state formation was the preserve of social scientists although later historians too began to engage with the concept of the growth of state power. Traditionally, historians have emphasised the importance of economic and/or geopolitical factors on the structure of early modern states and regimes with a significant body of scholarship that viewed state power in purely fiscal and military terms; indeed seventeenth-, eighteenth- and nineteenth-century historians have focused on the growth of government and bureaucracy, the fiscal-military state and the development of state apparatus. In so doing they regularly quote Max Weber who, in the early twentieth century, defined the state as a 'human community that (successfully) claims the monopoly of the legitimate use of physical force within a given territory'.[86] Recent studies have helpfully challenged

85 Immanuel Wallerstein, *The Modern World-System: Capitalist Agriculture and the Origins of the European World-Economy in the Sixteenth Century* (New York, 1974); *The Modern World System II: Mercantilism and the Consolidation of the European World-Economy, 1600–1750* (New York, 1980); *The Modern World-System III: The Second Era of Great Expansion of the Capitalist World-Economy, 1730–1840* (San Diego, 1989). Wallerstein's conceptual approach emphasised the dominance of the centre and the dependency of the periphery; a perspective that is evident also in Michael Hechter, *Internal Colonialism: The Celtic Fringe in British National Development, 1536–1966* (London, 1975). There are a number of critiques of and engagement with Wallerstein's work; for these and for a useful summary of various centre-periphery conceptual frameworks see 'Introduction' in Bernard Bailyn and Philip D. Morgan, eds, *Strangers within the Realm. Cultural Margins of the First British Empire* (Chapel Hill, 1991), 8 n.9; Amy Turner Bushnell and Jack P. Greene, 'Peripheries, Centers, and the Construction of Early Modern American Empires', in Christine Daniels and Michael V. Kennedy, eds, *Negotiated Empire. Centers and Peripheries in the Americas, 1500–1820* (New York and London, 2002), 1–14.

86 Max Weber, 'Politics as a Vocation' (1918).

these views arguing there is more to state formation than economic and geopolitics and instead emphasise the extent to which state power was 'negotiated'.[87] However, a common failure to define what is actually meant by state formation or state formation processes results in a tendency to focus on crown and government and the exercise of power, accompanied by arguments that suggest moves towards increased centralisation and uniformity.[88] As medieval historians have pointed out, with reference to the vast landed empire of the Plantagenet monarchy, centralisation and uniformity do not necessarily go hand-in-hand; while there were moves towards centralisation this did not always result in uniformity.[89] More helpful, however, have been the observations of J. H. Elliot who argued that the growing awareness of composite monarchies within Europe – that is 'monarchies composed of distinct units possessing their own distinctive characteristics and constitutional programme' – has meant what was once regarded as state formation is now viewed as the attempt of the crown or central government to enhance its authority, both on a national and international level.[90] The pre-occupation of sixteenth-century monarchs to assert

87 Philip S. Gorski, 'Beyond Marx and Hintze? Third-Wave Theories of Early Modern State Formation', *Society for the Comparative Study of Society and History* (2001), 851–61 at 853.

88 For an example of the discussions that arise concerning the state a number of articles, based on a seminar series of the Oxford Discussion Group on the State, give a useful introduction. They have been published in *Journal of Historical Sociology*, vol. 15: no.1 (2002). In addition to this, there is an abundance of literature discussing the state and state formation within early modern British and Irish historiography; for a helpful European perspective see Robert Frost, *The Oxford History of Poland-Lithuania. Volume I: The Making of the Polish-Lithuanian Union, 1385–1569* (Oxford, 2015), 36–46.

89 Much of the discussion of the 2014 Harlaxton conference centred on such themes, now helpfully published as Peter Crooks, David Green and W. Mark Ormrod, eds, *The Plantagenet Empire, 1259–1453: Proceedings of the 2014 Harlaxton Symposium* (Donington, 2016). For a Scottish perspective see Dauvit Broun, 'Statehood and lordship in 'Scotland' before the mid-twelfth century', *The Innes Review* 66/1 (2015), 1–71.

90 J. H. Elliot, 'Atlantic History: A Circumnavigation', in David Armitage and Michael J. Braddick, eds, *The British Atlantic World, 1500–1800* (Basingstoke, 2009), 260–1.

imperial status certainly aligns with the aim of extending royal authority within their kingdom, but there is acknowledgement that certain monarchs recognised the benefits of some degree of divergence.[91]

This perspective necessitates moving beyond the, now largely discredited, framework of centre-periphery as the evidence from the periphery needs to be integrated with that from the centre. Consequently, rather than simply analyse how the English or Scottish centre attempted to extend its authority throughout the outlying regions of their respective realms, localities also need to be recognised as alternative 'centres' where events influence overall political development as much as centralised government.[92] Recent work by Steve Hindle has brought a new dimension to studies of state formation. He argued that current studies of state formation suggest a 'linear progression from primitive to modern forms of political organisation' and so what developed is a teleological perspective of historical development. Instead Hindle has emphasised 'governance as a process' over 'government as an institution' and argued for the role that local elites played in this process. Rather than continuing a state-orientated understanding of processes of state formation, emphasis has been placed on the extent to which government relied on the co-operation of the people highlighting the need for an appreciation of what was going on at a parish level.[93] While, to some extent, this perpetuates the centre-periphery framework by positing a view that state formation is something formulated at the centre and developed through the co-opting of local elites

91 This is the focus of a forthcoming article but for some useful scholarship on this issue see Wormald, 'The Creation of Britain', 175–94; J. H. Elliot, 'A Europe of Composite Monarchies', *Past and Present*, 137 (1992), 48–71; J. S. Morrill, '*Uneasy Lies the Head that Wears a Crown': Dynastic Crises in Tudor and Stewart Britain, 1504–1746*, Stenton Lecture, University of Reading (Reading, 2005); Roger A. Mason, 'Debating Britain in Seventeenth-Century Scotland: Multiple Monarchy and Scottish Sovereignty', *Journal of Scottish Historical Studies* 35/1 (2015), 1–4.

92 My thanks to Dr Jackson Armstrong for discussions on this point.

93 Steve Hindle, *The State and Social Change in Early Modern England, 1550–1640* (Basingstoke, 2002); Michael J. Braddick, *State Formation in Early Modern England, c.1550–1700* (Cambridge, 2000).

into the process, it does attempt to present a more nuanced understanding of what is meant by 'state formation'.[94]

Continuing focus on the state as the 'centre' at best marginalises and at worst ignores the role of the individual or community on the so-called 'periphery'. State formation approaches lead to a reading of the past as more ordered than was the case. More misleading, however, is the resulting (no doubt unconscious) biased interpretation of the evidence, which can be selected to support a given argument. One example of this can be found in attempts to contextualise the 'civilising' agenda of James VI in relation to his Gaelic subjects in Scotland. Approached from a state-centred perspective this leaves little room for acknowledgement of the role of Gaels themselves in the process, and the extent to which the policies implemented in the region were the result of a two-way interaction.[95] This is not the only example as too often Scottish Gaeldom is viewed as peripheral to the mainstream political, social, cultural and economic development of Scotland. Unlike in Irish historiography where Gaelic society cannot be side-lined, general texts of Scottish history too readily relegate the western Highlands and Isles, a region which constitutes approximately half of Scotland, to a separate chapter or simply ignores the region altogether.[96] While it cannot be denied that there were differences in society, economy, culture, language and geography, and regardless of connections with Irish society, the western Highlands and Isles were part of the Scottish kingdom and

94 This perspective is also evident in Allan Kennedy, *Governing Gaeldom: The Scottish Highlands and the Restoration State, 1660–1688* (Leiden, 2014), 1–14 where Kennedy discusses the 'collaborative' and 'imperial' approaches to centre-periphery interaction.

95 Contrast the arguments put forward by Julian Goodare, *The Government of Scotland 1560–1625* (Oxford, 2005), chapter 11 with that of Thomas Brochard, 'Plantation: Its Process in Relation to Scotland's Atlantic Communities, 1590s–1630s', *Maritime Communities of the North Atlantic Arc in the Early Modern Period: Journal of the North Atlantic*, ed., Alison Cathcart, special volume 12 (2019), 73–94.

96 For example, Goodare, *Government of Scotland* deals with the Highlands in a separate chapter while Katie Stevenson, *Power and Propaganda: Scotland 1306–1488* (Edinburgh, 2014), in an otherwise excellent study, makes passing reference to successive Lords of the Isles and the Highlands but not in any sustained way, nor suggestive of the importance of the region for wider political development. The New Edinburgh History of Scotland series does make the effort to fully integrate the

more fully integrated than is suggested by how the region is treated within current historiography. The view of the Gaelic north and west as distinct, separate and, to an extent, inferior or irrelevant to wider developments, is the remnant of a centuries-old historiographical tradition.

This began, arguably, with the chronicles of John of Fordun and Walter Bower in the fourteenth and fifteenth centuries respectively.[97] In his *Chronicle of the Scottish Nation* Fordun made a clear distinction between the barbarous Highlander and the civilised and law-abiding Lowlander, a polarisation between two societies that was compounded by a geographic and linguistic separation. The mountains of Druim Alban and the Grampians provided a very real physical barrier between the south and east and the north and west but while there were '[s]harp cleavages' between the two regions, there was also considerable interaction.[98] Although the so-called Highland-Lowland divide served as the demarcation line between geographic, cultural, linguistic and political regions, it was and could be crossed readily as and when necessary. Over subsequent centuries stereotypical views of the unruly and barbaric Highlander became increasingly entrenched in the minds of Lowlanders and this historiographical tradition pervaded much of the historical writing on the region during the late nineteenth and twentieth centuries.[99] Indeed, the modern historiographical trend that views Highland society as different from, ultimately inferior to and defeated by that of the Lowlands was established in the

Highlands into the wider narrative: see in particular Richard Oram, *Domination and Lordship: Scotland 1070–1230* (Edinburgh, 2011); Michael Brown, *The Wars of Scotland, 1214–1371* (Edinburgh, 2004); Jane Dawson, *Scotland Re-formed, 1488–1587* (Edinburgh, 2007).

97 Dauvit Broun, 'Attitudes of *Gall* to *Gaedhel* in Scotland before John of Fordun', in Dauvit Broun and Martin MacGregor, eds, *Mìorun Mòr nan Gall, 'The Great Ill-Will of the Lowlander'? Lowland Perceptions of the Highlands Medieval and Modern* (Glasgow, 2009), 49–82.

98 Philip M. Dunshea, '*Druim Alban, Dorsun Britanniae* – 'the Spine of Britain'', *Scottish Historical Review* XCII:2/235 (2013), 275–89.

99 Jane Dawson, 'The Gaidhealtachd and the Emergence of the Scottish Highlands', in Bradshaw and Roberts, eds, *British Consciousness and Identity*, 259–300; Martin MacGregor, 'Gaelic Barbarity and Scottish Identity in the Later Middle Ages', in Broun and MacGregor, eds, *Mìorun Mòr nan Gall*, 7–48. Later treatment of the

nineteenth century with the publication of Patrick Fraser Tytler's *History of Scotland*.[100] Based on the chronicles of Fordun and Bower, Tytler viewed Highland society in general as a threat to the civility and good government found in the south and east of the kingdom.

There had been attempts to move beyond this ingrained prejudice towards Highland society since the late nineteenth century but such views made little headway in mainstream Scottish historiography.[101] It was the scholarship of John Bannerman in the 1970s that highlighted a strong artistic and literary tradition within Gaelic society and a perspective that did much to highlight the social, cultural and intellectual character of the MacDonald Lordship of the Isles and the Beaton kindred.[102] While shadows of the traditional view of the Highlanders, as a conservative, backward people cut off from mainstream political and economic developments, remain in modern historical writing recent decades have witnessed a proliferation of scholarship highlighting the strength of Gaelic culture, and literary and architectural heritage, alongside the extent to which economic development had occurred in the region.[103] Subsequent chapters will discuss in more detail the reasons why Scottish Gaelic, and also Irish, society was consistently regarded as primitive and barbaric by crown and government

---

Highlands in the historiography was influenced by the association of the region with Jacobitism.

100 P. F. Tytler, *History of Scotland*, 9 vols (Edinburgh, 1828–43); M. Ash, *The Strange Death of Scottish History* (Edinburgh, 1980), 22–6; Oram, 'A Celtic Dirk?', 5.

101 Oram, 'A Celtic Dirk?'.

102 J. W. M. Bannerman, 'The Lordship of the Isles', in J. M. Brown, ed., *Scottish Society in the Fifteenth Century* (London, 1977), 209–40; K. A. Steer and J. W. M. Bannerman, *Late Medieval Monumental Sculpture in the West Highlands* (RCAHMS, 1977); J. W. M. Bannerman, *The Beatons: A Medical Kindred in the Classical Gaelic Tradition* (Edinburgh, 1986); Jean Munro and R. W. Munro, eds, *The Acts of the Lords of the Isles*, series four, vol. XXII (Edinburgh: Scottish History Society, 1986).

103 Amongst a wealth of scholarship see Munro and Munro, eds, *Acts of the Lords of the Isles*; Allan I. Macinnes, *Clanship, Commerce and the House of Stuart, 1603–1788* (East Linton, 1996); Robert A. Dodgshon, *From Chiefs to Landlords. Social and Economic Change in the Western Highlands and Islands, c.1493–1820* (Edinburgh, 1998); Martin MacGregor, 'The Genealogical Histories of Gaelic

in both Edinburgh and London. The point to be made here is that the division between two societies, whether in Ireland or Scotland, is not helpful but often the result of national history. In addition, it further perpetuates a centre-periphery approach, whether implicit or explicit.

A number of specialised studies have focused on Gaelic society in both Ireland and Scotland. Far from advocating the existence of a pan-Gaelic world, as had been suggested in earlier work, this recent research has highlighted divergence and disconnect as much as contact and interaction.[104] Perhaps understandably there has been something of a focus on the MacDonalds who held lands in both kingdoms, while scholars in other disciplines, such as archaeology and literary studies, have made invaluable contributions too.[105] Much of this burgeoning literature consists of regional or local studies of an individual clan, lordship, or territory that together represents a substantial body of scholarship that enriches our understanding

Scotland', in Adam Fox and Daniel Woolf, eds, *The Spoken Word. Oral Culture in Britain, 1500–1850* (Manchester, 2002), 196–239; Wilson MacLeod, *Divided Gaels. Gaelic Cultural Identities in Scotland and Ireland, c.1200–c.1650* (Oxford, 2004); Stephen Boardman, *The Campbells, 1250–1513* (Edinburgh, 2006); Alison Cathcart, *Kinship and Clientage: Highland Clanship, 1451–1609* (Leiden, 2006); Fiona A. MacDonald, *Missions to the Gaels. Reformation and Counter Reformation in Ulster and the Highlands and Islands of Scotland, 1560–1760* (Edinburgh, 2006); David H. Caldwell, *Islay: The Land of the Lordship* (Edinburgh, 2008); MacDonald, *Clerics and Clansmen*; MacCoinnich, *Plantation and Civility in the North Atlantic World.*

104 For the existence of a pan-Gaelic world see Simon Kingston, *Ulster and the Isles in the Fifteenth Century: The Lordship of the Clann Domhnaill of Antrim* (Dublin, 2004); Ohlmeyer, *Civil War and Restoration*, 7. But compare with McLeod, *Divided Gaels*; Colin Breen, 'Maritime Connections: Landscape and Lordship along the Gaelic Atlantic Seaboard of Scotland and the North of Ireland during the Middle Ages', *Maritime Communities of the North Atlantic Arc in the Early Modern Period: Journal of the North Atlantic*, ed., Alison Cathcart, special volume 12 (2019), 3–15.

105 See, for example, Andrew Hadfield, *Edmund Spenser: A Life* (Oxford, 2012); Elizabeth Fitzpatrick, *Royal Inauguration in Gaelic Ireland, c.1100–1600: A Cultural Landscape Study* (Woodbridge, 2004); Horning, *Ireland in the Virginian Sea.*

of Gaelic society in both countries. Taken as a whole it also highlights the need for further studies of a similar kind, emphasising that Gaelic society was not homogenous, nor was there a unified response to crown intervention. Different clans, families and individuals followed divergent political agendas which changed through time.

These local and regional studies of Scottish Gaelic and Irish society also formed part of another historiographical trend that emerged from the New British and Irish Histories and utilisation of comparative contexts: the field of Irish-Scottish studies. Encouraged to a certain extent by political events during its inception, the growth of Irish-Scottish studies resulted in the establishment of a number of research centres.[106] This field continues to thrive but its emergence and the recognition of it as a valid discipline is said to have signalled the point at which both countries, and their respective histories, were no longer defined by their larger neighbour.[107] That may be so, and while there is much scholarly output in this area, it perpetuated the trend for comparison between Ireland and Scotland, rather than a truly archipelagic approach. Nonetheless, such local and regional studies have been invaluable, adding nuance to the general narrative and highlighting both commonalities and divergence.[108] This strength in local and regional studies is most noticeable in Irish historiography. The Maynooth Studies in Local History series has ensured academic rigour and respectability in local history studies; this stands in stark contrast to Scottish historiography where for too long local history has been regarded as parochial. Fortunately the tide is beginning to turn, but the field still has a long way to go to catch up with historians of early modern England and Ireland who have engaged more meaningfully with local and regional studies. To be fair, the lack of available source material does mitigate against the similar in-depth analysis of families, parishes, or counties that have been undertaken by historians of early modern England. Nonetheless, new dimensions to the field such

106 For example, the Research Institute of Irish-Scottish Studies, established at the University of Aberdeen in 1998 and formally opened in 1999 by the then President of Ireland Mary McAleese.

107 Liam McIlvaney and Ray Ryan, eds, *Ireland and Scotland: Culture and Society, 1700–2000* (Dublin, 2005), 11–22 especially p.17.

108 Smith, *Crisis and Survival.*

as landscape and spatial analysis, environmental, archaeological and geographic approaches have added much to our understanding the past.[109]

In contrast, some Scottish and Irish historiography has developed in a different direction to examine Scottish, including Highland, and Irish, communities abroad resulting in the burgeoning field of diaspora studies, exploring the military, economic, confessional and educational pull to places across Europe. This has challenged the general assumption that Ulster was the primary destination for the majority of Scots who migrated overseas during the early modern period, highlighting the vast numbers who left Scotland and headed east rather than west, to Europe rather than the Americas.[110] This growing trend to explore communities living beyond the territorial boundaries of the insular world is intimately intertwined with alternative historiographical and conceptual contexts that have developed rapidly in recent decades; that of Greater Britain and the Atlantic World, alongside imperial and, increasingly, transnational history.[111] Not without

109 See, for example, B. J. Graham and L. J. Proudfoot, eds, *An Historical Geography of Ireland* (London, 1993); Fitzpatrick, *Royal Inauguration in Gaelic Ireland*; T. C. Smout, *Exploring Environmental History: Selected Essays* (Edinburgh, 2009); Aidan O'Sullivan and Colin Breen, *Maritime Ireland: An Archaeology of Coastal Communities* (Stroud, 2011); Horning, *Ireland in the Virginian Sea*; Rachael Barrowman, ed., *Dùn Èistean, Ness, Isle of Lewis: The Excavation of a Late Medieval Clan Stronghold* (Stornoway, 2015); Rowan McLaughlin and James Lyttleton, eds, *An Archaeology of Northern Ireland 1600–1650* (Antrim, 2017).

110 Amongst a wealth of literature see T. M. Devine, *Scotland's Empire, 1600–1815* (London, 2003); Thomas O'Connor and Mary Ann Lyons, *Irish Migrants in Europe after Kinsale, 1602–1820* (Dublin, 2003); David Worthington, *Scots in the Habsburg Service, 1618–1648* (Leiden, 2004); Alexia Grosjean and Steve Murdoch, eds, *Scottish Communities Abroad in the Early Modern Period* (Leiden, 2005); Thomas O'Connor and Mary Ann Lyons, eds, *Irish Communities in Early Modern Europe* (Dublin, 2006); Esther Mijers, *'News from the Republick of Letters': Scottish Students, Charles Mackie, and the United Provinces, 1650–1750* (Leiden, 2012); David Worthington, *British and Irish Experiences and Impressions of Central Europe, c.1560–1688* (Farnham, 2012).

111 From a historiography almost as vast and deep as the Atlantic itself see David Armitage, 'Greater Britain: A Useful Category of Historical Analysis?', *American Historical Review* 104/2 (1999), 427–45; Jane Ohlmeyer, 'Seventeenth-Century Ireland and the New British and Atlantic Histories', *American Historical Review* 104/2 (1999), 446–62; J. G. A. Pocock, 'The New British History in Atlantic

its critics, the history of the Atlantic World has expanded considerably in recent years locating England and its colonies within wider frameworks and incorporating themes such as migration, empire, trade, slavery and gender as well as cultural, legal and political transmission between nations and peoples across the ocean.[112] Engagement with this Atlantic context by Irish historians commenced in the mid-to-late twentieth century with a focus on the 'westward expansion', examining plantation and settlement in Ireland as part of a wider overseas colonial development in the age of expansion; but there were renewed efforts in the late twentieth century.[113] Equally fruitful was the Scottish response. Relative late-comers to the Atlantic World, the Scottish involvement in empire has become a key focus of study, examining the extent to which Scots exploited the opportunities presented by imperial endeavour, while more recently highlighting Scottish

---

Perspective: An Antipodean Commentary', *American Historical Review* 104/2 (1999), 490–500; David Armitage and Michael J. Braddick, eds, *The British Atlantic World, 1500–1800* (Basingstoke, 2002); David Armitage, *Greater Britain, 1516–1776: Essays in Atlantic History* (Aldershot, 2004).

112 Kenneth R. Andrews, *Trade, Plunder and Settlement: Maritime Enterprise and the Genesis of the British Empire, 1480–1630* (Cambridge, 1984); David Armitage, ed., *Theories of Empire, 1450–1800* (Aldershot, 1998); Nicholas Canny, ed., *The Oxford History of the British Empire I: The Origins of Empire* (Oxford, 1998); Alison Games, *Migration and the origins of the English Atlantic world* (Cambridge, MA and London, 1999); David Armitage, *The Ideological Origins of the British Empire* (Cambridge, 2000); Armitage and Braddick, eds, *The British Atlantic World*.

113 D. B. Quinn, 'Ireland and Sixteenth Century Expansion', in T. Desmond Williams, ed., *Historical Studies* I (London, 1958), 21–32; Nicholas Canny, 'The Ideology of English Colonisation: From Ireland to America', *William and Mary Quarterly*, third series, 30 (1973), 575–98; K. R. Andrews, N. P. Canny and P. E. H. Hair, eds, *The Westward Enterprise: English Activities in Ireland, the Atlantic and America, 1480–1650* (Liverpool, 1978); David Cressy, *Coming Over: Migration and Communication between England and New England in the Sixteenth Century* (Cambridge, 1987); Nicholas Canny and Anthony Pagden, eds, *Colonial Identity in the Atlantic World, 1500–1800* (Princeton, 1987); Nicholas Canny, *Kingdom and Colony: Ireland in the Atlantic World 1500–1800* (Baltimore and London, 1988). For perspectives on efforts to locate Ireland within a wider Atlantic empire see Hiram Morgan, 'Mid-Atlantic Blues', *Irish Review* 11 (1991/92), 50–5; Andrew Hadfield, 'Rocking the Boat: A Response to Hiram Morgan', *Irish Review*, 14 (1993), 15–19.

participation in the slave trade.[114] Although we are not 'all Atlanticists now', it is a framework that offers useful parallels for this study.[115]

Atlanticist historiography facilitates an analysis which emphasises connections and comparisons across realms, and around a body of water, within a geographic region that lacks defined territorial, political, or national boundaries. This view of a region, without specific borders but given coherence by its location around the edges of a body of water, as being a legitimate subject for analysis resonates deeply with the scope of this current study. Indeed, much like the Atlantic World historiography, focus is not necessarily placed on the water itself, but on those communities that existed around, were brought together by, and utilised, the North Channel whether for political, military, social, economic or confessional reasons. This maritime perspective is important as it reinforces the fact that while it was one small part of the wider Atlantic World, the region at the heart of this study was far from being a remote littoral on the margins of Europe. Rather, the lands bounded together by the North Channel were in immediate proximity to a waterway that connected the region to Scandinavia, the continent and ultimately, the Atlantic itself.[116]

Given the approach outlined above, it will be clear that this study moves away from traditional nation-based approaches that have dominated early modern British and Irish history and instead takes a regional, geographic and transnational perspective centred on an area that lacks precise or readily defined borders. During the late sixteenth and early seventeenth

114 Andrew MacKillop, *More Fruitful than the Soil: Army, Empire and the Scottish Highlands, 1715–1815* (Edinburgh, 2000); Ned C. Landsman, *Nation and Province in the First British Empire: Scotland and the Americas 1600–1800* (Lewisburg, PA and London, 2001); Douglas J. Hamilton, *Scotland, the Caribbean and the Atlantic World, 1750–1820* (Manchester, 2005); T. M. Devine, ed., *Recovering Scotland's Slavery Past: The Caribbean Connection* (Edinburgh, 2015); Stephen Mullen, *Glasgow's Sugar Aristocracy in the British-Atlantic World, 1776–1838* (London, forthcoming, 2022).

115 David Armitage, 'Three Concepts of Atlantic History', in Armitage and Braddick, eds, *The British Atlantic World*, 13–29 at 11.

116 For more on the importance of the North Channel in the early modern period see *Maritime Communities of the North Atlantic Arc in the Early Modern Period: Journal of the North Atlantic*, ed., Alison Cathcart, special volume 12 (2019).

centuries the North Channel and the communities that existed around its rim were located on the edges of Europe and the Atlantic world, but were at the very nexus of this Atlantic archipelago where political, territorial, cultural, confessional, linguistic, social and economic boundaries coincided. As such this draws heavily on transnational approaches, examining peoples and processes operating across territorial, political and national boundaries. This is intentional, emphasising the permeability of frontier zones as the political, economic, confessional or cultural identities of the various communities (and the extent of their dominance) within this geographic region ebbed and flowed like the waters that bound them together. While the region and its peoples were regarded as peripheral by contemporaries, geographically remote from the centres of crown and government authority, this study aims to move beyond, and re-define, centre-periphery frameworks. It will do so, not by placing the periphery at the core (which would be an inversion of current approaches) but rather by regarding both core and periphery as 'centres' (or localities) within an undefined geographic region: what is peripheral is, after all, a matter of perspective. At the same time, the intention is not to examine these communities in isolation, amounting to the reverse of adopting a state-centred perspective, nor does it suggest that state-centred approaches are redundant. This type of analysis is possible only because it builds upon the scholarship of previous historians who have undertaken traditional, national histories. The aim is to integrate the perspective of these communities with that of the crown and government emphasising the interplay between crown and community or between different centres of power.

As well as drawing from different historiographical and methodological approaches, the present study also utilises the work and approaches of the Annales School. While it does not take the *longue durée* advocated by Fernand Braudel, it does take inspiration from Braudel's *La Méditerranée et le Monde Méditerranéen à l'Epoque de Philippe II* (1949), a work that focused on the sea, the lands around it and the people who lived there. Braudel also highlighted the different categories and speeds of change whether geographic and environmental, socio-economic and cultural, or the more immediate, and human, causal factors.[117] Like Braudel and *La*

117 Or *histoire événementielle* as the Annales termed it.

Méditerranée, this study explores the water, the land and people that existed around it. While for the large part it follows an empirical methodology, this research draws on a variety of approaches and perspectives from other disciplines and, where appropriate, incorporates non-traditional source material alongside documentary evidence.

This study has relied heavily on State Papers and other governmental records. While these offer the perspective of crown and government officials, whether in London, Edinburgh or in Ireland, when handled appropriately they reveal much about English and Scottish attitudes, the ineffectiveness of legislation and the situation on the ground in various localities. There is no doubt, researching this book took much longer on account of the availability of the State Papers Online, but without such access, this would have involved a considerably greater amount time spent at The National Archives and the British Library or a less nuanced analysis. Alongside these records, the analysis has sought to draw on a variety of source material ranging from Irish Annals, to cartography, to archaeological remains, and literature. When examined within a wider context, and with awareness of the intended audience and underlying agendas, such evidence provides a rich resource to illuminate perspectives too readily overlooked.[118]

For the most part, this book examines the development of a policy of plantation, both in theory and in practice, yet it does not aim to be a straightforward political history. The analysis has been shaped by a number of approaches including historical geography, environmental history and an appreciation of maritime considerations. Without seeking to diminish the inherent militaristic nature of much of the cross-channel migration, especially on the part of the Highlanders, the study emphasises economic drivers behind the plantation policy, as well as the role of individuals, while incorporating climate change and environmental and maritime factors that shaped the development of the archipelago. No doubt some of this evidence remains contentious and the significance of long-term, gradual

118 Although referring specifically to the 1641 depositions, the importance of such sources being 'read against themselves, and against the inherent bias they often convey' is eloquently expressed by Gerard Farrell, *The 'Mere Irish' and the Colonisation of Ulster, 1570–1641* (Cham, 2017), 16–17.

change needs to be offset by the adaptability of local communities and divergent responses to such change. Nonetheless, by weaving a variety of source material and different historical and disciplinary approaches into this study, it seeks to ask questions of current historiographical approaches yet emphasise the gradual evolution of what became a policy of plantation in Ireland. It questions assumptions about plantation as a process of state formation or extension of empire, and about who was involved, and why. Above all, the intention is to suggest an alternative approach to history, through the examination of regions bounded by geography rather than territorial boundaries, across borders rather than constrained by them, and highlight the extent to which the periphery was central to wider political, social and economic development within the archipelago during this period.

CHAPTER 2

Historical context[1]

At the end of the fifteenth century, the Tudor and Stewart monarchies in England and Scotland faced problems of a broadly similar nature. Both kings had succeeded to their respective thrones only recently, and after a period of turmoil. Admittedly the turmoil had been longer and more divisive in England as Henry VII's succession to the English throne, following his defeat of Richard III at the Battle of Bosworth in 1485, brought to an end a long and destructive civil war fought between the Yorkist and Lancastrian houses. His marriage to Elizabeth of York, eldest daughter of Edward IV, was intended to symbolise the end of unrest and the unification of rival claims. But Henry had to contend with a number of plots and rebellions against his rule led by Yorkist claimants to the English crown, two of which were supported by his Irish subjects. Such was the level of support for Lambert Simmel, who claimed to be Edward, Earl of Warwick, nephew of Edward IV, that in May 1487 Gerald FitzGerald, eighth Earl of Kildare, then Lord Deputy of Ireland, had Simmel proclaimed King Edward VI in Dublin.[2] In 1491 another rival, Perkin Warbeck, claiming to be Richard, Duke of York, younger son of Edward IV, initially received support in Ireland. This posed more of a threat and steps were taken to pacify England and Ireland while Warbeck made his way to Scotland where he was

1 It is not entirely necessary here to discuss in detail the historical background of the insular world prior to *c.*1550, however, some introduction to the wider context of these communities in the mid-sixteenth century, that takes account of previous interaction, is helpful.

2 S. J. Gunn, 'Henry VII (1457–1509)', *ODNB*, accessed 27 June 2016; Steven G. Ellis, 'Fitzgerald, Gerald, eighth earl of Kildare (1456?–1513), magnate and administrator', *ODNB*, accessed 20 July 2018.

welcomed and encouraged by James IV who exploited the opportunity to further weaken his English counterpart.[3] This was short-lived; James IV soon rid himself of Warbeck but the incident did bring immediate gains for the Scottish king who, in 1503, was married to Margaret, Henry VII's daughter.[4] While the two monarchs were able to put aside their differences, extending peace and stability within their own realms was another matter. Henry VII may have put down rebellion and reconciled the leading figures in the king's Irish administration but overall Ireland remained a problem for the English crown.[5] As well as being a drain on the crown's finances, continued resistance to English rule meant Ireland remained the proverbial back-door through which any hostile power would invade England.

In Scotland James IV was not without his own problems. While he exploited the opportunity presented by Perkin Warbeck to embarrass his southern neighbour, eventually bringing Henry VII to the negotiating table which resulted in the Treaty of Perpetual Peace and marriage to Henry's daughter, domestic matters were not progressing as smoothly as James might have hoped. He faced a law and order problem, a result of the 1493 forfeiture of the MacDonald lordship of the Isles. Although issued by his minority government, it was up to James to take steps to deal with the fall-out. While he embarked on a number of military expeditions, maintaining and garrisoning castles in the western Highlands and Isles and extracting submissions from a number of Highland chiefs, his divide-and-rule policy, along with the granting and regranting of lands and offices, exacerbated disputes between clans that formerly had been part of the lordship. The social and economic dislocation in the region, the result of internal division and inconsistent royal intervention, resulted in a number of rebellions in the west during the first half of the sixteenth century. Although none of

3 For more on the Warbeck conspiracy see Gunn, 'Henry VII'. James also carried out a number of border raids, see Norman Macdougall, *James III: A Political Study* (Edinburgh, 1982); Norman Macdougall, *James IV* (Edinburgh, 1997).

4 The, somewhat optimistically named, Treaty of Perpetual Peace was contracted the previous year in 1502.

5 In doing so, he replaced the earl of Kildare with Sir Edward Poynings as Lord Deputy, thereby resulting in the implementation of Poynings' Law.

them seriously threatened the crown, the unrest was significant enough to ensure that successive monarchs had to pay attention to matters in the west.[6]

Connections that crossed territorial and political boundaries were in play at this time; they were also connections that stretched back into previous centuries. The migration of Highland Scots to Ireland, known as galloglass, occurred frequently throughout the thirteenth and early fourteenth centuries. They went as a fighting force, bolstering the armies of Irish lords engaged in warfare either with their own local rivals or against English royal authority, and these martial connections often reinforced, and in turn were reinforced by, cultural, marital and confessional ties.[7] This period saw many galloglass settle permanently in Ireland, a consequence of a changing situation in Scotland and the reward of land in Ireland.[8] The result, as Kenneth Nicholls has argued, was the maintenance of long-standing alliances between Irish families and their Scottish galloglass supporters ensuring that certain Irish families could rely on the provision from particular Scottish clans. Most notable among the galloglass families who settled in Ireland were the MacSweens, who provided a permanent resource

6 K. A. Steer and J. W. M. Bannerman, *Late Medieval Monumental Sculpture in the West Highlands* (RCAHMS, 1977), 201–11; Jean Munro, 'The Lordship of the Isles', in L. Maclean, ed., *The Making of the Middle Ages in the Highlands* (Inverness, 1981), 23–37; Norman Macdougall, 'Achilles' Heel? The Earldom of Ross, the Lordship of the Isles, and the Stewart Kings, 1449–1507', in E. J. Cowan and R. A. McDonald, eds, *Alba. Celtic Scotland in the Medieval Era* (East Linton, 2000), 248–75; Alison Cathcart, 'A Spent Force? The Clan Donald in the Aftermath of 1493', in Richard D. Oram, ed., *The Lordship of the Isles* (Leiden, 2014), 254–70.

7 Seán Duffy, 'The Prehistory of the Galloglass', in Seán Duffy, ed., *The World of the Galloglass. Kings, Warlords and Warriors in Ireland and Scotland, 1200–1600* (Dublin, 2007), 15–16 argues that 'Hebridean lords … were, by 1247, a quotidian feature of warfare in the northwest of Ireland'.

8 Gerald A. Hayes-McCoy, *Scots Mercenary Forces in Ireland (1565–1603)* (Dublin, 1937; reprinted 1996), 15–76; James Lydon, 'The Scottish Soldier in Medieval Ireland: The Bruce Invasion and the Galloglass', in G. G. Simpson, ed., *The Scottish Soldier Abroad 1247–1967* (Edinburgh, 1992), 1–15; Kenneth Nicholls, 'Scottish Mercenary Kindreds in Ireland, 1250–1600', in Duffy, ed., *The World of the Galloglass*, 86–105; Michael A. Penman, 'The MacDonald Lordship and the Bruce Dynasty, *c.*1306–*c.*1371', in Oram, ed., *The Lordship of the Isles*, 62–87.

of men for the O'Donnell lords of Tyrconnell in northwest Ulster.[9] At the same time members of the MacDonald clan were active in Ulster also, providing galloglass for the O'Neills of Tyrone.[10]

Initially rather dispersed, the extent to which they had consolidated a presence in the area was highlighted in the late 1390s when John Mor MacDonald, second son of John, first lord of the Isles, and Margaret Stewart, daughter of Robert Stewart, later Robert II of Scotland, was married to Marjory, heiress of Hugh Bisset of the Glens.[11] An Anglo-Norman family, the Bissets are first recorded in Scotland in the late twelfth century having been granted the lands of Aird in Moray but by 1247 were established in northeast Ulster, although the means by which they did this is not clear. By the early fourteenth century they held lands in the Glens of Antrim along with Rathlin Island.[12] Although the marriage of John and Marjory is often put forward as the date the MacDonalds acquired lands in Antrim, it is likely the marriage was an indication of the strength of an established MacDonald presence in the area, as well as their dominant position across the channel.[13] Hugh Bisset would have been reluctant to marry his only daughter into the family unless the alliance offered significant, strategic (and probably military) advantages. Nonetheless, it was through this alliance that the MacDonalds are reputed to have gained the seven territories in the Glens of Antrim and, by the early 1400s, John Mor was referred to as 'Lord of Dunevege and the Glynnis'.[14] Though not immediately supplanted, the dominance of the Bissets in east Antrim began to decline as increasing

9 Hayes-McCoy, *Scots Mercenary Forces in Ireland*, 30–4; Nicholls, 'Scottish Mercenary Kindreds in Ireland', 91–7.

10 Nicholls, 'Scottish Mercenary Kindreds in Ireland', 97–103.

11 SP 63/1, fols 204–7 (206v).

12 Seán Duffy, 'The Lords of Galloway, Earls of Carrick, and the Bissets of the Glens: Scottish Settlement in Thirteenth-Century Ulster', in David Edwards, ed., *Regions and Rulers in Ireland, 1100–1650. Essays for Kenneth Nicholls* (Dublin, 2004), 37–50.

13 Duffy, 'The lords of Galloway', 48 suggests the Bissets had attempted previously to unite lands on either side of the channel.

14 Quoted in Colin Breen, *Dunluce Castle. History and Archaeology* (Dublin, 2012), 37; Simon Kingston, *Ulster and the Isles in the Fifteenth Century: The Lordship of the Clann Domhnaill of Antrim* (Dublin, 2004), 49–50.

numbers of MacDonalds settled in the Glens, a pattern that would continue into the sixteenth century.[15] The establishment of a branch of the Clan Donald in the Glens of Antrim became a thorn in the side for both English and Scottish monarchs. A MacDonald stronghold in the Glens facilitated further migration of Highland Scots into Ireland which contributed to ongoing unrest in the north. Over the course of the fifteenth and into the sixteenth century this consolidated the English view of the northern province as the most problematic region in Ireland and resulted in increasing animosity on the part of the English towards the presence of Highland Scots there. In the short-term, however, it was the Scottish monarchy who recognised the full implications of the existence of a MacDonald base in a land where the Scottish crown had no jurisdiction and lacked the authority to do very much about the situation.

In 1424 James I returned home after eighteen years in English captivity intent on taking firm action against those he felt had become too powerful in his absence, in particular the Albany Stewarts. During his imprisonment his uncle, Robert Stewart, Duke of Albany, and from 1420 Murdac Stewart, James' cousin and son of Robert, acted as Regent; James believed they had done little to secure his release and instead had furthered their own interests.[16] Despite the capture and execution of Duke Murdac and many of his kinsmen, the king was unable to seize the last remaining member of the family, Murdac's other son, James, known as 'the fat'. As a

15 Kingston, *Ulster and the Isles*, 49–53; George Hill, *An Historical Account of the Macdonnells of Antrim: Including Notices of Some Other Septs, Irish and Scottish* (Belfast, 1873), 17–37; Alison Cathcart, 'Scots and Ulster: The Late Medieval Context', in W. P. Kelly and J. R. Young, eds, *Scotland and the Ulster Plantations. Explorations in the British Settlements of Stuart Ireland* (Dublin, 2009), 62–83 at 64; Breen, *Dunluce Castle*, 34–47; Lydon, 'The Scottish Soldier in Medieval Ireland' 1, where Lydon states that, according to the Dublin parliament of March 1474, the number of Scots 'entred and dwellen in Ullester' was around 10,000.

16 Recent historiography has argued that Robert had been an effective and energetic regent in the king's absence although his son, Murdac, was unable to maintain the Albany regime in Scotland; see Stephen Boardman, 'Stewart, Robert, first duke of Albany (c. 1340–1420), prince and governor of Scotland' *ODNB*, accessed 31 July 2018; Michael Brown, 'Stewart, Murdoch [Murdac], second duke of Albany (c. 1362–1425), magnate' *ODNB*, accessed 31 July 2018.

close kinsman, the disinherited heir of the duchy of Albany, and a potential rival claimant for the crown, James 'the fat' posed a significant threat to the king: especially as, at this time, the king himself had no successor.[17] More troubling was the fact that James 'the fat', when he fled into exile, found refuge with the MacDonalds in Ireland. As a king determined to assert his royal authority after years of imprisonment in England and eliminate any opposition to his position, James I regarded the MacDonalds as another problematic and over-mighty kindred. Their settlement in the Glens of Antrim, a region beyond the king's reach, served to underline the seriousness of the situation. Although the king passed legislation forbidding unauthorised contact between Scotland and Ireland, in reality he was relatively powerless to do much to curtail the traffic between the western Highlands and Isles of Scotland and the north of Ireland.[18] Consequently, he turned instead to negotiation, sending one '[James] Campbell to know if John Mor of Kintyre', uncle to Alexander, third Lord of the Isles, 'would send to take al his nephew's lands'.[19] Whether the king really did intend such a course of action is unclear. In all probability he was hoping to come to some agreement with John Mor and, in so doing, neutralise the threat posed by the Albany Stewart. Unfortunately for the king, John Mor refused the offer but in the process was killed by Campbell, an act which fostered widespread resentment towards the king amongst the MacDonalds and undoubtedly contributed to the breakdown in relations between the two parties which occurred around this time.[20] Meanwhile, thankfully for the king, although

17 Michael Brown, *James I*, (Edinburgh, 1994), 17–71, 93–102; *Annála Rioghachta Éireann: Annals of the Kingdom of Ireland by the Four Masters, from the Earliest Period to the Year 1616*, ed. and trans., J. O'Donovan (Dublin, 2nd edn, 1856), IV, 1429 (875) [*AFM*] states that James 'had been banished from Scotland to Ireland'.

18 *RPS*, 1426/21; 1426/22; 1426/23; 1426/24, accessed 31 July 2018; Brown, *James I*, 75; Cathcart, 'Scots and Ulster', 65.

19 'History of the MacDonalds', in J. R. N. MacPhail, ed., *Highland Papers* I, series two, vol. V (Edinburgh: Scottish History Society, 1914), 38–9.

20 For a possible explanation of this see Brown, *James I*, 99–101.

a fleet came out of the isles in 1429 'to convey him [James 'the fat'] home that he might be made king', he died before arriving in Scotland.[21]

The episode contributed to a downturn in crown-MacDonald relations and while it forced James I to deploy additional troops towards Ireland, little could be done in the long-term to deal with the settlement of Highland Scots in Ulster. To be fair, in later decades Stewart monarchs paid little attention to this activity. At the end of the fifteenth century, however, events in Scotland again impacted directly on the settlement of the MacDonalds in the north of Ireland. Crown concern over increasing lawlessness in the west alongside the evident inability of John, fourth Lord of the Isles, to maintain stability in the region were factors that led to the final forfeiture of the Lordship of the Isles in 1493.[22] No doubt, there was significant internal fracturing within the wider Clan Donald but other satellite clans, notably the Mackenzies of Kintail in Ross, were acting increasingly independently.[23] This forfeiture was passed by the minority government of James IV, some members of which were the first to benefit from land grants of former lordship lands.[24] Although James himself had little to do with the disintegration of the lordship, it was left to him to clean up the mess. The main problem was how to fill the power vacuum left behind but crown policy was intermittent and inconsistent resulting in a deepening of divisions between former lordship clans and the various branches of the Clan Donald who began to jostle with one other for land and superiority. For the MacDonalds of Dunivaig and the Glens, their estates in Antrim provided the perfect refuge from the worsening situation in the Isles. This was most keenly felt in the last years of the fifteenth

21 *AFM*, 1429 (875); Art Cosgrove, 'Ireland beyond the Pale, 1399–1460', in Art Cosgrove, ed., *A New History of Ireland II: Medieval Ireland, 1169–1534* (Oxford, 1993), at 575–6 [*NHI*].

22 Already weakened by the loss of the earldom of Ross in 1476, internal divisions deepened. For more on this see Cathcart, 'Spent Force?', 254–70 at 254–5.

23 Aonghas MacCoinnich, "Kingis rabellis' to 'Cuidich 'n Rìgh'? Clann Choinnich: The Emergence of a Kindred, *c.* 1475–*c.*1514', in Steve Boardman and Alasdair Ross, eds, *The Exercise of Power in Medieval Scotland, c.1200–1500* (Dublin, 2003), 175–200.

24 Macdougall, 'Achilles Heel?', 265–6.

century when Alexander, the last remaining son of Sir John MacDonald of Dunivaig, escaped to Antrim.

The situation arose following John MacDonald's rebellious response to the actions of the king. In the later 1490s James IV had embarked on a number of naval expeditions to the Isles in an attempt to bring some degree of stability to the region. He stopped at various castles and strongholds of the main Hebridean chiefs, extracting promises of obedience and good behaviour. It was apparently on this voyage that, while on Islay in 1494, he knighted John MacDonald of Dunivaig but, before leaving also placed a royal garrison in Dunivaig Castle. This was an affront to the Highland chief who regarded Dunivaig as his own seat and, in full view of the departing king, hanged the newly appointed constable from the castle walls. The king was furious at this display of contempt for royal authority while the MacIans of Ardnamurchan, seeking favour in their claims to the lands of Sunart, arrested and handed over MacDonald of Dunivaig and his sons who were then hanged at Borrowmuir. Almost repeating the events of James I's reign, Alexander, the only male family member alive, fled to the family lands in Antrim, remaining there for some years while the fortunes of his family in Scotland were at something of a nadir.

In the early sixteenth century these long-standing cross-channel alliances between Irish and Scottish kindreds, cemented through regular and repeated movement of Highland Scots, began to break down, a result of the political instability and socio-economic dislocation that followed the forfeiture of 1493. These ongoing migration patterns had evolved into a temporary, seasonal movement as Highland Scots increasingly found short-term employment in the pay of an Irish lord, leaving them able to return to their lands in Scotland whenever their presence was required, notably spring-time and harvest, or during periods of significant unrest. At this time, Irish lords were willing and able to recruit ready armies of Highland forces for their own purposes but some, like O'Donnell, lord of Tyrconnell, were not prepared to jeopardise their long-standing friendship with the Scottish crown.[25] Aware of the ongoing turmoil in the western Isles, in April 1507 O'Donnell wrote to James requesting military

25 The O'Donnells of Tyrconnell were leading lords in the northwest of Ireland, a lordship more or less analogous to modern-day county Donegal, and long-standing enemies of the O'Neills of Tyrone. For more on both the lordship and county see

assistance from John MacIan of Ardnamurchan and his Highland allies.[26] At the time, MacIan was one of the chiefs in favour with the crown having arrested and handed over his own kinsmen, John of Dunivaig, and three of his sons. There is no doubt O'Donnell was fully aware of the situation in the Isles and hoped to benefit both from a surplus of unemployed Highland manpower and James' favour to the MacIan chief. It is probable the Irish lord sought military assistance against his long-standing foe, the O'Neills of Tyrone and their MacDonald galloglass, but on this occasion James refused the request. James blamed his inability to meet O'Donnell's needs on the time of year and the bad weather but, in truth, the king was

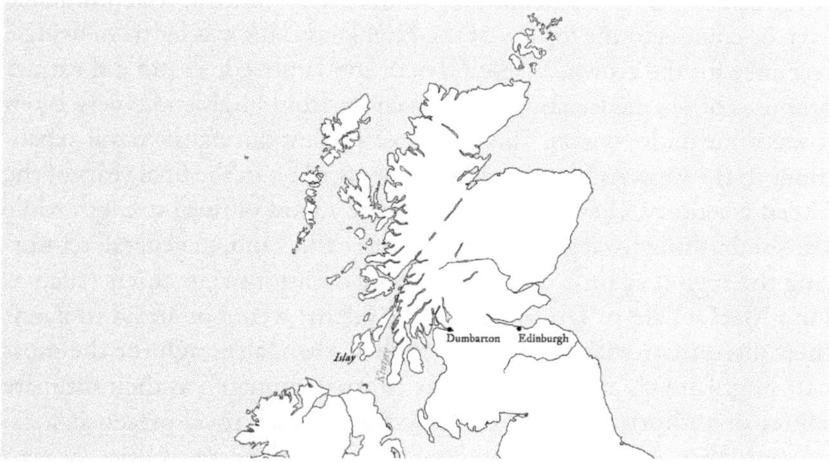

Map 2. The north of Ireland and Scotland

William Nolan, Liam Ronayne and Mairead Dunlevy, eds, *Donegal: History and Society. Interdisciplinary Essays on the History of an Irish County* (Dublin, 1995). Although the O'Donnells were a major kindred in the north of Ireland, in terms of this study of plantation, there is less focus on them than on the O'Neills of Tyrone. Their lands of Tyrconnell formed part of the lands escheated to the English crown following the Flight of the Earls in 1607 and settled during the official Plantation of Ulster.

26 R. K. Hannay and R. L. Mackie, eds, *The Letters of James the Fourth, 1505–1513*, series four, vol. XLV (Edinburgh: Scottish History Society, 1953), nos 104–6 (70–1).

being cautious. He did not want to refuse or deny his ally any assistance but he was well aware of the MacDonald presence in Ulster alongside the widespread rumblings of continued unrest in the west Highlands and Isles (see Map 2). He was unsure of the extent to which he could assert his royal authority over the cross-channel activity of his own subjects, but at the same time he wanted to retain MacIan manpower in the west at that time to suppress any further possible outbreak of rebellion.[27]

The Highlanders' martial prowess was a double-edged sword for successive Stewart monarchs. Lawlessness and disorder in their own realm was unwelcome and had been an issue for several of James' predecessors. When and if harnessed for the crown's own ends such militarism was viewed as advantageous and beneficial, but the ability to control, have influence over, or command the loyalty of the Highland clans was far from being a certainty for the crown. While on occasion James could and did extract promises of obedience and good behaviour from Highland chiefs, often it was done under duress. This was most evident during the naval expeditions to the western Isles that James embarked on in the final years of the fifteenth century. They were designed to be a show of royal strength while also establishing royal garrisons at various castles and, in general, reinforcing the region against unrest. On some occasions clan chiefs (such as John MacDonald of Dunivaig and the Glens) were not afraid to flaunt their discontent with the actions of the crown, although for the most part Highland chiefs recognised the Scottish monarch as their ultimate source of authority; but, when there was no such royal presence, local issues dominated. Land disputes, marital discord, petty rivalries, or economic matters were of greater priority than maintaining obedience to an absentee monarch, unless of course obedience to a monarch dovetailed with one's own agenda.

This was the case for the Campbells of Argyll.[28] Very much a traditional, Highland clan, the Campbell chiefs had risen to prominence in the

27 Performing such service for the crown may have brought short-term rewards, but it turned both kin and fellow clans against MacIan. He was later the focus of a rebellion in the west and subsequently murdered by his own kinsmen. See 'History of the MacDonalds' in *Highland Papers I*, 5–72.

28 Boardman, *The Campbells*.

previous century and a half, a reward for loyal service to the crown. It was James II who created Colin Campbell of Loch Awe first Earl of Argyll and subsequent Stewart monarchs relied on them for law and order in the west. James IV likewise turned to Archibald Campbell, second Earl of Argyll, in the aftermath of the 1493 forfeiture and post-1498 more or less delegated all Highland affairs to both Argyll in the South Isles and George Gordon, second Earl, and Alexander, third Earl of Huntly, in the North Isles.[29] The Campbells maintained good relations with other Highland clans and had numerous marital connections throughout the region, and success was predicated on their ability to align personal and clan interests with those of the crown. But Argyll also was keen to control the mercenary trade to Ireland that was developing in the wake of the 1493 forfeiture and sought to assert his position within the region and across the North Channel. It was difficult to get any sense of control over cross-channel activity in the opening decades of the sixteenth century, however, as rebellion broke out sporadically and Argyll was called upon to deal with the situation. Maintaining close ties with fellow Highland chiefs, while also performing loyal service to the crown and preserving national significance, was a delicate balancing act. As James IV preferred to delegate Highland affairs to his regional magnates, Argyll utilised this to further consolidate his position and influence in the west. It was a situation that would not be fully replicated or tolerated for long by James' son and heir.

Not long after his accession to the throne in 1528, following a protracted and troubled minority, James V recognised that the Campbell earls of Argyll had become rather too powerful in the west. Delegating royal authority to regional magnates may have been effective, but by the time James came to the throne, Archibald, fourth Earl of Argyll, was able to exploit his position and manipulate affairs to suit his own agenda. A dispute between Argyll and Alexander MacDonald of Dunivaig and the Glens that broke out in 1529 brought this to James' attention.[30] Consequently, James removed Argyll from the region, keeping him busy in Edinburgh with other affairs, and instigated a policy of direct personal communication with a number of Highland chiefs, notably MacDonald of Dunivaig

29 Cathcart, 'Spent Force?', 261–4.

30 Cathcart, 'Spent Force?', 260.

and the Glens himself and Hector Maclean of Duart. Crown-clan co-operation paid off. MacLean and MacDonald captured an English ship, the *Mary Willoughby*, off the Isle of Man in 1533, a vessel which later became the flagship of the Scottish fleet in 1540, despite the fact that the English had prior intelligence of the attack.[31] A few years later when MacDonald of Dunivaig and the Glens went to Ireland he remained in contact with his king which enabled James to interfere in Irish affairs. His direct support of Manus O'Donnell, writing to the papacy on behalf of the Irish lord, would not have gone unnoticed by his uncle, but Henry was pre-occupied with the aftermath of the FitzGerald rebellion, unrest in the north of England and a break-down in Anglo-French relations. In the summer of 1536 James' attentions were distracted by his own marital affairs and he sailed to France in September that year, later marrying Madeleine de Valois in January 1537. The premature death of his French bride only a few months after her arrival in Scotland meant James continued to be invested in other affairs, later marrying Marie de Guise in June 1538. By this time James had witnessed his uncle's harsh treatment of the FitzGeralds as Thomas and five of his uncles were executed in early 1537, a clear message that Henry would not tolerate such opposition. The Scottish king clearly felt he had pushed his uncle's boundaries far enough and, having benefitted financially from two large marriage dowries, was more concerned with projecting an image of his imperial monarchy to wider, European audience. As was so often the case, Ireland slipped down the agenda.[32]

The English continued to be concerned about the activities of the Scottish king, especially given the reports that he was preparing an expedition to head either to Ireland or to France in 1540. But that was only part of the matter. The more pressing issue was the reports that

31 The *Mary Willoughby* was retaken by the English later in 1547; see Richard Boulind, 'Ships of private origin in the mid-Tudor navy: the *Lartigue*, the *Salamander*, the *Mary Willoughby*, the *Bark Aucher* and the *Galley Blanchard*', *The Mariner's Mirror*, 59/4 (1973), 385–408, especially 393–5.

32 Roger A. Mason, '"This realm of Scotland is an empire?' Imperial Ideas and Iconography in Early Renaissance Scotland', in Barbara Crawford, ed., *Church, Chronicle and Learning in Medieval and Early Renaissance Scotland* (Edinburgh, 1999), 73–91; Andrea Thomas, *Princelie Majestie: The Court of James V of Scotland, 1528–1542* (Edinburgh, 2005).

> 8 gentylemen of Ierlande ... browght unto Hym [James V] the seales ... of all the greate men in Ierlande, that thay wolde houlde of Hym, and take Hym for thayre Kynge and Lorde, and that thay wolde come in to Scotlande to make hym omayge, and that He shulde have more proffet yerly than

Henry had ever received.[33] This may have been an attempt by the Geraldine League to gain James' continued support, perhaps hoping for a Catholic overlord, but certainly a less interventionist one. If so, it did not work out as they had hoped. The expedition was not destined for Ireland or France, but the western Isles to suppress rebellion in James' own kingdom. Despite encouragement from Pope Paul III to consider 'the weal of Ireland, which ... has a claim upon James' loyalty and touches his reputation', the Scottish king had clearly withdrawn from any involvement in Irish matters.[34] Nonetheless, the offer of the kingship of Ireland to James V in 1540 would have very real repercussions for the Irish the following year for there can be no doubt that these events also contributed to Henry's decision to pass the Act for the Kingly Title in 1541.[35]

33 *State Papers Published under the Authority of His Majesty's Commission, Volume V: King Henry VIII Part IV* (London, 1836), no.ccclxxii (178–9 at 178); *L&P Henry VIII*, XV, no.697 (326).

34 R. K. Hannay and D. Hays, eds, *The Letters of James V* (Edinburgh, 1954), 420: Letter from Paul III to James V, Rome, 24 February 1540–1. At the time Henry was facing opposition on numerous fronts, a consequence of his break from Rome in 1533–4. In 1536 the Pilgrimage of Grace saw disorder in the north of England, while unrest in Ireland, combined with international displeasure put increased pressure on Henry.

35 My thanks to Dr David Edwards for discussing this point with me on a number of occasions and encouraging me to pursue it. However, there is much more that needs to be examined on this issue, especially in relation to wider debates about contractual monarchy. For wider English, Irish and Scottish debates on this see Rory Rapple, 'Brinkmanship and bad luck: Ireland, the Nine Years' War and the succession' in Susan Doran and Paulina Kewes, eds, *Doubtful and Dangerous. The Question of Succession in Late Elizabeth England* (Manchester, 2014), 236–56; R. Malcolm Smuts, 'States, Monarchs and Dynastic Transitions: The Political Thought of John Hayward', in Susan Doran and Paulina Kewes, eds, *Doubtful and Dangerous. The Question of Succession in Late Elizabeth England* (Manchester, 2014), 276–94; Brendan Kane, 'The Nine Years' War in Ireland (1594–1603) as a problem of government' (forthcoming); Roger A. Mason, 'Beyond the Declaration of Arbroath: Kingship, Counsel and Consent in Late Medieval and Early Modern

While James was able to disentangle himself from involvement in Ireland with relative ease, such a luxury was not afforded to Henry VIII.[36] Ireland, as a lordship of the English crown, was his law and order problem. Concerns over the situation in the lordship, especially in the north of Ireland, were steadily increasing. The records of the State Papers are notable in that, from the early 1530s onwards, English officials in Ireland repeatedly express concern about the constant arrival of Scots in the north of Ireland.[37] This would have been encouraged by the Scottish king as a means of aggravating his uncle but was caused by a combination of the changing political scene in Ireland with Henry VIII's increased intervention there along with Highlanders readily seeking employment. Reports circulated of '4,000 Scotchmen' landing on the north coast while their numbers 'daily increase in Ulster'.[38] The regular arrival of Highland Scots in Ireland, and their involvement alongside the Irish who were resisting English authority, was a real problem for the English administration both in Ireland and England.

The English presence in Ireland had been diminishing since the fourteenth century. It was troubled further by deteriorating relations between

---

Scotland', in Steve Boardman and Julian Goodare, eds, *Kings, Lords and Men in Scotland and Britain, 1300–1625. Essays in Honour of Jenny Wormald* (Edinburgh, 2014), 265–82. James V, and the offer of the kingship of Ireland, is not discussed in any depth and is the focus of a forthcoming article. I am indebted to Associate Professor Brendan Kane for allowing me to read and cite his forthcoming article.

36 For detailed discussion of English policy towards Ireland during the mid-sixteenth century see Ciaran Brady, *The Chief Governors. The Rise and Fall of Reform Government in Tudor Ireland 1536–1588* (Cambridge, 1994), especially 11–158 which places policy on the part of the Lord Deputies towards the north into a wider Irish context. See also Colm Lennon, *Sixteenth-Century Ireland: The Incomplete Conquest* (Dublin, 2005); Steven G. Ellis, *Tudor Ireland: Crown, Community and the Conflict of Cultures, 1470–1603* (London, 1985); Steven G. Ellis, *Ireland in the Age of the Tudors, 1447–1603: English Expansion and the End of Gaelic Rule* (London and New York, 1998); S. J. Connolly, *Contested Island. Ireland 1460–1630* (Oxford, 2007).

37 This is how the English referred to them, not as Highland Scots. Nonetheless, the seasonal, migratory 'Scots' who arrived in the early sixteenth century were clearly distinguished from 'galloglass' who had been in Ireland for some time.

38 *L&P Henry VIII*, V, no.1246 (541); VI, no.1586 (645).

the English administration in Ireland and the Irish, and by the appointment of a Lord Deputy sent over from England which occurred on several occasions until the 1530s when this became standard practice. English settlers of the twelfth and thirteenth centuries had integrated into Irish society, marrying into ruling Irish dynasties, adopting Irish practices and customs, fostering their children with Irish families, trading with the Irish and maintaining Irish military retinues. The government in England viewed this as unwelcome and, with the decline of the colony in the fourteenth century, such integration was explicitly condemned in the 1367 Statutes of Kilkenny. The real reasons for weakening English authority and settlement in Ireland were more complex than cultural integration and intermarriage, and was impacted by absentee landlordism, the Bruce invasion, climatic change, cattle disease, famine and the Black Death, but the belief that the Old English had become degenerate on account of their interaction with the Irish persisted.[39] This 'degeneracy' was perceived to have contributed significantly to the decline of the English colony and, to rectify this, the Old English were called upon to renounce Irish customs, maintain English practice and law and curtail integration with Irish society. Instead of the English integrating into Irish society, the English wanted to reform Irish society and culture and ensure they adopted English practices, custom and law. In essence, Ireland was to be reformed along English lines and the inhabitants were to accept English royal authority and obey the Lord Deputy of Ireland as the representative of that authority in Ireland.

The role of the Lord Deputy in Ireland was a thankless one. By the fifteenth century the office of Lord Deputy passed from one family to another creating a host of additional problems as rivalries within the Old English community had wide-ranging repercussions due to long-standing factionalism. By the turn of the sixteenth century the office was held, almost as a hereditary position, by the FitzGerald earls of Kildare. For the most part, the earls of Kildare maintained a steady balance, although benefited themselves by manipulation of the fruits of the office and exploiting Irish custom

39 Seán Duffy ed., *Robert the Bruce's Irish Wars. The Invasions of Ireland 1306–1329* (Stroud, 2002); for cattle disease see Philip Slavin, 'The Great Bovine Pestilence and its Economic and Environmental Consequences in England and Wales, 1318–50', *Economic History Review* 65/4 (2012), 1239–66.

such as blackrents and coyne and livery, while also maintaining a retinue of galloglass. However, with Henry VIII's desire to reform Ireland there was a growing realisation that the monopoly of the position in the hands of the earls of Kildare was counter-productive as their influence extended across vast parts of the country, and they held significant political sway in Ireland. The decision in the 1530s to replace Gerald FitzGerald, ninth Earl of Kildare, with a Lord Deputy sent over from England resulted in the rebellion of his son Thomas, otherwise known as the 'Silken Thomas' revolt.[40] The rebellion demonstrated the extent of the power, political and military, of the FitzGeralds and although Henry dealt with the rebellion, executing every male member of the family bar one, it served to send a clear message to the English king concerning the level of resistance in Ireland to English authority.[41] The one surviving member of the family, Gerald FitzGerald, half-brother of Thomas, became something of a figurehead for resistance of a group that became known as the Geraldine League.[42] Gerald's aunt, Eleanor MacCarthy, had recently married Manus O'Donnell, head of his kindred. As one of the most powerful Irish lords in the north of Ireland, this marriage, and the close relationship to Gerald it afforded, catapulted Manus into a position of some significance, both locally and nationally. He became a key figure in the Geraldine League, an association of Irish

40 While Henry VII had appointed Sir Edward Poynings as Lord Deputy in the 1490s the position had become almost a hereditary position for the FitzGeralds of Kildare, one of the most powerful Old English families. The decision by Henry VIII to appoint Thomas Howard, Earl of Surrey, as Lord Lieutenant in 1520 was equally unpopular and he was recalled in 1521. Both times the Tudor monarchs reverted to reliance on the FitzGerald earls of Kildare.

41 For more on the Silken Thomas revolt see Steven G. Ellis, 'The Kildare Rebellion and the Early Henrician Reformation', *Historical Journal* 19/4 (1976), 807–30; Micheál Ó Siochrú, 'Foreign Involvement in the Revolt of Silken Thomas, 1534–5', *Proceedings of the Royal Irish Academy*, 96 C/2 (1996), 2–66; Laurence McCorristine, *The Revolt of Silken Thomas, a Challenge to Henry VIII* (Dublin, 1987).

42 Hiram Morgan, 'The End of Gaelic Ulster: A Thematic Interpretation of Events between 1534 and 1610', *Irish Historical Studies* 26/101 (1988), 8–32 at 10; Darren Mac Ettagáin, 'The Renaissance and the Late Medieval Lordship of Tír Chonaill, 1461–1555', in Nolan, Ronayne and Dunlevy, eds, *Donegal*, 211–12, 221; Lennon, *Sixteenth-Century Ireland*, 141, 150.

lords whose aim was to see the FitzGeralds back in influence. Nationally, however, the League became associated with resistance to both royal authority and Protestantism at a time when, following the Silken Thomas revolt, greater efforts were being made to bring reform to Ireland.

Henry's break from Rome with the 1533 Act of Appeals and 1534 Act of Supremacy may have ensured that the king was now free to divorce Catherine of Aragon and marry Anne Boleyn, but it brought with it a host of additional complications. Quite apart from the displeasure and hostility of the international community (primarily the papacy and Charles V, Catherine's uncle), there were problems within his own realm too. The Protestant Reformation and Henry's assertion of imperial authority enshrined in the declaration that 'this realm of England is an empire', overturned the very justification the English used for their presence in Ireland.[43] In the twelfth century Henry II had used papal instruction to reform Ireland as justification for his intervention there.[44] In overthrowing papal authority within his realm, including his lordship of Ireland, Henry VIII needed to re-configure Ireland's position within his dominions. At the same time, his knowledge that in 1540 the Irish had offered the overlordship of Ireland to his nephew must surely have helped focus the king's mind on such matters. The resolution came in 1541 with the Act for the Kingly Title and the accompanying policy of 'surrender and regrant' whereby Irish lords surrendered their lands in return for a regrant to held by an English title and, crucially, acknowledgement of English royal authority.[45] In passing this legislation, Henry changed Ireland's status from that of lordship of the English crown to that of kingdom on equal footing with England. The constitutional causes and implications of this change have been examined

43 For Henry's claims to imperial monarchy see Walter Ullman, 'This Realm of England Is an Empire', *Journal of Ecclesiastical History* 30/2 (1979), 175–203.

44 Maurice P. Sheehy, 'The Bull *Laudabiliter*: A Problem in Medieval Diplomatique and History', *Journal of the Galway Archaeological and Historical Society*, 29:3/4 (1961), 45–70.

45 For an excellent overview of this policy and the historiography surrounding it, see Christopher Maginn, ''Surrender and Regrant' in the Historiography of Sixteenth-Century Ireland', *Sixteenth Century Journal* 38/4 (2007), 955–74.

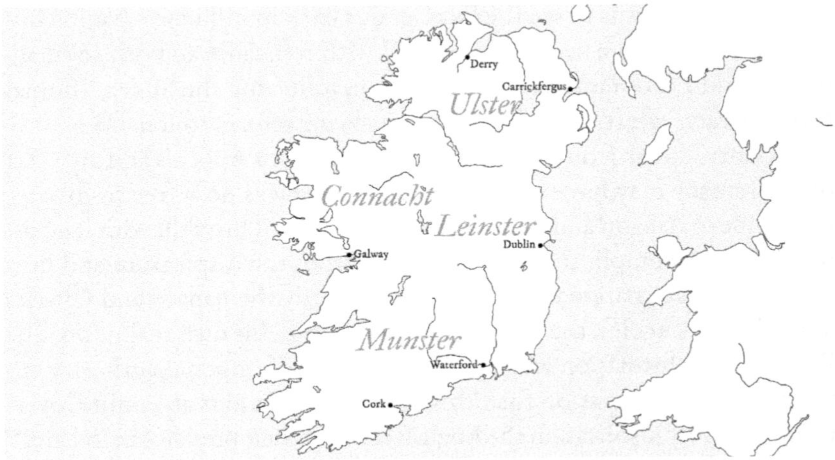

Map 3. Ireland

elsewhere.[46] It is more pertinent to discuss here the reasons why Henry embarked on this change. His advisors had argued that it was for the lack of being called the king's subjects that the Irish consistently rebelled. Instead, if Henry became their king, so the argument went, the Irish would be more naturally inclined to obey him – and it would prevent them offering the kingship to a rival.[47]

This was not to be the case as he, and his successors, would discover, although in the short-term the policy did appear to bear fruit. Manus O'Donnell of Tyrconnell was a politically astute individual and, sensing

46 Brendan Bradshaw, *The Irish Constitutional Revolution of the Sixteenth Century* (Cambridge, 1979). The implications were many and varied. For example, previously the Irish had little legal standing in English eyes. As subjects of the king, in theory this would now change.

47 Sir Thomas Cusack wrote to the Privy Council in England in 1541 that 'the Irishemen in Irelande … now … having ther lands of the Kingis Majestie, by His Graces letters patentes, whereby they may stande in assurance of ther lands, and being accepted as subjectes, where before they were taken as Irishe ennymies, which is the chiefest meane, by good wisdom, to contynewe them in peace and obedience'. See *State Papers Published under the Authority of His Majesty's Commission, Volume II: King Henry VIII Part III* (London, 1834), no.cccxlvii (326).

the way the political winds were blowing in the early 1540s, and without continued support from James V, he extricated himself from the Geraldine League and association with it by sending Gerald to France, after which he surrendered his lands and petitioned for the title of earl of Tyrconnell in return for his acceptance of the English settlement.[48] This was not capitulation; O'Donnell's actions were those of self-preservation in the political world of the north of Ireland, a policy the kindred would pursue throughout the century.[49] In 1542 Conn Bacach O'Neill similarly surrendered his lands and Gaelic title of 'the O'Neill' in return for English recognition of his lands and the title earl of Tyrone.[50] The O'Neills and O'Donnells were close neighbours with their lands of Tyrone and Tyrconnell respectively bordering each other but they remained fierce rivals and, although on a number of occasions during the sixteenth century enmity was put aside and efforts made to reconcile, these were short-lived until the latter years of the century. The English often sought to exploit this rivalry for their own ends, siding with one kindred in order to weaken the other, while the Irish lords themselves had little difficulty in doing likewise. Indeed, alliance with the English often came when one or other kindred needed the additional support of English forces to help take action against their rival. Such pragmatic, temporary alliances did little to foster longer-term trust between the various parties in the north of the country.

Petty rivalries and lingering animosity amongst the Irish themselves were exacerbated by English intervention and the contraction of alliances with one kindred against another. Above all, however, the policy known as surrender and regrant that accompanied the 1541 Act for the Kingly Title was the cause of significant unrest within Irish society itself, while also adding to the break-down of relations between the Irish and the English.

48 Indenture made 6 August 1541 between Sir Anthony St Leger, Deputy, and the Council, and Manus O'Donnell in *CCM*, I, no.159 (183–4). This action also resulted in estrangement from his wife.

49 James A. Mitchell, 'The O'Donnell lords of Tyrconnell, 1537–1603: a study of their efforts to maintain their local power in sixteenth-century Tudor Ireland' (University of Strathclyde, PhD, 2015).

50 SP 60/10, fol.272; Articles of the submission of Con O'Neill in *CCM*, I, no.167 (188–90).

The policy of the Lord Deputy, Anthony St Leger, the English failed to appreciate that surrender and regrant was completely incompatible with Irish succession practices and systems of landholding. While Irish lords might accept primogeniture and the succession of their heirs to the earldom, this undermined the landholding practices within Irish society, and the rights and claims of other members of the kindred to the headship.[51] The result was that Irish kindreds faced ongoing internal upheaval and dissent on account of surrender and regrant, while Irish lords also faced an inconsistent and insincere English government who were willing to make and break promises and policy when it was expedient to do so: a behaviour they were just as willing to accuse the 'barbaric' Irish of.[52] On their part, the English faced a society that had no unified leadership and dealing with numerous heads of kindreds was time-consuming, confusing and complex, especially as alliances between various Irish lords could change or alter at any time. At the same time, the Irish in general had no over-riding policy towards the English: resistance or co-operation and obedience depended on context and circumstance but, for the most part, was driven by efforts to maintain and defend their individual position and territories. It was in their efforts to preserve their society, culture and economy from ongoing English encroachment that Irish lords allied with Old English families and employed Scottish mercenaries, a trade the English wanted to put an end to.

The Act for the Kingly Title 1541 had few immediate consequences for Scotland as James V had already distanced himself from events across the channel, but his death in 1542 saw Henry embark on diplomatic efforts to persuade the Scots to marry their young queen, Mary, to his own son and heir, Prince Edward. As Henry had recently passed a body of legislation between 1536 and 1543 that became known as the Act of Union with Wales, when combined with the 1541 act concerning the kingship of Ireland, his proposal in 1543 of dynastic union with Scotland can suggest that Henry

51 Ciaran Brady, 'The Attainder of Shane O'Neill, Sir Henry Sidney and the Problems of Tudor State-Building in Ireland', in Ciaran Brady and Jane Ohlmeyer, eds, *British Interventions in Early Modern Ireland* (Cambridge, 2005), 28–48; Maginn, 'Surrender and Regrant', 955–74.

52 Giraldus Cambrensis, *The History and Topography of Ireland* ed. and trans., J. J. O'Meara (London, 1982), 106–7.

had a wider, imperial agenda here, seeking to do what Edward I had barely achieved and extend English rule and authority throughout the kingdoms of the insular world. As Scarisbrick has rightly pointed out, however, 'it is doubtful if Henry was ever either capable or guilty of such high statesmanship'.[53] Henry's main priority was English security followed by continental diplomacy but in 1543 he saw the opportunity for securing his northern border with Scotland. The Auld Alliance between Scotland and France had meant that for centuries successive English monarchs always risked a war on two fronts. Henry's anxiety had been further compounded by his break from Rome as he found himself surrounded by Catholic powers. With Mary, Queen of Scots, only an infant and the amenable, reform-minded James Hamilton, second Earl of Arran, heir-presumptive to the throne, as Regent, Henry wasted no time. Ultimately the Scots rejected the proposed Anglo-Scottish dynastic alliance put forward in the 1543 Treaties of Greenwich but this only served to push Henry to more extreme measures. If the Scots would not willingly accept dynastic union, he was determined to force them to do so. In 1544 he embarked on his 'rough wooing' of Scotland.

Henry's campaign was devastating for southern Scotland, but ultimately unsuccessful as it pushed a defeated and desperate Scotland into the open arms of an equally opportunistic Henri II of France who married Mary to his son, the dauphin, Francis. Henry's assault on his northern neighbour saw him look to various groups within Scotland to provide support and, crucially, enabled him to consider opening a second front in his war against the Scots. There were two main groups within Scotland he allied with: the first of these were the Highland Scots. Henry capitalised on the grievances of the Highland chiefs recently released from captivity, having been imprisoned by James V followed his expedition to the Isles in 1540. During the expedition James had embarked on a survey of the lands that formerly pertained to the lordship of the Isles, lands he had recently annexed to the Scottish crown. He wanted exact details of what the crown

53 J. J. Scarisbrick, *Henry VIII* (New Haven and London, 1997), 424. Scarisbrick goes on to argue that it was Thomas Cromwell who was responsible for union with Wales and serious efforts to reform Ireland.

was due from the region and in many cases it saw a significant rise in rentals for a number of Highland chiefs.[54] Combined with increased government intervention but decreased representation, as Campbell of Argyll had been restored as the main authority in the region, discontent in the Isles was ready for exploitation. Led by the heir to the forfeited lordship, Donald Dubh MacDonald, the Islesmen allied with Henry VIII against the ruling minority government, promising significant manpower.[55]

In opening a second front in his war on Scotland, Henry also tried to ally with another group of Scots: the lords from the 'westland'.[56] In regional terms it was predominantly such westland lords, individuals from the southwest of Scotland, that became involved in plantation in Ulster in the early seventeenth century. These lords did not suddenly appear in Ireland at the end of the sixteenth century, or during the plantations of the opening decades of the seventeenth century.[57] As early as the thirteenth century Scots

54 Martin Rorke, 'The Scottish Herring Trade, 1470–1600', *Scottish Historical Review*, LXXXIV:2/218 (2005), 159 and Aonghas MacCoinnich, 'The Maritime Dimension to Scotland's 'Highland Problem', ca.1540–1630', *Maritime Communities of the North Atlantic Arc in the Early Modern Period: Journal of the North Atlantic*, ed., Alison Cathcart, special volume 12 (2019), 44–72 both suggest the expedition was also an attempt to exploit the rich fishing of the region.

55 For a fuller discussion of this rebellion see Alison Cathcart, 'The Forgotten '45: Donald Dubh's Rebellion in an Archipelagic Context', *Scottish Historical Review*, XCI2/232 (2012), 239–64.

56 Landed families, such as the Hamiltons, the Cunninghams and the Montgomeries, were part of a group of Scottish lords that have been referred to, 'in a number of fifteenth-century chronicle and record sources', as the 'westland' lords; see Stephen Boardman, '"Pillars of the community": Campbell Lordship and Architectural Patronage in the Fifteenth Century', in R. D. Oram and Geoffrey Stell, eds, *Lordship and Architecture in Medieval and Renaissance Scotland* (Edinburgh, 2005), 123–59, at 138 n.95; *TA*, I, 92. The 'westland' itself encompassed Cunningham, Lanarkshire and probably other areas around the Clyde such as Ayrshire and Renfrewshire. During the fifteenth century these 'lords of the westland' engaged in occasional political and military activity in Argyll, the Clyde islands and the Hebrides, often acting in association with Gaelic lords from the latter areas.

57 Although recent historians have acknowledged a medieval precedent, too often connections between Ulster and the southwest of Scotland are regarding as having been established in the early seventeenth century (admittedly largely by post-1600

from Galloway had settled in the northeast of Ulster. Thomas of Galloway, Earl of Atholl, is mentioned as having 'plundered Derry-Columbkille, and carried off ... all the precious articles of the people of Derry' and the north of Ireland, which he brought to Coleraine in 1211–12, as part of his ambition to conquer significant territory in Ireland stretching from east of the River Bann to Lough Foyle.[58] Two years later, Thomas built a castle at Coleraine and in 1215 received confirmation of his right to lands there from King John. Although Thomas soon came under attack from the neighbouring Irish, his castle of Coleraine was said to have survived initially 'because of the surrounding settlement of Scots from Galloway'.[59] Coleraine Castle subsequently fell, however, to Hugh de Lacy, head of an Anglo-Norman family who had come north with a force intent on pressing his claims to the earldom of Ulster. He demolished Thomas' castle and ejected other Galloway Scots from their land. Four years later the Irish annals note that the castle had been rebuilt but Seán Duffy has argued that, as we hear nothing more of Thomas in Ireland, it was probably Hugh de Lacy himself who rebuilt it having expelled the Scots from the area. It was the Anglo-Normans, therefore, who thwarted the efforts of the men from Galloway to settle in the north but in the following century that colony too went into decline.

historians) and the earlier history treated in a very generalised and somewhat unhelpful way. Jane H. Ohlmeyer, *Civil War and Restoration in the Three Stuart Kingdoms. The Career of Randal MacDonnell, Marquis of Antrim* (Cambridge, 1993; reprinted Dublin, 2001), 7 argues that 'Gaelic Ireland and Gaelic Scotland ... had formed a single cultural, linguistic and even political entity since earliest times'; T. M. Devine, *Scotland's Empire 1600–1815* (London, 2003), 17 accepts that in 'medieval times relations between Scotland and Ireland had been close and enduring'.

58 *AFM*, III (Dublin, 1856), 1213 (177); Cathcart, 'Scots and Ulster', 79; Seán Duffy, 'The Bruce Brothers and the Irish Sea World, 1306–29', *Cambridge Medieval Celtic Studies* 21 (1991), 68.

59 F. X. Martin, 'John, Lord of Ireland, 1185–1216', in Cosgrove, ed., *NHI II: Medieval Ireland*, 147.

P/49 (25) (L9622): East part of Ulster [1601]. © National Maritime Museum, Greenwich, London.

In the fourteenth century another lord of Galloway arrived in Ireland: Edward Bruce. Duffy's excellent study of the Bruce invasion of Ireland and its aims and outcomes contextualises the invasion within the wider framework of the Irish Sea world.[60] In doing so he highlights the broader, archipelagic, ambitions of the Bruce brothers, but also the connections and interaction across the North Channel and throughout the Irish Sea region in earlier centuries. During his campaign of 1315–18 in Ireland, Edward was accompanied by men from both the western Isles and the southwest of Scotland, although men from both these regions also fought against Bruce in Ireland too. Bruce was supported by the MacRuaris and the Clan Donald and, although Thomas Randolph, Earl of Moray, was

60 Duffy, 'Bruce Brothers', 55–86.

Edward's lieutenant in Ireland, there were other Scots from the southwest in Edward's army such as Fergus of Ardrossan, killed in the battle at Skerries just south of Kildare, along with prominent members of the Stewart family too. The end of Edward Bruce's campaign in Ireland, with his unexpected death in battle in 1318, also signalled the end, for a time at least, of the involvement of men from the southwest of Scotland in Ulster. While the inheritance of estates in the Glens by John Mor MacDonald through his marriage to the heiress of the Bisset inheritance at the end of the fourteenth century cemented that family's ongoing connection with Ulster, in contrast there appears to have been no sustained pattern of migration to and settlement in Ulster on the part of men from regions such as Ayrshire or Galloway. Although Coleraine remained strategically important in Ulster, the decline of the English colony in Ireland from the fourteenth century onwards meant that Carrickfergus on the east coast of Ulster because the key English garrison in the north. The Ayrshire coast could be viewed easily from Carrickfergus Castle, situated between Belfast Lough and Larne Lough, a short distance along the coast from Olderfleet Castle, and only the North Channel between them.

Despite having played a minimal role in the political development of Ireland during previous centuries, the inhabitants of the southwest of Scotland remained part of the maritime world of the Irish Sea and the North Channel in particular, on account of their geographic proximity to Ulster, the South Isles and the Isle of Man. While they may have had little to do with affairs in Ireland during the later fourteenth and fifteenth centuries they were involved in affairs of the west of Scotland, acting in conjunction with Gaelic lords of the Clyde islands, Arran and Bute, and the western Isles.[61] This ability to participate with their Gaelic neighbours was a result of their significant maritime strength which would become increasingly evident throughout the sixteenth century. Indeed for many lords and merchants from Ayrshire and Galloway, maintaining a fleet of any size was of immense importance for commerce, fishing and on occasion

61 Boardman, 'Pillars of the community', 138 n.95; C. A. McGladdery, *James II* (Edinburgh, 1990), 166 quotes the Auchinleck Chronicle concerning James II who, in March 1455, 'past to glasgw and gaderit the westland men with part of the ereschery' in his campaign against the Douglases in 1455.

matters of defence. For those seeking to gain advancement through service to the crown, the ability to provide shipping when it was requested would be highly advantageous. Although the historiography would suggest that most maritime activity took place on the east coast, the western shires were often called upon to provide equipped vessels for defence, whether to deal with rebels from Ireland or invasion from Spain.[62] The Cunninghams of Glencairn are a useful example of this.

The family first appears in the records during the mid-to-late fourteenth century with their main estate of Kilmaurs in Cunningham, north Ayrshire, but also holding lands in mid-Renfrewshire and Kyle. Through marriage they were connected to other landed families and also held offices in the region, such as sheriff of Ayr and, in 1430, joint keeper of Kintyre and Knapdale with custody of the castles of Skipness and Sween. By the 1530s the Cunninghams of Glencairn had amassed a territorial base encompassing land in no less than nine sheriffdoms and, although an important family in Ayrshire, it was not until the mid-sixteenth century that the family had any role in national affairs. William Cunningham, Master of Glencairn, and from May 1541, third earl, was treasurer during the minority of King James V but it would be his reputation as a naval commander that saw him rise to prominence. Indeed, from the 1530s onwards it is clear that the Cunninghams, like other lords of the west of Scotland, recognised the need for naval power. Fishermen and merchants understood the importance of the waters of the west either as an economic resource to be exploited or as a means of trading that resource, but knowledge and mastery of the water itself was essential for political reasons too. William came to James' attention when in 1531 he offered to furnish five ships and equip 600 men at his own expense and sail to the assistance of the exiled Christian II of Denmark. Although the expedition did not take place, allegedly due to his ill-health, it suggested the extent of Cunningham's personal naval power; a maritime strength that the king appreciated and sought to exploit for his own purposes.[63] In 1538 William sailed to France with Robert,

62 As James VI did in 1605 prior to an expedition to the Isles; see *RPCS*, VII, 68–70.

63 *Letters of James V*, 186–7, 198–9. In return William would have received the castle of Tonsburg in Norway 'with its lordship and crown rights to be held freely' during his lifetime.

fifth Lord Maxwell, Admiral of Scotland, to escort the king's new bride, Mary of Guise, back to Scotland, departing from Le Havre and landing six days later at Balcomie in Fife.[64] William's son, Alexander, Master of Kilmaurs, was vice-admiral of James's expedition to the Isles in 1540. The earl himself also was in attendance and both men remained in Kintyre, with William as the king's commissioner, carrying out the survey of crown lands.[65] The *Little Forfar* was sent to the Isles for the Master of Kilmaurs' use and in 1543 Alexander was appointed as governor of Kintyre for one year.[66] Their growing political influence, along with their early conversion to Protestantism, brought them further into national prominence during the mid-1540s.

Reforming ideas had been circulating in Scotland since the 1520s but following the death of James V, Regent Arran allowed the bible in the vernacular to be circulated.[67] Protestantism had made significant converts in the west, including some of the main families, such as the Cunninghams of Glencairn, the Campbells of Loudoun and the Kennedys of Cassillis.

64 *Letters of James V*, 364. In February 1538 James V wrote to Pope Paul III regarding the vacant see of Lismore and outlined the situation. 'The land is mountainous and sterile, the rents small, and the people uncivilised .... It is adjacent to Ireland and the Isles, at the very back of the realm, and it is hard to preserve ecclesiastical discipline among a lawless fold.' For the position James recommended 'William Conynghame, twenty-six years of age and sprung from a neighbouring noble family, who promises to be a success and to keep the people in obedience to the crown'.

65 *RMS*, III, no.2233; *RPS*, 1540/12/26, accessed 31 July 2018.

66 *RSS*, II, no.4631; R. K. Hannay, ed., *Acts of the Lords of Council in Public Affairs, 1501–1554: Selections from the Acta Dominorum Concilii Introductory to the Register of the Privy Council of Scotland* (Edinburgh, 1932), 504; *ER*, XVII, 625–50; *RMS*, III, nos 345, 2816; *TA*, VII, 400.

67 Like Henry, however, Arran stopped short of permitting doctrinal debates. The Hamilton estates primarily stretched across Ayrshire, Lanarkshire, Renfrewshire and Kirkcudbrightshire along with holdings in Linlithgowshire and Roxburghshire, but the majority of the estate was concentrated in the west and included the island of Arran off the west coast of Scotland providing him with kin-based support in the region. See Marcus Merriman, 'Hamilton, James, second Earl of Arran, and Duke of Châtelherault in the French nobility (*c.*1519–1575)', *ODNB*, accessed 28 June 2016.

Henry tried to garner their support for dynastic union and use them in his campaign against Scotland because he, or rather his ambassador, Sir Ralph Sadler, recognised the west – the Firth of Clyde and Dumbarton Castle – as the key to the north of Scotland.[68] With allies among the major powers in the west of Scotland, whether in the South Isles, Ayrshire, or Galloway, Henry could ensure a safe passage to Dumbarton from the south. The west and its waterways became significant for him in these efforts to open a second front.[69] In addition, he would be able to capitalise on the maritime power of his Scottish allies and their mastery of the waters of the North Channel. That the Islesmen arrived at Carrickfergus, where they negotiated the agreement with Henry, with a fleet of 180 galleys was a clear show of naval strength, alongside a promise of a military force of up to 8,000 men. Henry's plan also included efforts to raise a force of 2,000 men in Ireland to assist the Islesmen, a decision based on the assumption they would have safe and easy passage to Scotland. Transporting the Irish army to Scotland may not have posed any difficulty as the Highland Scots clearly had the means to do so, although recruiting the force in the first place appears to have been problematic and, in the end, a force of only 200 was raised in Ireland.[70] In the light of the political situation there and long-standing links between Ireland and Scotland, it is perhaps unsurprising that English officials faced obstacles in raising an Irish force to fight for the English against Scotland.

In the negotiations that preceded the attempted rebellion of Donald Dubh, heir to the forfeited MacDonald lordship of the Isles, the Earl of Glencairn was among the westland lords who can be regarded as acting as a group, although ultimately individual allegiance was determined by local and personal factors.[71] This group of westland lords were connected

68 Joseph Bain, ed., *The Hamilton Papers: Letters and Papers illustrating the Political Relations of England and Scotland in the Sixteenth Century*, 2 vols (Edinburgh, 1890–92), II, no.4 (7).

69 For more on this: see Cathcart, 'Forgotten '45'.

70 *L&P Henry VIII*, XX (II), 562; *Hamilton Papers*, II, nos 261, 327; Cathcart, 'Forgotten '45', 257, 259.

71 For further details of the Donald Dubh rebellion and the role of the westland lords in it, see Cathcart, 'Forgotten '45', 251–3, 262–3.

with their Gaelic neighbours, including both the Campbells and the MacDonalds.[72] The 1545 rebellion highlighted the strategic importance of the west, not only as a crucial point of access to Scotland, but also on account of the strength of the westland lords themselves. These magnate families from the southwest of Scotland had consolidated a significant maritime presence which both the Scottish and English crowns wanted to utilise for their own ends, as evidenced by events of the 1540s. This decade also brought to light the interconnections between these families and their dominance in the west, particularly the Clyde estuary and Dumbarton Castle, the key fortress in the firth of Clyde, and their developing reformist perspectives which encouraged alliance with England during this period. Throughout the following decades, amidst the upheavals of the Reformation, these families of the west rarely achieved such cohesion in action again on account of rivalry and feuding, internal family concerns, religious differences and divergent responses to the Marian Civil War but they continued to intermarry and maintain regional prominence while intermittently involved in national affairs. The Hamiltons, despite forfeiture, mental health issues, exile and involvement in Catholic conspiracies, were later rehabilitated by James VI during the 1580s.[73] The Cunninghams and Montgomerys were involved in a bitter feud concerning the jurisdiction of the bailliary of Cunningham and later Kilwinning Abbey throughout

72 *RSS*, II, no.4628; Norman Macdougall, *James IV* (Edinburgh, 1997), 97–9; Hector L. MacQueen and John Simmons, 'Cunningham family (*per.* c.1340–1631)', *ODNB*, accessed 30 June 2012. By the sixteenth century the Campbells of Loudoun were hereditary sheriffs of Ayr. These contacts extended into the ecclesiastical sphere. Montgomery and Cunningham clergy were related through marriage to the earls of Argyll and the Campbells of Loudoun; see Iain G. MacDonald, *Clerics and Clansmen: The Diocese of Argyll between the Twelfth and Sixteenth Centuries* (Leiden, 2013), 118.

73 While the heads of the House of Hamilton remained committed to Protestantism, other members of the family remained Catholic, notably Lord Claud Hamilton, younger brother of James, third Earl of Arran, and father of James, first Earl of Abercorn. See Rosalind K. Marshall, 'Hamilton, James, third earl of Arran (1537/8?–1609)', *ODNB*, accessed 19 November 2015; Peter Holmes, 'Hamilton, Claud, first Lord Paisley (1546?–1621)', *ODNB*, accessed 19 November 2015.

much of the century, shifting between periods of greater or lesser intensity.[74] The Kennedys slowly built up their dominance throughout the southwest extending their influence across Galloway and Ayrshire.[75] The western perspective and a familiarity with the North Channel context ensured that the development of plantation endeavours across the water in the early seventeenth century offered new possibilities that some westland lords were keen to exploit. For the latter part of the sixteenth century, however, while there was little further involvement of the westland lords in Irish affairs, they were engaged in the developing trade across the North Channel and, on occasion, providing shipping for service to Ireland and victuals for both the English army in Ireland and the Irish who continued to resist the encroachments of English authority.

Following the failure of Henry's efforts to co-ordinate an Irish, Highland Scot and westland lords' force to open a second front in the war against Scotland, the king paid scant attention to Ireland. Pre-occupation with the war against Scotland and relations with France took priority until his death in 1547. While successive Lord Deputies continued with the policy of surrender and regrant in their efforts to spread reform throughout Ireland it was soon combined with efforts to spread Protestantism too. Associated with the imposition of English authority, the Reformation never took root which provided further justification for English involvement in Ireland. The failure of the Reformation, however, completely transformed how Ireland was viewed. No longer just the problematic, unruly and uncivilised neighbour to the west that was a drain on the English exchequer, it was now a source of heightened anxiety for

74 The dispute began in the mid-fifteenth century and was not settled until 1609 via royal arbitration. MacQueen and Simmons, 'Cunningham family (*per. c.*1340–1631)', *ODNB*, accessed 19 November 2015; Hector L. MacQueen, 'Montgomery family (*per. c.*1350–*c.*1485)', *ODNB*, accessed 19 November 2015; Keith M. Brown, *Bloodfeud in Scotland, 1573–1625: Violence, Justice, and Politics in an Early Modern Society* (Edinburgh, 1986), 85–105.

75 John Simmons, 'Kennedy, Gilbert, fourth earl of Cassillis (*c.*1541–1576)', *ODNB*, accessed 19 November 2015; Alan R. MacDonald, 'Kennedy, John, fifth earl of Cassillis (1574/5–1615)', *ODNB*, accessed 19 November 2015; K. M. Brown, 'A House Divided: Family and Feud in Carrick under John Kennedy, Fifth Earl of Cassillis', *Scottish Historical Review*, 75 (1996), 168–96.

the English who feared it could be used as the back-door for any foreign, Catholic or Counter-Reformation invasion force. Rumours of French or Spanish assistance for the Irish resurfaced regularly throughout the 1540s and 1550s. The brief reign of Mary might have alleviated fears of a foreign invasion, but it brought an international dimension to the Anglo-Scottish border as Scotland, then governed by the French, Catholic, Regent Mary of Guise, was allied with France while England was allied to Spain through Mary's marriage to Philip II. Mary's Catholicism may have brought respite for Catholics, although Protestants in England faced severe repression. In Ireland, however, it was during Mary's reign that the first attempts at plantation were implemented, in Laois and Offaly, where the people were to be 'kept in civil government'.[76] Mary's death and Elizabeth's succession brought another about-turn in religious policy and, once again, Ireland was viewed as the vulnerable back-door through which Catholic enemies could launch an attack on England, aimed at removing the illegitimate, 'heretic' queen from the throne. Despite these external threats, Elizabeth had to contend with the very real domestic problems posed by the consolidation of the MacDonald presence along the northern coast of Ulster and the rise of Shane O'Neill.

By the mid-sixteenth century the MacDonalds were well established in the local context of the Glens of Antrim but wanted to extend their influence east and aimed at Clandeboy, an area of land adjacent to the garrison town of Carrickfergus which included the Dufferin. MacDonald efforts to gain a foothold there is understandable. Clandeboy was a fertile region with ready access to the sea that would allow the MacDonalds to come and go with ease while offering additional lands for both arable and pastoral farming, vital if the MacDonalds were to provide for the wider clan. The lands had been granted previously to a branch of the O'Neill family who, at this time, was facing internal fracturing which the MacDonalds sought to exploit by undermining them further. Expansionist moves on the part of the MacDonalds were met with resistance from the English as

76 Alison Cathcart, 'The Maritime Dimension to Plantation in Ulster, ca.1550–ca.1600', *Maritime Communities of the North Atlantic Arc in the Early Modern Period: Journal of the North Atlantic*, ed., Alison Cathcart, special volume 12 (2019), 95–6.

they did not want to see consolidation of MacDonald settlement in the north of Ireland. But the English were unable to counter MacDonald raids into Clandeboy or expel them from the Dufferin, while an attack on their stronghold of Rathlin Island in 1551 failed on account of a lack of suitable shipping.[77] Throughout the 1550s the MacDonalds also extended their influence westward, countering the neighbouring O'Cahan and MacQuillan families, and taking hold of the MacQuillan castle at Dunluce by the 1550s or earlier.[78] This became the MacDonald base in Ulster and, along with other coastal fortifications, notably at Red Bay, was a vital stronghold for the maintenance of their position in Ireland throughout the latter half of the sixteenth century. Having successfully resisted English efforts to remove them and, in response, encroached further east into Clandeboy and west into the Route, James MacDonald sought to gain legal title for his Irish estates and in May 1552 petitioned the Privy Council in London to recognise his claims to the Glens of Antrim.[79]

Expanding east and west brought the MacDonalds into conflict with lesser, neighbouring clans like the O'Cahans and MacQuillans, but they also came up against the growing influence of Shane O'Neill. Shane's father, Conn Bacach O'Neill, had been married a number of times and fathered several children.[80] Under the terms of his submission to Henry VIII in

77 SP 61/3, fols 149, 151–5, where Croft outlines his reasons for the attack on the growing strength of the MacDonalds across the north of Antrim. SP 61/3, fol.181v; SP 61/4, fol.140. The source also mentions John White, heir of the Dufferin, as 'land lord' and who was 'disceiptfully murdred by Mac Ranyll boy is sonne, a Skotte; And since that murder he keapith possession of the said landes, by meane whereof, he is hable to dysturbe the countreis next adioyning on ev[er]y syde'. And see also *CCM*, I, no.200 (242); Breen, *Dunluce Castle*, 65–6, 68.

78 Hill, *Historical Account of the MacDonnells of Antrim*, 121–26; Breen, *Dunluce Castle*, 34–8, 41–2, 45–7, 63–70.

79 SP 61/4, fol.161r. In negotiations with Croft in September 1551, James had asked that his brothers be 'suffrd to dwell in the landes where they did inhabite in Ireland', holding them from the king and 'do his grace sarvice', SP 61/3, fol.152v.

80 During the 1520s Conn married Sorcha, daughter of Hugh Oge O'Neill, head of the O'Neills of Clandeboy, and Shane, born *c.*1530, was a product of this union. On account of these marital connections Shane and his father, Conn, were keen to support the Clandeboy branch of the O'Neill kindred; see Christopher Maginn, 'O'Neill, Conn Bacach, first earl of Tyrone (*c.*1482–1559)', *ODNB*, accessed 12

January 1542 by which Conn accepted the title of earl of Tyrone, it was his eldest son, Matthew, who was acknowledged as his father's heir and subsequently made Baron of Dungannon.[81] According to Gaelic laws of succession, however, there were four identifiable contenders for the position of O'Neill and it was Shane, the earl's youngest son, who rose to prominence during the 1550s. As Conn's position in the north weakened during this decade, largely because of his old age and absence from the earldom, the English began to promote Dungannon at his father's expense. This resulted in significant upheaval within Tyrone as rivalry between Dungannon and Shane spilled over while Conn's other younger, but illegitimate, sons also challenged for dominance. Shane's succession to his father was secured in 1558 when Dungannon was assassinated (largely on Shane's directions) and confirmed in 1559 when he was proclaimed as the O'Neill under Gaelic law.[82] This was not enough for Shane who was determined to pursue English recognition of him as legitimate heir to his father, but in doing so he faced an uphill struggle.

Shane's efforts to secure recognition of his right to the title and lands of the earldom of Tyrone, and thereby extend his influence as the O'Neill across the north of Ulster, met with disapproval from the English. His activities in this regard were interpreted through the lens of civility and confirmed English perceptions of their own superiority when compared with the perceived barbarity of the Irish. Any action on Shane's part that could be read as evidence of civility was overlooked and instead further proof of his degenerate character was highlighted. To be fair, Shane was not without

---

October 2015; Ciaran Brady, *Shane O'Neill* (Dundalk, 1996; reprinted Dublin, 2015), 22–8.

81 SP 60/10, fols 229–30, 268, 285v–6v. This ignored the fact that the tanist had been Niall Conallach, son of Art Oge O'Neill. Niall Conallach, Conn's cousin and rival, had opposed Conn's accession as O'Neill but he died in 1544. Shane O'Neill continually asserted that Matthew was illegitimate, the son of a blacksmith; see Brady, *Shane O'Neill*, 29. While Brady points out that no one ever questioned Conn's paternity, if Matthew was illegitimate, it was another example of the English conveniently overlooking their own laws that stated only a legitimate heir could inherit from his father. For more on the incompatibility of surrender and regrant with Irish society see n.51 above.

82 Maginn, 'Conn Bacach O'Neill'. See p.107 below.

fault and many of his actions would have reinforced the English view of him. Wasting the lands of his enemies was a well-used tactic in Ireland and Gaelic Scotland but its objectives were misunderstood by English observers. This was not simply mindless, wanton destruction, but a calculated act aimed at removing the economic resources, and thereby damaging the political standing and personal prestige, of an enemy.[83] The effect was to limit the ability to provide victuals for both followers and mercenary forces, thus ensuring the enemy had to concentrate on immediate issues of provision and protection rather than give attention to other matters.[84] Stealing the economic resources from an opponent weakened them and simultaneously strengthened O'Neill. Such actions, however, did little to improve Shane's standing with the English.

Within English government circles Shane was perceived as being full of 'pryid, stubbornness & all bent to do what he could to destroy the pore countrey'.[85] As such there was no agreement on how to deal with him. This had allowed Shane to shore up his influence in the north which even defeat at the hands of the O'Donnells in 1557 did little to hinder. Meanwhile he had tried to neutralise the MacDonalds by marrying Katherine, daughter of James MacDonald of Dunivaig and the Glens.[86] Although formal recognition from the English of the title and earldom of Tyrone lay beyond his reach, this mattered little in terms of local politics on the ground in Ulster. In 1559 Shane carried out a number of aggressive campaigns against the English across Ulster and, more worryingly, south of Ulster too, underlining

83 For further discussion of the socio-economic importance of food and economic resources, see Robert A. Dodgshon, *From Chiefs to Landlords: Social and Economic Change in the Western Highlands and Islands, c.1493–1820* (Edinburgh, 1998), 84–101.

84 For example, SP 63/15, fol.53 where Richard, Earl of Clanricard, wrote to Sir William Fitzwilliams that O'Neill had come 'to the lower parte of Connaught', camped in O'Rourke and O'Connor's country for six or seven days and 'ther he burnyt the corne & spoyled the holle contrye carrying thence aboue iii or iiii ai [thousand]… cattell'.

85 SP 61/4, fol.143.

86 Nicholas Maclean-Bristol, 'MacDonald, James, of Dunyvaig and the Glens (d. 1565), clan chief', *ODNB,* accessed 6 August 2018. Shane later sent her back on the grounds she was 'unsuitable'.

both the Lord Deputy's inability to deal effectively with the growing power of the Irish lord and Shane's ability to exert his strength outside of his own sphere of influence.[87] Looking at the situation in Ulster Elizabeth realised her options were limited, facing as she did the competing and expanding spheres of influence of the MacDonalds on one hand and the O'Neills on the other. The queen was open to alternative suggestions for how to deal with the problem of the north.[88]

A solution came from Scotland and would result in a complete volte-face in terms of English policy in the north of Ireland. Archibald Campbell, fifth Earl of Argyll, was one of the prominent Protestant lords in Scotland who, in 1559, formally joined the Lords of the Congregation in rebelling against the ruling government of Mary of Guise. In their efforts to remove the French military presence in Scotland and secure Protestantism, the Scottish Lords of the Congregation had looked to the Protestant, English queen, Elizabeth for support. Using arguments of protection, defence of Scotland's ancient rights and liberties, and maintenance of the unity between Scotland and England, Elizabeth was persuaded to intervene militarily in Scotland, securing the defeat of the pro-Catholic and pro-French faction and resulting in the repudiation of papal authority and the adoption of Protestantism by the Scottish parliament in 1560. In the process of persuading Elizabeth to embark on this course of action, offers on the part of the earl of Argyll to help settle the problem in Ireland were made. Argyll was in a strong position to do so on account of his connections both with key Irish lords and with Hebridean and west Highland clans, including the MacDonalds of Dunivaig and the Glens.

Unlike the MacSween(y)s and the MacDonalds, significant settlement of Campbells in Ulster had not occurred in earlier centuries, although members of the wider Campbell kindred had been and continued to be active in Ulster as hired fighting men, and were known by the name

87 Breen, *Dunluce Castle*, 79.

88 Mutual hostility and contempt between Sussex and Shane O'Neill did little to alleviate this stalemate. Brady, *Chief Governors*, 99 speaks of Sussex's 'inflexible determination to destroy Shane O'Neill'. For more on Sussex's time in Ireland see Brady, *Chief Governors*, 68–9, 72–111.

MacConnochie.[89] After communicating with James IV in 1507, closer contact between the O'Donnells of Tyrconnell and the earls of Argyll had emerged in 1513 when the O'Donnell chief visited the Scottish court of James IV.[90] From the 1520s onwards the earls of Argyll focused their energies on maintaining their connections with the west Highland and Hebridean chiefs and with Irish lords, while balancing that with their role in national affairs.[91] Indeed, in the wake of the forfeiture of the MacDonald lordship of the Isles, the Campbell chiefs had been careful not to succumb to a similar fate. Although James V had been wary of Argyll's prominence in the region, and specific mention was made of the Campbell chief in the negotiations of the Islesmen with the English in their planning for a rebellion in 1545, the Campbells remained fully integrated within Highland society.[92] Following the marriage of James MacDonald of Dunivaig and the Glens to Agnes Campbell, sister of Archibald, fourth earl, in 1545, close connections were once more renewed between the two clans and there was ongoing co-operation during the 1540s and 1550s. Across the North Channel too, relations had been revived in the early 1540s. In 1543, during the uncertainty that followed the death of James V and unrest in the Highlands, the English had intelligence that 'a gentleman of therle of Argyles' was 'lately repayred out of Scottelande to Odonell and … wer w[i]th the same Odonell at the haven of loghfoyle thre or foure daies what ther intent ys we knowe not but … of lykelyode yt is not good'.[93] The unrest of the mid-1540s in Scotland on account of the English invasion, combined with rumours that Gerald FitzGerald would return to Ireland leading an invasion force, fully pre-occupied the English throughout the decade and no doubt Argyll himself was caught up in matters north of the border.[94] Connections with Irish kindreds were revived again in 1555 when alliance was made between the fourth earl of Argyll, and Calvagh O'Donnell, a

89 Gerald A. Hayes-McCoy, *Scots Mercenary Forces in Ireland, 1565–1603* (Dublin, 1937, reprinted 1996), 234.

90 *The Letters of James the Fourth*, nos 105–6 (71); *ER*, XIII, lxxvi.

91 Cathcart, 'Spent force?', 262.

92 Cathcart, 'Forgotten '45', 246–7, 253–6, 259, 261.

93 SP 60/11, fol.51r although compare SP 60/11, fol.12r.

94 SP 61/1, fol.232r.

claimant to the lordship of Tyrconnell and head of the O'Donnell kindred. This was renewed on the death of the fourth earl and the succession of Archibald, fifth earl, and strengthened early in 1560 when Calvagh married Katherine MacLean, widow of the fourth earl. As well as reinforcing the alliance with the earl of Argyll, the marriage also brought Katherine's dowry of a Highland fighting force, crucial for Calvagh who was pushing his claims to Tyrconnell against those of his brother Hugh.[95]

Campbell connections with the MacDonalds of Duniviag and the Glens would have been viewed as an advantage by Elizabeth at this time as it would create an alliance of the earl of Argyll, the MacDonalds and the O'Donnells against Shane O'Neill, then regarded as the biggest threat to English policy at the time. This alignment of kindreds on either side of the channel with the English looked promising but it involved a dramatic shift in policy for the English who, for decades, had regarded the Highland Scots as the main obstacle to English policy in Ulster.[96] Their settlement in Ulster since, at least, the mid-fourteenth century, had been reinforced by successive waves of migration over the following two centuries. This process had been stimulated by both upheaval in Scotland and opportunity in Ireland. The MacDonald possession of land in the Glens and the Route was maintained by episodic and seasonal migration of Highlanders into Ulster as a hired, military force, and sustained by the maritime strength and expertise that afforded them unrivalled access to their Irish estates. For the English, this was an unwelcome presence in the land and one that heightened their security concerns. The dilemma was whether to continue to try to expel the Highland Scots or use them to curtail the activities of the equally unwelcome Shane O'Neill.

95 Mitchell, 'The O'Donnell lords of Tyrconnell, 1537–1603', 58–80. Both Hugh and Calvagh were sons of Manus O'Donnell.

96 *Selections from Unpublished Manuscripts in the College of Arms and the British Museum Illustrating the Reign of Mary Queen of Scots MDXLIII-MDLXVIII* (Glasgow: Maitland Club, 1837), 96. Indeed, according to Randolph, MacDonald advised there would be 'no greate good done agaynste Onel excepte he be invaded upon both sydes'; an opinion also held by Argyll.

CHAPTER 3

Removal and relocation
Alternative Ulster plantations

Economic, environmental and maritime considerations

The social and economic dislocation caused by the final forfeiture of the Lordship of the Isles in 1493 brought increased traffic across the North Channel as those affected by the changed circumstances in the western Highlands and Isles looked across the water for refuge, but also to take advantage of the opportunities Ireland offered. Meanwhile Irish lords were ready to exploit the situation for their own ends, supplementing their armies with Highland Scots who were willing to find employment in Ireland. The constantly shifting political context on both sides of the North Channel meant that this latter phase of military migration from Scotland to Ulster, albeit increasingly episodic and seasonal, was sustained throughout the sixteenth century. The Highlanders would seek temporary employment in Ireland at times when they were not needed to work their lands back in Scotland, but this was accompanied by the temporary displacement of clans from their estates on account of changing crown policy and internal clan feuding. Such a perspective focuses predominantly, if not entirely, on the political situation. Indeed, for the MacDonalds it has been argued that, while in general their lands were a 'source of cattle, men and booty' and a 'place of refuge in hard times', the primary significance of these lands was 'as a base for the deployment and employment in Gaelic Ulster of their expensive standing army when it was not in service in Scotland'.[1] This interpretation, however, perpetuates the

1 Ciaran Brady, 'East Ulster, the MacDonalds and the Provincial Strategies of Hugh O'Neill, Earl of Tyrone, 1585–1603', in William P. Kelly and John R. Young, eds,

view of the Highlanders as a militaristic society, and thus a problematic element from the perspective of Tudor and Stewart monarchs, and downplays a much wider economic and environmental dimension to these estates and to cross-channel migration that should not be overlooked.[2]

As early as the turn of the thirteenth century sea ice spread south from Greenland causing significant problems for Norse ships that travelled there but it was another century before the full impact of the Little Ice Age was felt across the archipelago. The onset of what is known as the Little Ice Age (LIA) at the end of the thirteenth century brought an end to the Medieval Warm Period (MPA) or the Medieval Climate Anomaly (MCA). In general, average summer and winter temperatures fell, resulting in shorter, harsher summers, periods of extremely cold winters and increased storminess in winds although there were periods of more 'normal' weather followed by times of extreme heat or cold. The LIA hit Ireland around 1315, coinciding perfectly with the worst rain and famine Europe had experienced and the devastation caused by the Bruce invasion and the unrest that followed, including a scorched earth policy. Crop yields diminished, harvests failed and cold winters saw livestock freezing to death. Following hard on the heels of war and famine came disease in the form of the Black Death that decimated the population followed by bovine pestilence.[3] As climatic conditions fluctuated significantly throughout the fourteenth century some areas recovered relatively quickly but elsewhere, as entire communities disappeared, land was left uncultivated. By the turn of the fifteenth century the combination of famine, plague and warfare meant many areas had suffered severe depopulation. Recurrent incidences of famine and plague, although often remaining localised, meant that population levels

---

Scotland and the Ulster Plantations. Explorations in the British Settlements of Stuart Ireland (Dublin, 2009), 46.

2 At the same time, this is not to diminish the militaristic dimension to Highlander involvement in Ireland at this time, but rather seeks to highlight other inter-connected aspects.

3 Timothy P. Newfield, 'A Cattle Panzootic in Early Fourteenth-Century Europe', *Agricultural History Review* 57 (2009), 155–90; Philip Slavin, 'The Great Bovine Pestilence and Its Economic and Environmental Consequences in England and Wales, 1318–50', *Economic History Review* 65/4 (2012), 1239–66.

were stagnant until the later part of the century when temperatures and weather patterns stabilised somewhat, conditions which lasted into the early sixteenth century.

The sixteenth century, in general, was characterised by an overall drop in temperature with continually unsettled and stormier weather. Conditions in the latter half of the century are uncertain. It has been suggested that they worsened with ongoing harvest failure, outbreaks of famine and disease and a significant increase in severe storms, with the 1580s and 1590s regarded as the coldest decades of the century and particularly harsh.[4] Extremely cold winters and severe storms were accompanied by a run of harvest failures with animals dying from disease; hunger and disease were common. While temperatures in England were likely around 1° higher than those in Scotland, many urban centres there witnessed food riots. At the same time, the weather became more unpredictable as winds in the Narrow Seas and the North Sea strengthened.[5] The period known as the

4 Brian Fagan, *The Little Ice Age. How Climate Made History 1300–1850* (New York, 2000), 23–44, 79–97; Richard D. Oram, 'Between a Rock and a Hard Place: Climate, Weather and the Rise of the Lordship of the Isles', in Richard D. Oram, ed., *The Lordship of the Isles* (Leiden, 2014), 40–61.

5 Research into ocean surface temperatures and the effect of the North Atlantic Oscillation (NAO) on prevailing wind patterns has highlighted that while a NAO positive index can result in increased wind strength in the north Atlantic and a negative NAO index can result in harsh winter conditions in Europe, the relationship was far from straightforward and some of the stormiest periods in history did not have a positive NAO index. See A. G. Dawson, K. Hickey, T. Holt, L. Elliot, S. Dawson, I. D. L. Foster, P. Wadhams, I. Jonsdottir, J. Wilkjinson, J. McKenna, N. R. Davis, and D. E. Smith, 'Complex North Atlantic Oscillation (NAO) Index Signal of Historic North Atlantic Storm-Track Changes', *The Holocene* 12/3 (2002), 363–9; A. G. Dawson, L. Elliot, P. Mayewski, P. Locket, S. Noone, K. Hickey, T. Holt, P. Wadhams, and I. Foster, 'Late-Holocene North Atlantic Climate 'seesaws', Storminess Changes and Greenland Ice Sheet (GISP2) Palaeoclimates', *The Holocene* 13/3 (2003), 381–92; A. G. Dawson, L. Elliot, S. Noone, K. Hickey, T. Holt, P. Wadhams, and I. Foster, 'Historical Storminess and Climate 'see-saws' in the North Atlantic Region', *Marine Geology* 201 (2004), 247–59; Robert A. Dodgshon, 'The Little Ice Age in the Scottish Highlands and Islands: Documenting Its Human Impact', *Scottish Geographical Journal* 121/4 (2005), 322–4.

Maunder Minimum, 1645 to 1715, saw a further drop in temperatures and this period is regarded as experiencing the worst weather of the LIA with cooler, windier, wetter weather all year round along with spells of extreme cold.[6] However, the evidence for individual years is rarely complete or indeed straightforward and some caution must be used when interpreting the data as the variations of views highlights: the sixteenth and seventeenth centuries were the worst of the LIA; the latter half of the sixteenth century saw higher than usual sea surface temperatures (SST) in the west of Scotland with mean temperatures returning to those of the medieval era; and while there were no periods of sustained or extremely severe conditions during the sixteenth century the latter decades were much colder and the winds much stormier.[7]

For the inhabitants of the archipelago, and farmers in particular who operated on a subsistence basis, these were difficult times. A run of bad harvests could be ruinous, and as prices rose those who were poorest were often the hardest hit. While there had been some improvement in farming methods, such as draining the land, in reality little had changed since medieval times, and with poor infrastructure there was little ability to move grain from one region to another. While this ensured that famine and outbreaks of disease remained localised, it also frustrated any attempt to alleviate the suffering of a particular region or locality. In such straitened circumstances the ability to rely on cattle and fish for diet was crucial. In upland areas, where there was less availability of fertile soil for arable production, communities continued to rely on pastoral farming, but even more so during the unstable and uncertain conditions of the sixteenth century. In Scotland, and also in England, there existed a rather basic division between the upland areas to the north and west and the more fertile lowlands to the

6 Robert A. Dodghson, 'The Little Ice Age'.

7 Fagan, *The Little Ice Age*, 47–97; Wolfgang Behringer, *A Cultural History of Climate* (Munche, 2007; translated and reprinted Cambridge, 2010), 85–115; Alastair Dawson, *So Foul and Fair a Day. A History of Scotland's weather and climate* (Edinburgh, 2009), 1–110; A. G. Cage, W. E. N. Austin, 'Marine Climate Variability during the Last Millennium: The Loch Sunart Record, Scotland, UK', *Quarternary Science Reviews* 29 (2010), 1633–47. My thanks to Dr Aonghas MacCoinnich for this reference.

south and east. While notable to sixteenth-century commentators, it is not appropriate to impose such an arbitrary division across the landscape as agricultural diversity is now more fully understood through knowledge of soil quality, mineral deposits, topography, climate, prevailing wind patterns and various other factors.[8] In many areas during the early modern period arable and pastoral farming operated hand-in-hand as almost all farmers, whether arable or not, needed animals even if only for the purposes of ploughing the soil. In England the south and east of the country saw more fertile lands where farmers concentrated on arable farming while in the north of the country there was a greater tendency towards pastoral farming where the land and climate was more amenable to livestock.[9] This regional diversity was evident across Scotland too.[10] The southwest Highlands and Isles was an area more suited to pastoral farming owing, amongst other factors, to the extent of rainfall and the quality of the soil; in contrast, the east and southeast of Scotland offered greater opportunity for agricultural development. In the south and southwest of Scotland, while there was still heavy rainfall in regions such as Galloway, there was varying soil quality also and pastoral farming predominated until effective draining of the land was introduced under later improvements. By then, however, the southwest was a region specialising in dairy farming.[11]

In economic terms, therefore, Scotland remained a regionalised country and harvest failures and incidences of famine remained localised. Nonetheless, as Scotland recovered from the decline and stagnation of the fourteenth and fifteenth centuries there was a shift towards a more grain-based diet across most of Scotland which provided for a burgeoning

8 *Report on the Present State of the Agriculture in Scotland, Arranged under the Auspices of the Highland Agricultural Society* (Edinburgh, 1878); Joan Thirsk, *England's Agricultural Regions and Agrarian History, 1500–1750* (Basingstoke, 1987), 12–17.

9 Mark Overton, *Agricultural Revolution in England. The Transformation of the Agrarian Economy 1500–1850* (Cambridge, 1996), 47–51.

10 David Turnock, *The Making of the Scottish Rural Landscape* (Aldershot, 1995), 180, 184–5; Fiona Watson and Piers W. Dixon, *A History of Scotland's Landscapes* (Edinburgh, 2018), 13–17, 79–95.

11 *Report on the present state of the agriculture in Scotland.* The first mention of the Ayrshire breed of cattle is said to date to the late sixteenth century (165).

population, although cattle and its produce and fish proved to be crucial supplements to the Scottish diet, along with imports from elsewhere, especially in years of harvest failure. The South Isles, as part of the Highland region, had much less land suitable for arable farming, but there were pockets of fertile land where crops could be and were cultivated, notably Islay, Kintyre, Tiree, Arran and Bute. Beyond these areas, however, due to soil quality, rainfall and climatic conditions, and regardless of improvement in farming techniques, a pastoral economy dominated. Cattle and its produce, whether hides or cheese, remained the bedrock of the Highland economy. While occasionally live cattle were taken to market where they were slaughtered and sold, in the sixteenth century most trade was in hides and cheese was a common commodity with which rents were paid.[12]

In Irish society, much like in western Scotland, there were a number of factors that ensured pastoral farming prevailed. Levels of rainfall had a direct impact on how land was best utilised in the north of Ireland but cultural and socio-political factors also had a significant role to play. Over preceding centuries cattle had remained a sign of social status, wealth and power within Irish society. Irish lords ensured their political dominance primarily through force but also their economic strength, extracting tribute and customs from tenants and others living under their protection, while billeting hired mercenaries on tenants' land. Cattle were a prize good and, although a valuable political and socio-economic commodity in Scotland also, in Ireland cattle had a much higher status.[13] Nonetheless, there was

12 ICA, Argyll Transcripts pre 1600, dated 21 August 1559; 21 May 1562; Robert A. Dodghson, *From Chiefs to Landlords. Social and Economic Change in the Western Highlands and Islands, c.1493–1820* (Edinburgh, 1998), 55–83.

13 Kenneth Nicholls, *Gaelic and Gaelicized Ireland in the Middle Ages* (Dublin, 2003), 34–40, 131–8; Nerys Patterson, *Cattle, Lords and Clansmen. The Social Structure of Early Ireland* (Notre Dame, 1994), 70–82, 90–8; Michael O'Connell, Fergus Kelly and James H. McAdam, eds, *Cattle in Ancient and Modern Ireland. Farming Practices, Environment and Economy* (Newcastle-upon-Tyne, 2018); Katharine Simms, *From Kings to Warlords* (Woodbridge, 1987, reprinted 2000), 96, 101, 103. For the Scottish experience see Dodghson, *From Chiefs to Landlords*, 55–101; Robert A. Dodgshon, 'West Highland Chiefdoms, 1500–1745: A Study in Redistributive Exchange', in Rosalind Mitchison and Peter Roebuck, eds, *Economy and Society in Scotland and Ireland, 1500–1939* (Edinburgh, 1988), 27–37.

little acknowledgement on the part of the English of the importance of cattle in Irish society where it was much more than simply livestock. Cattle were also a currency, one used by both Irish and Highland Scots in Ireland. Rent was paid in cattle while the Highland military forces in Ireland were paid, at times, in cattle.[14]

The MacDonald estates in Antrim afforded both arable and pastoral farming. The fertile areas suitable for agrarian cultivation would be exploited as a means to supplement the wider clan resources while less fertile parts afforded pasture for cattle. Thus, these lands were important to ensure the economic provision of the clan as a whole. Indeed, despite relatively high annual levels of rainfall, which impacted on the arable yield of the western Highlands and Isles, the north of Ireland was generally more productive than the west of Scotland.[15] In order to reap the economic benefits of the land, however, the MacDonalds had to maintain possession of their lands.[16] In Scotland, while clan chiefs held charters from the king for their land, thereby giving them legal title, this did not always mean the landholders could 'brukit and ioise' their estates. Inhabiting land for three generations or more gave people a customary right of possession, also known as 'kindly tenancy' in the Lowlands, which were acknowledged and respected.[17] As a result, land, and its economic resources, was often the cause of dispute.

14 SP 63/8, fol.66 where James MacDonald offered to pay rent to Elizabeth in cattle; SP 63/42, fol.43 where in September 1573 Walter Devereux, Earl of Essex, who was despatched to undertake the 'enterprise' of Ulster, commented that the Scots 'are riche in catteill being the price of their service'. *Annals of the Kingdom of Ireland by the Four Masters, from the Earliest Period to the Year 1616*, ed. and trans., John O'Donovan, vols IV and V (Dublin, 1856) contain numerous reference to exactions of payment of tribute in the form of cattle. For more on Essex in Ulster see pp. 142–6, 163–7 below; and R. C. Morton, 'The Enterprise of Ulster', *History Today* 17/2 (1967), 114–21.

15 Later, on occasion grain was imported from Ireland when there were incidences of shortage in England and Scotland, see Karen J. Cullen, *Famine in Scotland: The 'ill years' of the 1690s* (Edinburgh, 2010), 66, 68, 76–8.

16 Dodghson, *From Chiefs to Landlords*, 55–6.

17 Allan Macinnes, *Clanship, Commerce and the House of Stuart, 1603–1788* (East Linton, 1995), 16; Alison Cathcart, *Kinship and Clientage: Highland Clanship 1451–1609* (Leiden, 2006), 129–36. See also p.242 n.78 below.

Settlement of land was crucial if the economic benefits were to be reaped and the MacDonalds regarded their lands in Antrim as a vital part of the wider clan estate.

The establishment of the MacDonalds in the Glens had ensured continued clan possession of the lands and facilitated their economic exploitation. When, in the early sixteenth century, settlement in Antrim took on renewed significance in the light of the fluctuating fortunes of the clan in Scotland following the forfeiture of the lordship of the Isles, the economic resources of the clan were of increased importance.[18] No longer having legal right to their estates in Scotland meant that maintaining possession of, and thus reaping the economic resources of, their land would prove more difficult. In addition, the numerous rebellions that characterised the first half of the sixteenth century would have resulted in widespread wasting of lands and the theft of resources by enemies. The wider, uncertain environmental context meant that when they were deprived of their Scottish estates, the Glens of Antrim facilitated the very survival of the clan, economically and politically. The ability of the MacDonalds to exploit the land, both for pastoral and arable farming, and the fishing of the locality, was dependant on their maritime knowledge and prowess. As their estates in Scotland were separated by water, a short journey across the North Channel presented no obstacle; political or territorial borders mattered little.

The waters of the North Channel facilitated Highlander involvement in Ireland in general as well as the MacDonald presence in Antrim. This was a result of their familiarity with tidal streams and currents, prevailing wind patterns, and the coastline of the west of Scotland and the north of Ireland. The Irish Sea, and in particular the North Channel, was not an easy body of water to traverse. It is quite a unique stretch of water with its own tidal regime, a result of the waters of the Atlantic Ocean which enter from both north and south. In the north, the Atlantic tides are forced into the narrow passage between Torr Head in Antrim and Kintyre in Scotland. At this point the tidal streams are at their strongest, at times reaching up to

18 Breen, *Dunluce Castle*, 45, argues that in the early decades of the sixteenth century 'there was a renewed Scottish interest in northern Ulster'.

five knots. They are at their weakest between the Isle of Man and St John's Point on the Irish coast where, one-third of the way south through the Irish Sea, the tides from the north meet the Atlantic waters entering from the south. As St George's Channel is three times broader than the North Channel these waters extend much further into the Irish Sea. Consequently, even with 'fair winds, a day's sail from south to north … will be delayed by meeting an opposing tide at some point in the passage'.[19] The combination of challenging tidal conditions alongside unpredictable weather meant that anyone sailing west or north through the Irish Sea, when relying on sail alone, would find the journey to Dublin, Ulster, or the west of Scotland longer than distance might suggest.[20] These conditions, along with the heightened dangers of maritime violence in the west, added to the propensity to travel via the east coast when journeying between England and Scotland or to the continent. Even in wartime, patrolling the coasts of Ireland, the Irish Sea and the North Channel, in particular, was limited and usually only occurred when the English sought to intercept shipping between France and Scotland.[21] Frequent patrols in the North Sea and the Narrow Seas increased safety for English shipping in the east and, although the Isle of Man did not become a haven for pirates until later, there is some evidence to suggest that merchants were more likely to encounter pirates in the Irish Sea because of a lack of systematic patrols.[22] The waters of the

19 R. H. Buchanan, 'The Irish Sea: The Geographical Framework', in Michael McCaughan and John Appleby, eds, *The Irish Sea: Aspects of Maritime History* (Antrim, 1989), 3.

20 For more detail on the tidal conditions of the North Channel see Wallace Clark, 'Tides in the Waters of the Moyle', *The Glynns* (Journal of the Glens of Antrim Historical Society) 6 (1978), <http://antrimhistory.net/tides-in-the-waters-of-moyle-by-wallace-clark/>, accessed 9 August 2018.

21 David Loades, *The Tudor Navy: An Administrative, Political and Military History* (Aldershot, 1992), 14, 45, 111 and especially 144; N. A. M. Rodger, *The Safeguard of the Sea. A Naval History of Britain, 660–1649* (1997), 145–6, 179, 186.

22 Rodger, *The Safeguard of the Sea*, 182–8, 343–4, 347–51. There has been some examination of piracy in the waters around the archipelago; see H. Barnby, 'The Sack of Baltimore', *Journal of the Cork Historical and Archaeological Society* 74 (1969), 101–29; J. C. Appleby, 'Women and Piracy in Ireland: From Gráinne O'Malley to Anne Bonny', in M. MacCurtain and M. O'Dowd, eds, *Women in Early Modern*

west were less well known to sailors, merchants and crown officials who, on account of prevailing winds and currents and regular patrols, would prefer to make a quicker and safer journey via the east coast. Nonetheless, anyone wanting to travel between Scotland and the continent undetected by the English, would travel via the Irish Sea, especially if they were familiar with the waters, tides and coastlines.[23]

The ability of the Highlanders to dominate these waters and cross the North Channel with relative speed and ease was due to their tradition of naval architecture. Descended from the Viking longship, the birlinn, or Hebridean galley, had a distinctive shape and style.[24] Like the Mediterranean

Ireland (Edinburgh, 1991), 53–68; J. C. Appleby, 'The Problem of Piracy in Ireland, 1570–1630', in C. Jowitt, ed., *Pirates? The Politics of Plunder, 1550–1650* (Hampshire, 2007), 41–55; J. C. Appleby, *Under the Bloody Flag: Pirates of the Tudor Age* (Stroud, 2009), 66–77, 193–246; Keith Pluymers, "Pirates' and the Problems of Plantation in Seventeenth-Century Ireland', in Peter C. Mancall and Carole Shammas, eds, *Governing the Sea in the Early Modern Era: Essays in Honor of Robert C. Ritchie* (San Marino, 2015), 79–108 and more recently, albeit with a focus on Atlantic piracy, Connie Kelleher, *The Alliance of Pirates. Ireland and Atlantic Piracy in the early seventeenth century* (Cork, 2020).

23 See pp. 1–22 above. Although as Flavin and Jones have shown, trade from Ireland continued despite the obstacles and dangers; see Susan Flavin and Evan T. Jones, *Bristol's Trade with Ireland and the Continent 1503–1601: The Evidence of the Exchequer Customs Accounts* (Dublin, 2009).

24 The terms 'birlinn' and 'galley' have become somewhat interchangeable when discussing a variety of Highland vessels, although they referred to different sizes of craft. A birlinn was a vessel of between twelve to eighteen oars while a galley had between eighteen and twenty-six oars. The records also mention lymfads, a name that derives from the Norse word for longship, and a variety of smaller craft ranging from eight oars to two oars. See Denis Rixson, *The West Highland Galley* (Edinburgh, 1998), 64–78; Donald C. McWhannell, 'Ship Service and Indigenous Sea Power in the West of Scotland', *West Highland Notes & Queries: Special Maritime Issue*, series 3, 1 (2000), 3–18; D. C. McWhannell, 'The Galleys of Argyll', *The Mariner's Mirror* 88/1 (2002), 14–32; A. D. M. Forte, 'The Identification of Fifteenth-Century Ship Types in Scottish Legal Records', *The Mariner's Mirror* 84/1 (1998), 3–12; G. V. C. Young, *The Hebridean Birlinn, Nyvaig and Lymphad* (Peel, 1997); Colin Martin, 'A Maritime Dominion – Sea-Power and the Lordship', in Richard D. Oram, ed., *The Lordship of the Isles* (Leiden, 2014), 176–99.

galley which dated back to 3000 BC, these were originally oared vessels but the Vikings adopted the use of the sail around 700 AD. They were clinker-built, preferably from oak, had a sharp stem and stern, with a single mast, square sail and oars, and a rear or stern-rudder.[25] Different-sized vessels were required for different purposes and this influenced their construction, as did the availability of materials and the sea conditions within which these boats would operate. The prevailing historiography that presents Gaelic society in Scotland and Ireland as primitive, backward and uncivilised has suggested this form of maritime activity and shipbuilding continued because the area was cut off from mainstream development on the continent and in England and Scotland. This is not the case and the birlinn was not simply a remnant from a bygone era. Viking technology was extremely advanced for its time and innovation occurred when and where necessary. The side-rudder had been in use on Viking ships, but from the thirteenth century onwards, the stern-rudder became commonplace, a result of changes in ship design throughout northern Europe. While the stern-rudder today is often regarded as superior to the side-rudder this was not necessarily the case. The use of a side-rudder on vessels that sailed across the North Atlantic from Norway to Greenland was neither inefficient nor primitive. In a following sea the side-rudder would not jam, something that was a risk with the stern-rudder. From the existing evidence shipbuilding may not have developed much further between the thirteenth and seventeenth centuries but the birlinn remained the dominant form of seagoing vessel in the North Channel because it was perfectly suited to sea conditions and the uses to which the craft would be put.

25 Clinker-built boats were constructed from planks of wood that overlapped each other, as opposed to carvel-built vessels where the planks of wood lay flat against each other for a smooth finish, and allowed for greater flexibility, vital for the waters and tidal currents of the North Channel and North Sea.

Interior of Alexander MacLeod's tomb, Rodel, Harris. © Crown copyright: HES SC 973208.
The tomb was designed by Alexander MacLeod himself and incorporates biblical imagery along with hunting scenes and an image of a galley.

Ships used for raiding purposes, a common activity amongst the Vikings and Highlanders, were built for speed and manoeuvrability within the varied coastline of north and east Ireland, the western Highlands and Isles, and southwest Scotland, but they also needed to be large enough to transport a fighting force or goods to be traded. Like their Viking ancestors, the shallow draught allowed for easy manoeuvrability in sheltered coastal areas, inland rivers and sea lochs, yet it was deep enough to ensure the safe crossing of a short but turbulent body of water. The combination of sail and oar was key to the success of numerous raiding parties. While the use of sail was effective in favourable weather conditions, the ability to revert to oar to make a quick escape was of great importance, especially in situations where wind and wave were against the retreating party. Added to that was the short distances involved. Even if it was necessary to rely on manpower, the crossing between Ireland and Scotland was no more than twenty miles which, according to the contemporary English view, 'from Irland grounde to Scotlande is not vi howres sayling, no rowing, and to the best parts of Scotland not viii howres sayling', although obviously this depended on favourable weather conditions and tides.[26]

That all crossings were made in sight of land certainly made navigation easier and the close proximity of the MacDonald estates on either side of the North Channel allowed them to respond to urgent requests for assistance.[27] When under threat, either from a hostile Irish neighbour or a hosting from the English Lord Deputy, the Highland Scots in Ulster would light beacons on Torr Head, the most northerly headland on the coast of Antrim and in close proximity to the southern end of Kintyre and Islay, as a signal they needed help.[28] A map of Ulster produced *c.*1601 clearly marks the Scots' 'warninge fyres' on the headland near 'Faire-forland', Fair

26 SP 63/41, fol.160.

27 Rixson, *West Highland Galley*, 174 where he argues that '[f]inding land was less of a problem than coming safely to it'.

28 The English also believed the earl of Tyrone could get Scottish assistance in this way; see SP 63/173, fol.273; *CSPI*, V, 229, no.94. In March 1593–4 Dr Meredith Hanmer of Christ Church, Dublin, wrote to William Cecil, Lord Burghley, regarding the 'unsettled state of Ireland'. He mentioned the strength of the earl of Tyrone as consisting of 700 horse and 3,000 foot but added that if Tyrone made 'a fire upon the bank [*i.e.* if he light the beacons upon the rocks] within 7 hours he can have an endless supply of Scots, by whom he is greatly favoured'. Hanmer was 'the author of a Chronicle of Ireland from the earliest times to 1284, collected in the year 1571, and printed at Dublin 1633'.

Head in Antrim.[29] Even in quite poor visibility these fires could be seen from Kintyre where forces for a short-term campaign would be assembled quite easily and despatched quickly, albeit tide-dependent. Utilising this method of warning fires and capitalising on their maritime strength, the Highland Scots could be reinforced with fighting men at short notice. In contrast to the English whose ships were constantly delayed by adverse weather conditions, the adaptability of the birlinn was one of the reasons why it remained so important in this region for so long. It could be put to sea in different weather conditions, and was used for a variety of purposes, including the transportation of men – usually a trained military force but at other times, men escaping political, social, or economic dislocation and seeking refuge elsewhere – much to the frustration of the Tudor monarchy.

The turbulent waters of the North Channel represented something different for various groups of both English and Scots who traversed them. For individuals like Gilbert Thomson, living in a coastal trading community in the southwest of Scotland, there was no systematic or specialised training and merchants and mariners learned their craft through years of experience.[30] Their trade was earned through the combination of experience and knowledge passed down generation after generation. This was the case also for men like Thomson's attacker, Angus MacDonald of Dunivaig. While boat-building was a particular skill that, certainly in the seventeenth and eighteenth centuries, was the domain of the McWhannell family, the ability to maintain sea-worthy vessels was necessary for a community living in the western Highlands and Isles.[31] Most Scottish clan chiefs had disparate landed estates much like the MacDonalds whose main estate was

29 NMM Dartmouth Collection, P 49 (25), *c.*1601 [East part of Ulster]. For a helpful discussion of the map and its maker see Audrey Horning, *Ireland in the Virginian Sea. Colonialism in the British Atlantic* (Chapel Hill, 2013), 51, 76–84. The 'warning fyre' is also marked on TNA MPF 1/312. See pp. 99, 119–20 below.

30 Alfred W. Crosby, *Ecological Imperialism: The Biological Expansion of Europe, 900–1900* (Cambridge, 1986, 2nd edn 2004), 104–31, especially 111.

31 McWhannell, 'Ship Service and Indigenous Sea Power', 3–18; McWhannell, 'The Galleys of Argyll', 14–32; Donald C. McWhannell, 'Campbell of Breadalbane and Campbell of Argyll Boatbuilding Accounts 1600 to 1700', *The Mariner's Mirror* 89/4 (2003), 405–24.

Islay while also holding lands in Ireland and Kintyre. They were part of a wider maritime community that travelled frequently and easily from place to place. To them, and the men from the southwest of Scotland, the waters of the North Channel were primarily a bridge, a means of communication and connection, and an economic resource: in other words water, and the ability to cross it, was a basic need. It was through the processes of estate and resource management, the collection and redistribution of rents and tribute, as well as trade and military activity, that the west Highland and Island clans gained their knowledge and expertise in navigating the waters of the west; it was knowledge that offered a considerable advantage.

Prelude to plantation

The Campbell Earls of Argyll, as Highland chiefs and with an estate based around Kintyre, Lorn and the Cowal peninsula, also would have had maritime knowledge and prowess. Indeed, Campbell charter evidence points to a strategy of ensuring the provision of galleys around the region.[32] As magnates of national prominence too, the earls had a significant military potential and an influence that straddled the North Channel, facilitated by their maritime power. It was this influence that Archibald Campbell, fifth Earl of Argyll, hoped to utilise in his offer to work with Elizabeth I. Accepted in principle by the English queen, after the completion of the Treaty of Edinburgh in July 1560 it was left to her secretary, William Cecil, to negotiate the finer details of the agreement with Argyll that would afford Elizabeth an alliance which stretched across Ulster.[33] Co-operation with the Highland Scots, even via the acceptable

32 Steve Boardman, 'The Campbells and Charter Lordship in Medieval Argyll', in Steve Boardman and Alasdair Ross, eds, *The Exercise of Power in Late Medieval Scotland, c.1200–1500* (Dublin, 2003), 95–117; ICA Argyll Transcripts pre 1600, dated 29 July 1533; 23 May 1543; 24 June 1564.

33 The 1560 Treaty of Edinburgh secured the removal of French troops from Scotland. For the terms and conditions of the agreement between Argyll and the queen see SP 63/2, fols 58, 60; SP 63/3, fol.78; Jane Dawson, *The Politics of Religion in the Age*

face of Scottish Gaeldom in the shape of the Campbell earl of Argyll, was an abrupt about-turn for Elizabeth but it was her Lord Lieutenant in Ireland, Thomas Radcliffe, third Earl of Sussex, who baulked most at this policy, while Cecil also struggled to reconcile himself with the prospect of MacDonald settlement in Ulster.[34] Nevertheless, in the end Cecil was prepared to accept this in return for pacification of Ulster, but Sussex was not so amenable. As would prove the case in later episodes, the conflict of interests between London and Dublin ensured that policy agreed upon in London was not always followed through on the ground in Ireland.[35] Sussex simply avoided communication with Argyll and side-lined him.[36]

---

of Mary, Queen of Scots. The Earl of Argyll and the Struggle for Britain and Ireland (Cambridge, 2002), 96–110.

34 Thomas Radcliffe, Lord Fitzwalter, was appointed Lord Deputy in 1556 and succeeded to the title and earldom of Sussex in January in 1557. In 1560 Elizabeth appointed him as Lord Lieutenant of Ireland. Wallace T. MacCaffrey, 'Radcliffe, Thomas, third earl of Sussex (1526/7–1583)', *ODNB,* accessed 12 October 2015; Dawson, *Politics of Religion in the age of Mary, Queen of Scots*, 127–9.

35 Conflict of interests between London and Dublin also contributed to the failure of Sir Thomas Smith's attempt at plantation in the Ards in 1571. For more on Smith's plantation see pp. 137–42, 146–7 below.

36 Dawson, *Politics of Religion in the Age of Mary, Queen of Scots*, 126–37. Dawson argues (128) that Sussex regarded Ulster as 'a domestic problem of the kingdom of Ireland to be solved by its own governors'.

P/49 (25) (L9622): East part of Ulster [1601] with detail of Scots' warning fires. © National Maritime Museum, Greenwich, London.

Despite this unwillingness to countenance Argyll's involvement in Ulster, Sussex did begin negotiations with the MacDonalds in Ulster who had been petitioning for some time to have formal recognition of their claims to the lands they occupied. In January 1561 Elizabeth made an agreement with the MacDonalds, a tacit acknowledgement of their position in the region.[37] James MacDonald was to be granted the lands of the Route and the Glens (see Map 4), along with the 'captainship' of the Route for twenty-one years in return for a payment of 'threescore good fat ... beofs'.[38]

37 *Selections from Unpublished Manuscripts in the College of Arms and the British Museum illustrating the Reign of Mary, Queen of Scots, 1543–1568* (Maitland Club, Glasgow, 1837), 96. Sir Thomas Randolph wrote to Cecil on 12 September 1561 stating that MacDonald 'had refusall of a requeste he made unto the quene' but nonetheless promised he would 'at all tymes be at the queen my mestres devotion'.

38 SP 61/3, fol.152v; SP 63/2, fol.63; SP 63/3, fol.9; SP 63/8, fol.66; Jane Ohlmeyer, *Civil War and Restoration in the Three Stuart Kingdoms. The career of Randal MacDonnell, Marquis of Antrim* (Cambridge, 1993), 19; Dawson, *Politics of Religion in the Age of Mary, Queen of Scots*, 129. These lands consisted of those inherited

Sorley Boy and the all MacDonalds dwelling in the Glens and the Route were to become 'her M[ajes]tes subiect'; were to provide twenty-four horse and sixty footmen for all the Lord Lieutenant's hostings; and were to permit all other freeholders in the region to live peaceably on their lands and fish in the River Bann, paying no more rent than they had done formerly. In addition, James was to use the considerable MacDonald military force 'against all men dwellinge betwext Knockfergus Loughfoyle and [th]e Newry so oft as any of them shal rebel'.[39]

For a maritime kindred who traversed the North Channel easily and operated within two connected, yet distinct political worlds, becoming a subject of the queen of England was not complicated by issues of ideology or identity. In day-to-day realities such matters of sovereignty or territorial or legal jurisdiction were of little concern. This was a purely pragmatic decision, based on what best served the interests of the MacDonalds in Ulster at the time and was driven by the desire for security of settlement. Sorley Boy would become head of the MacDonalds of Antrim and a subject of the English crown, while his brother James would remain a subject of the Scottish crown and head of that branch of the clan. Indeed, being formally recognised as having a legal right to the Glens and the Route in Ulster would have further secured the ability of the clan as a whole to maintain their dominance over the North Channel world, enabling them to redistribute the economic resources of their disparate estate more easily. These negotiations, however, came to nothing. If they were an attempt by the English to appease or stall the activities of the MacDonalds it was counter-productive and resulted in the growing dominance of Shane O'Neill across Ulster.[40] At the same time, English failure to uphold their part of the agreement with Argyll and protect his allies allowed the internal dynastic rivalry of the O'Donnells of Tyrconnell to escalate, which further

through the Bisset marriage, along with additional lands in the Glens and the Route they had expanded into and continued to occupy.

39 SP 63/3, fol.9.

40 Jonathon Bardon, *A History of Ulster* (Belfast, 1996), 75–80; Breen, *Dunluce Castle*, 79–80 argues this was a temporary appeasement, long enough to enable Elizabeth to try to come to terms with Shane O'Neill.

benefitted O'Neill, while Argyll became gradually more disillusioned with Anglo-Scottish amity.

The Protestant and British agenda of the fifth earl of Argyll at this time has been skilfully outlined by Jane Dawson, highlighting how Argyll sought to work with Elizabeth to settle the problem in Ireland within a wider, British context. But Argyll also had a more immediate, local agenda as he sought to establish his dominance over the military trade across the North Channel. The fall-out from the 1545 rebellion suggests that while the vast majority of the Hebridean chiefs had come out in support of Donald Dubh's rebellion, whether or not it legitimately aimed at lordship restoration, it was the MacDonalds of Dunivaig and the Glens who controlled the military trade across the North Channel.[41] By allying closely with James MacDonald of Dunivaig and the Glens during the later 1540s and throughout the 1550s, Argyll sought to control that trade himself. Had the alliance with Elizabeth followed through, it would have catapulted Argyll, and indeed the MacDonalds, to prominence in the North Channel world, as well as in a wider archipelagic context also. Unfortunately for the earl, that was not to be the case.

Negotiations with the MacDonalds were underway but the English were more concerned by the realisation that all military efforts to deal with Shane O'Neill had failed. In his attempt to gain the title and earldom of Tyrone, Shane sought to portray himself as loyal to the queen while protecting his own position in Ulster. Rather than see the English allied to the Scots against himself, Shane wanted to use the English need for allies in the settlement of Ulster to his own advantage and turn it against the Scots. At the same time, he was aware of the economic benefits that could accrue to the crown should the Highland Scots be removed from the Glens and the Route. This would have been extremely attractive to Elizabeth as both the River Bann and Lough Foyle were well known as lucrative fishing grounds.[42] Fishing rights to both were fiercely guarded and

41 Alison Cathcart, 'The Forgotten '45: The Rebellion of Donald Dubh in an Archipelagic Context', *Scottish Historical Review*, XCI:2/232 (2012), 259.

42 Audrey J. Horning, 'On the Banks of the Bann: the Riverine Economy of an Ulster Plantation Village', *Historical Archaeology* 41/3 (2007), 95–6; Mark Gardiner and T. E. McNeill, 'Seaborne Trade and the Commercialisation of Fifteenth- and Sixteenth-Century Gaelic Ulster', *Proceedings of the Royal Irish Academy. Section*

disputes over them could be highly acrimonious. Shane was playing into the queen's hands by offering to remove the Scots, thus bringing stability to the north, while reaping economic benefits for the crown. Whether Elizabeth was fully taken in by Shane's show of loyalty is debatable but no doubt she felt compelled to accept. The number of soldiers she could (or would) commit to Ireland at this time, particularly in the north, was not enough to withstand the presence of the Highland Scots and their continued reinforcement from across the North Channel. Consequently, the queen decided to ally with the most powerful Irish lord in the north and, reversing English policy towards the Scots once more, looked to Shane to expel them from Ulster. By mid-August 1564 Shane, who likewise had 'nulie taken a byinge of the Scottes', regardless of his promises to the queen that he would not do so, was with 'an hoste and vyctuelles redie for v or syx weekes … to serve oppon the' MacDonalds.[43] By early November the queen was informed that Shane had moved against them 'and … burned part of ther contry'.[44]

Local and regional issues combined with self-interest and court factionalism had prompted Shane's offer to take action against the Scots but he was becoming increasingly frustrated by Elizabeth's failure to confirm him as earl of Tyrone. By February 1565 Sorley Boy had received reinforcements and was able to respond, inflicting defeat on Shane near Coleraine. Shane retreated, regrouped, recruited additional forces and, by May, the situation had been recovered. As Shane had gained the upper hand against his O'Donnell enemies in the west of Ulster he had the freedom to take action further east in the region without being too concerned with protecting his own lands in Tyrone. O'Neill moved against the Highland Scots,

---

C: Archaeology, Celtic Studies, History, Linguistics, Literature, (2016), 1–34, especially 10, 22–9.

43 SP 63/11, fols 68v, 138. Shane was not the only one amassing a fighting force. Sorley Boy recruited Gregor MacGregor of Glenstrae and his clan but did so without the knowledge or approval of either his brother James, or the earl of Argyll; see Dawson, *Politics of Religion in the age of Mary, Queen of Scots*, 132–4. This was probably on account of the outbreak of the feud between the MacDonalds and MacLeans that meant both forces, and any attention, were focused on Scotland.

44 SP 63/12, fol.114.

attacking all their key settlements: he turned first to Clandeboy, reportedly building 'a new and strong town', before surprising the MacDonalds in the Glens and the Route and pushing them back to their stronghold at Red Bay. After destroying Red Bay, Shane advanced to Ballycastle, defeating the Scottish forces in the valley of Glenshesk where he killed 700 of their men and captured James and Sorley Boy MacDonald, fatally wounding James in the process.[45] To further reinforce his victory Shane set about the destruction of all signs of Scottish occupation along the Antrim coast. If O'Neill had stopped there Elizabeth would have been delighted but, having removed the Scots from the east of Ulster, Shane wanted to ensure they would not return. In 'an unprecedented move by a Gaelic chief' at the end of May 1565 Shane was reported to be 'setlyng … hys people' in Clandeboy, the Glens and the Route, justified on the basis that, by June, he was busy resisting 'the Scots, who daily threaten to invade the kingdom'.[46] His agenda here was not so much economic exploitation but rather the expansion of his own influence across east Ulster which, in turn, would prevent the Scots from returning.

Opinion towards Shane was divided; many were inherently distrustful of the Irish lord while others continued to affirm his obedience to the queen. Terence Daniel, Dean of Armagh, wrote to Cecil arguing that, thanks to Shane, the north was now 'one of the questest contreye of Ireland and best ordred'.[47] The displacement of the Scots was welcome but Elizabeth was concerned at Shane's resettlement of the land and his imprisonment of James and Sorley Boy, especially when Fitzwilliam reported that Shane 'hath sent ocon[n]ores ould priest in to Scotland to the Q[ueen]'.[48] Nevertheless, Shane continued to profess his loyalty to the queen, suggesting that his

45 SP 63/13, fols 88, 113. Clark, 'Tides in the Waters of Moyle', argues that reinforcements from Scotland to repel Shane could not arrive in time on account of the tides needed to provide a safe and quick crossing of the North Channel. Therefore, on this occasion the tides and currents of the North Channel posed too much of an obstacle even for the Highland Scots.

46 SP 63/13, fol.116 (Fitzwilliams to Cecil); SP 63/13, fol.157 (Shane O'Neill to Cecil).

47 Compare attitude of Fitzwilliams (SP 63/13, fol.116) to that of Danyell (Daniel) (SP 63/13, fol.184).

48 SP 63/41, fol.56 (Fitzwilliams to Cecill).

actions were all for her service.[49] Such protestations of loyalty were treated with deep suspicion. While Elizabeth was keen to encourage Shane in his efforts to expel the Scots she had other ideas. As far as she was concerned the Scots, who had expelled '[th]e a[u]ncient ownors [th]e Irish' from the Glens, lands 'by them claymed as ther inheryta[n]ce, … have notoriossly forfeyted any right or title that they cold pretend'. Instead the queen wished to see '[tha]t co[un]trey w[i]t[h] the Iland of Raghty … brought to [th]e possession[n] and rule of some english subiect, or some Irish … of [th]e byrth of Irland [tha]t might kepe [th]e same to hir Ma[jes]tes use'.[50] Having attempted in recent years to utilise either the Highland Scots or Shane O'Neill against the other, on occasion tentatively recognising their claims to land, Elizabeth now sought to both expel the Scots and reduce O'Neill as neither party were trustworthy nor obedient.[51] This would not be easy, given the recent about-turns in English policy and, as Shane continued to make raids into Connacht and the Pale while building up his power within Tyrconnell, reports of Scots' galleys off the north coast of Ireland were far from reassuring for the queen. When the news came that James MacDonald was dead Shane sought to capitalise on this turn of affairs by asserting his position in the north both militarily and diplomatically.[52] His fortunes, however, were to change dramatically with the arrival of Sir Henry Sidney as Lord Deputy in January 1566.[53]

49 SP 63/14, fol.112; SP 63/14, fol.164v.

50 SP 63/14, fol.45.

51 SP 63/14, fol.44v. In an attempt to curtail O'Neill it was advised that O'Donnell 'shuld be restored to his Co[n]trie'.

52 *Annála Rioghachta Éireann: Annals of the Kingdom of Ireland by the Four Masters, from the Earliest Period to the Year 1616*, ed. and trans., J. O'Donovan, 7 vols (Dublin, 2nd edn, 1856), V, 1565 (1605–07) [*AFM*] recorded that the 'death of this gentleman was generally bewailed; he was a paragon of hospitality and prowess, a festive man of many troops, and a bountiful and munificent man. And his peer was not [to be found] at that time among the Clann-Donnell in Ireland or in Scotland; and his own people would not have deemed it too much to give his weight in gold for his ransom, if he could have been ransomed.'

53 SP 63/14, fols 163–6, especially 166r; Brady, *Chief Governors*, 113–58; Nicholas P. Canny, *The Elizabethan Conquest of Ireland: A Pattern Established 1565–76* (New York, 1976), 45–65. For more on Sidney and the factional politics he was

Sidney was stepping into a confused situation in Ulster that required immediate attention. He regarded Shane as a destructive force in the north that ought to be removed, a view that aligned neatly with that of the queen in the mid-1560s. In March 1566 Elizabeth was said to be 'very greatly heated and provoked to [th]e extirpat[io]n' of the Irish lord, a 'rebell' who, she declared, 'hath now manifested him self so contemptuous a traytor'.[54] Pragmatism had compelled Elizabeth to make an alliance with O'Neill, using him to rid Ulster of the Highland Scots, but his subsequent expansion into east Ulster raised the possibility of Shane becoming 'tyran of all Ireland' and brought another abrupt change in English policy.[55] Having engaged Shane to expel the Scots, his new dominance in the north threatened the English authorities and Elizabeth asked Sidney to 'employ your whole care, consideracion and wisdome how such a cankred dangerous rebell may be utterly extirpid'.[56] Sidney needed allies. He gained the support of Turlough Luineach O'Neill, Shane's kinsman and rival for the position as the O'Neill, and bolstered his neighbour and rival O'Donnell in Tyrconnell.[57] In addition, he tried to enlist the aid of Alexander Og MacDonald, brother of James and Sorley Boy, who had recently landed in Ireland, exploiting the animosity the MacDonalds had towards O'Neill. Given Shane's recent capture and imprisonment of James and Sorley Boy MacDonald, and the death of James while in captivity, it is not surprising the Highland Scots allied with the English at this time, but their alliance was shaped by more than just revenge.

embroiled in and fell victim to on account of his kin relations see Brady, *Chief Governors*, 113–16, 133; Canny, *Elizabethan Conquest of Ireland*, 45–7.

54 SP 63/16, fol.198r; SP 63/16, fol.206r.

55 SP 63/18, fol.1 (Sidney to Cecil 3 June 1566).

56 SP 63/16, fol.206r.

57 Turlough Luineach was the grandson of Art Og O'Neill who had been the O'Neill from 1513 to 1519. Following Art Og's death, he was succeeded by his half-brother, Conn Bacach O'Neill, while one of Art Og's sons, Niall Connallach O'Neill, became Conn's tainist. Niall had challenged Conn for the position as O'Neill during his lifetime but was unsuccessful and died in 1544. Turlough Luineach was Niall's son and, thus, a close relative of Shane.

In assisting the English, the MacDonalds once more were hoping for recognition of their claim to lands in the Glens and the Route.[58] Hope evolved into expectation when, on 2 June 1567, the MacDonalds met O'Neill at Cushendun on the Antrim coast, cut his throat and hacked him to pieces before burying him at Glenarm.[59] The Highland Scots looked for a reward but, while Elizabeth was greatly pleased by the news, there was little gratitude forthcoming. The queen acknowledged Alexander Og MacDonald 'hath very well servid in prayeng upon Shane' but would not countenance the MacDonalds having 'any habitacion or abode in Irland'.[60] Indeed, Sidney was 'to suffre as few Scotes to come into those partes as may be' while Elizabeth had 'an Intent[i]on to wryte to the Q[ueen] of Scotes to p[ro]hibit the frequentation and passage of her people into that our Realm'.[61] Shane's death was encouraging for Elizabeth, but news of a reinvigorated presence of Highland Scots in the north again was not. The Scots, like O'Neill, wanted recognition of claims to land and legal title, but the English were not prepared to capitulate. They continued to reinforce the earlier suggestion of 1563 that 'some number of well ordired people ... plant in those partes of the north' to avoid a resettling of the land by the Scots.[62] As for Alexander Og and his men, in July 1567 the queen informed Sidney they were to be 'well rewarded'; but if they did not leave willingly were to 'be expelled by force'.[63]

58 SP 63/20, fols 18v–19v. Elizabeth was keen to maintain the Scots' hopes of being granted title to their lands in Antrim as a means of ensuring their ongoing co-operation but, at the same time, they had to be prevented from making alliance with Shane.

59 SP 63/21, fol.17.

60 SP 63/20, fol.18v.

61 SP 63/20, fols 19r, 20v. This had been suggested earlier also, in 1563, see SP 63/9, fol.180r. Mary certainly seemed willing to co-operate with Elizabeth on this issue although, considering affairs in her own kingdom during early 1567, the Scottish queen would have been aware she needed to court Elizabeth's favour, not her hostility, see SP 63/20, fols 78r, 96r.

62 SP 63/9, fols 179–84; SP 63/20, fol.19r.

63 Concessions were to be offered to those Scots who had been settled in Ulster for some time; as they had performed good service and were 'well disposed to co[n]tynue in due obedience' they could be permitted to remain on the condition of paying 'reasonable rentes'. SP 63/21, fol.109; Memoranda by Sir Francis Knollys, 7

P/49 (25) (L9622): East part of Ulster [1601] with detail of O'Neill inauguration site. © National Maritime Museum, Greenwich, London.

This was an implicit acknowledgement that removal of the Scots from Antrim would not be straightforward despite the opinion that the Glens and Route should be planted with Englishmen. When under threat in Ireland the MacDonalds and their men could retreat across the North Channel, regroup and return to Ireland with reinforcements as they had done on numerous occasions. It was a tactic that Sorley Boy utilised when

July 1567 in *The Voyages and Colonising Enterprises of Sir Humphrey Gilbert: Volume I*, ed., David Beers Quinn (London, 1940), 121.

necessary. Having returned to Scotland after his release from captivity following the death of Shane O'Neill, throughout late 1567 and 1568 he was in constant movement across the North Channel between Scotland and Ulster. In November 1567 he was in the Glens with nearly 700 reinforcements and the next month with his men in Clandeboy.[64] In January 1568 he was reported to have 'gone to Rachline', in February he was in Kintyre, and later that year was settling members of the MacAlister clan in Cary and Glenarm.[65] By this time the English were aware of Sorley Boy's co-operation with Turlough Luineach, Shane's successor, and in March Elizabeth was told that Turlough was making 'a great fortification' to a castle Shane O'Neill had built at 'Dunalong, on this syde [east] of the Logh' Foyle'.[66] He also had allied with old rivals, the O'Donnells and the MacQuillans. Alongside alliance with the MacDonalds this presented a formidable united front against the English that stretched across much of the north of Ulster; a very unwelcome consequence of Shane's demise.[67]

Turlough Luineach had been waiting and was ready to step into Shane's shoes although his ability to fill them is questionable. His powerbase lay in western Tyrone and, although he had formed alliances with the neighbouring O'Donnells as well as the heads of lesser O'Neill branches in the region, he failed to assert any authority in east Tyrone and the key families there remained loyal to Shane.[68] In the immediate aftermath of Shane's death, 'Turlough Luineach … was styled O'Neill' although within a short time he had submitted to Lord Deputy Sidney and renounced the use of the title which, Turlough argued, 'he rather ignorantly than arrogantly toke upon hym' because it was 'the auncient custome'.[69] No doubt this

64 SP 63/22, fols 67, 112.

65 SP 63/23, fols 20 ii, 32 iii; Breen, *Dunluce Castle*, 81.

66 SP 63/23, fol.74 ix; SP 63/24, fol.20v. Dunalong was situated on the east side of Lough Foyle, about six miles south of Derry.

67 As a means of making peace with his MacQuillin neighbours, Turlough married one of his daughters to Rory MacQuillin; consequently, Turlough Luineach was allied with the MacQuillans, O'Donnells and MacDonalds.

68 SP 63/21, fol.17. Fitzwilliams wrote to Cecil in June 1567 of Turlough's 'p[ro] clamynge of him self as is sayd onell'.

69 *AFM*, V, 1567 (1623); SP 63/21, fols 17, 53. Henry A. Jefferies, 'O'Neill, Sir Turlough Luineach (*c.*1530–1595)', *ODNB*, accessed 24 July 2016, asserts that while Shane was

was done in an effort to gain English acknowledgement of his position, but the English were confident that stability would soon be restored now Shane was dead, so long as they could expel the Scots. Having received Turlough Luineach's submission, Sidney returned to court where he remained for almost a year, a sign of the confidence he had in the situation he left behind. Before the end of the year, however, conflicting reports were circulating regarding Turlough's loyalty. An alliance with Sorley Boy MacDonald in 1567 was followed by rumours Turlough was hoping to contract a Scottish marriage.[70] This O'Neill-MacDonald realignment was concerning. In late November 1567 Lord Justice Fitzwilliam wrote to Cecil stating that Turlough was 'lycke to be a mouche dangeroser rebell then was John [Shane?] onell, who neu[er] of him self lycked the Scottes'.[71] Despite the reports of him maintaining a force of Highland Scots in Ulster, Turlough attempted to portray himself as a loyal ally of the English. In reality, he was playing a double game. He made overtures of obedience and loyalty to the English in the hope his claim to the title and earldom of Tyrone would be acknowledged, but throughout 1568 was working with the MacDonalds and the Earl of Argyll.[72]

At some point in late 1567 to early 1568 plans began to be made for a marriage that would bring Turlough further political, military and kin connections across the North Channel. He was involved in negotiations concerning his marriage to Agnes Campbell, widow of James MacDonald of Dunivaig and the Glens, Sorley Boy's brother, and aunt of the fifth earl of Argyll. At the same time, another marriage was being proposed between Hugh O'Donnell, lord of Tyrconnell, and Finola, daughter of Agnes Campbell and James MacDonald.[73] Agnes was a formidable woman. Born

---

absent at the English court in 1562, Turlough was 'proclaimed as O'Neill at the traditional inauguration site at Tullyhogue'.

70 SP 63/22, fol.76r, SP 63/23, fol.73; Jefferies, 'Sir Turlough Luineach O'Neill', *ODNB*.

71 SP 63/22, fol.76 and see also SP 63/21, fol.17r where earlier in June 1567 Fitzwilliams described Turlough Luineach as being 'as valyante as any Iryshe in Ulster & w[i]thall as suttell & wyse as eu[er] was that rebell Shane'.

72 SP 63/23, fols 20 ii, 32 iii, 32 iv; SP 63/24, fols 20r, 119v. For further conflicting reports of Turlough's allegiances see SP 63/23, fols 32r, 37, 40r.

73 Finola was otherwise known as 'Inneen Dubh', the dark-haired daughter of Agnes and James.

into the powerful Campbell clan she was well-educated and had already played a useful role in Campbell politics through her previous marriage to James MacDonald in 1545. James' death in 1565 meant Agnes was again free to contract marriage that would further a wider Campbell agenda, alongside the marriage of her daughter, Finola.[74] These alliances would cement connections across the North Channel, drawing the main Highland Scots and Irish families into close ties of marital kinship. Throughout 1568 planning for the proposed marriages progressed while Turlough continued to keep all options open by also maintaining an outward show of obedience to the English queen.

Reports regarding the activities of the earl of Argyll and Sorley Boy MacDonald were far from comforting for the English. In the early months of 1568 there were several rumours concerning the imminent arrival in Ireland of Agnes Campbell and her daughter. The English were well aware of the number of galleys Sorley Boy had ready to transport large numbers of Highland Scots across the North Channel, ensuring 'that the arryvall of the Scottes is daylie looked for', while preparations were made along the coast to surprise them at any attempted landing.[75] In August 1568 the news that Sorley Boy was 'reddy preparing of a greate number of men to arryve in the Glyndes', alongside that of 'Thearle of Argyles diligence in making of galleys', prompted the council at Dublin to prohibit the export of timber from Carrickfergus and Wexford.[76] How far such legislation was enacted or the extent to which it could be enforced is debateable, but within a short time reports reached London that matters in Scotland might have saved the situation. They were informed that 'the Scottes w[hi]ch p[re]tended to sett in Rote here, are so busyed one against an other at home, as they can not intend hither, but haue broken of their enterprysse'.[77] It was neither parliamentary legislation nor a lack of timber that curtailed the activities

74 For more on marriage ties within Scottish Highland society see Cathcart, *Kinship and Clientage*, 99–112; for Campbell marriages see Dawson, *Politics of Religion in the Age of Mary, Queen of Scots*, 59–68.

75 SP 63/24, fols 20v–1r; SP 63/24, fols 15–16.

76 SP 63/25, fol.150.

77 SP 63/25, fols 42v, 87v–8r.

of Argyll at this time, but rather a last-ditch attempt to get the support of Elizabeth for his own queen, Mary Stuart.

Frustration caused by the breakdown of his agreement with Elizabeth earlier in the decade, combined with her refusal to offer support to him and his allies in the aftermath of the 1565 Chaseabout Raid, meant that relations between the earl of Argyll and the English were far from cordial. The deposition of Mary, Queen of Scots, in 1567 and her subsequent flight to England the following year saw Mary turn to Elizabeth for refuge and protection. By November, however, it was becoming clear that Mary was a prisoner of the English queen, a result of the York-Westminster conference which effectively became a trial to ascertain Mary's guilt in her own husband's murder.[78] Although Argyll had rebelled against his queen previously, unhappy with her marriage to Henry Stewart, Lord Darnley, and her subsequent remarriage to James Hepburn, fourth Earl of Bothwell, he was not prepared to condone the deposition of a divinely-appointed monarch and he rallied to Mary's cause. In an effort to get assistance from Elizabeth he sought to capitalise on his influence in Ireland once more. Late in 1568 an offer was made by Argyll to Sidney, requesting Elizabeth's aid in helping Mary 'to the enioyeng of her countrie'. If such support was forthcoming 'he woolde minister from tyme to tyme all good and neighbourely offices to this land; But if she woolde not he woolde be in Ireland in p[er]son w[i]t[h] 5000 men'.[79]

Sidney also informed Elizabeth of his meeting with Agnes Campbell who, like her nephew the earl, made a request and a threat at the same time. In order to persuade the English to support Argyll, and aware that her proposed marriage to Turlough Luineach would further frustrate English policy in Ulster, Agnes offered instead to 'matche w[i]t[h] some great man of this countrie birthe at the Quenes appointement'. In return Agnes asked that

> she and hers might enioye that inheritance that her husband and her auncestoures by the number of vii lynallie in dissent had occupied … sayeing furth[er] that if she

78 Julian Goodare, 'Mary (1542–1587)', *ODNB*, accessed 13 October 2015. Mary was not allowed to attend the conference and instead was detained at Bolton.

79 SP 63/26, fol.71.

> coulde not haue that graunte at the Quenes handes as longe as there were any of the Clandonnelles alyue they woolde neu[er] cease p[ro]seqution of that Title w[i]t[h] all the force they coulde.[80]

Threats and blackmail were what the English expected of the degenerate and uncivilised 'Irishe Scottes' but Agnes Campbell was regarded as an intelligent and well-educated woman.[81] This was a clear articulation on her part of MacDonald claims to sustained possession and occupation of land in Ireland over several generations. This may have received some legal recognition in Scotland but not necessarily in Ireland. Nonetheless, regardless of English inability to militarily remove the MacDonalds, it was a clear indication they would not remove of their own volition.

This communication with Agnes Campbell was particularly unsettling as the decision had already been taken to break up the O'Neill lordship of Tyrone and, in the process, reduce the size of Turlough's lordship and establish the young Hugh O'Neill, Baron of Dungannon, south of Lough Neagh.[82] News of this immediately pushed Turlough into opposition to the English, strengthening his desire to ally with both the Campbells and the MacDonalds through marriage. With little support for Mary, Queen of Scots, forthcoming from Elizabeth, and Turlough outwardly in opposition, Argyll now worked to thwart English policy in Ireland and in doing so he made full use of his own kin, his wider influence with neighbouring clans, and his cross-channel connections to negotiate the marriages of Agnes and Finola.[83] Thus, despite all English efforts to expel the Highland Scots from the north of Ireland, the 1560s had witnessed a constant shifting of alliances across Ulster with the English always seeking to gain the upper hand against both the Irish and the Scots. As the decade came to a close,

80 SP 63/26, fol.71.

81 Admittedly this was a view that emerged following the communication between Elizabeth and Agnes in 1571; see SP 63/31, fols 53, 55.

82 SP 63/21, fols 112r–13r, 144; Jefferies, 'Sir Turlough Luineach O'Neill', *ODNB*. Hugh was the son of Matthew, first Baron of Dungannon, son of Conn Bacach, who had been assassinated by Shane.

83 Dawson, *Politics of Religion in the Age of Mary, Queen of Scots*, 155–69; Gerald A. Hayes-McCoy, *Scots Mercenary Forces in Ireland, 1565–1603* (Dublin, 1937), 86–94.

it would appear that English policy in Ulster was very much on the back foot: the English faced a united opposition of Irish and Highland Scots combined with ongoing claims to land in Ulster.[84]

The English had become aware of the intended impending marriages and throughout 1568 and 1569 were watching the traffic across the channel closely, expecting the arrival of the Scotswomen at any time. In late summer 1569 they received further intelligence of the wedding plans. On 5 August William Pers, seneschal, reported 'that aboute one thowsand Scottes' had arrived in Ireland with Agnes Campbell 'sent hither by Therle of Argile'.[85] On 13 August Leonard Sumpter, a merchant from Bristol, reported having seen '32 galleys and many boats, and 4,000 Scots', which Sorley Boy was said to be the leader of, prepared at Islay ready to sail for Lough Foyle. It is unclear how seriously the English took such reports or what steps were made to prevent or monitor the Scots' arrival. It is likely that any and all efforts were simply ineffectual in trying to thwart the Highlanders arriving in Ireland. Indeed, regardless of attempts to intercept their arrival in Ireland, a month later on 12 September 1569 Lord Deputy William Fitzwilliam informed Cecil that Turlough Luineach had been in 'the raughlynes … xiiii dayes' where he 'concludyd hys maryage w[i]t[h] James McConelles late wyf'.[86] Settlement of the Highland Scots in Ulster was secured through marital connections with the O'Neills, an Irish kindred formerly hostile to their presence there, and the O'Donnells, now also allied to the O'Neills, all with Campbell support. The ability of the Highlanders to move back and forth across the channel at will to defend or expand their settlement meant the English would have to take alternative measures to deal effectively with the situation in the north of Ireland.

84 Elizabeth was reluctant to restore the Catholic Mary, Queen of Scots, to her throne in Scotland on account of the threat it posed to Anglo-Scottish stability and Protestantism across Britain. She was certainly encouraged in this by Cecil who regarded Mary as the most serious threat to Elizabeth's rule, and indeed to English security. See Jane Dawson, 'William Cecil and the British Dimension of Early Elizabeth Foreign Policy', *History*, 74 (1989), 196–216.

85 SP 63/29, fol.60.

86 SP 63/29, fol.117v.

Plantation by any other name …

The settlement of the MacDonalds in Antrim posed a threat to English policy in Ulster. Elizabeth was unable to expel the Highland Scots from Antrim due to their ability to retreat across the North Channel when under threat only to return, and with reinforcements, when circumstances had changed.[87] At the same time, the emergence of Shane O'Neill as head of the O'Neill kindred and his efforts to push his dominance across Ulster placed the MacDonalds under further pressure but, even more so, added to the concerns of the English regarding the situation in the north of Ireland. A consequence of English military support that enabled Scotland to push through with the reform of religion there, was the agreement with Archibald Campbell, fifth Earl of Argyll, regarding the pacification of Ulster. This provided Elizabeth with a potential solution to her Ulster problem but it would also facilitate Argyll's control over the movement of Highlanders across the channel and strengthen Campbell dominance in both the western Highlands and Isles of Scotland and the north of Ireland. English reluctance to see permanent Scottish settlements in Ulster meant the agreement would not be acted on. Thus, while the MacDonalds and Shane O'Neill fought their own local battle over control of the Route and the Glens, national events in Scotland and England had a direct impact on the situation in Ulster. Argyll's increasing frustration with the English queen and her administration's reticence

87 This was partly due to the fact that Elizabeth would not commit the military resources necessary to effectively implement policy, at least not until the end of the century during the rebellion of Hugh O'Neill, second Earl of Tyrone. Whether the English sought to fully conquer Ireland before the latter decades of the century remains much debated. For a nuanced appreciation of English aims and efforts in relation to Ireland, the evolution of policy from that of reform to conquest, and some of the historiographical debate on this see John McGurk, *The Elizabethan Conquest of Ireland. The 1590s Crisis* (Manchester, 1997), 3–28; Hiram Morgan, *Tyrone's Rebellion. The Outbreak of the Nine Years War in Tudor Ireland* (Woodbridge, 1993 reprinted 1999), 16–25; James O'Neill, *The Nine Years War 1593–1603* (Dublin, 2017), 13–24.

to exploit his cross-channel influence, Elizabeth's refusal to support the earl and his allies in 1565, and Elizabeth's reluctance to offer assistance to Mary, Queen of Scots, following her deposition, completely transformed politics across the North Channel during the 1560s. The death of James MacDonald of Dunivaig and the Glens and the growing dominance of Sorley Boy MacDonald in Ulster, the MacDonald murder of Shane O'Neill, and the MacDonald alliance with Shane's successor, Turlough Luineach O'Neill, posed further problems for the English. Argyll's involvement in this alliance served to exacerbate the situation as he placed himself at the centre, not simply of national or 'British' politics, but of cross-channel politics. The earl negotiated marriages that brought about a Campbell-MacDonald-O'Neill-O'Donnell axis while also providing him with increased leverage over the movement of Highland fighting men from Scotland into Ulster.[88] In 1560 Argyll had offered Elizabeth resolution, by 1569 he exacerbated the threats she faced in Ireland.

Within this context of archipelagic politics, the efforts of the MacDonalds to maintain their settlement in Antrim was not only driven by the political or military matters that had previously ensured continued occupation of lands in east Antrim.[89] It has been argued that earlier expansion was not simply the result of strategic marriage or political opportunism.[90] Rather climate change, disease and environmental conditions that caused deteriorating weather patterns, crop failures and depletion of livestock meant that the Islesmen were more than ready to respond to any opportunity for landed expansion on account of the need to find additional economic resources by which to maintain the wider clan. This was no less the case in the sixteenth century and, although by this time

88 Argyll was also closely connected to the MacLeans, who became a key provider of manpower for the O'Neills, on account of kinship ties following the marriage of Shane to Katherine MacLean, widow of Archibald Campbell, the fourth Earl of Argyll, in 1561. The MacDonald-MacLean feud, that would shape local politics in the southern Highlands and Isles for much of the latter decades of the sixteenth century, spilled over into Ulster as well. For more on this see pp. 226–35 below.

89 In the fifteenth and early sixteenth centuries the Antrim estate had provided a refuge for the clan, and other Scottish exiles, when facing opposition at home.

90 Oram, 'Between a Rock and a Hard Place', 40–61.

the inhabitants of the North Channel region had adapted somewhat to cycles of poor weather, shorter growing seasons, repeated harvest failures and stronger winds, this was a challenging time.[91] Nonetheless, while not diminishing the militaristic drivers for this cross-channel activity, by the mid-sixteenth century a clear economic dimension to MacDonald settlement in the Glens of Antrim is evident. While Islay and Kintyre were both relatively fertile regions in comparison to many west Highland and Island estates, unpredictable weather conditions including high levels of rainfall, combined with localised harvest failures and subsistence crises, meant that these Irish estates could have a significant economic importance through redistribution of food resources around the entire clan, facilitated by their ability to cross the North Channel quickly and frequently.[92] It was the continued settlement of these lands that allowed for the economic resources to be utilised effectively by the wider clan, whether in Ireland or Scotland.

Rathlin Island, a core part of the MacDonald Irish estates, was regarded as the location where the clan stored both arable produce and livestock. In November 1568 Lord Deputy Sir Henry Sidney wrote to Cecil concerning 'the Ila of Raughlynes' where, he said, would be found 'corne and cattell … sufficient'.[93] At the same time, the MacDonalds were keen to exploit what

91 Fagan, *The Little Ice Age*, 73–112; A. Crone and F. Watson, 'Sufficiency to Scarcity: Medieval Scotland 500–1600', T. C. Smout, ed., *People and Woods in Scotland: A History* (Edinburgh, 2003), 60–81; R. Oram and P. Adderley, 'Lordship and Environmental Change in Central Highland Scotland, c.1300–c.1450', *Journal of the North Atlantic*, 1 (2008), 78–84; Richard C. Hoffman, *An Environmental History of Medieval Europe* (Cambridge, 2014); B. Campbell, *The Great Transition: Climate, Disease and Society in the Late-Medieval World* (Cambridge, 2016).

92 Robert A. Dodgshon, 'West Highland Chiefdoms, 1500–1745: A Study in Redistributive Exchange', in Rosalind Mitchison and Peter Roebuck, eds, *Economy and Society in Scotland and Ireland, 1500–1939* (Edinburgh, 1988), 27–37.

93 SP 63/26, fol.72r. Sidney also advocated that Rathlin 'of necessetie muste be taken and fortified for it is the verie Staple and bayteng place of the Scottes'. See also SP 61/3, fols 151r–5r. In his report of the hosting into Ulster led by the Lord Deputy Sir James Croft, Sir Thomas Cusacke, Chancellor, made mention of the cattle and corn the MacDonalds had. He reported of the recent MacDonald raid into Clandeboy when 'all the kyne of that contre was … taken by the … Skottes' before moving on towards the Glens to 'a villadge called the M[ar]ket towne, where James

fertile land they had in the Glens too. Although the English conveniently ignored evidence of the Irish or Highland Scots engaged in arable farming (a key indicator of a civil society), in January 1568 Elizabeth was informed that Sorley Boy had 'gone to Rachline' [Rathlin Island] leaving 'as muche peopill as he could gether manuring the land'.[94] Maintaining their presence in Antrim ensured they could reap the economic resources of their lands of the Glens and also the Route and Clandeboy when they extended their influence further west and east. Suitable for arable farming, these lands also afforded pasture for cattle.[95] Given the importance of cattle in Irish society as a symbol of both wealth and status, and an economic resource, it is understandable that the MacDonalds utilised their lands as pasture for cattle which could then be either traded internally, exported as hides, or redistributed in other parts of their estate across the North Channel if necessary. Alongside this pastoral farming, their presence in Antrim allowed them to exploit economic resources that, in theory, were in the hands of the English crown.

During their expansion west from the Glens into the Route the MacDonalds had taken control of the Bann fisheries and income from fishing would have supplemented provision for the clan as a whole. While the English were fully aware of the economic potential of the fisheries of Ulster, there was little Elizabeth could do if the MacDonalds controlled the water and its resources. In 1564, when trying to present himself as a loyal subject in return for recognition as earl of Tyrone, Shane O'Neill promised Elizabeth that when he had removed the MacDonalds from Antrim, he would restore to her all 'the proffite' of 'the fishing of the Bane & Loghfoyll, her Ma[jes]ties auncie[n]t enheritaunce'. In doing so, 'the proffite thereof, hitherto taken by the Scottes may hensforthe be converted to her ma[jes]

McConnell brether[e]n had their chief inhabitans. And the contre round about the same well manured & occupied. Wherein was more store of corn then in all Clanneboy.' They then received reports that James and his men were 'all togidder in the Iland of Raghlyn & had w[i]th them the moost p[ar]te of all the praies of kyne & garrans that … were taken by them out of Clanneboy'.

94 SP 63/23, fol.20 ii

95 See n.14 above.

ties use'.[96] But while Shane's death may have been welcomed by the queen, it saw continued MacDonald dominance in the north enabling them to further reap the benefits of the rich fishing. Alongside this, the English were keen to exploit timber resources in Ireland and forests were often reserved for the use of the crown. Implementing such reserved status, however, in a region where the authority of the crown was rarely respected, was another matter. In June 1568 the English were unable to prevent Sorley Boy coming 'to the Glynnes w[i]th a … company' where he 'contynewed … two nyghtes' with the 'purpose to cawse wattyll to be cutt to bylde in the Rawghlyns', probably in preparation for the forthcoming marriages that had recently been contracted or, like Argyll, for the 'making of galleys'.[97]

The economic potential of Ulster had already been recognised by Shane O'Neill. His efforts to exploit the economic potential of the region led Terence Donnelly, Dean of Armagh, to inform Elizabeth of 'all kind of husbandry sowing of wheit wheare none was sowen this hundredth yeares' by Shane along with 'buyldinges and all other thinges w[hi]ch tendethe to all quiettness'.[98] All this was viewed with contempt by Elizabeth, who was unable to look at Ireland in any other way than through the lens of accepted concepts of civil society.[99] Thus there was no recognition of the attempts by Shane to cultivate the land. It was with greater concern that, in 1564, she learned Shane was settling his own people in the Glens and the Route. This came about after Shane had pushed the MacDonalds out of their lands in Ulster and, in order to secure possession of the land, had started 'colonising the Glens and the Route, settling his own people there in large numbers'. As Ciaran Brady went on to argue, the 'first sixteenth century plantation of Ulster had begun'.[100] Except this is not quite accurate.

Although not recognised by the English as such, probably because it did not involve the building of cities or engaging with other forms of economic exploitation, the first plantation of Ulster was undertaken by

96 SP 63/11, fol.1. In return for 'the enterteyneme[n]t of fowrty men' and for the queen and council to 'followe his counsaill & advice for one yiere'.

97 SP 63/25, fol.97r; SP 63/25, fols 150, 152. See p.156 below.

98 SP 63/10, fol.152r.

99 This is developed fully in Chapter 4.

100 Ciaran Brady, *Shane O'Neill* (Dundalk, 1996; reprinted Dublin, 2015), 74.

the Highland Scots. A combination of cartographic, archaeological and architectural evidence identifies where the MacDonalds lit beacons to send messages to their kinsmen across the North Channel: a permanent settlement on the cliff above Murlough Bay in Goodland townland, Antrim.[101] Comparison with settlement sites at Finlaggan, Islay, clearly points to a distinctly Scottish type of dwelling, while the location offered the MacDonalds unrivalled views of Rathlin Island and across the channel to Islay and Kintyre. Audrey Horning has argued that archaeological evidence suggests a 'permanent 17th-century Highland Scottish village'.[102] Indeed Colin Breen has argued the area was settled by Scots throughout previous centuries as all efforts by Shane and by the English to permanently expel the MacDonalds from Ulster were frustrated.[103] Continued possession of the lands for over seven generations and their integral part in the wider clan economy, combined with MacDonald maritime dominance and their ability to move back and forth across the North Channel

101 NMM Dartmouth Collection, P 49(25), c.1601 [East part of Ulster]. See p.95 n.28, p.96 n.29 and p.99 above. A. J. Horning, 'Archaeological Explorations of Cultural Identity and Rural Economy in the North of Ireland: Goodland, County Antrim', *International Journal of Historical Archaeology* 8 (2004), 199–215 at 204–13; A. Horning, 'Telling Tales?: Islay and the Archaeology of Goodland, North Antrim', unpublished paper presented at Scottish Society for Northern Studies Islay Conference: From Gall to Gael and Galloglass, April 2012; Audrey J. Horning, *Ireland in the Virginian Sea. Colonialism in the British Atlantic* (Chapel Hill, 2013), 52–84.

102 Horning, 'Archaeological Explorations: Goodland, County Antrim', 204, 209; A. Horning and N. Brannon, 'Summary report on excavations at Goodland, Co. Antrim', Unpublished excavation report for Department of Communities: Historical Environment Division Lic. AE/07/67 (2007), 13–17; E. M. Jope, 'Scottish Influences in the North of Ireland: Castles with Scottish Features, 1580–1640', *Ulster Journal of Archaeology*, third series 14 (1951), 32–9, 52–84; Rowan McLaughlin and James Lyttleton, *An Archaeology of Northern Ireland 1600–1650* (Newtownards, 2017), 353–4. Earlier excavations in 1949 and 1950 revealed a sixteenth-century silver broach which perhaps points to a slightly earlier settlement of these lands prior to the plantation era. My thanks to Professor Audrey Horning for allowing me to see a copy of the unpublished excavation report.

103 Colin Breen, 'Maritime Connections'.

with ease, secured their position in Antrim.[104] Cliff-top fires and beacons, for which there is documentary and cartographic evidence, would have been seen twelve to thirteen miles away in the western Isles and, utilising this method of warning fires, the Scots could be reinforced with fighting men at short notice, thus enabling them to defend the lands when under attack.[105] When necessary they could retreat back to Scotland, retuning to Ulster when the situation had calmed down. The MacDonalds, however, did more than simply occupy the land: they also reaped its economic resources, especially at a time when such utilisation of land was vital for survival.[106] This was a crucial component of plantation for the English but while sustained occupation and exploitation of the economic resources of the land were methods employed by both the Highland Scots and the Irish, this was ignored by the English who viewed Gaelic society as 'barbaric', lawless and lacking in commercial endeavour. Settlement of people to ensure control of land and people, or 'plantation', alongside economic endeavour, has been regarded as the preserve of the English or of so-called 'civilised' societies. In their efforts to expel the Highland Scots and reform the Irish it would be to a policy of plantation that the English would soon turn.

104 For more on this see pp. 89–97 above; and Alison Cathcart, 'The Maritime Dimension to Plantation in Ulster, c.1550–1600', *Maritime Communities of the North Atlantic Arc in the Early Modern Period: Journal of the North Atlantic*, ed., Alison Cathcart, special volume 12 (2019), 95–111.

105 HL Ellesmere and Bridgewater Collection 1126, 'A treatise on the port and east coast of England and its defences. With a letter to the Earl of Essex' discusses the role of beacons in warning the inhabitants of England upon discovery of any potential invasion fleet off the coast, 'whereupon thaie Alarum beinge thus geven aswell into the land as alongst the coaste both sudden feares tumults hurlie burlies and other dangers are prevented, that to burnynge of beacons are insidente and w[i]thall in excedinge short tyme'. Beacons for such defensive purposes were common, although A. H. W. Robinson, *Marine Cartography in Britain: A History of the Sea Chart to 1855* (Leicester, 1962), 23–4, points out that they were also used to aid 'coastwise' navigation'. See also Horning, 'Archaeological Explorations of Cultural Identity and Rural Economy', 204, 209; Horning and Brannon, 'Summary report on excavations at Goodland, Co. Antrim', 14;

106 For further development of this argument see Cathcart, 'Maritime dimension to plantation'.

Map 4. Locations in Ulster pre-plantation

CHAPTER 4

The English in Ulster

Plantation policies and processes

Raised as early as 1521 in a report for Henry VIII by Thomas Howard, Earl of Surrey and Lord Lieutenant of Ireland, plantation was not a policy the English crown pursued until the mid-sixteenth century.[1]

1 *State Papers Published under the Authority of His Majesty's Commission, Volume II: King Henry VIII Part III* (London, 1834), no.xx (72–5 at 74). According to Surrey's own 'poure opinion' Ireland would never 'be broght to goode order and dew subjeccion, but only by conquest'. After conquering the land, he advised that 'onles Your Grace send enhabitantes off your owne natural subjects, to enhabite such countrees as shalbe won, all your charges shuld be but wastfully spent'. There is a wealth of scholarship on English policy in Ireland throughout the sixteenth century. The main debate is the extent to which the English adopted policies of 'reform' as opposed to policies of conquest and coercion. Key works include Brendan Bradshaw, *The Irish Constitutional Revolution of the Sixteenth Century* (Cambridge, 1979); Brendan Bradshaw, 'The Tudor Reformation and Revolution in Wales and Ireland: the origins of the British problem', in Brendan Bradshaw and John Morrill, eds, *The British Problem, c. 1534–1707, State Formation in the Atlantic Archipelago* (London, 1996), 39–66; Ciaran Brady and Raymond Gillespie, eds, *Natives & Newcomers: The Making of Irish Colonial Society* (Dublin, 1986); Ciaran Brady, *The Chief Governors. The Rise and Fall of Reform Government in Tudor Ireland, 1536–1588* (Cambridge, 1994); Ciaran Brady, 'Comparable Histories?: Tudor Reform in Wales and Ireland', in Steven Ellis and Sarah Barber, eds, *Conquest and Union: Fashioning a British State, 1485–1725* (London, 1995), 64–86. The work of David Edwards, which highlighted the extensive use of martial law in Ireland, has challenged this reform agenda. See David Edwards, Clodagh Tait and Vincent Carey, eds, *Age of Atrocity: Violence and Political Conflict in Early Modern Ireland* (Dublin, 2007); Rory Rapple, *Marital Power and Elizabethan Political Culture: Military Men in England and Ireland, 1558–1594* (Cambridge, 2009); the excellent historiographical review article that touches on this debate, R. Rapple, 'Writing about Violence in the Tudor Kingdoms', *The Historical Journal*

Henry VIII's break from Rome and the wider Reformation context from the mid-1530s onwards brought an added dimension to security concerns, with Ireland perceived to be the weak back-door through which an external power would launch an attack on England.[2] The security threat of the 1540s, caused by rumours of the return to Ireland of the exiled Gerald FitzGerald, heir to the forfeited Kildare inheritance, with Scottish and French assistance, brought home to the English the vulnerability of their Irish coastline.[3] This resulted in a baseline policy that emphasised the strengthening and reinforcement of coastal garrisons with greater naval patrols and an increased military presence in Ireland when rumours of invasion were rife but, as the English crown was reluctant to commit the necessary funds to Ireland, progress was stilted and sporadic.[4] First devised by Edward VI, it was Mary Tudor who implemented plantation in counties Laois and Offaly in the 1550s.[5] The policy, initiated under Lord Deputy Thomas Radcliffe, Lord Fitzwalter,

---

54/3 (2011), 829–54; Brendan Kane, 'Ordinary Violence? Ireland as Emergency in the Tudor State', *History* 99/3 (2014), 444–67. See also recent publications on the English in Ireland: Christopher Maginn, *William Cecil, Ireland, and the Tudor State* (Oxford, 2012); Gerard Farrell, *The 'mere Irish' and the colonisation of Ulster, 1570–1641* (Basingstoke, 2017); David Heffernan, *Debating Tudor Policy in Sixteenth-Century Ireland: 'Reform' treatises and political discourse* (Manchester, 2018). For the most recent position on the reform debate by one of its key participants see David Edwards, 'Questioning the viceroys: towards a new module of English government in Tudor Ireland, 1536–1594' in Sarah Covington, Vincent P. Carey and Valerie McGowan-Doyle, eds, *Early Modern Ireland. New Sources, Methods and Perspectives* (London, 2019), 147–65.

2 Concern over foreign invasion would continue throughout the rest of the century, particularly heightened at times depending on wider context. While more attention has been given to Spanish intrigue and intervention in Ireland, for the French dimension to the Irish context see Mary Ann Lyons, *Franco-Irish Relations, 1500–1601. Politics, Migration and Trade* (Woodbridge, 2003; reprinted 2015).

3 SP 60/11, fols 141, 143; SP 60/12, fol.18r.

4 Wallace T. MacCaffrey, 'Radcliffe, Thomas, third earl of Sussex (1526/7–1583)', *ODNB*, accessed 12 October 2015.

5 Ciaran Brady, *The Chief Governors. The Rise and Fall of Reform Government in Tudor Ireland 1536–1588* (Cambridge, 1994), 94–6.

was far from a success and shelved during the early years of Elizabeth's reign partly because of the financial commitment it involved. Instead, in the northern part of Ireland, that most problematic of provinces, alternative policies were in place in an effort to extend English royal authority, law and order. By the end of the 1560s it was clear that more concerted action was required.[6] Initial suggestions for plantation in Ulster during Elizabeth's reign were the result of a need for greater defence of the province from the constant influx of Highland Scots who, in the mid-sixteenth century, were regarded as a real and consistent threat to English policy in the region.[7] Following the creation of an O'Neill-O'Donnell-Macdonald-Campbell alliance that stretched across Ulster and into the South Isles and southwest Highlands of Scotland, a more strenuous effort was needed in order to deal with the situation in the north. The policy of plantation that eventually emerged had evolved over previous decades and, in the 1570s, was one that Elizabeth could consider implementing in Ulster.

Political context and origins of a policy

Thomas Radcliffe, Lord Fitzwalter, was appointed Lord Deputy in 1556 by Mary Tudor and in January the following year succeeded to the title and earldom of Sussex.[8] Although generally regarded as an ineffective

6 Around 1551 Sir James Croft, Lord Deputy, suggested a colony of married English soldiers and their families be settled at Baltimore in west Munster, a proposal based on the example of the English garrison at Calais; see Richard Bagwell, *Ireland Under the Tudors: With a Succinct Account of Earlier History*, 3 vols (London, 1885–90; reprinted 1963), I, 360; Howard Mumford Jones, 'Origins of the Colonial Idea in England', *Proceedings of the American Philosophical Society* 85/5 (1942), 448–51, 454 n.35.

7 Brady, *Chief Governors*, 96.

8 Hiram Morgan, 'Overmighty Officers: The Irish Lord Deputyship in the Early Modern British State', *History Ireland* 7/4 (1999), 17–21; MacCaffrey, 'Radcliffe, Thomas, third earl of Sussex'. Thomas Radcliffe, Lord Fitzwalter, succeeded to

Lord Lieutenant, Sussex did have an appreciation of the need for an amphibious campaign reinforced by suitable coastal defences, all necessary to rid Ulster of the Scots.[9] On 2 January 1557, shortly after his arrival in Ireland, Sussex wrote to Mary reiterating the need for coastal defences to be fortified and inhabited, mentioning specifically the havens of Carlingford, Strangford, Carrickfergus, Olderfleet, the Bann and Lough Foyle.[10] He recognised the need to fortify and maintain garrisons along the northern coast of Ireland as a means of enhancing security and keeping the Scots out. Although the English garrison in Ireland had increased to 2,500 men shortly after Sussex's arrival there, his suggestions for greater fortifications and reinforcements along the north coast, on top of the need for greater resources elsewhere in Ireland, would require significant investment.[11] Queen Mary had other concerns apart from Ireland, primarily the war between France and Spain that England was embroiled in on account of her marriage to Philip II, alongside a possible Scottish invasion, declining trade and a succession of bad harvests.[12] Following the loss

the earldom of Sussex in 1557, shortly after his appointment as Lord Lieutenant of Ireland. To avoid confusion throughout the rest of this chapter Radcliffe will be referred to as the earl of Sussex. In 1560, following her accession to the English throne, Elizabeth promoted him to the position of Lord Lieutenant of Ireland. He was the first English earl, born in England, to hold the post since the time of the earl of Surrey in the 1520s and pleaded with Elizabeth in 1559 to allow him to resign the position: she refused.

9 MacCaffrey, 'Radcliffe, Thomas, third earl of Sussex'; Brady, *Chief Governors*, 72–112, argued for the earl's 'intellectual progress' and his nuanced appreciation of the state of Irish affairs (76); *The Irish sections of Fynes Moryson's Unpublished Itinerary*, ed., Graham Kew (Dublin, 1998), fols 250–4 (28–32).

10 SP 62/1, fol.71v. Earlier in 1551 it had been suggested that the 'ii principall places' in the north to be fortified were 'Wold[er]fleete and also at an abbey upon the Banne'. Olderfleet was situated on the east Antrim coast not far from Carrickfergus, while the mouth of the River Bann was one of the main havens on the north Antrim coast; the river Bann flows from Lough Neagh into the sea. The report continued that if 'bothe those ii havens may be possessed … the Scottes w[i]th James McOnell there … may be brought to obedience'; see SP 61/3, fols 3v–4r.

11 For more on this see Brady, *Chief Governors*, 85. Anthony St Leger had 500 men in early 1556; but by mid-1558 the garrison had risen to 2,500 men.

12 Ann Weikel, 'Mary I (1516–1558)', *ODNB*, accessed 13 October 2015.

of Calais at the beginning of 1558 plus Mary's deteriorating health, Sussex realised that waiting for garrisons to be fortified was futile.

In his efforts to curtail the Highland Scots who frequently arrived in Ireland, in 1557 Sussex first led an attack on Rathlin Ireland, just a few miles from the north Antrim coast, which was followed up the next year with an expedition aimed at making a pre-emptive strike against them in the Isles.[13] On 13 September 1558 he wrote to the queen from Dublin informing her he was about to set sail for Scotland 'trustyng to acco[m]plysh y[ou]r Highnes c[om]mandment yf wynd and wether s[er]ve'.[14] In early October, while on board the *Mary Willoughby*, Sussex wrote again to update the queen of his progress.[15] Having arrived at 'Lowghe Gylkeran' in Kintyre he 'burned eight myles of leynght, and therw[i]th James McConnelles chief howse, called Saudell, a fayre pyle and a stronge'. The following day he 'crossed over the lande and burned twelve myles a leynght on the other syde of the lowghe wherin were burned a fayre howse of his called Mawher Imore and a strong castell called Donalvere'. As he reported to Mary, he burned Kintyre 'from sea to sea'.[16] After this a storm arose and, 'the wynde being contrarye', he was unable to go to Islay so he made his way to Arran 'and did the lyke there', before moving on to the Cumbraes to waste lands there also. While anchored between the Cumbraes and Bute, Sussex 'susteyned sume losse' in a 'terrybell tempeste'.[17] The 'losse' must have been considerable as,

13 Little attention has been paid to this attack on Rathlin but was the focus of an unpublished paper by David Edwards presented at 'Beyond the Pale and Highland line: new narratives in archipelagic history, *c*.1350–*c*.1630', a conference hosted 13–14 July 2020. Amy Blakeway, 'The Anglo-Scottish war of 1558 and the Scottish Reformation', *History: The Journal of the Historical Association* 102/350 (2017), 201–24.

14 SP 62/1, fol.158.

15 This was the vessel taken by MacDonald and MacLean at the Isle of Man in 1533. It had been retaken by the English in the Firth of Forth in September 1547. See Richard Boulind, 'Ships of Private Origin in the Mid-Tudor Navy: the *Lartigue*, the *Salamander*, the *Mary Willoughby*, the *Bark Aucher* and the *Galley Blanchard*', *The Mariner's Mirror*, LIX: no.3 (1973), 385–408 at 393–5.

16 Sussex arrived at Campbeltown ('Lowghe Gylkeran') and made his way up the Kintyre peninsula burning Saddell, another house at Machrimuir and the MacDonald stronghold at Dunaverty.

17 SP 62/1, fol.160.

having returned to Carrickfergus, Sussex was unable to carry out his initial plan to return to the Isles to wreak havoc in Islay and Bute. The reasoning that he was required to stay in Ireland on account of 'certain exploytes to be don against the Scottes in these querters' suggests that his efforts in Rathlin Island and the South Isles were, at best, ineffective and, at worst, counter-productive.[18] Overall, Sussex's failure to achieve much militarily, his alienation of a significant element of the Old English establishment in Dublin, his perceived mismanagement of finances and the army, combined with ill-health and a weakening of his position at court, saw his recall to England in April 1564.[19] He was replaced as Lord Deputy by Sir Henry Sidney who arrived in Ireland in 1566 with a clear programme, largely based on that outlined by Sussex in 1562, although Sidney claimed he would be more efficient and spend less.[20]

While Sidney was focused on a wider, overall reform agenda, another individual was enlisted to help with the more specific Ulster problem. Humphrey Gilbert arrived in Ulster in 1566 to assist Sidney's military campaign against Shane O'Neill. Following O'Neill's assassination by the Scots in 1567, Gilbert became involved in plantation schemes for Ulster and Munster.[21] Gilbert had been an advocate of the northwest passage to the Pacific, in opposition to those who advocated a northeast passage. He was the author of *Discourse of a Discoverie for a New Passage to Cataia* (1566) which advocated colonisation in the New World as a remedy to the socio-economic ills of England. A contemporary of Richard Hakluyt, Gilbert was actively engaged in 'western discoverie', unlike Hakluyt who preferred

18 SP 62/1, fols 161r–2r. On 3 October Sussex wrote a brief initial report while on board the *Mary Willoughby*, adding further details a few days later when he was back in Carrickfergus. See also *The Book of Islay. Documents Illustrating the History of the Island*, ed., G. Gregory Smith (Edinburgh, 1895), no.XXXI.

19 Brady, *Chief Governors*, 101–7. By this time he had been Lord Deputy/Lord Lieutenant for eight years.

20 Wallace T. MacCaffrey, 'Sidney, Sir Henry (1529–1586)', *ODNB*, accessed 13 October 2015; Brady, *Chief Governors*, 73, 116–17, 119; Nicholas Canny, *The Elizabethan Conquest of Ireland: A Pattern Established, 1565–76* (Hassocks, 1976), 47–8.

21 Canny, *Elizabethan Conquest of Ireland*, 60, 67, 72, 79, 101–2, 119, 121, 127, 131, 160.

to stay on land and write about the benefits that would accrue from it.[22] In essence, he was a product of the 'age of exploration' and was intimately connected to Elizabethan maritime explorations.[23] Although he later was involved in discussions concerning various schemes in Ireland, Gilbert had not advocated plantation across the Atlantic, but rather emphasised the need for new markets and the importance of extending English influence into the Americas.[24] Like many of his contemporaries, the need for new markets was connected to the desire to spread Protestantism across the ocean, to counter the growing dominance of the Catholic powers, Spain and Portugal, that had been involved in colonisation in the Americas for some time.[25] Those advocating overseas endeavours argued English involvement in the Americas would be beneficial for both the inhabitants and for England. As well as establishing 'true religion' (as opposed to Catholicism), the English would facilitate development of the land and encourage cultivation which would be advantageous for the Indigenous Peoples as well as contributing to market opportunities for the English. This stood in sharp

22 *A Discourse Concerning Western Planting Written in the Year 1584 by Richard Hakluyt*, ed. and introduced, Charles Deane and Leonard Woods (Cambridge, MA, 1877); David Harris Sacks, 'Discourses of Western Planting: Richard Hakluyt and the Marking of the Atlantic World', in Peter C. Mancall, ed., *The Atlantic World and Virginia, 1550–1624* (Chapel Hill, 2007), 410–53; David Armitage, 'Literature and Empire', in Nicholas Canny, ed., *The Origins of Empire. British Overseas Enterprise to the Close of the Seventeenth Century: The Oxford History of the British Empire I* (Oxford, 1998), 107–8; Peter C. Mancall, *Hakluyt's Promise. An Elizabethan's Obsession for an English America* (New Haven and London, 2007), especially 128–55; Anthony Payne, 'Hakluyt, Richard (1552?–1616)', *ODNB*, accessed 7 August 2015. Hakluyt did travel as far as Paris where he spent time at the embassy there.

23 In 1572 Gilbert also penned 'The Discourse of Ireland' which emphasised an economic agenda for Ireland. For Humphrey Gilbert see David B. Quinn, ed., *The Voyages and Colonising Enterprises of Sir Humphrey Gilbert: Volume I* (London, 1940), introduction, especially 12–19 and 124–8 for 'The Discourse of Ireland'; Rory Rapple, 'Gilbert, Sir Humphrey (1537–1583)', *ODNB*, accessed 22 July 2012.

24 Mumford Jones, 'Origins of the Colonial Idea in England', 460–2.

25 Mancall, *Hakluyt's Promise*, 35. As far as Hakluyt was concerned, English monarchs were 'obliged' to maintain Protestantism.

contrast to the Spanish and Portuguese who, Hakluyt asserted, oppressed the people and exploited the resources of the land.

Plantation in Ireland, therefore, coincided with initial English efforts across the Atlantic and there is a significant body of literature that places plantation in Ireland within a wider, Atlantic context, emphasising the development of colonial, 'westward expansion', and comparison can be drawn between English attitudes to Ireland and arguments supporting English colonisation schemes in America.[26] While comparison between the colonial experience in Ireland and the Americas has been illuminating, a school of thought has developed arguing that the early Irish plantations set a precedent, a model to be followed in the emerging colonies across the Atlantic.[27] That there were men involved in plantation in Ireland who later moved across the Atlantic suggests Ireland was a 'laboratory for empire'.[28]

26 John C. Appleby, 'War, Politics, and Colonization, 1558–1625', in Canny, ed., *The Origins of Empire*, 55–78; Armitage, 'Literature and Empire', 99–123; Nicholas P. Canny, 'The Ideology of English Colonization: From Ireland to America', *The William and Mary Quarterly* 30/4 (1973), 575–98; Nicholas Canny, 'The Origins of Empire: An Introduction', in Canny, ed., *The Origins of Empire*, 1–33; Nicholas Canny, *Kingdom and Colony. Ireland in the Atlantic World, 1560–1800* (Baltimore and London, 1988); Nicholas Canny, 'The Permissive Frontier: Social Control in English Settlements in Ireland and Virginia, 155–1650', in K. R. Andrews, N. P. Canny, and P. E. H. Hair, eds, *The Westward Enterprise. English Activities in Ireland, the Atlantic and America, 1480–1650* (Liverpool, 1978), 17–44.

27 For an analysis of colonial experiences on either side of the Atlantic see Audrey J. Horning, *Ireland in the Virginian Sea. Colonialism in the British Atlantic* (Chapel Hill, 2013); and especially 1–16 for the debate regarding the extent to which Ireland was a 'laboratory' for colonial endeavour in the Americas. For different perspectives on this, amongst a wealth of literature, see David B. Quinn, 'Sir Thomas Smith and the Beginnings of English Colonial Theory', *Proceedings of the American Historical Society* 89/4 (1945), 543–60; Canny, 'The Ideology of English Colonization: From Ireland to America'; Canny, *Elizabethan conquest of Ireland*, 65–92; Allan Macinnes, 'Making the Plantations British, 1603–38', in Steven G. Ellis and Raingard Esser, eds, *Frontiers and the Writing of History, 1500–1850* (Hannover-Laatzen, 2006), 95–125; Hiram Morgan, 'Mid-Atlantic Blues', *The Irish Review (Cork)* 11 (1991/2), 50–5; Farrell, *The 'mere Irish'*, 27–61.

28 Jane H. Ohlymeyer, 'A Laboratory for Empire?: Early Modern Ireland and England Imperialism', in Kevin Kenny, ed., *Ireland and the British Empire* (Oxford, 2005), 26–60.

There were similarities, such as the problem of clear property boundaries, low population levels, and the issue of dealing with the inhabitants, but there were considerably more, and more pronounced, differences.[29] As the work of Karen Kupperman has shown, plantation was not first implemented in Ireland before being transferred into the North American context as plantation endeavours occurred on both sides of the Atlantic at different times, under different models and with different outcomes. Indeed, few were able to put their experience of Ireland into practice across the Atlantic.[30] Settlers in Ireland were affected by the resistance on the part of the Irish, and were constrained in their actions by royal officials and the implementation of English law into Ireland; in the American colonies there was little infrastructure. Ireland was relatively well known to the English crown and had experienced varying levels of English intervention since the twelfth century; the Americas really were a *terra incognita*. Another major distinction between settler society in Ireland and the Americas was that of geography. Ireland was situated in close proximity to England and Scotland and contact between the communities at home and in the new plantations could be readily maintained. In contrast, the settlements in the Americas remained isolated and separate on account of the distances involved and the transatlantic crossing. It was harder to maintain communication with, and regulate and control how the plantations developed when such a distance from England.[31] It was also more challenging to supply, defend and support fledgling plantations emerging so far away. Nonetheless, there was one similarity as, on both sides of the Atlantic, plantation was not necessarily a policy formulated in London and imposed onto the periphery. Rather, on occasion, plantation as a policy emerged as a by-product. In the Americas, specifically Newfoundland, in some cases the real aim had been to establish

29 D. B. Quinn and A. Quinn, eds, *The Virginia Voyages of Hakluyt* (Oxford, 1973), 92. Hakluyt argued that America would be easier to settle than Ireland because the Irish were too 'warlike' a people.

30 Karen O. Kupperman, *The Jamestown Project* (Cambridge, MA and London, 2007); Raymond Gillespie, *Colonial Ulster: The Settlement of East Ulster 1600–1641* (Cork, 1985), 219–22.

31 For more on the importance of geography in relation to the plantations see pp. 146–67 below.

markets. Settlements that grew up around these were intended to be seasonal, only in place during the time of year that transatlantic voyages could be undertaken safely. As a result of the distances involved, these temporary settlements became permanent.[32] It was around this time that plantation began to be taken more seriously as policy for Ulster because it came to be regarded as the best way to ensure security and realise the expulsion of the Scots.[33] Thus, the policy emerged initially out of security concerns rather than for any other reason. It was also a policy that, regardless of the aims and agendas of those in government or of any individual Lord Deputy, was shaped largely by events that occurred on the ground, in the locality.

Sidney had always been enthusiastic about plantation. Despite the personal animosity between the Lord Deputy and his predecessor, for the most part Sidney had adopted Sussex's policies for Ireland.[34] According to Sidney, Sussex's earlier efforts to establish plantations in Laois and Offaly, renamed Queen's County and King's County respectively, were to be replicated elsewhere. Indeed, Sidney agreed that the settlement of English colonies in the northeast of Antrim between the Scots and the sea was the best way to ensure their removal from the north of Ireland. In 1565 Captain William Piers, Constable of Carrickfergus Castle, put forward proposals

32 Peter Pope, *Fish into Wine. The Newfoundland Plantation of the Seventeenth Century* (Chapel Hill, 2004), 48–51, 349–59; L. Turgeon, 'Codfish, Consumption and Colonisation. The Creation of the French Atlantic World during the Sixteenth Century', in C. A. Williams, ed., *Bridging the Early Modern Atlantic World. People, Products and Practices on the Move* (Ashgate, 2009), 33–56.

33 Much in the same way as Sir James Croft advocated settlement in Baltimore, west Munster in the early 1550s (see n.6 above). All attempts at plantation took place within the wider context of English efforts to govern Ireland during the sixteenth century. While at times there were individuals who called for conciliation, negotiation and co-operation that does not take away from the more gradual, long-term drift of English policy in Ireland towards harsher measures.

34 For an assessment of Sidney's tenure as Lord Deputy see Brady, *Chief Governors*, 113–58; Canny, *Elizabethan Conquest of Ireland*. Indeed, much of what follows on Sidney is taken from Brady. As Brady has argued (115), 'Sussex had fundamentally transformed the way in which the Tudor problem in Ireland was to be perceived. … Sussex had produced a model of government that was immensely attractive in its simplicity, economy and apparent conclusiveness'.

to 'plant ffowur thowsand inhabit[a]untes of her natural subjectes' in the 'Northe parte of Ireland in the chiefe place of the Scottes'. In doing so the aim was to 'expel them [the Highland Scots] from all possession in that realme'. With this plantation, 'continuall warre' could be made against the Scottish or Irish inhabitants of the north until they 'submitt themselves to order' otherwise their lands would be forfeit.[35] Piers' proposal may have been a response to Elizabeth's assertion in July of that year that the Glens and Rathlin Island ought to be 'brought to the possessio[n] and rule of some English subiect, or some Irish … of the byrth of Irland'.[36] A further request for financial assistance in order to 'wall the towne of Knokfargus stronglie w[i]t[h] stone and reinforce the castell in good strength w[hi]ch nowe ys all in decaye' perhaps betrayed his underlying motive. Piers previously had petitioned repeatedly for further troops to support the English garrison at Carrickfergus which had been subjected to a number of assaults by both the Irish and the Highland Scots. As such, his experience of the MacDonalds was not a positive one and he was keen to see them removed from east Antrim. Shane O'Neill's attempts to resettle his dependants in east Antrim after he had forced the Scots out earlier in the 1560s may have helped to persuade Elizabeth of the importance of plantation if undertaken by English men; but Elizabeth was still not fully committed to the idea.[37]

35 SP 63/9, fols 179–80, 181–4. Piers also referred to the fishing and trade that would bring benefits to the crown following plantation in Ulster. Dawson argues that, although this report is calendared as 1563, it is likely to date from March 1565 (see Jane E. A. Dawson, *The Politics of Religion in the Age of Mary, Queen of Scots. The Fifth Earl of Argyll and the Struggle for Britain and Ireland* (Cambridge, 2002), 134). The report itself discusses the advantages plantation in Ulster would afford for security of the coastline, as it would enable them 'tanoye the Ffrenche' sailing through St George's Channel 'yf occasion shall serve' (fols 179v–80r).

36 SP 63/14, fol.44. This proposal to remove the Highland Scots coincided with a change in English policy which once more regarded the Scots, not Shane, as the problem in Ulster who needed to be expelled. Although the English had for some time tried to work with Shane they had maintained an outward show of co-operation with the Scots; see pp. 101–8 above.

37 For Shane's settlement of his own dependants in east Antrim see pp. 101–4 above and Brady, *Chief Governors*, 111.

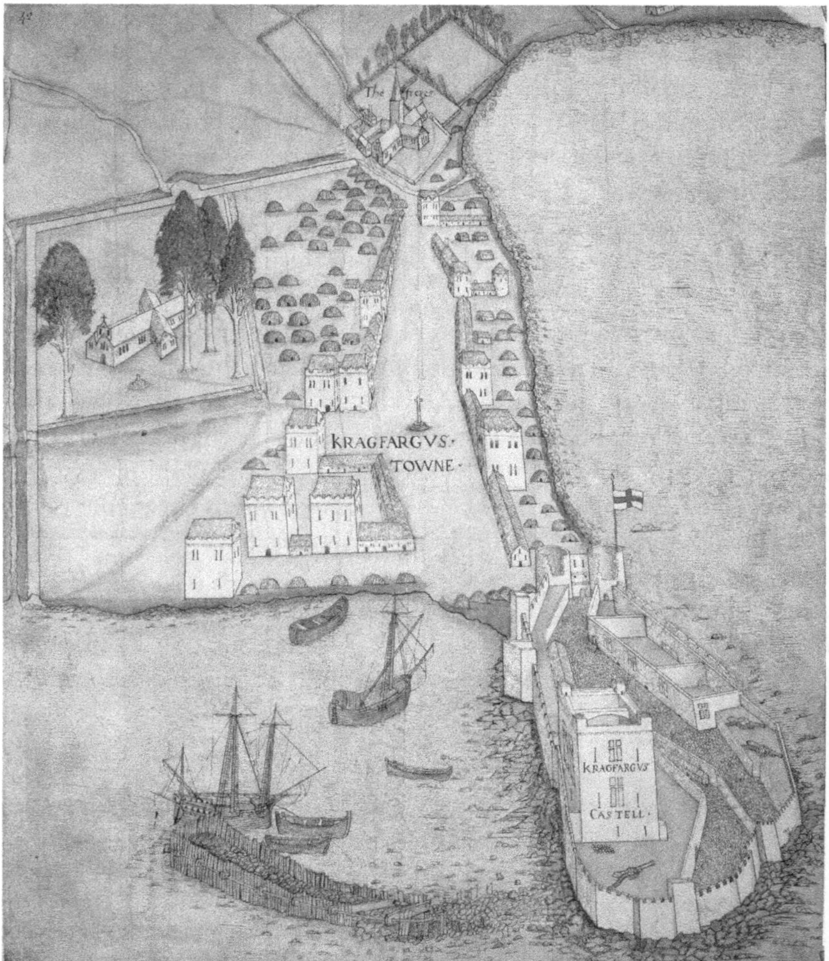

Carrickfergus, 1560. © The British Library Board, Cotton Augustus I, ii, f.42.

Sidney's promise to save money, combined with factionalism at court in England and Elizabeth's refusal to commit more resources than necessary, ensured little progress was made and resulted in a clear lack of support for his wider reform agenda. Shane's death at the hands of the MacDonalds in June 1567 enabled Sidney to repeat his recommendations for Ulster including the planting of colonies as a means of removing the Scots and preventing their return.[38] The following month Elizabeth acknowledged the only way to prevent the Scots 'from retourning out of Scotla[n]d' was 'either by keeping of garis[s]ons there to our contynuall charge, or elles by planting the sea coastes … with Englishe subjectes'.[39] She added that Humphrey Gilbert had been 'instructid from certen gent[lemen] in the west partes' to negotiate with Sidney concerning plantation, no doubt hoping to exploit his knowledge and experience in this regard.[40] Expelling the Scots in the short-term was one matter, keeping them out permanently was something different altogether. By this time, Sidney had come to the realisation that any recommendations had to be formulated and presented in such a way as to ensure the support of the crown on financial grounds. For economic reasons, therefore, Sidney encouraged private individuals to put forward proposals for plantation as he believed this was the best means of ensuring Elizabeth's support. If plantation were to commence in Ulster, then Sidney could begin to work towards the expulsion of the Scots.[41]

Offers concerning plantation in the northeast were received at court in the later 1560s, most of which Sidney had personally encouraged.[42] Captain George Thornton was familiar with the situation in Ireland as he had served against the Scots in patrolling the waters of the North Channel. Having outlined this service to Cecil, which included seizing the pirate 'Wolsall his shyppe & one pryese' he had encountered at the Isle of Man, Thornton put forward his 'simple suete' for 'the Ile of Magy' for him and his lieutenant, John Potter, in July 1568. The two men had already 'buylded a forte for the savegard of the harbrowe' and intended to 'have a fisher towne inhabited

38 SP 63/21/20, fol.48.

39 SP 63/21, fol.110r.

40 SP 63/21, fol.110v; Quinn, ed., *The Voyages and Colonising Enterprises of Sir Humphrey Gilbert*, 120. For arguments concerning the involvement of men from the West Country see J. Michael Hill, 'The Origins of the Scottish Plantations in Ulster to 1625: a Reinterpretation', *Journal of British Studies* 32/1 (1993), 24–43.

41 Canny, *Elizabethan Conquest of Ireland*, 46–75, 97–116, 140–53, highlights Sidney's dislike of landed interests of the great magnates in Ireland and the wider context of conquest as a prelude to plantation in Munster.

42 Brady, *Chief Governors*, 132.

w[i]th Englyshmen alwayes readye to serve the quenes ma[jes]tie at sea'.[43] Thornton's proposal, however, did not find much favour at court. Indeed, Cecil was to comment to Sidney in early January 1569 that his plan 'for Ulster to people it w[i]t[h] Collonyes is here better liked than thought lykly to be obteyned'.[44] On 15 March 1570 offers were received from Sir Thomas Gerrard regarding plantation in the Glens and part of Clandeboy. While Gerrard said he would 'people & fortyfie suffycientlie against any rebell of that contrey or Scotland' he asked for '100 horsemen and 400 footemen … untyll three cropes may be gatherid' along with 'the Queenes Ma[jes]tes shipes … for their defence against the Scottes'.[45] In 1571 Captain Nicholas Malby asked for Macartan's country and Thomas Chatterton of Wiltshire asked for O'Hanlon's country, while Captains Thomas Browne and Thomas Borrowe petitioned the queen for 'the Arde … from the mouthe of the river of Strongford to the River at Belfast, including castell Rewgh and the woodes from by east that river adioyning to Kylwarling and to the Dufferne' to be held in fee farm.[46] Most of these men had served in Ireland in a military capacity. They hoped to be rewarded for their efforts with grants of land and that their knowledge of the region and ability to defend their lands would be considered an advantage in any plantation scheme.[47] There were clear objections to the majority of these proposals,

43 SP 63/25, fol.35.

44 SP 63/27, fol.3.

45 SP 63/30, fol.62. Gerrard also requested 'com[m]yssion to levie the soldio[r]s … w[i]t[h] convenient nombers of laborers and artyfycers, w[i]thin the counties of Yorke Lancaster and Chester'.

46 SP 63/34, fols 116, 117, 118. Browne later petitioned the council in 1572 stating that he had formerly leased 'Ilande Machye' from the late Bishop of Down who had promised him a grant of the lands in fee farm. Browne added he had been 'the first of o[u]r nacyon that did in a daungerous and rebellious time … sett downe in the wast place of Clandeboye' and had built there 'a castle that cost him fowre hundredth markes & upwardes', thereby requesting a grant of the lands in fee farm as had been promised; see SP 63/38, fol.172r; Canny, *Elizabethan Conquest of Ireland*, 77.

47 Increasing numbers of Englishmen who had been active in Ireland, either in a military or administrative capacity, were being granted lands there as a reward for their services.

however, largely because they all requested crown support of some kind or another, primarily the crown's shipping to protect the coasts from Scottish attacks. On account of this, Elizabeth was reluctant to progress with any.[48] Her attitude would soon change, however, when proposals were received from Sir Thomas Smith, a 'scholar, diplomat … political theorist' and, perhaps most crucially, a member of the Privy Council.[49] What made Smith's proposals attractive to Elizabeth was that they were to be financed entirely by private individuals, thus eliminating any need for economic support from the crown.[50]

Despite humble beginnings, Smith had been educated at Cambridge where his intellectual ability brought him to the attention of the court as he established himself as a humanist scholar and an effective administrator. His career experienced the fluctuating highs and lows of being in and out of royal favour; at times this was due to the uncertainty of the middle decades of the sixteenth century and factionalism at court, but on other occasions it was said to be a result of his own temperament and beliefs. Clerk of the Privy Council, MP for Marlborough, and secretary of state during the late 1540s, Smith fell out of favour in the 1550s. Rehabilitated during the reign of Elizabeth he had a few brief spells as ambassador in France in the 1560s but in 1571 he was granted the lands of Clandeboy and the Ards peninsula, situated around Strangford Lough in east Ulster, despite having little experience of Ireland at all.[51] In the following year, Smith put forward his

48 SP 63/30, fols 78r, 463–4; SP 63/39, fol.87. Malby was granted Kinelarty and Chatterton was granted Orior; see Hiram Morgan, 'The Colonial Venture of Sir Thomas Smith in Ulster, 1571–75', *The Historical Journal* 28 (1985), 263; Canny, *Elizabethan Conquest of Ireland*, 85. Other Englishmen received lands in Ulster such as John Sankye who in 1570 was granted the 'in fee tayle … a castle w[i]t[h] certen landes … otherwise called … by the name of the howse of the Narrowe Water', then referred to as being in Magennis' country. But, Morgan argues (264), Captains Browne and Borrowe were unsuccessful because they had less influence at court and because they requested one hundred footmen and fifty horse.

49 Ian W. Archer, 'Smith, Sir Thomas (1513–1577), *scholar, diplomat and political theorist*', *ODNB*, accessed 25 July 2012.

50 Canny, *Elizabethan Conquest of Ireland*, 74–87.

51 SP 63/34, fols 144r–5r; SP 63/35, fol.19. For more on Smith's choice of location see Alison Cathcart, 'The maritime dimension to plantation in Ulster, *c.*1550–1600',

proposals to establish a colony of Englishmen in the Ards through publication of a tract that outlined his plantation project.[52] Emphasising his humanist education and scholarship, the work was written as an account of a conversation between two individuals, and contained both biblical and classical references, as well as the odd phrase of Latin. Although printed and circulated anonymously, it was clear that the arguments outlined were those of Smith himself.[53]

The tract began with an explanation of why the English colony in Ireland had declined over previous centuries and why England's government of Ireland at the present time was unsuccessful. In doing so Smith made reference to how the English had become 'degenerate' through alliance with and fosterage amongst the Irish, thereby 'choosing rather to maintain themselues in the Irish mans beastly libertie'. In more recent times the 'lack of sufficient forces' and the attitude towards 'Ireland as a matter of smal importance' were the reasons why the English, as yet, had failed to subdue Ireland. This could be easily rectified, argued Smith, and without any charge to the crown. The cost would be borne by those six or seven hundred men who would volunteer to participate and the colony

---

Maritime Communities of the North Atlantic Arc in the Early Modern Period: Journal of the North Atlantic, ed., Alison Cathcart, special volume 12 (2019), 95–111.

52 Anon., *A letter sent by I. B. Gentleman unto his very frende Mayster R. C. Esquire, wherein is conteined a large discourse of the peopling & inhabiting the Cuntrie called the Ardes, and other adiacent in the North of Ireland, and taken in hand by Sir Thomas Smith, one of the Queenes Majesties priuie Counsel, and Thomas Smith Esquire, his Sonne* (London, 1572), available via Early English Books Online; <historicaltexts@jisc.ac.uk>, accessed 4 August 2016.

53 D. B. Quinn, 'Sir Thomas Smith (1513–1577) and the Beginnings of English Colonial Theory', *Proceedings of the American Philosophical Society* 89/4 (1945), 543–60 at 550–1. Quinn suggests that although containing the arguments of Sir Thomas Smith, the letter, in its published form, was probably drafted by Smith's son. When published without royal approval Sir Thomas tried to distance himself from the work writing to Burghley on 10 April 1572 that the 'little book which my son sent out was evil done. I did not like it at the first myself … '; see *CCM*, I, no.285 (421). Quinn, 'Sir Thomas Smith and the Beginnings of English Colonial Theory', 543–60 also discusses Smith's other writings and letters showing the influence of Roman history, including his emphasis on 'colonels' and his desire for a principal city called 'Elizabetha'.

would begin to pay rents to the crown in 1576, four years after the proposed project was expected to commence. The rest of the tract outlined Smith's plans for plantation and, while it contained very clear economic reasons why plantation should be undertaken in Ireland, it was perhaps understandably vague on certain aspects of how it would proceed and why it would be successful. Plantation in Ireland, he argued, would solve some of England's social and economic ills, the most pressing being overpopulation and the issue of numerous younger sons. The reformation of religion in England had resulted in an increase in marriage while also causing religious exiles from other countries to seek refuge in England.[54] This was compounded by the dissolution of the monasteries, places where younger sons 'were wonte to be thruste'; instead they 'must nowe seeke some other place to live in'. Due to the increase in the population 'many lacke abode' with 'few dwellings emptie' but the solution to England's ills lay across the sea in Ireland where 'many countreis … lye almost desolate'. The endeavour would bring benefits to both countries. If Ireland were 'replenished with Englishe men', it would bring significant 'profite … to the estate of Englande' while to 'inhabite & reforme so barbarous a nation as' Ireland would bring the Irish 'to the knowledge and lawe' which 'were bothe a godly and commendable deede, and a sufficie[n]t worke for our age'. Regardless of his own lack of experience in such matters, Smith asserted that 'God did make apte and prepare this nation for such a purpose'. With God on their side, how could such an adventure fail? But fail it did.

Shortly after Smith received his grant of Clandeboy and the Ards he was sent to France once more in an ambassadorial role. While this left his illegitimate son and heir, Thomas, to commence with the project by himself and to deal with various obstacles, Sir Thomas remained involved, albeit from a distance and not always productively. Once news of Smith's grant reached Ireland Sir Brian MacPhelim O'Neill, chief of the Clandeboy O'Neills who lived in the Ards, requested its revocation on the basis he was a loyal subject and previously had been granted these lands by the queen. In an attempt to alleviate the situation, although actually underlining

54 In addition, there was a general increase in population across Scotland and England during the sixteenth century.

his lack of appreciation of the Irish situation, Sir Thomas Smith wrote to MacPhelim O'Neill in May, informing the Irish lord of Smith's claim to the Ards and that he would 'shortly come to live near him [O'Neill] as a good neighbour'. Smith added his desire that they would 'live on friendly terms'.[55] O'Neill, however, was far from welcoming and unlikely to so readily relinquish his lands to an outsider. Combined with the half-hearted response from Elizabeth to O'Neill's request for Smith's grant to be revoked, this meant the Irish were prepared to oppose the plantation from the outset.[56] The endeavour also faced resistance from the Lord Deputy, Sir William Fitzwilliam, who had taken up his position in January 1572 and, as he did not view the project favourably, offered little help. Fitzwilliam was not against plantation in principle, but was opposed to the private venture of Smith for two main reasons: he had not been consulted about it in advance, and his authority as deputy was curtailed by the extensive powers granted to Smith for the purposes of the plantation attempt. He was also wary. The endeavour had the potential to result in rebellion by the Irish, and he would be responsible for suppressing any unrest.[57]

On his appointment as Lord Deputy, Fitzwilliam had been warned 'that when the newes [of Sir Thomas Smith's grant] shalbe more open unto S[i]r Bryan he shold ioyne w[i]th the rest and revolt'.[58] A few months later in April 1572 Captain William Piers wrote to Fitzwilliam highlighting the 'knytting of Tirelaghe Lennaghe, S[i]r Bryan and others w[i]th the Scottes' which were 'greate cawses to be concydered on and p[re]vented'.[59] An alliance of the Scots and Irish against the plantation endeavour was exactly what the English did not want to see, especially before the project commenced.[60] While Fitzwilliam harboured these concerns, the queen

55 SP 63/36, fol.46; *CSPI*, I, 472, no.22.

56 Morgan, 'The Colonial Venture of Sir Thomas Smith', 271. Turlough Luineach O'Neill wrote to the Lord Deputy in October 1572 that Thomas Smith should not be allowed to settle on the lands of Sir Brian MacPhelim; see SP 63/38, fol.26.

57 Archer, 'Smith, Sir Thomas (1513–1577)'.

58 SP 63/35, fol.19r.

59 SP 63/36, fol.13r.

60 Indeed, the Scots were 'the most dangerous enemyes that can be to the crowne of Englande'; see SP 63/34, fol.144v.

was remarkably confident of success, and did 'marvell much' at the Lord Deputy's request for eight hundred additional troops, adding that he should be perfectly capable of dealing with the situation 'w[i]th those forces that ye have all redy'.[61] Fitzwilliam responded, stating the desire for reinforcements was 'necessarie' and 'not w[i]th owte great cawse', and also referred to the numbers of Scots recently arrived in the north.[62] Sir Thomas Smith himself then wrote to Fitzwilliam, trying to allay his fears and sought to persuade him of the advantages of plantation. Smith argued that the plantation did not aim 'to destroy the Yrish race, but to kepe them ... in order, in virtuous labor, and in justice, and to teach them ... English lawes and civilite, And leave robbying & stealyng & killyng one of an other'.[63] Smith's words did little to further his project and, on account of Fitzwilliam's concerns regarding, and resentment of, the venture, the Lord Deputy only added to Thomas Smith's difficulties; the younger Smith's departure in the summer months of 1572 was delayed.

Bad management and poor planning on the part of the young Thomas, alongside Fitzwilliam's opposition, meant that when the expedition finally departed from Liverpool at the end of August 1572 it consisted of little over one hundred men, a far cry from the number of around eight hundred that had been recruited initially at the start of the summer.[64] By 10 September Smith was already complaining to Lord Burghley that Sir Brian 'would not departe w[i]t[h] one foote of the lande', as a result of which Smith withdrew his men 'from the Newton in the Ardes ... unto to Renoughaddy [Ringhaddy] in the Duffren'.[65] In October 1572, by which time Smith, the son, had stumbled from one mistake to another, O'Neill and his allies wasted the lands of the Ards.[66] Meanwhile, Sir Thomas, the father, was trying various ways of gaining support within Ulster. In May 1573 he attempted to marry his niece to Rowland White's son. White held lands in the Ards and Dufferin and Sir Thomas saw this match as a means

61 SP 63/37, fol.56.
62 SP 63/37, fol.123.
63 SP 63/38, fol.69v.
64 Morgan, 'The Colonial Venture of Sir Thomas Smith', 264.
65 SP 63/37, fols 56, 117.
66 SP 63/38, fol.28r.

by which to 'joyne the Arde, and the Duffer in affynitie'.[67] Unfortunately he would not be given the opportunity to utilise kinship ties to implement his plantation more fully for the very same month Elizabeth granted 'Clandeboy, Rowt, Glynnes, Rawghlyns and als[o] landes in the countie of Knokferg[us]' along with 'the fishinges of the Band [River Ban] and Lough Eagh [Neagh]' to her favourite Walter Devereux, the recently created Earl of Essex.[68] Back in Ulster, Smith's son had a brief respite in spring 1573 but reinforcements to capitalise on this were not forthcoming. On 20 October 1573 his efforts ended in tragedy when he was murdered by one of the Irish he himself had employed.[69] By this time, the queen had already despatched Essex to Ulster to undertake his own colonisation enterprise.[70]

Despite the fact he was being sent to clean up the mess created by Smith, Essex was full of confidence, perhaps buoyed by some level of crown support. He was granted much of Antrim, from Carrickfergus to Lough Neagh, including the Glens and the Route, but excluding Carrickfergus Castle, and with the fishing of the Bann and Lough Neagh; was licensed to transport victuals and munitions out of England into Ireland; and given a loan of £10,000 for three years.[71] In addition, he was to have an army of 1,200 men and, once established, his colony was to be exempt from taxation for a total of seven years. Essex estimated his plantation in Ulster would realise an annual rent of £5,000, an amount that would easily offset any monies the queen had invested at the outset. Essex was encouraged

67 SP 63/40, fol.77.

68 SP 63/40, fol.173. The grant excepted 'the castell of Knokfergus w[i]th thapp[er]-ten[a]nces and all mynes of gold and silu[er]'. J. J. N. McGurk, 'Devereux, Walter, first earl of Essex (1539–1576)', *ODNB*, accessed 26 July 2012.

69 SP 63/42, fol.118.

70 R. C. Morton, 'The Enterprise of Ulster', *History Today* 17/2 (1967), 114–21; Herbert F. Hore, 'The Earl of Essex's Enterprise for the Recovery of Ulster', *Ulster Journal of Archaeology*, first series 9 (1861/2), 245–55.

71 SP 63/41, fols 125, 127, 129; McGurk, 'Devereux, Walter, first earl of Essex'. Essex was permitted to transport quantities of 'grayn, butter, chese and other victaills and sundry other thinges as armure, munition, his plate and money'. The loan of £10,000 was a mortgage of his estates in Buckinghamshire and Essex. If the earl failed to repay the money within three years, these estates would be forfeited. McGurk states this extended to about one-third of his entire landed estate.

further by the wide support from men who helped to enlist volunteers for the plantation and his desire was for each adventurer to 'build a small castle with a bawn of stone and intrench a town'.[72] He departed Liverpool in early September, but had his 'companie and victualls … scattered by tempest' with his shipping 'dispersed, some to the Isle of Man, and some to Cork'. More corn had to be sent.[73] The initial optimism quickly dissipated as affairs deteriorated rapidly for Essex, and he wrote to the council in London with some proposals.[74] During the short time he had been in Ulster he had witnessed first-hand the ability of the Highland Scots to come and go as they pleased, and to gain reinforcements at short notice. In a significant departure from the policy of planting English settlements in the region and reinforcing coastal garrisons, Essex suggested Sorley Boy be granted the lands of the Glens, which he claimed as an inheritance, and the captainship of the Route; in addition he proposed the queen 'make him [Sorley Boy] a denizen and assigne him a service in lieu of rent as captaine of Her Ma[jes]tes kerne, w[hi]ch he being a m[er]cenarye man, and a soldio[r], will easelie consent unto'. In return, Sorley Boy 'would serve her Ma[jes]tie against all other[s]'.[75]

It may have been a departure from English policy, but Essex's proposal was not new. On 29 May 1573 Sir Thomas Smith had sent a report concerning negotiations with Sorley Boy during which Sorley expressed his desire that 'himself and his [be] made denizens' by the queen's patent 'and enjoy all liberties of mariage' with the new settlers. Sorley Boy also wanted his claims to the inheritance of the Glens confirmed by the queen in return for his service.[76] Essex's suggestion likewise conveyed recognition of Sorley Boy's position in the north, his possession of the Glens and the

72 BL Add MS 48015: Papers relating to Ireland, 1538–1600, fols 296–300; McGurk, 'Devereux, Walter, first earl of Essex'.

73 SP 63/42, fols 40, 43; SP 63/48, fol.131.

74 For more on the career of Edward Waterhouse see Andrew Lyall, 'Waterhouse, Sir Edward (1535–1591)', *ODNB*, accessed 20 October 2015.

75 SP 63/42, fols 116, 118v, 142v. Sorley Boy promised to abide by the terms of the grant agreed between his elder brother, James, and the earl of Sussex, some years earlier.

76 SP 63/40, fols 196–7r.

Route and his ability to provide a significant fighting force as and when necessary. The desire of both Smith and Essex to succeed in their endeavours in Ireland compelled them to suggest such an alliance; they would rather work with Sorley Boy than oppose him and had come to the realisation that the MacDonald settlement would not be so easily removed from the north. With Shane O'Neill out of the way, and a policy of plantation failing to gain any traction, there were emerging voices suggesting that perhaps the best policy was to work with the Highland Scots rather than against them.[77] Part of the motivation for this proposal was the number of problems Essex was encountering, many of which were the perennial problems of the English in Ireland: a lack of support from Lord Deputy Fitzwilliam; diminishing troops on account of desertions without sufficient resupply (this forced him into agreeing a truce with Turlough Luineach O'Neill); ongoing resistance of the Irish and the Highland Scots; and a lack of steady supply of victual from England; all of which were compounded by the outbreak of plague at Carrickfergus.[78] With the project facing imminent failure Elizabeth contemplated recalling him but Essex was determined to persevere. He borrowed additional money by mortgaging more of his estates in England and requested more troops; he also asked for a grant of Magee Island at a small rent, which Elizabeth granted, along with pay for 600 foot and 100 horse.[79]

Essex remained personally committed but realised his days in Ulster were numbered.[80] On 1 June, he provided an update on the situation in Ireland and offered his opinion on various matters including where garrisons should be established and why. He also advised that, as the queen was not going to follow through with plantation in Ulster, then agreement should be reached with Sorley Boy MacDonald. In his view Sorley Boy was 'the lesse ill … more inclinable to civility, though more daungerous to the state if the n[um]bers shold be great'. Indeed, if Sorley Boy 'be made

77 On this occasion, Elizabeth was far from enamoured of the proposal.

78 SP 63/44, fols 65, 168; SP 63/45, fols 21–2; SP 63/46, fols 29, 31. Essex also complained that his commission was 'not half so longe and liberall as the Presidents of Mounster and Connaghe' (see SP 63/48, fol.132).

79 SP 63/45, fols 21r–2r, 118.

80 SP63/45, fol.21r.

trewe' he and his men would 'be better kerne then enie of this countrey [Irish] birth'.[81] He may have advocated reaching an agreement with Sorley Boy, but Essex's patience with the MacDonalds was running out as they continued to frustrate his efforts to establish garrisons and defences in the north.[82] With one final move, Essex succeeded in pushing the Scots out of Clandeboy after which, in an effort to prevent their return, he launched a naval attack on Rathlin Island, much like Croft and Sussex had done previously.[83] The attack was led by Captain John Norris who took 300 foot and eighty horse on three frigates to the island.[84] The people on the island took refuge in the castle although they surrendered following a two-day siege. Norris responded by slaughtering all the inhabitants he could find, to a total of 300–400 which included Sorley Boy's men, and their wives and children, who had been sent there for their safety.[85] Norris placed a garrison in the castle and burned a number of Scottish galleys but, unable to hold the island for long, he was soon forced to abandon the garrison. Sorley Boy, who had been able only to stand on the mainland and watch the attack, retaliated soon after by attacking Carrickfergus, taking the cattle of the townspeople and killing 100 soldiers.[86] The Rathlin massacre brought an end to Essex's time in Ireland for he was recalled to England in September 1575.[87] Around the same time Sir Henry Sidney returned to

81 SP 63/52, fols 7v–8r.

82 For Essex's plans see SP 63/52 fols 6–8. At the time the MacDonalds were facing their own internal disputes with the Scottish and Irish branches of the family competing for precedence in their lands in the Glens. For more on this see Brady, 'East Ulster, the MacDonalds and the provincial strategies of Hugh O'Neill'.

83 See p.76 and n.77; p.127 and n.13 above.

84 SP 63/52, fols 202–3, 204, 206.

85 Some survived by hiding in caves around the coast.

86 SP 63/52, fols 202–3, 204, 206.

87 McGurk, 'Devereux, Walter, first earl of Essex'. Elizabeth did not comment directly on his actions at Rathlin but, writing to Essex on 6 August 1575, she assured him that his efforts in Ireland 'hath not been bestowed on so ungrateful a prince that will not both consider the one and reward the other'; Walter Bourchier, *Lives and Letters of the Devereux, Earls of Essex: In the Reigns of Elizabeth, James I, and Charles I, 1540–1646*, 2 vols (London, 1853), I, 118–19. At the time the event secured his recall to England, and in the long-term his reputation never recovered from the Rathlin massacre.

Ireland to replace Fitzwilliam as Lord Deputy, signalling a return to a more persuasive means of enforcing English policy. Despite initial enthusiasm and confidence, and her own reluctance to fund plantation endeavours, Essex's plantation project had cost Elizabeth over £130,000.[88] Most accounts of Essex's time in Ireland focus on the failure of his endeavours, the reasons for that failure and the massacre on Rathlin. While contemporaries commented on his courage and determination, his time in Ireland generally has been regarded as having achieved little of note.[89] Nonetheless, without diminishing the severity of his actions against the Irish and the Highland Scots, or ignoring the overall failure of his and Sir Thomas Smith's efforts in Ulster, it is important to recognise the appreciation both he and Smith had of economic, geographic and maritime considerations.

Economic, geographic and maritime considerations

In his writings Sir Thomas Smith made various references to the need to bring civility to the barbarous Irish. Much of his reasoning for establishing a colony in Ulster rested, not simply on classical precedent, or biblical authority, but on economic arguments.[90] For him, civility and economic

88 McGurk, 'Devereux, Walter, first earl of Essex'.

89 McGurk, 'Devereux, Walter, first earl of Essex'.

90 There is a wealth of literature concerning the issue of 'civility'; of particular relevance to this context see J. Leersen, 'Wildness, Wilderness and Ireland: Medieval and Early-Modern Patterns in the Demarcation of Civility', *Journal of the History of Ideas* 56 (1995), 25–39; John Montaño, *The Roots of English Colonialism in Ireland* (Cambridge, 2011); Hiram Morgan, 'Giraldus Cambrensis and the Tudor Conquest of Ireland', in Hiram Morgan, ed., *Political Ideology in Ireland, 1541–1641* (Dublin, 1999), 22–44; Jane H. Ohlmeyer, '"Civilizinge of those rude partes": Colonisation within Britain and Ireland, 1580s–1640s', in Canny, ed., *The Origins of Empire*, 124–47; Anthony Pagden, *The Fall of Natural Man: The American Indian and the Origins of Comparative Ethnology* (Cambridge, 1982); D. B. Quinn, 'Sir Thomas Smith (1513–77) and the Beginnings of English Colonial Theory', *Proceedings of the American Historical Society* 89/4 (1945), 543–60; D. B. Quinn, 'Renaissance Influences in English Colonisation', *Transactions of the Royal Historical Society*,

development went hand-in-hand with plantation efforts. After all Ireland was, as Smith declared,

> a lande that floweth with milke and hony, [with] a fertile soile … whether it be manured to corne, or left to grasse … a country full of springs, riuers and lakes bothe small and greate, full of excellent fishe and foule, no parte of the country distant aboue, viii. miles from a moste plentifull sea, or land water able to beare lode.[91]

Most sixteenth-century attempts at plantation were articulated in such a way as to emphasise a concern with extending good government, law and order and bringing reform to a rebellious and backward people. As a result the 'agriculturalist' dimension to plantation is often overlooked because of the rhetoric of civility that was used to justify such schemes.[92] Indeed, unless the land was waste and empty (as the English often claimed the north of Ireland to be), plantation had to be preceded by the 'rooting out' of something else.[93] Regardless of how the policy was

fifth series 26 (1976), 73–92; Quentin Skinner, 'Sir Thomas More's *Utopia* and the Language of Renaissance Humanism', in Anthony Pagden, ed., *The Languages of Political Theory in Early Modern Europe* (Cambridge, 1987), 123–57; Keith Thomas, *In Pursuit of Civility: Manners and Civilisation in Early Modern England* (New Haven, 2018); Arthur Williamson, 'Scots, Indians and Empire: The Scottish Politics of Civilization, 1519–1609', *Past and Present*, 150 (February, 1996), 46–83; Phil Withington, *Society in Early Modern England. The Vernacular Origins of Some Powerful Ideas* (Cambridge, 2010); Phil Withington, 'Plantation and Civil Society', in Éamonn Ó Ciardha and Micheál Ó Siochrú, eds, *The Plantation of Ulster. Ideology and Practice* (Manchester, 2012), 55–77.

91 *A letter sent by I. B. Gentleman*. This was also a direct biblical reference to the Promised Land that would have been immediately understood by contemporaries; see NIV Exodus 3:8 and numerous Old Testament references thereafter.

92 'Plantation' was used freely at this time although rarely defined and often used interchangeably with 'colony' or 'colonisation'. Although it developed during the sixteenth century from the Roman *colonia*, more fully articulated in Sir Thomas Smith's tract advocating plantation in the Great Ards in 1571, plantation was an accurate description of what became part of English policy towards Ireland. For more on this and the 'agriculturalist' aspect to it see Mumford Jones, 'Origins of the Colonial Idea in England', 448–51; *A Letter by I.B. Gentleman*.

93 Throughout the sixteenth century successive Stuart monarchs had been attempting to get their Highland subjects to acknowledge royal authority and pay their rents while also granting legal title to their lands. James VI, therefore, could not argue that

presented, in sixteenth-century Ireland plantation referred not only to the people living on the land, but also to what could be reaped from it whether produce, natural resources or mineral wealth. Before the English could develop plans for plantation in Ulster, and extract any economic benefit, they had to contend with the Irish who inhabited the land and the settlement of Highland Scots in the region, both of which concerned them greatly throughout the century. Thus, although plantation evolved initially as a response to the need for greater security of and a desire to pacify the north, in time, the English increasingly became concerned with plantation's role in the development of the Irish economy.

By the turn of the sixteenth century, Ireland was a serious drain on the English exchequer and had been since the early fourteenth century.[94] At the very least the aim was to make Ireland pay for itself, although it was hoped that, if reformed, it might make a profit for the English crown. When the English looked to Ireland they saw a rich and fertile land but one that remained unproductive on account of the indolence of its inhabitants.[95] This view of the Irish as lazy and backward was unquestioned as the English generally accepted the Irish displayed 'barbaric' characteristics. When discussing English perceptions of the Irish, Giraldus Cambrensis', *Topography of Ireland* is most commonly brought into play.[96] Cambrensis had travelled

---

the western Highlands and Isles were empty and waste. Consequently, writing in *Basilicon Doron* in 1598, James articulated the need to root out his unruly Highland subjects before he could plant the 'civilitie' of Lowlanders 'in their roomes'; see Johann P. Sommerville, ed., *King James VI and I: Political Writings* (Cambridge, 1994), 24.

94 James Lydon, 'The Impact of the Bruce Invasion, 1315–27', in Art Cosgrove, ed., *A New History of Ireland, Volume II: Medieval Ireland 1169–1534* (Oxford, 1987), chapter 10 reprinted in Seán Duffy, ed., *Robert the Bruce's Irish Wars. The Invasions of Ireland, 1360–1329* (Stroud, 2002), 119–52.

95 Such attitudes were also evident across the Atlantic, see William Cronon, *Changes in the Land. Indians, Colonists, and the Ecology of New England* (New York, rev. edn 2003).

96 Giraldus Cambrensis, *The History and Topography of Ireland*, trans., John J. O'Meara (London, 1982). By the mid sixteenth century humanist-educated Englishmen like Smith would have had a well-developed understanding of their own civil society as well as an awareness of the defining characteristics of the barbaric 'other'. And, as Debora Shuger, 'Irishmen, Aristocrats, and Other White Barbarians', *Renaissance*

to Ireland in the late twelfth century and set out to describe the society he came into contact with. Like other eleventh- and twelfth-century commentators who provided ethnographic accounts of the 'other', he described the 'barbarous' qualities of the Irish.[97] In doing so Cambrensis utilised views passed down from classical antiquity that were reinforced further over time.[98] His *Topography* was a crucial text and it shaped English views of their Irish neighbour considerably. Thus, when Elizabethan Englishmen went to Ireland they interpreted what they saw within a well-established conceptual framework and through the particular lens of English civility.[99] The politically fragmented nature of Irish society horrified and frustrated the English in equal measure. In keeping with classical views of a barbarous society, the English regarded the lack of a unified source of authority as evidence the Irish would be more vulnerable to conquest by another power. In reality, the English had to conquer, bribe or negotiate with many individual Irish lords or captains of kingroups whose allegiances could swiftly change. Thus, efforts to extend English royal authority throughout the land were piecemeal and painfully slow. At the same time Irish customs, lifestyle and legal and religious practices further confirmed the belief of the English that they were dealing with a primitive, backward people, ignorant of God and in need of good government. These attitudes towards the Irish were compounded by the perceived 'degeneracy' of the Old English, regarded as responsible for the earlier decline of the English colony, and the continued adherence of the Irish and Old English to Rome, which reinforced the belief that Ireland would benefit from English intervention.

The wider confessional context created security issues but, above all, it was the lack of economic activity that confirmed for the English the status

Quarterly 50/1 (1997), 494–525 points out, 'civility', as a program of reform, was not limited to the Gaels of Ireland and Scotland. See also Morgan, 'Giraldus Cambrensis and the Tudor Conquest of Ireland'.

97 *Topography of Ireland*, 100–3, 106–18.

98 Robert Bartlett, *Gerald of Wales, 1146–1223* (Oxford, 1982), 177 argues that the efforts of these eleventh- and twelfth-century writers sought 'to create a hostile stereotype to salve their consciences and justify their conquests'.

99 Mumford Jones, 'Origins of the Colonial Idea in England', 451–7; Withington, 'Plantation and Civil Society', 65.

of the Irish as barbaric and in need of reform. Indeed, economic factors provided crucial justification for the actions of the English in Ireland, offering not only a legal argument for their involvement there, but also fostered a sense of duty. While Cambrensis wrote extensively on the natural wealth of Ireland, detailing the temperate climate and wealth of livestock alongside birdlife and rich fishings, the underdeveloped Irish economy and lack of market centres stood out as a clear sign of barbarity, and the unproductivity of both land and sea was frequently commented on.[100] Fynes Moryson, writing at the end of the sixteenth century, confirmed these prejudices asserting that 'the Irish might have abundance of excellent sea and fresh-water fish, if the fishermen were not so possessed with the natural fault of slothfulness', adding that the Irish in general, 'being idle', refused to 'till their grounds or plant trees'.[101] Further evidence with which to condemn the Irish was found not only in their predominant pastoral economy but also in the practice of booleying or transhumance, whereby the Irish moved with their livestock to new pastures, living with and, so the English argued, like beasts.[102] The inability to realise this was a planned or

100 *Topography of Ireland*, 14–19, 34–8.

101 *A Description of Ireland by Fynes Moryson, Secretary to the Lord Mountjoy, then Lord Deputy. 1600–1603*, in Henry Morlay, ed., *Ireland under Elizabeth and James the First, Described by Edmund Spenser, Sir John Davies and Fynes Moryson* (London, 1890), 419, 423.

102 Keith Thomas, *Man and the Natural World. Changing Attitudes in England 1500–1800* (London, 1984), 30–50; Rolf Loeber, 'An Architectural History of Gaelic Castles and Settlements, 1370–1600', in Patrick J. Duffy, David Edwards, and Elizabeth FitzPatrick, eds, *Gaelic Ireland c.1250–c.1650: Land, Lordship & Settlement* (Dublin, 2004), 275 where Loeber argues this 'was a feature only of the lower strata of Gaelic society'. For more on this practice see Aidan Clarke, 'The Irish Economy, 1600–60', in T. W. Moody, F. X. Martin and F. J. Byrne, eds, *A New History of Ireland Volume III: Early Modern Ireland 1534–1691* (Oxford, first published 1979, online 2011), 172–3; Audrey Horning, '"Dwelling houses in the old Irish barbarous manner": Archaeological Evidence for Gaelic Architecture in an Ulster Plantation Village', in Duffy, Edwards and FitzPatrick, eds, *Gaelic Ireland c.1250–c.1650*, 375–96, at 377; Eugene Costello, 'Seasonal Management of Cattle in the Booleying System: New Insights from Connemara, Western Ireland', in Michael O'Connell, Fergus Kelly and James H. McAdam, eds, *Cattle in Ancient and Modern Ireland: Farming Practices, Environment and Economy* (Newcastle

controlled practice, or indeed an attempt to make best use of the available land meant the English were deeply suspicious of a people they perceived as being unwilling and unable to settle, cultivate the land and develop an agrarian economy.[103] Although the English commented regularly on the corn growing in Ireland, the dominance of a pastoral economy, the practice of transhumance and the lack of recognisable towns or market centres (in the eyes of the English) would override any acknowledgement of the extent of agricultural activity. To put it crudely, from an English perspective the Irish had not progressed from eating meat to making bread and instead a predominantly pastoral economy persisted, resulting in an arrested commercial development.[104]

Instead, according to the English, if they were to establish a firm foothold in Ireland they could develop agriculture, establish market centres and gain proper custom from trade, exploit the mineral wealth and encourage manufacturing.[105] The country's resources could then be fully utilised and traded as a means to benefit both the Irish inhabitants and the English economy. It was the English desire and ability to exploit the natural resources of Ireland that provided the justification for their actions.[106] If the

upon Tyne, 2016), 66–74; Theresa McDonald, 'The 'Ups and Downs' of Booleying in Achill, Co. Mayo, Ireland', in O'Connell, Kelly and McAdam, eds, *Cattle in Ancient and Modern Ireland*, 56–65; D. B. Quinn and K. W. Nicholls, 'Ireland in 1534' in Moody, Martin and Byrne, eds, *NHI III*, 35; Montaño, *Roots of English Colonialism*, 31, 216–17.

103 There was little contemporary understanding that much of the landscape, climatic conditions, and soil quality of Ireland favoured a pastoral economy.

104 Bartlett, *Gerald of Wales*, 161–2; SP 63/35, fol.19r. Captain William Piers wrote to the Lord Deputy in 1572: 'as yo[u]r L[ordship] doth knowe the nature of the Irishe is such as rather they would have there contrie to lie altogether wast than any man but them selves to inhabite'. According to the later work of Adam Smith, *An Inquiry into the Nature and Causes of the Wealth of Nations* (1776), they had progressed from hunter gather to pastoral farming but no further.

105 There are numerous references in the State Papers to the early search for mineral wealth in Ireland. See, for example, SP 61/2, fols 131, 200; SP 61/4, fols 1, 38, 159; SP 63/8, fols 109–10; SP 63/16, fols 118, 120; SP 63/23, fol.68.

106 Thomas, *Man and the Natural World*, 254–69. The full exploitation of the land's natural resources and cultivation of barren landscapes was a growing concern within sixteenth-century England.

Irish refused, as according to the English they evidently did, to exploit the fertile land on which they lived, leaving it waste and unproductive, the English had a right to take it over and utilise it for their own benefit. Declaring the land was *res nullus*, an 'empty thing', did not necessarily mean the land was devoid of inhabitants, although population levels in Ireland were significantly lower than in England at the time.[107] Rather the English were asserting that the land remained uncultivated and unproductive, and in doing so they conveniently overlooked the arable farming undertaken by the Irish and Highland Scots in Ulster.[108] Plantation of people went hand-in-hand with, not just a civilising process but also, a process of economic development. It was this aspect of plantation that legitimised the English presence in Ireland and their settlement on the land at the expense of the Irish and justification for this 'agriculturalist' argument was found in other sources too. In *Utopia* (1516) Sir Thomas More had expounded a similar view, arguing that its inhabitants had a right to engage in warfare

> when any people holdeth a piece of ground void and vacant to no good nor profitable use, keeping others from the use and possession of it which notwithstanding by the law of nature ought therefore to be nourished and relived.[109]

107 Anthony Pagden, *Lords of all the World. Ideologies of Empire in Spain, Britain and France c.1500–c.1800* (New Haven and London, 1995), 76. Nonetheless, by the end of the sixteenth century many parts had witnessed severe depopulation on account of the ravages of war inflicted during the rebellion of Hugh O'Neill, second Earl of Tyrone.

108 See p.117 above for reference to Sorley Boy 'manuring the land'.

109 Susan Bruce, ed., *Three Early Modern Utopias:* Utopia, New Atlantis *and* The Isle of Pines (Oxford, 1996), 63; George M. Logan and Robert M. Adams, eds, *More: Utopia* (Cambridge, rev. edn 2002), 54; David B. Quinn, 'Renaissance Influences in English Colonization: The Prothero Lecture' *Transactions of the Royal Historical Society*, fifth series, 26 (1976), 75 where Quinn asserts More was the first Englishman to use the word *colonia* in a Roman meaning and suggests More's view was that 'to colonize can be legitimate, even good'; Armitage, 'Literature and Empire', 108. Hiram Morgan, 'The Colonial Venture of Sir Thomas Smith', 268–71, 274–8 directly links More's *Utopia* to Smith's emphasis on 'waste' land. See also SP 63/31, fols 84v–5r, 90r–1v; Nicholas Canny, 'Rowland White's *Discors touching Ireland*, c.1569', *Irish Historical Studies*, XXIV (1977), 439–63; Pagden, *Lords of all the World*, 76–7.

At the same time, early modern Englishmen could find biblical support for their actions. After the Fall of Man God expelled Adam from the Garden of Eden telling him: 'Cursed is the ground because of you; through painful toil you will eat food from it all the days of your life', adding that for evermore he was 'to work the ground from which he had been taken'.[110] Working the land was a God-given command. Furthermore, the utilisation of the land and its resources was not simply a means of bringing reform to Ireland but also a means by which they could distance themselves from the exploitative behaviour of the Spanish and Portuguese in the Americas.[111] The English, therefore, had a duty and an obligation to their Irish neighbours to bring reform, civility, Protestantism and commercial development, much in the same way the Romans had brought civility to Britain centuries previously.[112] In general, however, this underlying economic agenda was hidden beneath the rhetorical veneer of civility and beneficial reform.[113]

Failing to recognise the trade and agricultural activity on the part of the Irish and the Highland Scots, the English came to view Ireland as an economic resource that could be exploited for their own ends. In the light of prevailing English attitudes regarding the Irish and their lack of utilisation and cultivation of the land in Ireland, the English did not hesitate to view Ireland's rich natural resources as a providential benefit to

110 NIV Genesis 3:17b, 23b; Thomas, *Man and the Natural World*, 254–5.

111 In the Americas during the early establishment of colonies much of the concern of the English was to develop agriculture and there was an increased focus on the crops grown and the animals being raised. While there is a significant body of literature on this, for an engaging study that explores the desire for agrarian cultivation which evolved into a need for pastoral farming see Virginia DeJohn Anderson, *Creatures of Empire. How Domestic Animals Transformed Early America* (Oxford, 2004), especially 77–83.

112 As put forward by Geoffrey of Monmouth, *The History of the Kings of Britain* (translated by) Lewis Thorpe (London, 1964).

113 For a fuller discussion of this see Thomas, *Man and the Natural World*, 254–69; deJohn Anderson, *Creatures of Empire*, suggests this came more or less full circle in the New England and Chesapeake Bay colonies when pastoral farming re-emerged as the sign of a civilised society due to the difficulties of growing crops.

the kingdom.[114] Alongside the arable and pastoral produce they sought to cultivate, the English regarded Ireland as a useful source of timber.[115] Exploitation of Ireland's timber reserves was not new at this stage for throughout the sixteenth century the English had viewed this particular natural resource greedily. Timber was needed in Ireland for building projects, whether boat-building or reinforcement of garrisons, and regarded as a resource to meet demand back in England where the combination of building works and enclosure had used up much of the available wood.[116] Demand increased throughout the sixteenth century as timber was needed to support the developing manufacturing industries on both sides of the Irish Sea and supplies were regularly exported to England from Wexford in the southwest of Ireland.[117] It has been suggested that rapid devastation of timber supplies in Ireland is evidence of 'the "colonial" attitude of the

114 SP 63/201, fols 343–51. In a tract by John Bell, Vicar of Christ Church entitled, 'How Irish rebels may be taught to be obedient to her Majesty' he asserted that 'hauing a speciall loue unto us, God hath giuen the Kingdoom of Ireland to hir Maiestie; a Countrey most sweet, most wholesome, and most fruietfull to dwell in; so full of springes, so full of riuers, so full of lakes, so full of fish, so full of cattell, and so full of fowle; that thear is not a Countrey upon the face of the earth, more beneficiall to the life of man, than that is'.

115 An attitude also seen in relation to the "excellent good timber" found in New England; see Cronon, *Changes in the Land*, 24–30.

116 SP 63/3, fol.174. In May 1561 Thomas Smythe wrote to Cecil from Dublin, requesting a 'flatt bottomed hoy … of xl or l ton the same to draw not aboue v or vi foote water at the moste'. This hoy would help carry cut wood necessary for the works he was involved in, which was 'to repaire suche decayes of houses furnaces and chymneys as ar nedefull to be amended and also … to cut woode for the fynars and for coale'.

117 Kenneth Nicholls, 'Woodland Cover in Pre-modern Ireland', in Duffy, Edwards, and Fitzpatrick, eds, *Gaelic Ireland c.1250–c.1650*, 181–206, especially 198–202. Timber also was exported to Scotland as evidenced by a contract of 7 October 1606 between John, Earl of Cassillis, Lord Kennedy on one part, and Nyc[o]las and William Sy[er]met of Wexford regarding the export of timber from Ireland to Innermessan, on the southwest of Loch Ryan; see NRS GD25 Ailsa Muniments/9/box 21. It was also needed to support other activity in Ireland, see SP 63/16, fol.120. On 5 March 1566 Thomas Lancaster wrote to Cecil following discussions with 'Rowland Whiet … the owners of the Duffer [Dufferin] and dyverse others concerning woode for your myne of Skedo in Com[b]erland'.

English towards the Irish economy'.[118] Possibly on account of this escalating exploitation of woodland, forests came to be guarded carefully and a number were 'continuewed in her Ma[jes]ties ryall possession', such as, the forest of Glenconkeyne in Ulster.[119] It was mentioned on numerous occasions as being profitable but limited to the use of the crown while wooded regions elsewhere, such as Wicklow, were regarded similarly.[120] The woods of Glenconkeyne were much coveted and although the English could declare them to be in crown hands, in the light of the fluctuating political situation in Ireland, making that a reality, much like control of the fishing of the Bann, was not always possible. Numerous prohibitions were imposed on the taking and transportation of timber, such as the restraint on the 'great quantities of shipplancks and pypestaves transported … into the territories of the King of Spaine', but the English settlers and the artificers they brought over also required timber for their plantations.[121] Controlling the

118 Quoted in Nicholls, 'Woodland cover in pre-modern Ireland', 203; and see 204 where Nicholls argues 'unmanaged unsustainable exploitation remained the norm'. Audrey J. Horning, 'On the Banks of the Bann: The Riverine Economy of an Ulster Plantation Village', *Historical Archaeology* 41/3 (2007), 94–114 has argued (101) there 'is clear evidence that the woods of Killatrough, Loughinsholin, and Glenconkeyne were being excessively damaged through overzealous and often illegal felling in the early years' of official plantation in the seventeenth century. See also Thomas, *Man and the Natural World*, 192–212. For an introduction to woodland cover and its uses in Scotland see T. C. Smout, ed., *Scottish Woodland History* (Edinburgh 1997); T. C. Smout, Alan R. MacDonald and Fiona Watson, eds, *A History of the Native Woodland of Scotland, 1500–1920* (Edinburgh, 2005).

119 SP 63/160, fol.61. Glenconkeyne is in the southeast of modern-day county of Derry.

120 Rolf Loeber, 'Settlers' Utilisation of the Natural Resources', in Ken Hannigan and William Nolan, eds, *Wicklow, History and Society* (Dublin, 1994), 267–304. Other areas were not so rich in woodland. Robert Lythe, the map-maker, described the lands in Down from Strangford Lough to Carlingford as containing only 'underwoods as hasell, holye, alder, elder, thorne, crabtre and byrche with such lyke. But no great hoke neyther great building timber'; see Robert Dunlop, 'Sixteenth-Century Maps of Ireland', *English Historical Review* 20/78 (1905), 327. Heavily wooded areas in Ireland were quickly ring-fenced for the state and, during the years of the plantation, various forests were reserved for the settlers.

121 SP 63/191, fols 228–9. Sir Henry Wallop wrote to Cecil concerning his plantation at Enniscorthy. Nicholls, 'Woodland cover in pre-Modern Ireland', 199 comments

taking, use and transportation of timber across Ireland was something of a challenge. After all, in June 1568 the English were unable to prevent Sorley Boy coming 'to the Glynnes w[i]th a few company and contynewed there but two nyghtes' with the 'purpose to cawse wattyll to be cutt to bylde in the Rawghlyns'.[122] However, following reports in August 1568 of the earl of Argyll's 'diligence in making of galleys, for whose furnyture of bourdes not to be prepared eny more either from Karickfergus or Wexford' the English authorities gave 'order for precise restreynt of the same' so that the earl 'maye be prevented of those provisions, and of his other purposes'.[123]

For the English, cutting timber also facilitated transport and communication links, and provided greater safety against Irish attacks. Forests and woodland, like mountains, regarded as the refuge of thieves and lawbreakers in general, was one of the 'strengths' of the Irish where they could retreat for safety and from where they could launch attacks on the English.[124] If woods were not reserved for the crown, cutting them down, or at least cutting passes through them, would assist the English campaign by weakening the strongholds of the Irish.[125] Establishing passes through woods and mountainous regions and locating where rivers could be forded diminished the advantage of familiarity with the terrain that the Irish had over the English. It enabled the English to traverse the north with greater confidence and make inroads into territory not previously explored. At the same time,

that Wallop, along with Henry Pyne in Munster, was among the first to recognise the upsurge in demand for casks and organised a trade in cask-staves.

122 SP 63/25, fol. 97r; see p.118 above.

123 SP 63/25, fols 150, 152. For his 'other purposes' see p.118 above.

124 SP 63/179, fol.160v. In May 1595 Sir Ralph Lane, muster master, informed the queen that the 'finall retraite of Therle [Tyrone] and of all his cowes … and his forces, as well Irish as Skottishe … wilbe within the fastnes of wooddes Glynnes and Bogges in the two counties of Downe and Antrim'. On the association of the lawless Irish with woods see Nicholls, 'Woodland cover in pre-Modern Ireland', 182 where he argues '*sylvaticus*, synonymous with *sylvestris*, 'belonging to a wood', is the root of our word 'savage'; Montaño, *Roots of English Colonialism*, 32, 213, 215; Thomas, *Man and the Natural World*, 194.

125 SP 63/53, fol.21r. On 16 August 1575 Essex wrote to Elizabeth that Turlough Luineach had assured the earl that 'whosoeu[er] distimbeth the worke at the Black water or molesteth such as drawe the tymber shalbe hanged w[i]thout excuse'.

however, there was considerable emphasis placed on the garrisoning and strengthening of strategic locations, especially coastal defences as a means of keeping the Scots out; Essex would advocate establishing garrisons in inland areas also as the best way of bringing control to Ulster. This policy of strategic security quickly dovetailed with the economic agenda of the English as they sought to reap the advantages that Ireland offered.[126] Alongside repeated proposals to plant at the Bann, Lough Foyle and Strangford was the growing recognition that these were lucrative fishing areas and the English needed to ensure that they, and not the Irish, reaped the benefits.[127]

That fishing rights to coastal regions and rivers were highly valued but equally highly contentious is well known. Although they bemoaned the fact that, in their eyes, the Irish were lazy, indolent inhabitants who failed to cultivate land, develop fisheries or market opportunities, the English would have been well aware of the strong trade in fish from Tyrconnell, via the O'Donnell lordship, to the continent.[128] Throughout the west of Ireland, English officials often lamented the loss of revenue to the crown due to the lack of customs paid on this trade by the Irish or by the Scots, Spanish and Dutch who frequented the waters around Ireland to fish and

126 While the significance of coastal locations is obvious, the English sought to reinforce other sites for good reason. Coleraine had long been recognised as a strategic site, and a castle had been first built there by Thomas of Galloway in 1214; see Alison Cathcart, 'Scots and Ulster: the late medieval context' in William P. Kelly and John R. Young, eds, *Scotland and the Ulster Plantations. Explorations in the British Settlements of Stuart Ireland* (Dublin, 2009), 79–80. Located on the River Bann further upstream from the estuary it was built at a point where the river could be crossed. Castle Toome, now Toome Bridge, likewise was situated on the Bann but further inland where the river left its source at Lough Neagh. Massereene was located on the eastern shores of Lough Neagh, while Newry was also situated on a river at a crucial crossing point between the Mourne mountains.

127 SP 63/21, fols 109–11, 129. For a discussion of later plantation efforts to exploit the Bann fisheries see Horning, 'On the Banks of the Bann', 94–114.

128 For more on efforts by the Irish to exploit the economic resources, including fisheries, and develop trade see Mark Gardiner and T. E. McNeill, 'Seaborne Trade and the Commercialisation of Fifteenth- and Sixteenth-Century Gaelic Ulster', *Proceedings of the Royal Irish Academy. Section C: Archaeology, Celtic Studies, History, Linguistics, Literature*, 116 (2016), 1–34.

thus deprived the English of a raw material regarded as their own.[129] There was fishing activity also in the east of Ulster around Strangford Lough and Carlingford, and the English were keen to gain control of Lough Neagh, the Foyle and the Bann.[130] In 1564, during the time of co-operation between Shane O'Neill and the crown, Shane had promised 'to expulse all the Scottes out of Ireland' and restore to the queen's use all 'the proffite … hitherto taken by the Scottes' of 'the fishing of the Bane & Loghfoyll, her Ma[jes]ties auncie[n]t enheritaunce'.[131] How much progress Shane was able to make in this respect is not clear but in 1567 Elizabeth wrote to Lord Deputy Sidney concerning a recent request to take 'the fisshing of the Ban … in farme' and wanted to know 'the best auncient rent'. While the queen was content to lease the fishing of the Bann to whoever Sidney thought 'meetest', it was to be for one year only.[132] In 1573, the fishing of the Bann and Lough Neagh was part of the grant made to Essex although again, little progress was made in fully exploiting the potential of these fisheries because he was unable to subdue the surrounding area.[133] Ongoing political turmoil caused by unrest and ultimately war in the 1590s meant the English were not able to fully reap the benefit of the lucrative fishing in these rivers and loughs.

A further dimension to the commercial agenda of the English in Ireland was the exploitation of the natural mineral wealth of the land. A number of agents were active in Ireland, taking a note of silver and lead

129 SP 61/2, fol.155. Indeed in October 1550 Lord Deputy Sir Anthony St Leger and the council in Dublin informed the Privy Council in London that they had 'stayed' the 'conveyance of woll, tallowe, butters, lynnen yarne and other suche lyke co[m]modyties' from Ireland 'to other outewarde p[ar]tes' because it encouraged 'ydlenes'. For comments on the Spanish taking away fishing from Irish waters with no customs paid to the queen see SP 63/27, fol.136; for comments on the losses caused by Irish merchants see SP 63/49, fol.83.

130 From early in the reign of Henry VIII there had been attention on the fishing of the Bann and the desire to exploit it fully; see Horning, 'On the Banks of the Bann', 95. See also SP 63/160, fol.61 for the desire to exploit the fishing and timber resources of the lands around Lough Neagh.

131 SP 63/11, fol.11. This was in return for 'the enterteyneme[n]t of fowrty men'.

132 SP 63/20, fol.22v.

133 SP 63/40, fol.173.

deposits, making enquiries about mining and materials that could be exported back to England and granting licences for manufacturing.[134] Indeed, in comparison to the exploitation of the fisheries, more progress was made, for a time at least, in ascertaining Ireland's natural mineral wealth. Most evidence for the development of mines and other industries comes from the early seventeenth century but it is possible to date such activity to the late sixteenth century. Certainly efforts were being made from the mid-century onwards to discover the natural mineral deposits in Ireland.[135] In 1550 a memorandum was produced for 'certain artificers required for working the mines in Ireland', while two years later the Privy Council received information from a Joachim Gundelfiner regarding 'their proceedings in the mines'.[136] Silver, lead and ore were found at Clonmines and molten at Ross in Wexford according to Robert Record, Surveyor of the Mines, in 1552.[137] Soon it was not simply the government who sought to exploit these natural resources. In May 1563 John Chaloner wrote to Cecil asking for a 'licence & commission', along the same lines as that 'granted to Walter Pepperd for … Clonmyne', allowing him to work the 'sundrie large veynes of copper myne' he discovered in his 'yle of Lambaye'.[138] In 1567 Peter Back of Brabant wrote to the queen requesting a patent for twenty years to 'carry on the manufacture of madder, … the converting of stags', kids', goats' and calves' skins into morocco leather' and also the manufacture of salt. He was granted a twenty-eight-year patent for the 'preparation of madder and dressing of skins'.[139] Preparatory investigations continued with the Privy Council writing to the council in Dublin in March that same year for information regarding the patent granted to the 'L[ord] Montioye … for

134 Encouragement and regulation of trade and industry continued into the seventeenth century along with the granting of patents for the development of industries. For example, see HL Hastings Irish Papers, Box 1: HA16052, HA15066, HA16069, HA16074; Box 2: HA16089, HA16103, HA16105; Box 3: HA16144, HA16200.

135 SP 61/4, fols 53–6, 62.

136 SP 61/2, fol.200; SP 61/4, fol.1.

137 SP 61/4, fols 38, 39–41.

138 SP 63/8, fol.110.

139 *CSPI*, I, 338, nos 31–2; 340, no.43; SP 63/21, fols 73, 98.

the serching digging fynyng and making of alum and coperas'.[140] Alongside these endeavours to develop extraction and mining industries in Ireland were the more traditional manufactures such as saltpans.[141] Salt was in great demand, partly due to the curing of fish and meat, and it was necessary to import it from England along with other victuals.[142] As the situation in Ireland deteriorated during the later decades of the sixteenth century, the desire to exploit minerals and develop other industries, while ongoing, was superseded by the constant need for replenishing essential needs in Ireland, such as men, munition and victuals.[143] Nonetheless, efforts to exploit the economic resources of Ireland remained the underlying agenda of the English in Ireland as reform and conquest were the precursors to plantation and economic development.

This agenda of economic exploitation was evident in the proposals put forward by Sir Thomas Smith concerning his plantation project. In outlining the benefits, Smith asserted that Clandeboy and the Ards offered 'Timber, stone plaister, & slate commodious for bulding' which was 'euery where aboundant'. While the volunteers who embarked on this plantation would be able to 'reap … Corne, Butter … Cattle & such like', Smith's emphasis, understandably, was on arable farming. He advised that all colonists with arable land 'should continue the same vnder tillage … because it settleth the occupier, and what with tending his fallowe, reaptyde, seede time, & thrashing, it bindeth always the occupier to the Lande, and is a continuall occupation of a great number of persons, a helper and a mainteyner of Ciuilitie'. Thus, those with military experience could acquire

140 SP 63/23, fol.68.

141 For example, in 1575 the council requested 'iii or iiii salte pannes from Tynmowth w[hi]ch lye there Idle and unoccupied … to be sent unto Irelande for the making of salt, and a salter therw[i]thall'; see SP 63/51, fol.59. Demand for salt was recognised by Randal MacDonnell in the early seventeenth century in Ireland and it is likely he developed a saltpans at his lands at Ballycastle to supply these demands. See p.275 below. My thanks to Hector MacDonnell for discussing this with me on a number of occasions and showing me what remains of the saltpans today. The desire to establish a salt-pans was likely an effort to supply the ongoing demand for imports of salt for curing and preserving purposes.

142 SP 63/51, fol.59; SP 63/53, fol.17.

143 See pp. 185–96 below.

land, invest in it through building and agriculture which, 'if he keepe and defende …, hee is a Gentleman, a man of liuelyhode & of enheritaunce' and ultimately become 'the patron & first founder of a familie in that cuntrie'. For Smith, plantation of men on the ground as well as crops in the ground was justified on the grounds that Ireland 'lacketh only inhabitants, manurance, and pollicie'.[144] According to the maxim of *res nullus*, uninhabited land could be possessed by those who wanted to settle there. Uncultivated land remained in common hands until it was invested in through agriculture.[145] This provided crucial justification for his project.

Clandeboy and the Ards were fertile lands and suitable for arable cultivation, while easy access to Strangford Lough would provide the colonists with a solid supply of fish.[146] Indeed, Smith argued his endeavour was providential, almost as if 'it were of purpose'. The main obstacle to the colonisation of the Ards, however, faced by Smith's son and later also by Essex was the resistance from the O'Neills, Turlough Luineach in Tyrone and Sir Brian McPhelim in Clandeboy, and the Highland Scots, all of whom often allied together against the incomers. Nonetheless, Sir Thomas had a strong rationale for selecting the Ards as the location for his settlement paying attention to the importance of geography.[147] In his proposal for colonisation Smith elaborated more fully on this:

144 *A Letter by I.B. Gentleman*. Smith himself noted that 'great numbers of the Husbandmen which they call Churles, [will] come and offer to liue vnder vs, & to ferme out grounds: both such as are of the Cuntry birth, and others, bothe out of the wilde Irishe and the Englyshe pale'.

145 This argument was used time and again in the colonies across the Atlantic.

146 Marshal Bagenal, Herbert F. Hore and Lord Burghely, 'Marshal Bagenal's Description of Ulster, Anno 1586', *Ulster Journal of Archaeology*, first series 2 (1854), 137–60, at 153–4, referred to the Ards as 'a fertile champion countrey'. The lands around Strangford Lough were a key part of Smith's proposed plantation while the remains of some sites in the area today are evidence of attempts to establish English settlements; see Horning, *Ireland in the Virginian Sea*, 65–8; Rowan McLaughlin and James Lyttleton, *An Archaeology of Northern Ireland, 1600–1650* (Newtownards, 2017), 115–17, 123–4. For more on the strategic importance of Strangford Lough see pp. 204–5 below.

147 It is likely he had paid close to attention to the advice of those advocating plantation across the Atlantic. See Richard Hakluyt, 'Notes on Colonisation (1578)', in

> The Arde which is my demaund, and the nearest parte of all Ireland to Lancashere, and the Easte parte of England, I take to be a peece of ground as easie to be wonne, inhabited, safely kepte and defended, as any platte within the Realme of Ireland, being a reache of land (as it were of purpose bayed out from the mayne into the Sea, to wall in so muche of it as woulde make so faire and commodious a lake and herber as the hauen of Strangford is) fashioned like an Arme bente in the Elbowe, annexed no where to the mayne but at the one ende as the Arme to the shoulder. The bredth of whiche entrie is aboute fiue Miles, as by the platte here vnto annexed may be more plainlye seene. That straight once kept and defended, all the reste of the Countrie muste of necessitie become quiet and safe, and thus shall it be defended.[148]

In other words, apart from the small isthmus connecting the Ards peninsula to the rest of county Down, the territory was surrounded entirely by water. Although there is now no knowledge of the 'platte' Smith had attached to his tract, he put forward clear geographic reasons why the Ards was a suitable location for a colony.[149] Bounded almost completely by sea, and a short sail across the Irish Sea from Liverpool, the English would have ready access by sea. As the land border to the peninsula was only five miles in breadth, defending the Ards would be relatively straightforward

D. B. Quinn, ed., *The Voyages and Colonising Enterprises of Sir Humphrey Gilbert*, 2 vols (London: Hakluyt Society, 1940), I, 181–6.

148 *A letter sent by I. B. gentleman.*

149 On 6 January 1569 Sir William Cecil had requested 'some larger and more p[ar]ticular descriptio[n] topographically of Ulster'. Although Cecil never held any formal office in the Irish administration, throughout his long career as Elizabeth's secretary he maintained an interest in Irish matters, one that had begun back in the reign of her half-brother, Edward. Cecil was careful to ensure he remained informed of the political situation there while also collecting and commissioning maps of the country. The fact that so many maps of Ulster remain is testament to the efforts of the English to extend royal authority in Ireland and to justify their presence there, but also to Cecil's concern to collect and utilise them. Treatises written by men such as Sir Thomas Smith were often accompanied by a 'platt'. These maps no longer accompany the tracts they were originally meant to, largely because Cecil collected them separately, but that so many of them survive is due to the interest in geographic matters of men like Sidney and Cecil. See SP 63/27, fol.3; Maginn, *William Cecil, Ireland*, 56, 75–6; Wallace T. MacCaffrey, 'Cecil, William, first Baron Burghley (15202/1–1598), *royal minister*', *ODNB*, accessed 19 July 2012.

which the colonists, Smith argued, could easily do.[150] Alongside the economic resources of the region, geography offered both security for the settlers, and access to the sea for trade, providing further reasons for attempting plantation in the area.[151]

Like Smith, Essex understood the geographic significance of the Ards but he had a more nuanced appreciation of the maritime context and wider strategic security concerns. Having failed to deal effectively with the situation in Clandeboy and the Ards, in March 1574 Essex requested and was granted 'the Ile of McGuy' or Magee Island, now known as Islandmagee.[152] This small piece of land on the east coast of Antrim just north of Carrickfergus, anciently known as Rin Sevne (a peninsula and territory of the Semhne), is said to take its name from its early settlers, the MacAedha (Magees).[153] Essex's request for Magee Island is often overlooked, but when compared to Sir Thomas Smith's proposal for plantation in the Ards peninsula, Essex's reasons for wanting this piece of land becomes clear.[154] Like a smaller, inverted version of the Ards peninsula, Magee Island

150 Although the colonists could readily defend the short corridor of land connecting the peninsula to the mainland, Smith did not elaborate on how the colonists might defend their settlement from the arrival of the Highland Scots by ship.

151 Geographic considerations were a crucial although often neglected aspect in discussion of English efforts at plantation in Ulster. However, early maps of Ireland have been the focus of a number of studies. See, for example, G. A. Hayes-McCoy, ed., *Ulster and other Irish Maps, c.1600* (Dublin: Irish Manuscripts Commission, 1964); and more recently Annaleigh Margey, 'Representing Plantation Landscapes: The Case of Ulster, c.1560–1640', in C. Rynne and J. Lyttleton, eds, *Plantation Ireland: Settlement and Material Culture, c.1550–1700* (Dublin, 2009), 140–64; 'Representing Colonial Landscapes: Early English maps of Ulster and Virginia, 1580–1612', in B. MacCuartha, ed., *Reshaping Ireland: Colonization and Its Consequences 1550–1700 (Essays Presented to Nicholas Canny)* (Dublin, 2011), 61–81; J. H. Andrews, *The Queen's Last Map-Maker: Richard Bartlett in Ireland, 1600–03* (Dublin, 2008); William J. Smyth, *Map-Making, Landscapes and Memory; a Geography of Colonial and Early Modern Ireland, c.1530–1750* (Cork, 2006). See pp. 176–84 below.

152 SP 63/45, fol.21v.

153 Dixon Donaldson, *Historical, Traditional and Descriptive Account of Islandmagee* (published privately, Islandmagee, 1927), 7–8.

154 Essex was not the first to petition the queen for Islandmagee. In 1568 Captain Thornton asked for the land, stating that he would establish a 'fysher towne

was a promontory of land that jutted northwards into the North Channel joined to the mainland by a small strip of land for Islandmagee, at its southerly end, is almost cut off by Larne Lough and Whitehead Water.[155] As such it is bounded by the Irish Sea to the east and Larne Lough to the west, and located between Carrickfergus Castle to the south and Olderfleet Castle to the north. It was also close to Belfast, the place where Essex believed a strong garrison should be established, rather than at Coleraine or the Blackwater.[156] Surrounded almost entirely by water, Essex argued, would make the land easier to defend. In addition, he hoped to reap the benefit of the fertility of the land as well as the fishing of Larne Lough as he had had little opportunity to exploit his grant of the fishing of the Bann and Lough Neagh. The land itself was 'not above 3000 acres' and Essex offered £500 'towardes the wallinge of any Townes' that might be established there.[157] According to Captain Thornton's bid for the same lands in 1568, whose plan had been to establish a fishing industry, there was some English settlement in the region already. Given the situation in the Ards and in the Glens of Antrim, Essex no doubt hoped he would encounter no immediate opposition from Irish or Highland Scot neighbours.

inhabited w[i]th Englyshmen', having already 'buylded a forte for the savegarde of the harbrowe'. See SP 63/25, fol.35 and pp. 135–7 above.

155 Donaldson, *Account of Islandmagee*, 6.

156 SP 63/52, fol.6v. A small town at Belfast would 'Releive Knockergus w[i]t[h] wood and horssemen being laid there shall com[m]and the plaines of Clandeboy & w[i]t[h] fotemen may kepe the passage open betweene that & the Newrie, and kepe … Duffrin in obedience, and may be victualled at pleasure by sea w[i]t[h]out daunger of Scott or pirate'.

157 SP 63/45, fol.21v. Islandmagee is an area of 'about 7,020 acres' see Donaldson, *Account of Islandmagee*, 6.

P/49 (25) (L9622): East part of Ulster [1601] with detail of Islandmagee and Olderfleet. © National Maritime Museum, Greenwich, London.

Above all, however, the desire to have the lands of Islandmagee would have been stimulated by Essex's appreciation of the maritime context. The island afforded Essex a vast marine horizon from Kintyre and Islay to the north, Scotland to the east and the Isle of Man to the south. At the northerly tip of the peninsula lies Port Muck with a very small island off its east coast called Muck Isle, almost accessible by foot at low tide. On the coastal cliff path at Port Muck, opposite Muck Isle, are the remains of a castle said to have been built in the eleventh, although certainly in existence in the thirteenth, century.[158] Firm evidence relating to the castle is found in maps dating to the mid-sixteenth century when it took on greater significance

158 Sue Anderson, Alastair Roy Rees, Catherine M. Dunne, Sarah Gormley, Shelia Hamilton-Dyer, Eileen M. Murphy, Eiméar L. Nelis and Mark Noel, 'The Excavation of a Medieval Rural Settlement at Portmuck, Islandmagee, County Antrim', *Ulster Journal of Archaeology*, third series 63 (2004), 76–113 especially 93, 101–04. My thanks to Dr Colin Breen for this reference. Pottery remains, fired at a kiln in Carrickfergus, suggest significant medieval activity at this site.

after the Reformation as the lands at Port Muck would have passed from the church to secular control. The Magees, the inhabitants of the region and under the overlordship of the O'Neills of Clandeboy, may have been responsible for the castle's construction and its location suggests it was built in an attempt to control the harbour at Port Muck.[159] Although little remains now, as much of the stone has been taken over subsequent centuries to build houses in the locality, it is possible that Essex would have commandeered this castle for his own purposes had he spent much time in the area. It would have provided the earl with a strategic look-out post and, if regular watches were maintained, weather permitting, the English would have had intelligence of the extent of maritime traffic between Ireland and Scotland. Despite all these considerations, it is unclear how much time, if any, Essex spent in Islandmagee for between 1573 and 1575 he had his hands full trying to negotiate with the Irish.

Without diminishing the severity of his actions against the Irish and the Scots, while also acknowledging the overall failure of his plantation attempt, it is important to recognise Essex's appreciation of geographic considerations. He understood that any moves against the Highland Scots had to proceed through a combination of land and naval forces to be able to counter them effectively. Essex recognised the importance of cutting passes through inland regions, he attacked crannogs, and he tried to establish a fort and build a bridge over the Blackwater, south of Armagh, but as he was constantly under attack from the Irish in this endeavour the work remained unfinished.[160] He also attempted to fortify coastal defences and maintain a watch of the seas. Unfortunately for Essex, and indeed for the various attempts made by the English authorities, without additional resources of men, victuals and ammunition, all of which would mean greater financial investment by Elizabeth, it would prove challenging to gain the upper hand. On account of such chronic under-resourcing their efforts, regardless of whether they were ill-conceived or well-planned, were thwarted

159 For more on this and the nearby abbey; see Northern Ireland Sites and Momument Record Ref: Ant 041:003 at <http://www.bnfc.org.uk/BNFC/Islandmagee.html>; accessed 14 October 2016. My thanks to Dr Colin Breen for this reference.

160 Morton, 'Enterprise of Ulster', 119. For more on the significance of crannogs, see pp. 179–83 below.

by the realities of geography and environment. The simple fact of the proximity of the north of Ireland to the west Highlands and Isles of Scotland continued to be the proverbial thorn in the side of the English. Essex may have appreciated the maritime perspective afforded to him by establishing a base on Islandmagee, but such a strategic outlook did not bring with it the necessary, and appropriate, manpower, intelligence or shipping required to prevent movement of Highland Scots across the channel. In contrast, aided by maritime strength and knowledge of the tides and currents of the channel the Highlanders were able to retreat rapidly when necessary, or to send aid from Scotland to Ireland at short notice when requested. Their system of beacons or 'warning fires' across the narrow stretch between Fair Head and Dunaverty Castle on the southern tip of Kintyre allowed for a very simple, but highly effective communication system which out-manoeuvred any efforts by the English to patrol or contain maritime activity in the North Channel.[161] Successive failures for the English led to a gradual increasing awareness, although not formally articulated, that they needed to assert their authority more fully, not only on land but also at sea.

161 For a fuller analysis of the problems facing the English due to geographic and maritime considerations see Cathcart, 'The maritime dimension to plantation in Ulster'.

CHAPTER 5

Of military men, merchants and mariners

By the closing decades of the sixteenth century it was evident that the issues of security and defence of the sea coasts in Ulster had been left unresolved. Following the failure of both the plantation scheme of Sir Thomas Smith and the 'enterprise' of Walter Devereux, Earl of Essex, by the mid-1570s the crown had been forced to accept that private endeavours (with or without limited crown support) would not be enough to bring stability and reform to Ulster. Elizabeth and her advisors were gradually reaching the conclusion that conquest needed to come before reform.[1] The English had forged some level of co-operation with various regional and local Irish lords, but it was piecemeal and

1 Ciaran Brady and James Murray, 'Sir Henry Sidney and the Reformation in Ireland', in Elizabethanne Boran and Crawford Gribben, eds, *Enforcing Reformation in Ireland and Scotland, 1550–1700* (Aldershot, 2006), 26 argue that despite the act of 1541, 'the English conquest of Ireland remained more or less a fiction'. The only way to make progress in Ireland was through 'tolerance of and compromise with the political and cultural mores pertaining in the provincial lordships'. By the end of the century, however, it was recognised that piecemeal agreements with Irish lords was not enough and a full conquest of the kingdom was necessary before reform could be realised. For more on the development of English policy towards Ireland see p.123 n.1; and Ciaran Brady and Raymond Gillespie, eds, *Natives & Newcomers: The Making of Irish Colonial Society* (Dublin, 1986); Ciaran Brady, *The Chief Governors. The Rise and Fall of Reform Government in Tudor Ireland, 1536–1588* (Cambridge, 1994); Nicholas Canny, *The Elizabethan Conquest of Ireland: A Pattern Established 1565–76* (Hassocks, 1976); Nicholas Canny, *Making Ireland British, 1580–1650* (Oxford, 2001), 1–120; S. J. Connolly, *Contested Island. Ireland 1460–1630* (Oxford, 2007); Steven G. Ellis, *Tudor Ireland. Crown, Community and the Conflict of Cultures, 1470–1603* (London, 1985); Steven G. Ellis, *Ireland in the Age of the Tudors, 1447–1603: English Expansion and the End of Gaelic Rule* (London, 1998); David Heffernan, *Debating Tudor Policy in Sixteenth-Century Ireland: 'Reform' Treatises and Political Discourse* (Manchester, 2018).

incoherent while sustained Irish resistance to English authority in the north mirrored the situation across the whole kingdom, most notably in the south, specifically in Munster with the Desmond rebellions.[2] In Ulster, however, this was further compounded by the Highland Scots who remained an unwanted element in the mix, while the exile and imprisonment in England of the Catholic Scottish queen, Mary Stuart, ensured that during the 1570s and 1580s she would remain a focus for Catholics throughout the three kingdoms seeking the overthrow of the Protestant, 'heretic' Elizabeth. This brought with it rumours of French or Spanish assistance to liberate Mary and place her on the thrones of England, Ireland and Scotland. Fear of the Spanish threat intensified as the English moved closer to involvement in the Low Countries while Philip II's inheritance, albeit through force, of the Portuguese crown in 1580 and the unification of the two empires saw a reinforced Spanish maritime presence which could challenge Elizabethan shipping in Atlantic waters.[3] During these decades the finances of the crown would

2 These rebellions were met with harsh repression from the English and resulted in the subsequent plantation of Munster in the 1580s. For more on the Desmond rebellions and the Munster plantation see Canny, *Making Ireland British*, 121–64; Robert Dunlop, 'The plantation of Munster, 1584–89', *English Historical Review* 3/10 (1888), 250–69; G. A. Hayes-McCoy, 'Conciliation, Coercion and the Protestant Reformation, 1547–71', in T. W. Moody, F. X. Martin and F. J. Byrne, eds, *A New History of Ireland Volume III: Early Modern Ireland 1534–1691* (Oxford, first published 1979, online 2011), 69–93, especially 86–93 [*NHI III*]; G. A. Hayes-McCoy, 'The Completion of the Tudor Conquest and the Advance of the Counter-Reformation, 1571–1603', in Moody, Martin, and Byrne, eds, *NHI III*, 94–141, especially 99–109, 113–15; Michael MacCarthy-Morrough, *The Munster Plantation: Migration to Southern Ireland 1583–1641* (Oxford, 1986); Keith Pluymers, 'Colonizing lands and landscapes in the English Atlantic, c.1580–c.1640' (University of Southern California, PhD, 2015), 67–94; D. B. Quinn, 'The Munster Plantation: Problems and Opportunities', *Journal of Cork Historical & Archaeological Society* 71 (1966), 19–40. For a concise summary of the harsh policies of the English see David Edwards, 'Beyond Reform: Martial Law and the Tudor Reconquest of Ireland', *History Ireland* 5/2 (1997), 16–21; Heffernan, *Debating Tudor Policy in Sixteenth-Century Ireland*, 174–206.

3 N. A. M. Rodger, *The Safeguard of the Sea. A Naval History of Britain, 660–1649* (London, 1997, reprinted 2004), 219–20, 245–8.

be stretched even further and yet greater investment in Ireland was required if the English were to ever realise their aims there.

On paper maintaining a presence in Ireland should not have presented too much of an obstacle for the English. After all, until 1558 England had maintained its garrison at Calais while English claims to sovereignty over France dated back centuries to when a very real English maritime empire existed encompassing Gascony, Normandy and Aquitaine under the dominions of the English crown.[4] During the 1580s, although much was made of England's position as a powerful sea-faring nation, the Spanish flaunted their prowess both in the Mediterranean and in open Atlantic waters, while in the Irish Sea and North Channel England's maritime power was being seriously challenged by the Scottish Highlanders largely because the queen would not commit the appropriate shipping required.[5] Patrolling the Irish Sea was not a priority for Elizabeth, nor had it been for her predecessors; throughout the sixteenth century systematic patrols of the waters off the west coast was rare, even during times of warfare.[6] Meanwhile, Elizabeth gave careful, albeit sporadic, encouragement to the private enterprises of

4 Although King John (1199–1216), is regarded as having ruled over a vast overseas empire, claims can be traced back to 1066 when William the Conqueror united the duchy of Normandy with the English crown.

5 A shipbuilding programme, started by Mary Tudor, was continued during the reign of Elizabeth but the majority of English shipping remained in private hands unless commandeered by the crown. The victory of the Marquis of Santa Cruz, the Spanish admiral, over a Portuguese-French fleet on 26 July 1580 saw the Spanish gain control of the Azores and highlighted to European powers that Spanish maritime power was not confined to the Mediterranean (see Rodger, *Safeguard of the Sea*, 246), while Spanish shipping regularly made the return journey to the Americas. Meanwhile, at the end of the decade, the Armada of 1588 had been less of a victory for the English than a failure for the Spanish. See Tom Glasgow Jr., 'The Shape of the ships that defeated the Spanish Armada', *The Mariner's Mirror*, 50:3 (1964), 177–87; Geoffrey Parker, 'The *Dreadnought* Revolution of Tudor England', *The Mariner's Mirror* 82/3 (1996), 269–300; Simon Adams, *The Armada Campaign of 1588* (Historical Association, 1988); Colin Martin and Geoffrey Parker, *The Spanish Armada* (London, 1988).

6 David Loades, *The Making of the Elizabethan Navy 1540–1590. From the Solent to the Armada* (Woodbridge, 2009), 73, 85, 109; David Loades, *The Tudor Navy. An Administrative, Political and Military History* (Aldershot, 1992), 14, 45, 111, 144.

men like Martin Frobisher, the Hawkins family, Humphrey Gilbert and of course Francis Drake and Walter Ralegh, in their overseas endeavours primarily because this offered 'immediate and tangible monetary gain'.[7] This was especially so if successful attacks were carried out on Spanish shipping returning from the Americas with a lucrative cargo. In contrast, Ireland offered little immediate financial incentive although, if conquered, could be fully exploited to provide a welcome relief to the ongoing drain on resources it had been since the early fourteenth century.[8] Regardless of the financial situation, however, the political and confessional situation in Ireland had to be addressed. English officials on the ground were increasingly aware of the need to gain the upper hand if they were to expel the Highlanders from Ulster and defend the coasts of Ireland in order to prevent it becoming the 'back door' through which hostile, Catholic powers could launch an attack on England.[9] In the 1580s, however, the decision was taken to grant lands in the Route to Sorley Boy MacDonnell.[10] No doubt, as has been argued, the threat of a Spanish invasion spurred the then Lord Deputy, John Perrot, to reach this accommodation but the situation was

7 E. G. R. Taylor, *Late Tudor and Early Stuart Geography 1583–1650. A Sequel to Tudor Geography, 1485–1583* (London, 1934), 2; Loades, *The Tudor Navy*; Loades, *The Making of the Elizabethan Navy*; Rodger, *Safeguard of the Sea*, 254–96; Peter C. Mancall, *Hakluyt's Promise. An Elizabethan Obsession for an English America* (New Haven and London, 2007).

8 As highlighted in Humphrey Gilbert, 'The Discourse of Ireland (1572)', in David B. Quinn, ed., *The Voyages and Colonising Enterprises of Sir Humphrey Gilbert: Volume I* (London, 1940), 124–8.

9 Patrick Collinson, 'Elizabeth I (1533–1603)', *ODNB*, accessed 27 October 2015. While the Spanish squadron that landed at Smerwick in the Dingle peninsula had been massacred, the ability of the Spanish to land forces on Ireland was not a comforting reality; see Vincent P. Carey, 'Atrocity and History: Grey, Spenser and the Slaughter at Smerwick (1580)', in David Edwards, Pádraig Lenihan and Clodagh Tait, eds, *Age of Atrocity. Violence and Political Conflict in Early Modern Ireland* (Dublin, 2007), 79–94.

10 The Irish branch of the family became known as the MacDonnells. As 1586 is regarded as the date when the Irish and Scottish branches of the family split and became distinct clans, to avoid further confusion the Irish family will now be referred to as the MacDonnells.

more complex.[11] With both the Atlantic and the North Channel contexts providing challenges and threats for the English, the agreement with the MacDonnells was the result of local, national and international concerns regarding security, supply and supremacy of the seas.

Security …

Aware of concerns over security of the north coast, Elizabeth wrote to Lord Deputy Sir Henry Sidney in January 1567 asking him to inform her 'who possessith the landing places betwixt Logh Foyle and Knokfargus', as these were 'the principall places by w[hi]ch the Scotes make their entree into Irland', and how those places should be recovered.[12] Although reluctant to commit more ships to the North Channel, in March 1567 barks were to be sent to secure Strangford Lough from Turlough Luineach O'Neill while in June ongoing plans to secure the north Antrim coast would also require a greater numbers of vessels.[13] The crown acknowledged the importance of fortifying Carrickfergus, Belfast and the Bann in order to prevent 'succors' that came to the Irish 'by sea', but Sidney recognised that much more was needed.[14] He was instrumental in establishing a garrison on the banks of Lough Foyle as a means of gaining

11 In August 1585 Elizabeth signed the Treaty of Nonsuch, formally committing men and money in support of the Dutch fighting against Spanish rule. This was regarded as a declaration of war by Philip II resulting in the Anglo-Spanish war of 1584–1604 which enabled Elizabeth to exploit English attacks on Spanish shipping in the transatlantic trade. See José Luis Casada Soto, 'Atlantic Shipping in Sixteenth-Century Spain and the 1588 Armada', in M. J. Rodríguez-Salgado and Simon Adams, eds, *England, Spain and the Gran Armada, 1585–1604* (Edinburgh, 1991), 95–132; Simon Adams, 'The Outbreak of the Elizabethan Naval War against the Spanish Empire: The embargo of May 185 and Sir Francis Drake's West Indies Voyage', in Rodríguez-Salgado and Adams, eds, *England, Spain and the Gran Armada*, 173–96.

12 SP 63/20, fol.20r.

13 SP 63/20, fols 104, 148; SP 63/21, fol.66.

14 SP 63/17, fol.55v.

a greater presence in the northwest of Ulster in order to keep an eye on the activities of the O'Neill and O'Donnell kindreds.[15] They were fierce and historic rivals but both were willing to ally with the English if it gave them the upper hand against the other. The subsequent destruction of the garrison at Derry in 1567 is said to have hit Sidney very hard, on account of his personal dedication to the project, but it reinforced the need for garrisons in such places if English policy and plantation was to succeed. In communicating with William Cecil, Lord Burghley, Sidney advocated 'some collany … to the number of 2000 men or more' to be established in Ulster and raised the need for the reinforcement of Carrickfergus, Olderfleet, Glenarm, Red Bay, Market-town Bay, the Skerries, Portrush and the bridge over the Bann river 'w[i]th a castell upon it', no doubt all aimed at keeping out the Scots.[16] Upon Sidney's arrival in Ireland for his second term as Lord Deputy, 1575–78, he immediately concerned himself with coastal defences and, in the light of the situation in Ulster, made that province a priority. His view that the English presence in Ireland required greater reinforcement was strengthened by the various requests he, as Lord Deputy, had to handle from members of the English army in Ireland, from naval captains, from members of the Irish parliament in Dublin, and also from the Irish who had allied with the English. Alongside these requests for additional resources was the need to deploy them more effectively. Indeed, in maritime terms, Sidney appreciated that it was not simply a case of more ships, but rather the situation in Ireland necessitated a variety of, often smaller, vessels to meet the demands of English policy.

Sidney's time in office was regarded as a failure by contemporaries, despite his ambitious and wide-ranging outlook and programme for reform. His record, therefore, as far as Ireland was concerned was fairly dismal, despite all his efforts, but such an evaluation of his role as Lord Deputy

15 For the O'Donnell kindred and their alliances with the English see James Alexander Mitchell, 'The O'Donnell lords of Tyrconnell, 1537–1603: a study of their efforts to maintain their local power in sixteenth-century Tudor Ireland' (University of Strathclyde, PhD, 2015).

16 SP 63/26, fols 71–5, at 72r. The Skerries are a small group of islands just off the north coast of Antrim, opposite Portrush and nearby Dunluce on the mainland.

overlooks his maritime perspective.[17] Like some of his predecessors, Sidney's early career hints at a maritime perspective that was further developed and put to good use during his time in Ireland. Before service in Ireland Sidney had enjoyed a long and varied career, including commanding the right wing at Flodden Field in 1513, acting as messenger for Cardinal Thomas Wolsey in his French affairs, and sitting on juries during the Pilgrimage of Grace in 1536. His maritime experience had begun early in 1512–13 when he was captain of a royal ship and fought against the French in a naval battle off Brest, for which he was knighted; in later years he was charged with the supervision of coastal defences.[18] Given that Sidney has been responsible for maintaining coastal defences in England, it is unsurprising he should focus on this in Ireland too. He also had a very useful personal and kin network. Sidney first arrived in Ireland in 1555 when he accompanied his brother-in-law Thomas Radcliffe, Lord Fitzwalter, then soon to be, third Earl of Sussex. How far Sussex and Sidney influenced each other is unclear but they appear to have shared a concern for maritime matters. It was Sussex who had launched the naval attack on the Highland Scots in 1557 and 1558, an attempt to both expel them from, and deter them returning to, Ulster. There were other notable kin connections back in England too that may have influenced Sidney's perspective. In 1551 he married Mary Dudley, daughter of John Dudley, Viscount Lisle and later Duke of Northumberland. Northumberland had been appointed Vice-Admiral of the Narrow Seas in 1537, warden-general of the Scottish marches in 1542 and, later in 1543, Lord High Admiral.[19] Closely connected to the Dudley

17 For more on Sidney see Canny, *The Elizabethan Conquest of Ireland*, especially 46–75, 97–116, 140–63; Wallace T. MacCaffrey, 'Sidney, Sir Henry (1529–1586)', *ODNB*, accessed 10 February 2017; Hiram Morgan, 'Overmighty Officers. The Irish Lord Deputyship in the Early Modern British State', *History Ireland* 7/4 (1999), 17–21. For the challenges in faced in relation to the ecclesiastical state of Ireland see Brady and Murray, 'Sir Henry Sidney and the Reformation in Ireland', 14–39; Henry A. Jefferies, 'Why the Reformation Failed in Ireland', *Irish Historical Studies* 40/158 (2016), 151–70.

18 MacCaffrey, 'Sir Henry Sidney'.

19 David Loades, 'Dudley, John, duke of Northumberland (1504–1553), *royal servant*', *ODNB*, accessed 8 February 2019; E. G. R. Taylor, *Tudor Geography 1485–1583* (London, 1930), 72–3.

family was John Dee. Dee had gone to Louvain to study 'mathematics, geography, astronomical observation and … civil law', but returned to England in 1551. He went on to make a significant contribution to knowledge as well as overseas exploration and discovery, advocating expansion into the Americas.[20] Thus, Sidney was well-connected to a wider circle of men with maritime, geographic and navigational experience and interests. While Northumberland was involved in maritime and naval strategy in relation to the Narrow Seas, Sidney, Northumberland's son-in-law, would develop similar approaches to affairs in Ireland.

Sidney is said to have had an 'unfailing' interest in geographic matters and during his time as Lord Deputy 'took steps to collect and preserve' Ireland's past and current records.[21] It was during Sidney's time in office that John Gough made his map of 1567, many details of which were incorporated into the large-scale map made later by Robert Lythe, and the Lord Deputy is said to have accompanied Lythe during the production of this map between 1569 and 1571.[22] Sidney's interest in geographic matters and indeed his interest in Ireland was crucial given his position there, but so too was such interest in Ireland from others at the time, primarily William Cecil, Lord Burghley. Aware of the need for a more comprehensive understanding of the extent of land in Ireland, its topography and economic potential, individuals like Burghley insisted on the need for detailed maps in order to support English policy there.[23] While maps were used to justify English involvement in Ireland, by showing vast, empty, uncultivated areas of land, Sidney's appreciation of the need for greater knowledge of

20 R. Julian Roberts, 'Dee, John (1527–1609), *mathematician, astrologer, and antiquary*', *ODNB* accessed 8 February 2019; Robert C. H. Baldwin, 'John Dee's Interest in the Application of Nautical Science, Mathematics and Law to English Naval Affairs', *International Archives of the History of Ideas* 193 (2006), 97–130.

21 Taylor, *Tudor Geography*, 31.

22 Taylor, *Tudor Geography*, 31–2. Taylor also notes that Sidney's secretary at this time was Emery Molyneux who went on to make the first English globe twenty years later.

23 For an interesting discussion of the role of geography in policy development towards Ireland see J. H. Andrews, 'Geography and Government in Elizabethan Ireland', in N. Stephens and R. E. Glasscock, eds, *Irish Geographical Studies in Honour of E. Estyn Evans* (Belfast, 1970), 178–91; see p.162 n.149 above.

Ulster's geography, topography and coastline had a more practical basis.[24] Control, maintenance and consolidation of coastal defences in the north was necessary against an external threat such as Spain or the Highland Scots, but to secure successful plantation within Ulster the English needed more detailed geographical information of the landscape of the region beyond the coastal areas and main rivers. They needed intimate knowledge of the land and its contours. This demanded specific knowledge of the location and extent of woodland, mountainous and bog regions, and where passes could be cut through them; the size and location of rivers and loughs, where bridges or fords could be made; and of course, in whose

24 There is a wealth of literature on maps and map-making both in general and specifically in relation to Ireland. See, for example, J. H. Andrews, 'The Irish Surveys of Robert Lythe', *Imago Mundi*, 19 (1965), 22–31; J. H. Andrews, 'The Maps of the Escheated Counties of Ulster, 1609–10', *Proceedings of the Royal Irish Academy. Section C: Archaeology, Celtic Studies, History, Linguistics, Literature* 74 (1974), 113–70; J. H. Andrews, *Shapes of Ireland: Maps and Their Makers 1564–1839* (Dublin, 1997); John H. Andrews, 'The Mapping of Ireland's Cultural Landscape, 1550–1630' in Patrick J. Duffy, David Edwards and Elizabeth Fitzpatrick, eds, *Gaelic Ireland, c.1250-c.1650: Land, Lordship and Settlement* (Dublin, 2004), 153–80; J. H. Andrews, *The Queen's Last Map-Maker: Richard Bartlett in Ireland, 1600–3* (Dublin, 2008); Bernhard Klein, 'English Cartographers and the Mapping of Ireland in the Early Modern Period', *Journal for the Study of British Cultures* II (1995), 115–39; Annaleigh Margey, 'Representing Plantation Landscapes: The Mapping of Ulster, *c.*1560–1640', in James Lyttleton and Colin Rynne, eds, *Plantation Ireland. Settlement and Material Culture,* c.*1550–*c.*1700* (Dublin, 2009), 140–64; Annaleigh Margey, 'After the Flight: The Impact of Plantation on the Ulster landscape', in David Finnegan, Éamonn Ó Ciardha and Marie-Claire Harrigan, eds, *The Flight of the Earls: Imeacht na nIarlaí* (Derry, 2010), 247–58; William J. Smyth, *Map-Making, Landscapes and Memory: A Geography of Colonial and Early Modern Ireland,* c.*1530–1750* (Cork, 2006). For the wider context see Jeremy Black, *Maps and History: Constructing Images of the Past* (New Haven, CT, 1997); David Buisseret, ed., *Monarchs, Ministers and Maps: The Emergence of Cartography as a Tool of Government in Early Modern Europe* (Chicago and London, 1992). For a lovely discussion of maps and what they tell us about Gaelic lordship in Ulster and their involvement in trade (especially trade in fish) see Mark Gardiner and T. E. McNeill, 'Seaborne Trade and the Commercialisation of Fifteenth- and Sixteenth-Century Gaelic Ulster', *Proceedings of the Royal Irish Academy. Section C: Archaeology, Celtic Studies, History, Linguistics, Literature*, (2016), 11–34.

territory woods, rivers and loughs lay.[25] Focusing on coastal fortifications may have assisted in repulsing the enemy in the short-term but it did not help in furthering English efforts to extend authority inland across the rest of Ulster; after all, it was familiarity with the landscape that enabled the Irish (and Highland Scots) to retreat quickly across rivers and bogs, through forests and into mountainous terrain. Indeed, during his first term of office Sidney had made agreements with Sir Brian McPhelim and Brian Carragh in Clandeboy to assist in building a 'good and sufficient bridge, that men, horsses … w[i]th all man[n]er of cariage, maie safelie pass' over the Laggan river at Belfast; 'to cutt or cause to be cutt and hewen downe the paces and highe waie through the wod' at Kilwarten; 'to deffend all artificers working or framing of tymber in eu[er]y off the wodds' for furnishing the town of Carrickfergus; and to 'defend from spoile & burning all shipps, boates & other vessells' there.[26] As this highlights, Sidney knew that alongside effective utilisation of the landscape, navigation of inland areas and waterways was also crucial.[27]

English patrols of the North Channel sought to intercept the arrival of shipping from Scotland during times of perceived threat but it was far from satisfactory. In reality, the infrequent and minimal patrols that were undertaken bordered on being dangerously negligent and there was a gradual realisation that, even if done effectively, it would not be enough to support English policy in Ireland.[28] Smaller vessels were needed to transport

25 SP 63/179, fols 160–1r at 160v. On 5 May 1595 Sir Ralph Lane, muster master, sent the queen by Captain James Carlyle 'a plotte of yo[u]r highnes province of Vllester … and all the p[ar]tes of it, then with the septes and factions of the same, as well Skottishe as Irish'. Nonetheless, as highlighted by Andrews, 'Geography and Government', 182, 184–5, Essex too had been aware of the need to take the key strongholds of other Irish chiefs, whether castles or island dwellings, bridges, river fordings or passes cut through forests and mountains.

26 SP 63/26, fol.30r.

27 D. J. B. Trim, 'Medieval and Early-Modern Inshore, Estuarine, Riverine and Lacustrine Warfare', in D. J. B. Trim and Mark Charles Fissel, eds, *Amphibious Warfare 1000–1750. Commerce, State Formation and European Expansion* (Leiden, 2006), 357–419.

28 The English may well have been dependent on 'the commodity of the sea' as Charles Blount, Lord Mountjoy, put it, but sea-power on its own was not enough; see

men and supplies around the coast, while others were needed to navigate inland rivers and loughs, especially in the more remote northwest of Ireland where knowledge of the landscape was limited and the English presence barely noticeable.[29] In 1575 the earl of Essex, had requested 'flatt bottomed boates to be made or gotten abowt Liverpoole for caryages in the bane and blackwater', emphasising the need for different types of shipping, especially vessels suitable for inland navigation.[30] Sidney went further and attempted to build boats on Lough Neagh as a means to control the region and also afford access, via the River Bann at Toome, to Coleraine. This was vital as there were few suitable fording places across the Bann.[31] Late sixteenth-century maps of Ulster show that for a time the lough was called Lough Sidney, a result of Sidney's own endeavours there.[32] In addition, as some maps indicate, an island in the lough was called Island Sidney. While this is most likely a reflection of Sidney's relentless self-promotion it also points to the exploitation of natural or man-made resources by the English.[33] Utilisation of crannogs or natural islands in loughs was something the English Lord Deputy had learned from the Irish. Indeed, before his first term of office came to an end, in December 1567, Sidney had entered into negotiations with Turlough Luineach O'Neill during which O'Neill requested 'insulam illam sitam sup[er] loch each' [Lough Neagh], 'in which Sidney left his men'.[34]

John McGurk, *The Elizabethan Conquest of Ireland: The 1590s Crisis* (Manchester, 1997), 54.

29 SP 63/20, fols 51r–2v, 104; SP 63/21, fol.145r.

30 SP 63/50, fols 168–9. Essex also stated that for building projects 'masons, carpentars, lyme burners, & two principall men in fortification, & especiallie water woorckes, to be sent'. The boats requested were duly sent, arriving a few months later at Carrickfergus; see SP 63/51, fols 19r–20r.

31 Audrey J. Horning, 'On the Banks of the Bann: The Riverine Economy of an Ulster Plantation Village', *Historical Archaeology* 41/3 (2007), 94–114.

32 TCD University Archives, Hardiman Collection, 1209/1; 1209/14; 1209/16; 1209/17; 1209/19; 1209/83; TNA, MPF 1/35.

33 Morgan, 'Overmighty Officers', 18.

34 SP 63/22, fol.131; *CSP Ireland*, I, no. 577.

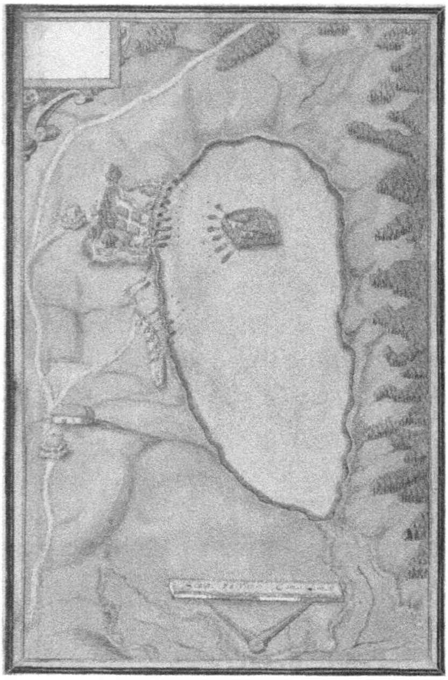

Maps, drawings and plans by Richard Bartlett (Barthelet) and others, 1587–1625, Drawing of attacks on crannogs in Ulster, c.1602. Reproduced courtesy of the National Library of Ireland, NLI MS 2656 (11).

As the majority of crannogs appear to date from prehistory their use during the early modern period has been neglected. More recent scholarship by archaeologists has highlighted that although crannogs may have been constructed during the period from 1000BC to 500AD, evidence from a number of them point to a later development and utilisation of crannogs in the medieval period.[35] Nonetheless, the use of crannogs for both defensive

35 J. W. Barber and B. A. Crone, 'Crannogs: A Diminishing Resource? A Survey of the Crannogs of Southwest Scotland and Excavations at Buiston Crannog', *Antiquity* 67/256 (1993), 520–33; Jon C. Henderson, 'Islets Through Time: The Definition, Dating and Distribution of Scottish Crannogs', *Oxford Journal of Archaeology* 17/2 (1998), 227–44; A. Crone, *The History of a Scottish Lowland Crannog: Excavations at Buiston, Ayrshire, 1989–90* (Edinburgh, 2000); Aidan O'Sullivan, 'Crannogs in Late Medieval Gaelic Ireland, *c.*1350–*c.*1650', in Duffy, Edwards and FitzPatrick,

and offensive purposes is often overlooked by historians although not by archaeologists. A notable exception is Gerald A. Hayes-McCoy who brought them to attention, and to life, in his study of early Irish maps, one of which portrays an attack by the English against the Irish.[36] Indeed, both early maps of Ulster and documentary evidence point to the extensive use of island dwellings, whether crannogs or natural islands, for various purposes during the late sixteenth and early seventeenth centuries.[37] On occasion it would appear these were used to store munitions or were a place to retreat to before launching a counter-attack on the English.[38] At other times it was clearly a safe refuge for livestock, or simply a place of security or habitation.[39] Castles and forts on Ulster maps were clearly lacking in the northwest of Ulster, but they can be found around Lough Earn, Lough Derg and, of course, at Derry and on Lough Neagh, suggesting the widespread use of island dwellings by the Irish.[40] In the Scottish Highlands

---

eds, *Gaelic Ireland* c.*1250*–c.*1650*, 397–417; Anne Crone and Ewan Campbell with Colleen Batey et al., *A Crannog of the First Millennium AD: Excavations by Jack Scott at Loch Glashan, Argyll, 1960* (Edinburgh, 2005); John Raven, 'Medieval Landscapes and Lordship in South Uist' (University of Glasgow, PhD, 2005).

36 G. A. Hayes-McCoy, *Ulster and other Irish Maps, c.1600*, Irish Manuscripts Commission (Dublin, 1964); NLI MS 2656(5), unidentified crannog and Dungannon Castle by Richard Bartlett, 1602, reproduced in John H. Andrews, 'The Mapping of Ireland's Cultural Landscape, 1550–1630', in Duffy, Edwards, and Fitzpatrick, eds, *Gaelic Ireland c.1250–c.1650*, 153–80 at 163; and at p.180 above.

37 John McGurk, *Sir Henry Docwra, 1564–1631. Derry' Second Founder* (Dublin, 2006), 30–1, D 28. For example, Thomas Roe Burke had a castle on an island in Lough Mask. The O'Donnell lords had a crannog in Lough Eske, four miles upriver from their main castle in Donegal town, that was used 'as a bolt-hole and storehouse'; see Gardiner and McNeill, 'Seaborne trade and the commercialisation of fifteenth- and sixteenth-century Gaelic Ulster', 1–34 at 26.

38 SP 63/190, fol.163.

39 Hayes-McCoy, *Ulster and other Irish Maps*; McGurk, *Sir Henry Docwra*, 84; SP 63/173, fol.56. SP 63/22, fol.148r recounts that in August 1566 Richard Creagh, titular Archbishop of Armagh went on a visit to 'Shan O neyle being in an Iland called Inishdavell in cu[m]pany w[i]t[h] B[ishop] of Downe and dyned w[i]t[h] Shan'. The bishop was a 'friar, Meyler Magrath'. According to Creagh, Shane preferred his own foster-brother, Terence Danyell, for the position of Bishop of Down and Connor (SP 63/12, fols 0093r, 0094r).

40 For more on Derry as an island see p.211 n.149 below.

and Isles the role of crannogs in North Uist has been emphasised and there was utilisation of natural islands in loughs, as evidenced by the use of Innis Chonnel Castle in Loch Awe, Finlaggan in Loch Finlaggan and a number of other locations in Islay; perhaps most notably Donald Gorm is said to have had a building of some sort on an island in Loch Gorm in Islay.[41] Island dwellings, whether natural or man-made, were exploited in the central and eastern Highlands also. William, seventh chief of the Mackintoshes and Clan Chattan, is said to have been buried 'in the island of' Loch Arkaig in 1368; in 1580 'in order that he might subdue the insolence of the Lochaber men', Lauchlan, sixteenth chief,

> caused an island in the loch commonly called Loch Lochy, to be constructed, which was called Alan-darrach, that is, the oaken island: for it was built upon oaken beams .... In that island he placed a garrison, and while it was there, all the people of Lochaber were very submissive and obedient to their superiors: but as soon as the island was broken down they relapsed into their wonted rebellion and mischief.[42]

Given the number of lochs/loughs in both Scotland and Ireland, it is unsurprising that such sites became strategically important although the Irish evidence for their use in the early modern period is more compelling than that from Scotland.[43]

41 David Caldwell, *Islay: The Land of the Lordship* (Edinburgh, 2008), 20–1, 39, 70–1, 79, 100–1, 170–1; 'History of the MacDonalds', in *Highland Papers I*, ed., J. R. N. MacPhail, series two, vol. V (Edinburgh: Scottish History Society, 1914), 24–5, 50; 'Extracts from the collection of State Papers in the Advocates' Library known as the Denmylne MSS', in *Highland Papers III*, ed. J. R. N. MacPhail, series two, vol. XX (Edinburgh: Scottish History Society, 1920), 273; *The Book of Islay. Documents Illustrating the History of the Island*, ed., G. Gregory Smith (Edinburgh, 1895), no. LXXXV, n.6; Ross Crawford, 'Warfare in the West Highlands and Isles of Scotland, *c.* 1544–1615' (University of Glasgow, PhD, 2016), 221.

42 'Epitome of the Origin and Increase of the Mackintoshes', in *Genealogical Collections Concerning Families in Scotland, Made by Walter Macfarlane 1750–51*, ed., J. T. Clark, series one, vol. XXXIII (Edinburgh: Scottish History Society, 1900), 173, 242; on how to read such histories see M. MacGregor, 'The genealogical histories of Gaelic Scotland', in A. Fox and D. Woolf, eds, *The Spoken word. Oral culture in Britain, 1500–1850* (Manchester, 2002), 196–239.

43 That does not mean, however, that crannogs and island dwellings were not used in Scotland during this period. For crannogs or lake islands and suggestions they may

The use of crannogs by the Irish necessitated suitable vessels to access them and if the English were to gain the upper hand, they needed to be able, quite literally, to out-manoeuvre the Irish on both land and water. Sidney's efforts to build vessels on Lough Neagh, alongside additional flat-bottomed boats sent from England, were vital in order to allow the English to traverse Ulster through navigation of inland waters. Increased demand for knowledge of, combined with growing interest in and appreciation of, Ireland's landscape and natural resources resulted in a greater determination to map the country more accurately during the 1580s and 1590s. The mapping carried out by the English, particularly men like Richard Bartlett, during the last years of the sixteenth century was undoubtedly beneficial for the forces there in their efforts to bring the Irish to submission but, considering the misinformation maps often contained, little could compensate for a working knowledge of the area.[44] While the constant changing of personnel did not help the English cause, for those individuals who experienced a longer career of service in Ireland their knowledge was invaluable and the actions of such individuals remained of significant importance.

In June 1584 Sir John Perrot arrived in Ireland as Lord Deputy. He was both well connected and experienced. His service to the crown began in 1552 as sheriff of Pembrokeshire although his first experience of Ireland came between 1571 and 1573 when he succeeded Sir Humphrey Gilbert as President of Munster. Following the rebellion of James FitzMaurice FitzGerald in 1569 Perrot had the task of attempting to stabilise the region before plantation could commence. In dealing with FitzGerald he governed with brute force despite a lack of resources and was glad to return to England when he did. Nonetheless, he remained interested in Irish affairs and, in August 1579, was given command of a number of ships with the aim of intercepting Spanish or pirate vessels along the southern coast of

have been a royal dwelling or associated with kingship in some way see R. Warner, 'On Crannogs and Kings (Part I)', *Ulster Journal of Archaeology*, third series, vol. 57 (1994), 61–9.

44 See pp. 208–13 below; for more on Bartlett see Thomas Herron, 'Orpheus in Ulster: Richard Bartlett's Colonial art', in Thomas Herron and Michael Potterton, eds, *Ireland in the Renaissance, c.1540–1660* (Dublin, 2007), 289–308; Andrews, *The Queen's Last Map-Maker*.

Ireland.[45] With experience of service in Ireland by land and sea under his belt alongside friends and patrons that included former Lord Deputies Sir Henry Sidney and Thomas Radcliffe, Earl of Sussex, it was a treatise of 1581 whereby Perrot put forward his views as to how effective government in Ireland would be achieved that ensured his return to Ireland once again in 1584.[46] During his time in office Perrot put into effect his military and naval expertise and built upon the efforts of his predecessors. Five months after his arrival, Perrot wrote to inform the Privy Council that he intended to keep boats 'upon Logh-ewe and Logh-ern' while also pointing out to Burghley that the use of 'the boates upon the Shannon … is verie necessarie'.[47] Smaller vessels were vital for internal navigation but also for the more practical movement of men, munitions and victuals.[48] Given that Perrot embarked on the complete suppression of dissent in Ulster in anticipation of subsequent plantation there, internal transportation of supplies was crucial.

45 Roger Turvey, 'Perrot, Sir John (1528–1592)', *ODNB*, accessed 20 March 2017. His son would later 'concede that his father's accomplishments were fatally flawed by choler and tactlessness' in Sir James Perrot, *Chronicle of Ireland, 1584–1608*, ed., H. Wood (Irish Manuscripts Commission, 1933); quotation from Victor Treadwell, 'Sir John Perrot and the Irish Parliament of 1585–6', *Proceedings of the Royal Irish Academy Section C: Archaeology, Celtic Studies, History, Linguistics, Literature*, vol. 85 (1985), 259. For the rise of piracy in the south and west of Ireland see John C. Appleby, 'The Problem of Piracy in Ireland, 1570–1630', in Claire Jowitt, ed., *Pirates? The Politics of Plunder 1550–1650* (Basingstoke, 2007), 41–55; Keith Pluymers, "Pirates' and the Problems of Plantation in Seventeenth-Century Ireland', in Peter C. Mancall and Carole Shammas, eds, *Governing the Sea in the Early Modern Era. Essays in Honor of Robert C. Ritchie* (San Marino, 2015), 79–108.

46 Turvey, 'Sir John Perrot'; Brady, *The Chief Governors*, 291–300, especially 293. The father of his first wife, Sir Thomas Cheyney of Shurland, Kent, had been Lord Warden of the Cinque Ports while Perrot was also connected to Robert Dudley, Earl of Leicester, and Sir Francis Walsingham.

47 SP 63/112, fols 150, 155.

48 SP 63/200, fol.32. In 1597, in order to cross the Blackwater, the Lord Deputy Thomas Burgh 'had framed a flat botom vessel … that was able to transport … 150 men at once'.

… supply …

Throughout the sixteenth century the English presence in Ireland relied on victuals being sent from England but, on account of ongoing requests for supplies coupled with the unreliability of regular provisions arriving in Ireland, efforts to be as 'self-sufficient' as possible were encouraged.[49] This involved collecting rents, usually beeves, from Irish lords who had submitted to the English but on other occasions there were efforts to either reap the harvest of Irish before they did or simply take what they could from the land.[50] This stemmed in part from the need to supply the army in Ireland, rather than wait for infrequent and delayed victuals to arrive, but also from English policy which was to starve the Irish into submission.[51] On 8 February 1567 Colonel Edward Sayntloo wrote to Lord Deputy Sidney, updating him on recent activities in the north of Ulster and recounted how he had 'made a jornaye into the Ocanes countrye, burned to the bande [Bann], prayed and spoyled … tene thousande catle and vii hundrethe gar[r]ons and receyuiede to yo[u]r honno[r]s mercye one Richard Occane'.[52] Wilful destruction of crops and livestock, although part of English policy, was something the English criticised

49 SP 63/23, fol.20. Reports such as that of January 1568 from the Lord Justices of Ireland, informing the queen that 'notwithstanding the proportion of victels and store of grayne' it would 'not hold owt the tyme appoyncted', were not uncommon.

50 SP 63/38, fol.14. In October 1572 some of the Clandeboy O'Neills offered 'twoo hundred cowes bothe for the ransome of the said Con [McNeyll Oge], and the firste yeres rente of Claneboy'. They also asked that Con 'keepe the Island of Baile Galloglay in his handes as he ought'. See also McGurk, *Elizabethan Conquest of Ireland*, 205.

51 'A Description of Ireland by Fynes Moryson, Secretary to the Lord Mountjoy, then Lord Deputy. 1600–1603', in *Ireland under Elizabeth and James the First, Described by Edmund Spenser, Sir John Davies and Fynes Moryson*, ed., Henry Morley (London, 1890), 419–20. Although Moryson stated that the Irish 'take less pleasure to till their grounds or plant trees, content to live for the day' he noted that the land did 'yield … great increase of corn'.

52 SP 63/20, fol.62.

the Irish for.[53] In August 1580 when Hugh Magennis complained that Turlough Luineach O'Neill had taken from him, 'by pray', 400 cattle, 60 mares, 200 swine, and 300 sheep, 'killed xvi of my [Magennis'] poore followeres', and went into the 'borderes' of Magennis' land and 'cutt all [the] greene corne', the English condemned it.[54] They were not above such measures themselves but, while on occasion the English would destroy the goods and livestock of the Irish, when the opportunity arose they would try to take it for themselves. This was not without some difficulty. On 3 September 1566 Colonel Edward Randolfe wrote to William Cecil from Bristol, where he waited for passage to Ireland, and described his 'enymyes the wynde' that would prevent him gathering Shane's harvest.[55] Just two weeks later a rather frustrated Hugh Brady, Bishop of Meath, informed Cecil that 'the corne in the enemies Countrey is gotten, and hid in woodes and caves', but the English 'corne Liethe in o[u]r yards, gathered together … burned … by the meanes of the traytors', the O'Reillys. Further victuals from England would be required.[56] Burning and wasting of land, a scorched earth policy, and the slaughter of cattle were tactics employed against the Irish although ultimately counter-productive. While it led to constant requests for more provisions it also reinforced the English view of Ireland as a waste, uncultivated land and often resulted in retaliation by the Irish. With little progress being made in terms of the English becoming self-sufficient, they needed to maintain a steady supply of men, munitions and victuals. Repeated destruction of foodstuffs through warfare combined with a population that demanded to be fed, left Ireland struggling to provide.

The wider climatic context of the later sixteenth century did not alleviate the situation in Ireland at all. Evidence of lands lying waste in the western Highlands and Isles is found in the account given by Angus

53 The same was true also of the Scottish crown who condemned the perceived lawlessness of the Highlanders without understanding the social, political and economic significance of the destruction of livestock and foodstuff.

54 SP 63/75, fol.166. Magennis asked Lord Deputy Grey to 'license' him 'to be revenged'.

55 SP 63/19, fol.3r.

56 SP 63/19, fol.27.

MacDonald of Dunivaig (although still styled 'of Dunnavage and Glenis') to Sir William Stewart of Houston in 1596. This concerned his lands in Kintyre and MacDonald 'grantit and confessit that ane pairte of the landis of South and North Keantyre war occupyit and possessit be thame and ilkane of thame ... and ane uther pairte thairof war lyand waist unoccupyit be thame or ony utheris'.[57] Robert Dodgshon has argued that the amount of land counted as 'waste' suggests something of the harsher weather conditions that impacted directly on the ability to produce enough to subsist on or make rental payments.[58] This wider context of harsh climatic and environmental conditions, combined with famine, disease and stormier weather, needs to be borne in mind when considering the ability of the English to supply an army in Ireland whose policy for some time had been contradictory and that was, in the 1590s, in quite desperate circumstances.[59]

In order to alleviate shortages, and because of delays in victuals arriving in Ireland, the English had no alternative than to trade with the Irish themselves. This was far from straightforward as often the Irish were unwilling to enter into transactions with the English, a combination of their own need for sufficient foodstuffs, a reluctance to provide succour to the enemy and a growing distrust. On 27 October 1566 Colonel Randolfe, having arrived in Derry, wrote to Cecil stating he could not purchase provisions 'ether for money or love'.[60] It was not only in Ireland that the English experienced problems in acquiring sufficient foodstuffs to be sent. Local and regional factors alongside the unpopularity of the Irish situation meant that at times it was difficult to raise the necessary victuals in England to support

57 'Papers relating to Kintyre' in *Highland Papers III*, ed., J. R. N. MacPhail, series two, vol. XII (Edinburgh: Scottish History Society, 1920), 72–3.

58 Dodgshon, 'The Little Ice Age'.

59 While the later decades of the sixteenth century, especially the 1590s, are generally regarded to have been years of cold winters, wet summers and poor harvests, the sixteenth and seventeenth centuries in general appear to have experienced stronger, more challenging, winds although the winds are regarded as being at their worst during the Maunder Minimum, 1645–1715; see Wolfgang Behringer, *A Cultural History of Climate* (Cambridge, 2010), 85–115; Brian Fagan, *The Little Ice Age. How Climate Made History 1300–1850* (New York, 2000), 77–8, 83–97; Dodgshon, 'The Little Ice Age', 321–37; McGurk, *Elizabethan Conquest of Ireland*, 51.

60 SP 63/19, fol.63r.

the forces in Ireland.[61] In November 1577 Lady Drury (signed M[a]rgery Wyllms), wrote to Sir Francis Walsingham, then Elizabeth's principal secretary, concerning the 'corne butter and chese' requested from Norfolk and asked that he find 'a doble proportion in some other of the countries which are opposit to Irland'.[62] The government also issued commissions to merchants to purchase necessary foodstuffs and transport them directly to Ireland. An example of such an agreement was that reached with Henry and Thomas Sackford in 1575 regarding victuals to be shipped to Ireland, although negotiations on this occasion were fraught due to the situation in Ireland.[63] Other merchants were reluctant to enter this trade usually because pay was not forthcoming. In 1573 Nicholas Wyse, a merchant of Dublin, petitioned the council in London for a payment of £130 4 shillings for 'wheate, salte, otes and wyne' delivered three years earlier for the 'provision of her highenes Garrison at the newrye in the northe p[ar]tes' of Ireland following orders from the then Lord Deputy Sidney.[64] Given the hardships and dangers merchants often had to endure, English perceptions of the 'greate losse & hinderance' to the country, on account of the 'Irysh marchantes & others' who 'deceaved' the queen of her 'customes for wares & marchandizes transported from' Ireland into England hardly helped, while lack of payment forthcoming from the English further compounded hostility and distrust between the two communities.[65]

In addition to the need for a regular supply of foodstuffs there was a constant need for soldiers and mariners to serve in Ireland, replenishing the numbers lost through death, on account of warfare, disease, outbreak of plague, or desertion, as well as requests for masons, carpenters, labourers, brewers, bakers and other skilled individuals to work on the garrisons and develop towns and industry too.[66] The continuous recruitment of men

61 SP 63/38, fol.121.
62 SP 63/59, fol.118.
63 SP 63/45, fol.30; SP 63/51, fols, 41, 43–51, 130; SP 63/52, fol.64; SP 63/53, fol.17; SP 63/55, fol.73.
64 SP 63/43, fol.138.
65 SP 63/49, fol.83r.
66 SP 63/45, fol.241r; SP 63/50, fol.168r; SP 63/51, fols 19–20r; SP 63/52, fols 6–8r; SP 63/55, fol.73; SP 63/59, fol.39; SP 63/61, fols 3–5; SP 63/75, fol.128.

for service in Ireland was increasingly unpopular, especially considering the numbers who had been killed there and the financial drain Ireland placed on the English economy. This unpopularity was most evident in ports such as Bristol, Chester and Liverpool where soldiers and mariners gathered before being transported across the Irish Sea (see Map 5).[67] Lack of discipline and unlawful behaviour in these locations on the part of troops destined for Ireland was a recurring problem while many deserted before they ever set sail. Amassing the men, munitions and victuals to be sent to Ireland, however, was only part of the difficulty. Another part of the process that faced various obstacles was transportation. The most obvious need was for suitable shipping to transport the victuals within an appropriate timeframe to meet the needs in Ireland, and for it to be done without mishap so the goods did not spoil. In order to make most efficient use of what shipping was available men, munitions and victuals were usually transported together.[68] Unfortunately, any delay in the provision of suitable shipping could have severe implications, and not just on account of shortage of supplies in Ireland. The combination of soldiers (with or without pay and provisions) and a lack of munitions and victuals made for a potentially volatile situation as many, including Thomas Smith, found to their cost.[69]

Even after suitable transportation was made available, the English were powerless against the vagaries of the weather. Delays were common on account of the 'contrary winds' that Englishmen continually complained about and which could play havoc with the best laid plans.[70] Walsingham was informed from Bristol on 31 August 1567 of the 'staye … off men …

67 SP 63/60, fol.155; SP 63/68, fols 43, 68, 102; SP 63/75, fols 127–8. For a detailed study of the demands placed on English ports such as Bristol and Chester, as well as the burden on places like Kent, Lancashire and Cheshire see McGurk, *Elizabethan Conquest of Ireland*, 81–188.

68 SP 63/60, fol.155; SP 63/65, fol.148; SP 63/68, fols 41, 43; SP 63/75, fol.127.

69 Hiram Morgan, 'The Colonial Venture of Sir Thomas Smith in Ulster, 1571–1575', *The Historical Journal* 28/2 (1985), 261–78; and see p.141 above.

70 SP 63/10, fol.23; SP 63/10, fol.25; SP 63/19, fol.5v. On 9 March 1580 the Council in Ireland wrote to the Privy Council that 'the queens shippe having lyen here thes vi weekes ready to dep[ar]te … could never yett get wynde and weather'; see SP 63/72, fol.20v.

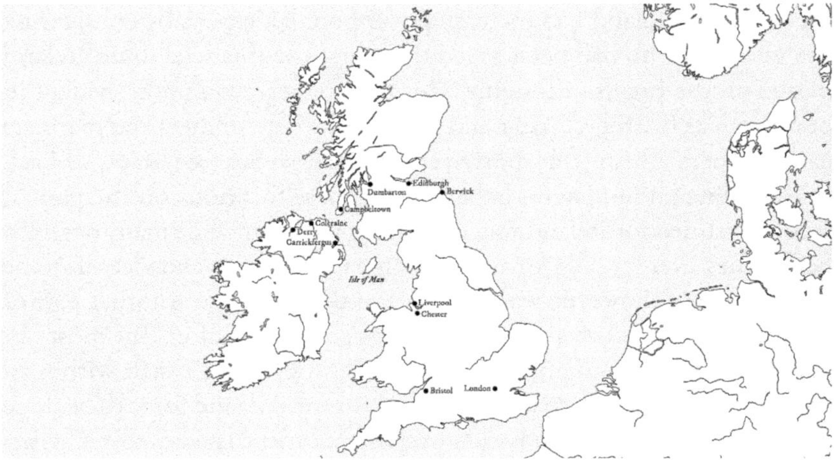

Map 5. Key ports

ffor Ireland', along with soldiers and victuals; while the aim was to leave the next day 'w[i]t[h] the tyde' this was dependant on 'the wynde', and wind was not so reliable as the tide.[71] When Essex had travelled to Ireland in 1573 to deal with the situation in Ulster following the failed plantation by Sir Thomas Smith and his son, a storm scattered his fleet across the Irish Sea from the Isle of Man to Cork. Essex was particularly fortunate as, in the immediate aftermath, the Privy Council prevented the export of corn to France and Spain, instead ordering it to be sent to him in Ireland.[72] Such intervention was rare and, in most cases, delays in transportation on account of unpredictable and stormy weather meant that provisions sent to Ireland often were ruined by the time they reached their destination. In September 1566, Sidney informed Cecil concerning victuals 'arrived at Carlingford … the wheat is utterly lost and not to be accompted of and

71 SP 63/68, fol.119v.

72 SP 63/42, fol.47. In order to ensure they did not suffer a shortage of victuals, military personnel as well as private individuals, like Sir Thomas Smith and the earl of Essex, who were heading to Ireland for a period of service there often requested the rights to reap the harvest, or to import victuals as required without paying customs; see SP 63/30, fols 62–3r; SP 63/40, fol.194r; SP 63/41, fol.125; and see p.143 above.

the malt hardly brought to serve to eny use'; consequently he requested 'some new propor[ti]on may be sent to serve that toune'.[73] In July 1580 it was reported that while wheat and malt had recently been sent to Youghal, of the cargo of wheat just arrived at Waterford from Bristol, 'tenne weys therof nought and nott s[er]vissable by reason that it is so fustie and perished'; the beef also recently arrived at Waterford was 'not good'.[74] The spoiling of foodstuffs was also due to the lack of suitable harbours for loading and unloading goods, although this was more acute in the north where there were not any developed ports.[75] Alongside the repeated demands for victuals and accounts of the deteriorating situation in Ireland, Burghley received reports of the 'wast of victuals' on the northern coast where 'the marrino[u]rs haue been driven to unlade the victualls upon[n] raffs ... wading up to the necks where bootes wolde not serve'.[76] Thus, despite the relative geographic proximity of the two kingdoms the difficulty encountered in efforts to supply the English presence in Ireland served to reinforce the wider difficulties facing the English in Ireland in general.

The situation in Ireland, much like the weather, gradually deteriorated during the later sixteenth century but it was the outbreak of rebellion led by Hugh O'Neill, second Earl of Tyrone, in the mid-1590s that forced Elizabeth to finally commit additional forces to service in Ireland.[77] Tyrone's rebellion

73 SP 63/19, fol.29.

74 SP 63/74, fols 11, 16.

75 SP 63/74, fol.16. The problems of transportation were heightened in winter; after the end of September the Irish coast was 'comonly so stormie, as hardlie shall enny shipping come ... as in somer'; see also McGurk, *Elizabethan Conquest of Ireland*, 174, 207–8.

76 SP 63/114, fol.88v. Indeed in January 1585 Sir Henry Wallop confirmed these reports, writing to Walsingham of the 'iniquity' of 'Marckingtonbaie' [Marketown Bay on the north coast of Antrim] where 'marrino[u]rs weare constrained to unloode the victualls upon a raff w[i]th much traveill & wading'. This was on account of 'Rocks that no boote cann serve'; see SP 63/114, fol.92.

77 For more on Tyrone and his rebellion, see Darren McGettigan, *Red Hugh O'Donnell and the Nine Years War in Ireland, 1594–1603* (Dublin, 2005); Hiram Morgan, *Tyrone's Rebellion: The Outbreak of the Nine Years War in Tudor Ireland* (Woodbridge, 1993), 3–15, 85–112 (especially 94), 212–21; Hiram Morgan, 'Hugh O'Neill and the Nine Years' War in Tudor Ireland', *The Historical Journal* 36/1 (1993), 21–37; Hiram Moran, ''Never any realm worse governed': Queen Elizabeth

also coincided with the coldest decades of the sixteenth century and a run of bad harvests from 1591 to 1597. While many counties in England experienced food riots, the English scorched-earth policy as a means of bringing the Irish to submission meant that resources were increasingly stretched.[78] The addition of a growing Spanish threat put further demands on shipping and defence.[79] In October 1596 Lord Chancellor Loftus and the council in Dublin wrote to London concerning the situation in Ireland which, quite simply, was dire. They had received reports of the arrival of a Spanish ship in the northwest, the territory of Red Hugh O'Donnell of Tyrconnell, and that O'Neill and O'Donnell were ready to join with the Spanish in an attack, while the Irish mariners would serve 'for guides and pylottes'. They requested that 'speedy care may be had … for sending men, vitles and money'. While they reported later that 'ten companies of foote … together w[i]th 64 barrells of meale and 6000 waight of cheese' had arrived, they commented on 'how lytle good yt will do to comfort so great a companie and in so great a skarcety and darth of all manner of vitles'. They further informed the Privy Council of the situation across other parts of Ulster, stating that 'Knockfergus, the Newry, Armaghe and all other places held by hir ma[jes]ty in the north wilbe abandoned for want of vitles, and the lyke daunger wilbe to the frontyre townes of the borders'.[80] A few months later in January 1596–7 Sir Henry Wallop, treasurer, also wrote from Dublin informing Cecil of the lack of provisions, the rising costs of wheat and beeves and that, at Waterford, 'the fysshing fayled'. As a result, he could not see 'how the Armye can be maintayned'.[81] By September 1597 little had changed. Lord Deputy Thomas Burgh wrote to Cecil, again with the usual request for victuals, 'of corne and chese espetially' but also detailing the state of horse and foot companies, their provisions and clothing in advance of the onset of winter. The silver lining of this particular cloud, according

and Ireland', *Transactions of the Royal Historical Society* 14 (2004), 295–308; James O'Neill, *The Nine Years War, 1593–1603* (Dublin, 2017). For the English forces committed to service in Ireland, see McGurk, *Elizabethan Conquest of Ireland*, 220–39.

78 Fagan, *The Little Ice Age*, 94–6.

79 SP 63/191, fol.173v.

80 SP 63/194, fol.233.

81 SP 63/197, fol.88r.

to Burgh, was that the Irish were at breaking point. Indeed he advised that O'Neill had 'cessed [th]e countrey almost to [th]e utmost penye, to kepe his bonnaghtes together [th]is sommer. To applye all against him [th]is winter must nedes breake his neck … [th]e countrey can yelde frute no longer when it is afflicted w[i]th co[n]tineuall incursions'.[82]

The policy of starving the Irish into submission was close to success but, given the situation in both countries, reaching that point had almost caused the English to starve themselves into defeat. The following month, Sir Henry Bagenall, Marshall of Ulster, wrote to Cecil acknowledging that the queen 'w[i]th a most Christian princlyk care' had sent over 'fforces sufficient for a p[ro]seqution' in early May. However, until the beginning of July these men, and the rest of the army in Ulster, 'were driven for want of competent p[ro]vision of victual to live only upon bread and water'. The men were 'utterly decayed' leading to 'the greate weakning of the body of tharmye'. Bagenall disregarded any suggestion that this was the result of 'the altera[ti]on of the climate' arguing instead that 'the wante of sufficient p[ro]vision of victuall for the souldier … is only and alone the very cause that o[u]r Englysh doe here so soone decaye'.[83] To rectify the situation in Ireland trade was vital and Lord Deputy Burgh suggested merchants should be encouraged to trade with '[th]e Hollanders' who 'transporte much butter and more chese owt of there province'. The English, however, were not the only ones seeking to gain provisions, and not just foodstuffs, from overseas.[84]

Given the dire situation within Ireland, it was perhaps unsurprising, albeit unwelcome, for the English to learn that '[th]e rebells … buye out of Denmarke, Skotland, and other partes, pouder, and munition to maintaine ther rebellion'.[85] Powder, like foodstuffs, spoiled easily in bad weather and was of limited supply. The situation in Ireland, combined with the threat

82 SP 63/200, fols 302v–3r.

83 SP 63/201, fol.33r. Thus, Bagenall was unable to recognise that climate and sufficient provision of victual were inextricably connected.

84 SP 63/200, fol.259v.

85 SP 63/200, fol.259v. The confession of Mahon MacDonogh in 1596 also highlighted the 'munition and weapons' the Irish gained through trade with Spain; see SP 63/192, fol.55r.

of invasion from Spain, meant that a constant supply of powder was required in England, in Ireland and at sea. During the late 1580s the English had attempted to make saltpetre in Ireland, as a means of ensuring a good and ready supply. In the wake of the Spanish Armada of 1588, and in response to ongoing requests for more powder to be sent to Ireland, the Privy Council in London tried to find an alternative solution. As the immediate Spanish threat had been removed, and to avoid the difficulty of supply and transportation, it was decided there would be 'no great use' of powder in Ireland over the winter of 1588 so a new supply would be sent in the spring of 1589. In the meantime, however, the council urged Lord Deputy William Fitzwilliam to

> inquier, whither their bee not some of that contrie birth or some borne w[i]thin this realm, *residy[n]g ther* that can skill of making salte peter, and will *mak [th]e same in [tha]t realme and* deliuer it at some reasonable price to bee converted into powder, wherby the charges of the carriage, the annoyance of the contrie here w[i]thin this realme, and the hassarde of the transportation may bee avoyded.[86]

Rather than rely on the infrequent and unreliable transportation of powder from England, the council sought to encourage manufacture of powder within Ireland. At this point such efforts were less likely to be about making Ireland self-sufficient but rather, at the very least, to ensure it could provide for its own campaigning needs over the winter.

In contrast, the Irish had no need to try to develop such manufacturing as they had a more reliable supply of powder from Scotland. In June 1595 the Privy Council in Edinburgh had complained about the inhabitants of a number of sheriffdoms in the southwest of Scotland, including Dumbarton, Tarbert, Bute, Ayr and Wigton, who 'daylie furnissis the rebellis of Irland with victuallis, waponis, poulder, bullet and uthir munitioun of weir'. Proclamation was made forbidding anyone, under pain of treason, to 'furneis and sell' either to the Highlanders and Islesmen or to the 'rebellious people of Irland' because the 'peace and amitie' between James and Elizabeth was 'gritelie endangerit' by this trade.[87] While aimed at preventing

86 SP 63/136, fols 115v–16r. The text in italics was added later and is in Cecil's hand.

87 *RPCS*, V, 223–4. This proclamation was made at this time because of reports that a force of Highlanders were 'myndit … to transporte thameselffis ouer to Irland, and

the sale of powder and munitions to the Irish, it also expressly forbade the burghs of Glagow, Ayr, Irvine, Renfrew and Dumbarton to sell 'ony kynd of victuaill', thus, hindering legitimate trade with communities in Ireland.[88] Throughout 1597 there were numerous comments on the support Tyrone and his allies received from Scotland while Cecil was informed that 'Allexander Steward a Scott dwellinge in the toune of Glasco … at one time sold to [Tyrone] … gunn powder worth two thowsand pound ster[ling] … and brought to therle from Scottland iii Scottishe workmen who maketh musketts callvers and pistolls'.[89] Before his death, Lord Deputy Burgh had planned to 'prevent the coming of powder, muni[ti]on and artillerie to therle of Tirone, and … cause to be app[re]hended one Allexander Steward (aman that doth muche furnishe the Erle w[i]th powder & muni[ti]on) … or anie other that should com thether for the hurt of' Ireland.[90] Burgh had also requested a number of times that the queen write to James VI asking him to 'restrayne his subiects' as all Tyrone's powder 'comes out of Skotland'.[91] Given past experience, this was more likely an attempt to cauterise Tyrone's source of powder than a means of getting the Scottish king to deal with his subjects. Once again, matters were interrupted, this time by Burgh's death and in October 1597 Bagenall informed Cecil of the 'intelligence that Tyrone hath greate store of powder, leade and match come to hym out of Scottland … landed at Loghfoile'.[92]

The mercenary trade between Ireland and Scotland may have been diminishing during the last years of the sixteenth century, but there was a gradual increase in trading activity across the North Channel.[93] Powder

to joyne with the Erll of Tyrrowne, O'Doneill, and uthiris of the rebellious people of that land, for the troubling of the quyet estate thairof'.

88 See p.231 n.46 below.

89 SP 63/200, fol.198.

90 SP 63/201, fol.79.

91 SP 63/200, fols 293v, 302v.

92 SP 63/201, fol.88v; SP 63/202/2, fol.29v.

93 The diminishing frequency with which Highland forces arrived into Ireland from Scotland is generally regarded as a result of the increase in clan feuding in the western Highlands and Isles. This may be so, but the feuding, no doubt, was exacerbated by the severe economic conditions caused by the harsh weather of the 1590s and the resulting run of harvest failures. See pp. 83–9 above.

along with other goods, including foodstuffs, formed much of the cargo imported into Ireland at this time. Gilbert Thomson was one of the many merchants and mariners from the southwest of Scotland who increasingly came to exploit the markets in the north of Ireland, trading with both England and Irish communities there. Indeed, during the closing years of the sixteenth century the English in Ulster would come to depend heavily on the developing trade between Scotland and Ulster, an intercourse that would be vital to their survival, and to the later plantations of the early seventeenth century. Before that trade could thrive fully, however, the English had to gain dominance of the waters of the North Channel in order to curtail the disruptive activity of the Highland Scots.

… and supremacy of the seas

During his time as Lord Deputy, John Perrot faced ongoing Irish resistance, increased unrest in the Isles, and a steady stream of Highland Scots arriving in the north, although this traffic did become more infrequent and, therefore, less reliable for the Irish. Despite having little personal experience of the Ulster context Perrot was quick to act against the Scots. Although, ultimately, he failed to expel them, it has been argued that the outbreak of war with Spain encouraged Perrot, and Elizabeth, to conclude agreement with the Scots in 1586. Under the terms of this agreement Sorley Boy MacDonnell was granted the territory of the Route which he would hold from the queen having been 'reconstituted … as an independent Irish subject with a patrimony of his own held under the Irish crown over which his Scottish relations could make no claim'. Meanwhile, the lands of the Glens of Antrim were granted to his uncle, Angus MacDonald, who 'was explicitly recognized as a subject of the Scottish crown'.[94] Brady has argued the English hoped the terms of the agreement would cause such dissent between the two branches of

94 SP 63/124, fols 60–1r; 176–7r; Ciaran Brady, 'East Ulster, the MacDonalds and the Provincial Strategies of Hugh O'Neill, Earl of Tyrone, 1585–1603', in William

the MacDonalds that they would turn in on themselves, destroy each other through infighting and thus eliminate the threat they posed to the English. There may be some truth to this but the wider situation should not be marginalised.

The threat of Spanish dominance in Atlantic waters along with the possibility of a Spanish invasion, following Elizabeth's support of the Dutch against Philip II and the outbreak of the Anglo-Spanish war in 1585, was compounded by the dominance of the Highland Scots in the North Channel which exacerbated an already tense situation.[95] Meanwhile, Perrot was just as concerned about an alliance between the Catholic Mary, Queen of Scots, and the Highlanders in the west of Scotland and north Ulster, and the possibility of a combined French or Spanish threat as well. Perrot undertook a hosting against the MacDonnells, maintaining a three-day siege of Dunluce Castle in September 1584 and garrisoning Coleraine, Carrickfergus and the friary at Bonemargy. It was an expensive campaign, however, and Elizabeth was less than pleased, especially when the following year Sorley Boy easily took back control of Dunluce. Barely pausing to catch his breath, Sorley Boy made his way to Dublin to submit to Perrot and reiterate his claim to the lands of the Route.[96] That Perrot, and Elizabeth, finally conceded to the long-repeated requests of the MacDonnells to recognise their occupation of land in Antrim and, then, to grant the Route to Sorley Boy as a subject of the English queen, speaks to the inability of the English to expel the Highland Scots. It was the end point of a policy that had been evolving ever since Elizabeth first tried to work with them in Antrim in the 1560s, as a counter to Shane O'Neill. The agreement also

---

P. Kelly and John R. Young, eds, *Scotland and the Ulster Plantations. Explorations in the British Settlements of Stuart Ireland* (Dublin, 2009), 48–9.

95 Despite the view of the superiority of English maritime power, this was not a reality at the time. Kenneth R. Andrews, *Elizabethan Privateering: English Privateering during the Spanish War 1585–1603* (Cambridge, 1964); Kenneth Andrews, *Trade, Plunder and Settlement: Maritime Enterprise and the Genesis of the British Empire, 1480–1630* (Cambridge, 1984); N. A. M. Rodger, 'Queen Elizabeth and the Myth of Sea-Power in English History', *Transactions of the Royal Historical Society* 14(2004), 153–74.

96 Breen, *Dunluce Castle*, 82–6.

underlined the problem of the fairly rapid turnover of Lord Deputies and others who served in Ireland. While men like Smith and Essex had previously advocated coming to an agreement with the MacDonnells, none of them remained in post long enough or held sustained influence in government to bring such a proposal to fruition.[97] The grant to Sorley Boy underlined local issues but also English concerns over the wider implications of a hostile presence within Ulster if it had external support. While the grant may have removed one obstacle in the north in the closing years of the sixteenth century, the English faced several more.

By 1588 Perrot had argued with and alienated many in the Dublin administration, resulting in his return to England and, although the situation with Sorley Boy MacDonnell had been fundamentally altered, this brought little relief from the, albeit increasingly sporadic, movement of Highlanders across the North Channel.[98] Indeed, while at times both the O'Neill and O'Donnell lords were eager to receive more reinforcements, on occasion the appearance of more Highlanders was unwelcome, especially if the Irish lords had promised not to recruit them as part of an agreement or truce with the English.[99] It was this wider involvement of the Highland Scots in Ulster that was so frustrating to Elizabeth and her deputies. While they could reach agreement with the MacDonnells, this did little to prevent the MacLeods, MacLeans, or other Highland clans crossing the channel to seek

97 See pp. 143–6 above.

98 For more on Perrot and his time in Ireland see amongst others Turvey, 'Perrot, Sir John (1528–1592)'; Ciaran Brady, *The Chief Governors: The Rise and Fall of Reform Government in Tudor Ireland, 1536–1588* (Cambridge, 1994); Hiram Morgan, 'The fall of Sir John Perrot', in John Guy, ed., *The Reign of Elizabeth: Court and Culture in the Last Decade* (Cambridge, 1995), 109–25; Treadwell, 'Sir John Perrot and the Irish parliament of 1585–6', 259–308.

99 SP 63/191, fol.171v. Despite hostilities the English often tried to get O'Neill and O'Donnell to agree not to hire Scottish mercenaries, but any such agreements only lasted as long as it suited the Irish lords; see Morgan, *Tyrone's Rebellion*, 163, 179–80. At the same time, Elizabeth went to significant lengths to try to prevent the Highland Scots joining with the Irish 'rebels'; see Ross Crawford, 'Noble Power in the West Highlands and Isles. James VI and the End of the Mercenary Trade with Ireland, 1594–96', in Miles Kerr-Peterson and Steven J. Reid, eds, *James VI and Noble Power in Scotland, 1578–1603* (Abingdon, 2017), 117–35.

employment in Ireland and a concerted effort was required by the English in the light of the dominance of the Highlanders in the North Channel. In general, the extent of English shipping in the North Channel was not sufficient to intercept or challenge the movement of the Highland Scots while the lack of any suitable harbour or haven on the north Antrim coast, other than Carrickfergus or Olderfleet, was problematic and caused further difficulties. The location of both these garrisons on the east coast did little to facilitate English penetration into the west or hamper Highlander traffic into Lough Foyle, now their main destination.[100] The naval presence charged with patrolling the North Channel consisted largely of one pinnace, the *Popinjay*, throughout the later 1580s and 1590s.[101] During a time of increased unrest across Ulster leading to the outbreak of rebellion led by the earl of Tyrone, combined with ongoing disorder in the Isles with widespread clan feuding, most notably between the MacDonalds of Dunivaig and the MacLeans of Duart, this was far from adequate.[102] The North Channel situation needs to be placed within the wider archipelagic context of ongoing fear and suspicion regarding a Spanish invasion force, alongside the hardship caused by harvest failure and harsh weather conditions. Consequently, anxiety within the English ruling administration reached something of a crescendo in 1596.

Patience with the Highland Scots and their involvement in Ulster was, understandably, wearing thin on the part of the English government by the mid-1590s. Sir Geoffrey Fenton, a senior civil servant in Ireland and commissioner for Ulster and Connacht, wrote disparagingly of the Highland Scots, referring to them as 'a needy and beggarly people … not easely expelled owt of a contrey, where they haue once taken footing', mentioning specifically 'the Rowte and the Glynnes in the north of Ulster' where they

100 The preferred route was from Lochindaal in Islay to Lough Foyle in Ulster, taking them from MacDonald territory to the lands of Tyrone and Tyrconnell.

101 SP 63/209/1, fol.54r. On 12 August 1601 Sir Henry Docwra noted the *Tramontane* was also patrolling the Irish seas although it is likely *Tramontane* replaced *Popinjay*; see Rodger, *Safeguard of the Sea*, 289; McGurk, *Elizabethan Conquest of Ireland*, appendix.

102 Gerald A. Hayes-McCoy, *Scots Mercenary Forces in Ireland (1565–1603)* (Dublin, 1937), 181–5, 187–262.

had 'setled longe since and yet the Crowne of England can not to this day expulse them'. He added that it had always been 'an auncient … rule' of England 'to kepe the Scottes out of the north, for ther wyld and barbarous pretences they haue to some p[ar]tes there'.[103] According to the terms of the 1586 grant to Sorley Boy, the MacDonnells were now subjects of the English crown but Fenton could not envisage any advantage in working with the Highland Scots against the Irish, as Elizabeth had done briefly in the 1560s. He advocated their expulsion from Ulster arguing that the Irish 'rebells of Ulster' would not 'be puld downe by the Scotts of Cantyre or the Ilandes, for dogges will not eate dogges flesh'.[104] To contend with the regular arrival of Highlanders into Ulster the English reverted to traditional policy, sending 'the Popinjay … to occupie the northern seas, to attend the doinges of the Scottes, and to cross their cominge asmuch as she maii'.[105] Reliance on the *Popinjay* and Captain Thornton was simply inadequate given the maritime superiority of the Highlanders and their galleys.[106]

By the end of the sixteenth century shipbuilding developments meant the English crown could call on a technically advanced fleet of warships, alongside smaller galleys and pinnaces.[107] In the North Channel, however, alongside the ever-faithful *Popinjay*, the English continued to deploy old, traditional vessels that were unsuited to the conditions there and no match for the Highland galleys. Despite this, the English inflicted a notable and significant defeat on the Highlanders and Islesmen in 1595. Earlier in the summer of that year a force of around 3,000 Highland Scots had assembled,

103 SP 63/197, fol.298r.
104 SP 63/197, fol.298v.
105 SP 63/191, fol.174.
106 The English also struggled to counter the Irish off the west coast. In September 1600 Myghell Lynch, Mayor of Galway, wrote to Sir Robert Cecil complaining about 'the contyning roades used by the Maylies and Fflaherties w[i]th their gallies, alonge our costes, where they have taken sondrye shippes and barques bounde for this poore towne'; see SP 63/207/5, fol.168.
107 Alison Cathcart, 'The Maritime Dimension to Plantation in Ulster, ca.1550–ca.1600', *Maritime Communities of the North Atlantic Arc in the Early Modern Period: Journal of the North Atlantic,* ed., Alison Cathcart, special volume 12 (2019), 104.

ready to sail to Ireland.[108] Internal dissent resulted in some delay and disorientation with the fleet divided. One section arrived in Lough Foyle, were met by Red Hugh O'Donnell, and carried out some service before returning to Scotland.[109] The main force, however, landed at Carrickfergus much to the frustration of Tyrone who had been awaiting its arrival for some months. This section of the fleet moored off the Copelands Islands, at the southern entrance to Belfast Lough, just a short distance away and within sight of the town.[110] The ever-reliable Captain Thornton on the *Popinjay* and Captain Gregory Rigges on the *Charles*, who had been at Olderfleet, received intelligence of their location from a merchant ship; a vessel the Highlanders had not long before attacked, relieving the captain of its cargo.[111] The Highlanders and Islesmen were hindered by the tidal currents around the islands which Thornton, having the advantage of surprise, was able to navigate more effectively.[112] Cut off from the mainland, unable to make contact with Tyrone, and unable to escape they were surrounded by Thornton and his fleet who gained assistance from the garrison

108 *CSP Scotland*, XI, no.85, and appendix (694). In July 1593 Robert Bowes wrote to Cecil informing him that 'a rabble of thieves of Kintyre, Argyle and the Isle of Arran, to the number of 500 men' were 'gathered together purposing to invade the Isle of Man'. Notice had been given to 'the Captain of the Isle of Man' in an effort to repel this force. Given the increasing concerns about the Spanish and the Highlanders more attention was being paid to the waters of the North Channel.

109 SP 52/56, fol.92.

110 The Copeland Islands are situated off the southern entrance to Belfast Lough. On 3 August 1595 Sir Ralph Lane wrote to Cecil that 'in the greate Ardis, there are landed 55 Scottish gallies with Skottes (as they said) 4000 – but not beleved to be soemany'; see SP 63/182, fol.121r. Tyrone was said to be 'in Clandeboy, taking up cowes for' the Scots; see SP 63/182, fol.46.

111 SP 52/56, fols 92, 94–5; SP 63/182, fol.6v. The attack occurred on 28 July.

112 The tidal currents around the islands may have contributed significantly. S. A. Royle, 'Island Life off Co. Down: The Copeland Islands', *Ulster Journal of Archaeology*, third series 57 (1994), 177–82 states (177) 'the sounds between the islands and the coast and within the archipelago are treacherous and there have been a number of shipwrecks'. That said, the Highlanders had spent the previous evening drinking the wine they had acquired from the merchant vessel and possibly were in no fit state to repel Thornton's early morning attack.

at Carrickfergus just across the lough.[113] During the attack a number of gallies were sunk and some men were killed.[114] The Islesmen themselves were forced to take refuge on the Copeland Islands and, although there was some fighting, the size and landscape of the islands did not offer any hope of resistance.[115] Realising the situation, the Islesmen surrendered and gave hostages for their return to Scotland, although not before they offered themselves in service to the queen.[116] Indeed, even after they had been allowed to return to Scotland, Donald Gorm MacDonald of Sleat wrote to the Lord Deputy clearly stating his intention to provide men for the queen's service, so long as he was satisfied with the conditions of pay.[117] Later they went a step further and offered to switch sides to fight for Elizabeth.[118] Having given pledges the main leaders were allowed to return to Scotland under certain

113 *CSP Scotland*, XI, no.633; *CSP Ireland*, V, 364 (26 I).

114 Writing with news of the defeat John Morgan declared that 'seaven of their gallies [were] suncke'; SP 63/182, fol.46. A later report from Rowland Savage, however, stated that two gallies were sunk, two were taken by the English and one ran ashore as it tried to escape; see SP 63/182, fol.110. Captain Thorton stated that twelve gallies were damaged and thirteen or fourteen men were killed; see SP 63/182, fol.197r. See also SP 63/182, fol.200.

115 On 10 August Nicolson wrote to inform Bowes that Captain Thornton had previously 'sunk, near the Isle of Rathlin, thirteen of the islesmen's galleys'. The rest of the fleet had 'spoiled Clandeboy's country and … gone with the spoils to the isle of Copeland' where they were ambushed; see *CSP Scotland*, XI, no.633 (676–8). It is highly likely that the fleet had been separated with some ending up at Rathlin, others at Carrickfergus and others at Lough Foyle. As reported to Nicolson, since the fleet of Islesmen left for Ireland, the storms had been 'sua great in thir partes'; see SP 52/56, fol.67v.

116 *CSP Ireland*, V, 359, no.9; 369–70, no.43 I-IV; 370, no.44.

117 *CSP Ireland*, V, 359, no.9. MacLean reiterated his offers to the queen (see *CSP Scotland*, XI, no.641), and wrote to James assuring his loyalty to the Scottish crown (see NLS Adv. MS 29.2.6., fol.116).

118 SP 63/182, fol.43. In doing so, Donald Gorm MacDonald highlighted the 'ould band betwixt the Crowne of England' and his predecessors, adding that he now wanted to 'uphold that course'. In offering to serve the queen, however, MacDonald did state that his obedience to 'the king of Scottes' was 'excepted'.

conditions.[119]

It has been argued that 'the 1595 campaign had emphatically told the islanders that they would no longer be able to sail unchallenged' but such a view needs greater nuance.[120] On the face of it, the defeat signalled the growing dominance of a superior English fleet but, in reality, it was a combination of luck and circumstance: good intelligence, the ever-present Captain Thornton and factors beyond the control of the English, namely weather conditions, tidal currents and the earlier opportunistic plundering of an unfortunate passing merchant ship.[121] Aside from such opportunistic attacks, the English could only hope to contend fully with the Highlanders at sea if they were prepared to commit the men, appropriate vessels and resources required. This defeat has also been regarded as a factor in the decline of the Scottish mercenary trade to Ireland. This may be so, but it was only a part of a much larger, more complex and gradual process taking place across the archipelago during the latter years of the sixteenth century.[122] Nonetheless, victory was important for the English, affording them the confidence that they could challenge the Highlanders at sea. This was much needed as the following year rumours of a renewed Spanish invasion intensified.

Any euphoria at the victory over the Highland Scots at the Copeland Islands was short-lived. While the Highland Scots would return, increasingly arriving into Lough Foyle in the northwest, rumours regarding

119 SP 63/182, fols 46, 196–7, 198, 199, 200. MacDonald stated that his intention to return to Scotland was because he had 'no vittles' in Ireland and said he 'would not hurt anie of her Ma[jes]tes' subjects; see SP 63/182, fol.43.

120 Crawford, 'Noble Power in the West Highlands and Isles', 126.

121 Royle, 'Island Life off Co. Down', 177 and n.112 above highlights the challenging currents around the Copelands, much like those between Rathlin Island and the north Antrim coast. While there also had been reports of storms at the time this was certainly not a shipwreck. Given the conditions of wind and wave, probably the Highlanders felt safe mooring where they did. The English were able to inflict defeat because of intelligence regarding the location of the Highland fleet, the element of surprise and the fact the fleet was stationary.

122 For more on this see Crawford, 'Noble Power in the West Highlands and Isles', 125–7.

Strangford Lough in the southeast of Ulster heightened English concern in August 1596. The English were informed that

> Odonell hath undertaken to the Spanish king to entertayne in to his service; out of his Mothers Allyence in Kenteere … 3000 redshanks with theyr gallis; with which hee [the Spanish king] will possesse him of such a porte in Ulster as being putt in to the possession of 1,000 Spanyardes, maye by them alone be holden unrecou[er]-ably against all the forces by land or sea that cann bee brought against them; that shall give him entrie in to Dublin when hee will, and … footing for garrisons bothe in England and Scotland …. [123]

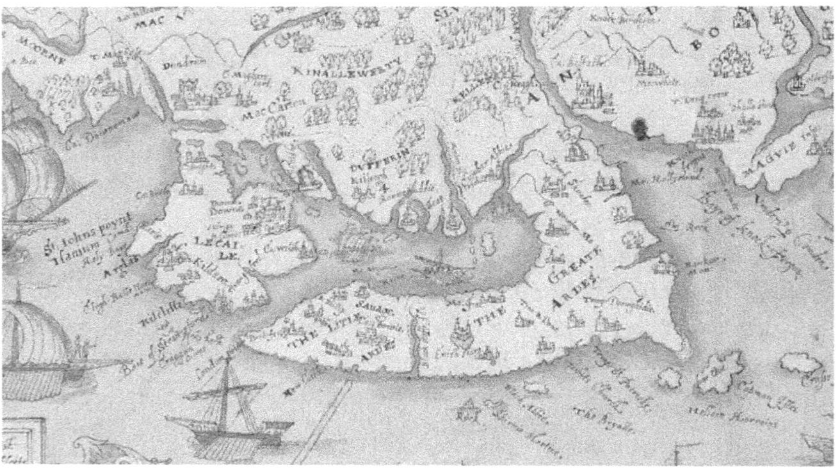

P/49 (25) (L9622): East part of Ulster [1601] with detail of Strangford Lough. © National Maritime Museum, Greenwich, London.

This 'porte' was Strangford Lough and the English believed Philip II would try to take it, recognising its numerous advantages as a base for naval and military operations throughout the three kingdoms, so the need to fortify 'the mouthe of yt' was of utmost importance.[124] Indeed, there had been repeated attempts to strengthen the English presence in

123 SP 63/192, fol.124r.
124 SP 63/192, fol.124v.

this area in previous decades. Ringhaddy Castle, Mahee Castle and Castle Ward are remains that point to English efforts to establish settlements around the lough during the 1570s.[125] In the light of English fears of a renewed Spanish invasion, the ongoing rebellion in Ireland and the links between Ireland and Spain, there was a growing concern over the vulnerability of Strangford Lough. The Spanish could not be allowed to gain a foothold in Ireland but reports that Tyrone was seeking information on the area, attempting to ascertain 'what harbo[u]r the river of Stranford was, and whether ane great shipping might come into yt' and 'whether the Castle of Strangford were of ane strength' were disconcerting for the English.[126] The Castle of Dundrum, located further south on the coast, if 'possessed by therle of Tyrone' could be 'deliu[er]ed unto … anie other forrane nation'.[127] Indeed, if Strangford Lough, albeit a safe haven and able 'to contayne all the fleetes of shippes or gallis that England hathe or Spayne can make', were to fall under Spanish control it would be extremely dangerous for the English both in Ireland and at home.[128]

Co-operation between Tyrone and the Spanish would not be welcome, though hardly unsurprising given the ongoing support (albeit little that was tangible) the Irish had received from Spain since the 1530s. The possibility of such an eventuality was exacerbated by rumours emerging late in 1597 of 'a capitula[ti]on betwixt hyme [Tyrone] and the Scottes' and 'the coming of a great number of' Highland Scots into Ulster.[129] Further reports of the Highlanders' arrival, alongside rumours of a Spanish attack, and the arrival of Spanish aid for Tyrone and his allies were rife at court during the late 1590s and increased efforts were made to defend Ireland. The triangulation of England's enemies turned the focus once more on Ulster and, despite concerns over the vulnerability of Strangford Lough,

125 Audrey Horning, *Ireland in the Virginian Sea. Colonialism in the British Atlantic* (Chapel Hill, 2013), 67–8.

126 SP 63/192, fols 31r–2r, at 31v.

127 SP 63/192, fol.32r. Its location meant it could be well supplied by ship. Previously the English believed Shane O'Neill had desired to take control of Strangford Lough; see SP 63/20, fols 104, 113v.

128 SP 63/192, fol.124r.

129 SP 63/201, fol.88v.

increasingly to Lough Foyle and Lough Swilly in the northwest where the Scots frequently arrived, largely unhindered. To secure Ireland from external threats, to turn the tide against the Scots and to make any progress against Tyrone, the English needed to make inroads into this northwest region and command greater supremacy of those seas.[130] However, despite advances in shipbuilding technology, the reliance on typical larger, traditional-style galleys that, for the most part, were unsuitable for those waters, the coastline and tidal streams ensured limited effectiveness of English efforts in the North Channel. With these vessels, individuals like Thornton were unable to take action against pirates when the opportunity presented itself, and despite the unexpected victories such as that off the Copeland Islands in 1595, a sustained, secure presence in the region required greater resources and more effective action if the English were to counter the maritime dominance of the Highland Scots and their galleys.

The shortest crossing between Ulster and Scotland remained that between Torr Head on the north Antrim Coast and Kintyre, but for a number of reasons the preferred destination for the Scots was Lough Foyle and Lough Swilly. Tidal currents in these waters were notoriously difficult to navigate, especially those between the northern coast and Rathlin

130 Concern over the vulnerability of Strangford Lough remained; see Horning, *Ireland in the Virginian Sea*, 78–81. Sir Ralph Lane began petitioning the queen shortly after his return from the failed Roanoke endeavour but it was not until 1598 that he was granted lands between Belfast and Carrickfergus. By the terms of the grant he was 'empowered to take from the woodmen of those parts, such bonnaghts as they have answered to the earl of Tyrone or the Scots, if he can win the good will of the captains of those countries' ('Entry 6235' in *The Irish Fiants of the Tudor Sovereigns during the Reigns of Henry VIII, Edward VI, Philip and Mary, and Elizabeth I*, III, *1585–1603* (Dublin, 1875, reprinted 1994), 326 quoted in Horning, *Ireland in the Virginian Sea*, 78). However, as argued by Horning, Lane recognised the 'greater economic and political significance' of the lands around Strangford Lough and, later in 1602, wrote to Cecil expounding on the fertility of the region (SP 63/210, fol.154), while also including a document (fols 156r–8v) entitled 'A Discouery of an unavoydable ruyn to both the kingdoms, no less of England then of Ireland in the Riuer of Strangford, and the Lough Cone [Strangford Lough], lefte open to be entred, if the Spanish fleete (expected in Ulster) should aryue at Calebegg; And a Proiect to [th]e meanes to secure and saue all, so as the tyme be not forslowed till theire aryuall … '.

Island, at times even for the Highlanders themselves whose knowledge of the waters and their galleys gave them mastery of the North Channel.[131] Thus, the less challenging route took them straight to the west of Ulster where, in a region with a minimal English presence, there was less chance of encountering English vessels; both loughs also offered shelter from bad weather. The earlier attempt to establish a garrison at Derry, on the edge of the River Foyle in the 1560s, as a means of gaining a foothold in the northwest region had ended in abject failure. Poorly resourced from the outset and left isolated without shipping, it is no surprise the garrison was unable to withstand an assault that resulted in the garrison being burned.[132] Although the earl of Essex advised the queen that a garrison at Lough Foyle would be best placed to impede the Irish and the Highland Scots, it was not until Tyrone's rebellion in the 1590s that concerted efforts were made to follow that up. In October 1597 Bagenall advised Cecil to set up strong garrisons in locations 'where they may both border nearest the rebell to annoy hym, and by sea be relieued w[i]th victuall … w[i]thout any … daunger'.[133] The English needed to extend their authority into the northwest to counter the (albeit already diminishing) flow of Highland mercenaries into that region but there was an awareness of the difficulties they faced in establishing a garrison at Derry.[134] In 1598 a 'discource' argued that the Dutch were 'the fittest and aptest' to colonise Ulster because they had 'the greatest store of shippes of any men' and were the 'best staplers of victuaille in all the worlde'. In short, the discourse argued, the 'unaptness' of the English nation to do so meant that ongoing attempts to establish a

131 Wallace Clark, 'Tides in the Waters of the Moyle', *The Glynns: Journal of the Glens of Antrim Historical Society*, 6 (1978), <https://antrimhistory.net/index-of-the-glynns-volume-6-1978/>, accessed 18 February 2019; see p.103 n.45 above.

132 SP 63/20, fols 51–2, 104, 113, 148, 174. The report of 12 May 1567 stated that the fire began 'in a smithes forge'.

133 SP 63/201, fols 33–4. For other proposals regarding the establishment of a garrison there see SP 63/191, fols 239v–40v. At this point Bagenal was feeling the full strength of O'Neill's power in the north. He had had to relieve and revictual the garrisons at Newry and Armagh, but in attempting to supply the Blackwater Fort in August 1598 he was killed by O'Neill's forces at the Battle of Yellow Ford.

134 SP 63/202/2, fol.90r.

garrison at Derry would 'expose themself to … much hassarde and small certeinty'.[135]

Soon after the arrival of Charles Blount, Lord Mountjoy, as Lord Deputy in February 1600, however, Sir Henry Docwra received his commission to plant garrisons at Derry and along the River Foyle, and in Lough Erne towards Beleek and Ballyshannon.[136] Docwra had served previously in Ireland under Sir Richard Bingham when the latter was appointed as President of Connacht. Indeed it was during his time in Connacht with Bingham that Docwra gained experience of 'amphibious tactics, siege techniques, ambushes, open-field fighting, and the hunting down of rebel forces in bogland and thickets', and this was invaluable in his later efforts to establish a garrison at Derry.[137] Bingham, like Sidney, Sussex, Essex and others, is one of a number of English officials who gained a reputation for being harsh or ineffective. Nonetheless, while these interpretations may be fair, it is important to acknowledge their appreciation of geographic awareness and the need for a maritime strategy.[138] Bingham had enjoyed a successful and varied military, naval and diplomatic career prior to his arrival in Ireland in 1579 to assist in supressing the Desmond rebellion. His career began when he was part of a force that accompanied Protector Somerset to Scotland in 1547; afterwards he fought alongside the Spanish against the French at the battle of St Quentin in 1557; he later fought with the Spanish and Venetians under Don John of Austria against the Turks, and may have fought at the Battle of Lepanto in 1572; in 1573–74 he was in the Low Countries reporting to Cecil on the conflict with the Spanish. As well as this international service, he had some experience of the North Channel context, having been part of the expedition to the western Isles of Scotland in 1558 led by the then Lord Deputy Sussex.[139] His naval experience

135 SP 63/202/4, fols 232–6, at 233v–4r. This was reinforced in 1604 when Richard Hudson advocated inviting the Dutch to inhabit Lough Foyle; see SP 63/216, fols 180r–1v, 'A Discourse presented to the King's Majesty touching Ireland' by Richard Hudson; see pp. 253–7 below.

136 SP 63/207/1, fol.200r; McGurk, *Sir Henry Docwra*, fig. 1.

137 McGurk, *Sir Henry Docwra*, 29.

138 McGurk, *Elizabethan Conquest of Ireland*, 7.

139 Bernadette Cunningham, 'Bingham, Sir Richard (1527/8–1599), *soldier and president of Connacht*', *ODNB*, accessed 19 August 2016.

and expertise contributed to his appointment as captain of the *Swiftsure* in 1580. Having countered the Spanish and Italian forces who landed at Smerwick Harbour in Kerry to support James FitzMaurice FitzGerald, he was still on the *Swiftsure* three years later, although by this time he was admiral with orders to apprehend pirates on the Narrow Seas. In 1584 he was appointed as President of Connacht and it is from this period of service that Bingham acquired his reputation: his presidency is said to have pushed the Irish into open rebellion. Described in the Irish annals as 'the greatest monster of all the English that were then in Ireland', much of the criticism levelled at him was also the result of factionalism, having fallen victim to 'personal animosities' within the Dublin administration.[140] Indeed Sir John Perrot, during his time as Lord Deputy, resented Bingham's success to the extent that Bingham believed all of his military successes in Connacht had been undermined by Perrot.[141] A different view of Bingham, however, is gained if close attention is paid to an alternative 'eyewitness' perspective.[142]

Sir Henry Docwra's *The Narration of Services done by the Army Ymployed to Lough-Foyle*, a tract written before Bingham's appointment as President, details his service and the experience Docwra gained serving under him.[143] Bingham recognised the need for knowledge of the terrain and geography of Connacht and commissioned John Browne to draw up a map of Mayo for him although, as more recently suggested, the 'topographical inaccuracies'

140 Cunningham, 'Bingham, Sir Richard' quoting from L. Ó Cléirigh, *The life of Aodh Ruadh Ó Domhnaill*, ed., P. Walsh and C. Ó Lochlainn, 2 vols, (Dublin: Irish Text Society, 1948–57), I, 101.

141 Cunningham, 'Bingham, Sir Richard'. However, at the end of 1596 when the English were planning a three-pronged attack against the Irish in the north, with one army sent to Armagh, another to Connacht and the third to Lough Foyle, members of the council in Dublin advised Cecil that Sir Richard Bingham 'in regard of his goode experience & knowledge of all the portes of the north, mighte have the charge' of the army sent to Derry; see SP 63/195, fol.71v.

142 McGurk, *Sir Henry Docwra*, 23–37.

143 For the *Narration of Services done …* see 'Docwra's Tracts', in *Miscellany of the Celtic* Society, ed. J. O'Donovan (Dublin, 1849), 187–325; *Docwra's Derry: A Narration of Events in North-West Ulster 1600–1604: The 1849 O'Donovan Edition*, ed. William P. Kelly (Belfast, 2003), preface. An interesting analysis of *Narration* has been provided by McGurk, *Sir Henry Docwra*, 23–37.

must have proved more of a hindrance than a help to military men.[144] Nonetheless, Docwra also recorded how, having intelligence of a Scottish attack, Bingham gathered 'information on their movements from the Erne loughs and rivers into Sligo', while Docwra received experience of military strategy, combined hostings of horse and foot, and 'the use of flat-bottomed boats, such as the long Highland galleys', all of which would be utilised later in Ulster.[145] Part of the plan incorporating the commission to Docwra to establish a garrison at Derry was to take English forces into the heartland of the northwest to frustrate the activities of both O'Donnell of Tyrconnell and Tyrone. Indeed, the plantation at Lough Foyle was to be 'an iron hook in the nostrils of Tyrone to hold him hard and entangle him at home'.[146] Despite the various, and usual, setbacks of lack of pay, lack of victuals, poor weather and a lack of experienced pilots to navigate into Lough Foyle, Docwra arrived at Derry in mid-May 1600.[147] Although Derry was the main focus of Docwra's commission, further garrisons were established at Culmore, the Inishowen headland at the mouth of Lough Foyle, and further upstream at Donnalong.[148] In doing so Docwra certainly was not the first English officer in Ireland to utilise amphibious methods to deal with the Irish but he was best placed to do so, located as he was in the remote northwest, on the banks of the River Foyle with direct access to Lough Foyle, and a short distance from Lough Swilly and the sea. Here

144 McGurk, *Sir Henry Docwra*, 30.

145 McGurk, *Sir Henry Docwra*, 34–5. Docwra went on to gain additional experience, serving with Essex in the Netherlands before his appointment to Derry. Thus, the military men appointed to service in Ireland often had cut their teeth elsewhere, bringing to the country a range of experience and perspective, yet required to adjust that to the specifics of the Irish context.

146 O'Donovan, *Miscellany of the Celtic Society*, 238; McGurk, *Sir Henry Docwra*, 51–2, 54, 56.

147 SP 63/207/3, fols 156–71.

148 SP 63/23, fol.74 ix; SP 63/24, fols 20, 25. For locations of these garrisons see Hayes-McCoy, *Early Irish Maps*, no.XVI; and p. 211 below. Donnalong had been built by Turlough Luineach O'Neill just further north along the River Foyle from the old settlement at Strabane. The garrison at Lifford was situated on the opposite banks of the River Foyle from Strabane, obviously intended to strengthen the area as Lifford Castle had been a stronghold of the O'Donnells.

he put into practice much of what he learned from his time in Connacht where fords, island dwellings, loughs and rivers were an all too frequent encounter.[149]

Maps, drawings and plans by Richard Bartlett (Barthelet) and others, 1587–1625, A plot of Logh Foyle brought over by Cap. Covert, 1600. Reproduced courtesy of the National Library of Ireland, NLI MS 2656 (16).

149 Docwra's account of an attack on Derry by the O'Donnells in 1600 highlights how the the horses 'were visually euery night brought into the Iland to Graze'; see Kelly, ed., *Docwra's Derry*, 77. Derry was referred to as an island (or 'the Derry') at this stage because, before the reclamation and draining of land in later centuries, the settlement was encompassed by the River Foyle on three sides with a bog to the west side (hence the 'Bogside'). The following year Docwra successfully made inroads into the Inishowen peninsula and secured the only island in Lough Swilly, Inch Island, and placed a number of soldiers from Sir Richard Bingham's garrison at Rathmullan; see McGurk, *Sir Henry Docwra*, 108. For references to the English taking islands in loughs from the Irish, see SP 63/208/3, fol.223v.

Docwra had an uphill battle on his hands in his attempt to establish a garrison at Lough Foyle and in the early months he expressed concern about supply of powder. While Derry was militarily strategic in the war against Tyrone and his allies and in efforts to counter the Highland Scots, the English were keen to exploit the natural resources of the region although this would not be straightforward. During his time at Derry, Docwra regularly sent reports to London with 'fulsome descriptions of the natural richness of his location' but, at the same time, was quick to reiterate the devastation inflicted on the land during the rebellion, compounded by successive harvest failures, and the difficulty in reaping what resources survived. He pointedly remarked that while there was a good source of timber nearby, 'there was not a sticke brought home but was first well fought for'.[150] Docwra also noted the excellent fishing grounds the Foyle offered ranging from cod and herring at the estuary to salmon and trout further upstream; there were slate and stone quarries and an abundance of lime too.[151] Docwra was not the first to recognise the potential of Derry as a port and the commercial activity that could develop there. Previous O'Donnell lords of Tyrconnell had maintained a thriving trade with the continent from their base on the banks of the Foyle and Swilly, with Manus O'Donnell regarded by the English as the 'best lord of fish in Ireland' which he 'exchangeth … with foreign merchants for wine, by which [he] is called … the king of fish'.[152] From the English perspective Lough Foyle was more suitable for access by their larger vessels because of its deep waters, providing plenty of safe anchorage, unlike the River Bann to the east; further inland towards Derry, Lifford and Strabane the river becomes shallower with a narrow channel suitable only for smaller craft. Indeed, in 1595 the *Popinjay* was sent to Strabane to take Turlough Luineach

150 McGurk, *Sir Henry Docwra*, 67; Kelly, ed., *Docwra's Derry*, 44.

151 SP 63/207/3, fols 146–9; SP 63/207/6, fols 221–3r.

152 *CCM*, I, no.229; Brendan Bradshaw, 'Manus 'The Magnificent': O'Donnell as Renaissance Prince', in Art Cosgrove and Donal McCartney, eds, *Studies in Irish History Presented to R. Dudley Edwards* (Dublin, 1979), 15–36, at 18; for a fuller discussion of the fish trade that Irish lords engaged in, either directly or indirectly, see Gardiner and McNeill, 'Seaborne trade'.

O'Neill to Dublin following his surrender in 1593 in return for a pension, while contemporary sketch maps of the garrisons Docwra established show boats in the water at both Derry and Donnalong.[153] With the river suitable for navigation, and the island of Derry a strategic location for a garrison, the English regarded the whole valley of the River Foyle as rich in natural resources that could be exploited fully either by the settlements there or exported. Within a short time, Docwra's enthusiasm at the potential for a thriving garrison at Derry soon dissipated, only to be replaced with a growing desperation at the state of affairs.[154] His lengthy reports detailed the scarcity at Derry and the need for provisions.[155] In November 1600 he informed the Privy Council that he and his men had been relieved only through trade with a Dutchman who brought 'biefe, hearing, cabages' and other provisions from Scotland.[156] This was an early indication of the growing trade at Derry but few could have predicted the events that would ensure significant development at Derry over the next two decades.

During this brief period, the opening decade of the seventeenth century, Ireland was changed irrevocably. The defeat of the Irish forces at Kinsale in 1601 and the subsequent submission of Tyrone to Mountjoy, Lord Lieutenant of Ireland, in early 1603 brought an end to war in Ireland. Unknown to him, Tyrone's submission coincided with the death of Elizabeth and was followed by the succession of James VI of Scotland to the thrones of England and Ireland. These events overtook Docwra's concerns regarding Derry as the cross-channel context was changed entirely almost overnight. The ending of Tyrone's rebellion was a catalyst,

153 Henry A. Jefferies, 'O'Neill, Sir Turlough Luineach (*c.*1530–1595)', *ODNB*, accessed 4 July 2017; McGurk, *Sir Henry Docwra*, 63, 64, 72. Turlough Luineach received prior information and fled to 'a neighbouring ruin' where he stayed until his death in September that year. See p.211 above.

154 Early in September 1601 Docwra wrote that they had been 'abandoned from all trade and traffique of marchannts, since the yssuyng of this newe coyne'; see SP 63/209/1, fol.131. Consequently, on 15 October 1601 the want of victuals and men at Lough Foyle was highlighted; see SP 63/209/2, fol.73r. On 23 February Docwra wrote that the 'miseries of the place increase daiely'; see SP 63/212, fol.327v.

155 SP 63/207/4, fols 34r, 253r–4r; SP 63/207/5, fols 3r–5v.

156 SP 63/207/6, fol.26r.

ensuring an abrupt halt to the already diminishing travel of mercenaries from Scotland into Ireland; while Tyrone himself went from 'rebel' to rehabilitation at the court of James VI and I, much to the disgust of many in England.[157] The English had failed to alleviate their concerns about the security of Ireland, and the arrival of the Spanish in 1601 only confirmed those fears; they had failed to adequately supply their army in Ireland with either munitions, men or victuals; and they had completely failed to assert their supremacy of the seas. Indeed, while the fleet patrolling the Narrow Seas may have been more technologically advanced and nimble in the water, Dowcra wrote to the Privy Council in November 1600 informing them of the arrival of 180 Highland Scots who looked for employment with O'Donnell. In response, Docwra had commanded Captain Thornton to 'ly in waight … for their returne' but lamented on how ineffective this would be: Thornton's 'ship so yll indures the seas, that he complaynes he is not able to ly out in a storme, nor can doe good upon those [Highland] galleys, they are so swifte of sayle, and he so slowe'.[158] Within a few years, however, and in the context of the early seventeenth century, such supremacy of the North Channel mattered less and less as new communities began to establish their presence on those waters.[159]

157 Only to join Rory O'Donnell and Cuconnaught Maguire in the 'Flight' to Spain in September 1607. This event, followed the next year by the rebellion of Sir Cahir O'Doherty in Derry in April 1068, left the way clear for James to consider plantation in Ulster on a much grander scale than previously envisaged. There is significant debate over the causes of the flight but on this see David Finnegan, Éamonn Ó Ciardha and Marie-Claire Peters, eds, *The Flight of the Earls: Imeacht na nIarlaí* (Derry, 2010). For more on these events within an archipelagic context see my own article in that volume ('The view from Scotland: the Scottish context to the flight of the earls', 132–39) and Alison Cathcart, 'The Statutes of Iona: The Archipelagic Context', *Journal of British Studies* 49/1 (2010), 4–27.

158 SP 63/207/6, fol.28.

159 SP 63/209/1, fol.213r.

P/49 (25) (L9622): East part of Ulster [1601] with detail of North Channel.

CHAPTER 6

Clanship and commerce

Plantation in a North Channel context

The extent to which James VI offered real and tangible support for Hugh O'Neill, second Earl of Tyrone, during his rebellion against the English crown in the 1590s is difficult to ascertain from the evidence. Given James' reluctance, and arguably his inability, to prevent his Highland subjects moving freely and readily across the North Channel (largely because in the 1580s he had been quite happy to turn a blind eye to any disorder they caused in Ireland), Elizabeth and her council were wary of the Scottish king's motives. By the 1590s, James was more concerned with pacifying unrest on both sides of the channel, but he was not in a position to effect any meaningful change and needed to delegate this to his ruling regional lords. The English interpreted James' inaction as complicity in assisting Tyrone, but they also had concerns about James' pardoning of his Catholic earls on account of the rumours of Spanish aid for an invasion involving Scottish and Irish allies, and the king's own flirtation with conversion to Catholicism.[1] Viewed within this wider

1 Jenny Wormald, 'James VI and I (1566–1625), king of Scotland, England and Ireland', *ODNB*, accessed 26 February 2019. As argued by Wormald, and evidence in correspondence in *Calendar of Letters and State Papers Relating to English Affairs Preserved in, or Originally Belonging to, the Archives of Simancas,* ed., Martin A. S. Hume, vol. IV (London, 1899), there were rumours the king was open to conversion to Catholicism but could not display this publicly. The real motive was to prevent a Catholic contender for the English throne coming forward but rumours that James would convert continued for a decade. However, most foreign ambassadors were unconvinced by such suggestions. See *CSP Simancas*, IV, nos 5 (4), 31 (30), 33 (32), 52 (51–4), 65 (65), 71 (71), 90 (86), 93 (92), 108 (107), 173 (167), 367 (362); and see also no.617 (603–6).

context, James' support for Tyrone, whether apparent or real, was a significant threat to English security; but there was another important dimension to this rumoured cross-channel co-operation. If, as the reports suggested, Tyrone was getting powder from Scotland it was further evidence of the growing trade between the west of Scotland and north of Ireland during the closing years of the sixteenth century. The mercenary trade was already in a gradual decline as the English continued their efforts to patrol the narrow stretch of water; meanwhile Scottish merchants saw potential markets among the new settlements and English garrisons along the north coast. Men like Gilbert Thomson in the late 1580s and 1590s tried to capitalise on the developing trade with Ireland and the opportunities markets there offered. While Tyrone may have acquired powder in the 1590s in his war against the English, Sir Henry Docwra's garrison at Derry survived from 1600 onwards because of the victuals he could procure from these merchants. The opening years of the seventeenth century saw the situation in the North Channel dramatically altered. Ireland no longer offered Highland Scots the same opportunity for employment as a fighting force and while some took to piracy, thus potentially exacerbating maritime violence in the western Isles and North Channel, James VI and I had to make a more sustained effort to pacify his Highlands and Isles which were 'farre out of order'.[2] Given the proximity of Ulster to the western Isles, the North Channel context increasingly demanded his attention. How best to deal with his Gaelic subjects while asserting some level of control over them and their involvement in Ireland developed throughout the 1580s and 1590s and came to involve the 'rooting out or transporting the barbarous and stubborne sort, and planting ciuilitie in their roomes'.[3]

2 SP63/53, fol.62. The problem of piracy in the Irish Sea is the subject of an ESRC-funded PhD studentship at the University of Stirling, see Scott Carballo, 'Piracy in the Irish Sea: Sovereignty, Economy and the Scottish Western Burghs, 1560–1630' (in progress).

3 James VI, *Basilicon Doran* in Johann P. Sommerville, ed., *King James VI and I. Political Writings* (Cambridge, 1994), 24.

James VI, the Highland 'dilemma' and his 'civilising' policy in Scotland (1585–1597)[4]

James viewed himself as the lineal descendant of a long, illustrious and unbroken line of kings that had governed Scotland and which could be traced back to Fergus, first king of the Scots in 330BC. James was more than willing to sign-up to the ancient Dalriadic origins of his kingdom, but his attitude towards his contemporary Gaelic subjects was rather more ambiguous.[5] Since the fourteenth century the inhabitants of the Lowlands of Scotland had increasingly sought to distance themselves from their unruly neighbours while maintaining the belief in the Gaelic origins of the kingdom. John of Fordun wrote his *Chronica Gentis Scotorum* in the late fourteenth century and utilised the Gaelic origins of the kingdom as a means of refuting English claims to overlordship of Scotland, founded in the Brutus origin legend, yet described the Highlanders as 'a savage and untamed nation'.[6] Two centuries later, while elaborating considerably on the lives of the early kings of Scots as a means of educating James V on the virtues of good kingship, Hector Boece's 1528 *Scotorum Historia,* praised the Spartan discipline of the Highlanders (who he equated with ancient

4 Colin Kidd, *British Identities before Nationalism: Ethnicity and Nationhood in the Atlantic World, 1600–1800* (Cambridge, 1999), 123–45, the chapter entitled 'The Gaelic Dilemma in Early Modern Scotland'.

5 Martin MacGregor, 'Gaelic Barbarity and Scottish Identity in the Later Middle Ages' in Dauvit Broun and Martin MacGregor, eds, *Mìorun Mòr nan Gall, 'The Great Ill-Will of the Lowlander'? Lowland Perceptions of the Highlands, Medieval and Modern* (Glasgow, 2009), 43. Other historians have perceived James' attitude towards his Gaelic subjects in starker terms. See Kidd, *British Identities before Nationalism*, 127 where he describes James VI as 'the hammer of the Highlanders'; Roger A. Mason, 'Civil Society and the Celts', in Edward J. Cowan and Richard J. Finlay, eds, *Scottish History. The Power of the Past* (Edinburgh, 2002), 119; Edward J. Cowan, 'The Discovery of the Gàidhealtachd in Sixteenth Century Scotland', *Transactions of the Gaelic Society of Inverness*, lx (1997–98), 281–2.

6 John of Fordun, *Chronicle of the Scottish Nation*, ed., W. F. Skene, 2 vols (Edinburgh, 1872), I, 38; Roger A. Mason, 'Scotching the Brut', in Roger A. Mason, ed., *Scotland and England* (Edinburgh, 1987), 60–84.

Scots), but stopped far short of advocating 'the wholesale rehabilitation' of them.[7] George Buchanan, one of Europe's most renowned humanists, likewise utilised the myth of Fergus although in seeking to expound his resistance theories he argued that Fergus had been chosen to rule by clan chiefs thereby conveniently claiming the Scottish monarchy was an ancient elective one.[8]

For a king who asserted the imperial nature of his kingship and indefeasible hereditary right, perhaps it is understandable why he later banned Buchanan's works.[9] But that does little to unpick the king's attitude towards his Highland subjects. No doubt James spoke firmly about the lawlessness of his Gaelic subjects, but he also articulated similarly strong views about the 'feckless, arrogant conceit' of his nobility who were too ready to 'bang it out bravely' in 'barbarous feuds'.[10] As for his reformed Protestant kirk and the more radical Presbyterian element within it, James believed he would 'never find with any Highland or Border thieves greater ingratitude, and more lies and vile perjuries' than with such 'fanatic spirits'.[11] All that said, with James, what he articulated in written word and in speech was often

7 MacGregor, 'Gaelic Barbarity and Scottish Identity', 46.

8 Kidd, *British Identities before Nationalism*, 125; for Buchanan's positive view of the Highlands see George Buchanan, *History of Scotland*, trans., J. Aikman, 4 vols (Glasgow, 1827), I, 55.

9 Buchanan had been tutor to James during the king's minority. As well as a curriculum of Greek, Latin, history, composition, theology and arithmetic, cosmography, dialectics and rhetoric, Buchanan also found time to lecture the young king on the failings of his mother and on the contractual nature of monarchy. See Maurice Lee Jnr, *Great Britain's Solomon: James VI and I in His Three Kingdoms* (Urbana, 1990), 32.

10 James VI, *Basilicon Doran*, 24–9.

11 James VI, *Basilicon Doran*, 24–9; Jenny Wormald, 'The Headaches of Monarchy: Kingship and the Kirk in the Early Seventeenth Century', in Julian Goodare and Alasdair A. MacDonald, eds, *Sixteenth-Century Scotland. Essays in Honour of Michael Lynch* (Leiden, 2008), 377. The radical Protestant minority within the kirk advocated a 'two-kingdoms' theory which sought to place the king, as representative of God's temporal kingdom on earth, in a subordinate position to the kirk, as the representative of God's spiritual kingdom on earth.

rather different to how he behaved in practice.[12] Nonetheless, despite his desire to rule above the factionalism that had so shaped his years of minority, James could take harsh action when he felt his royal authority was not acknowledged.[13] Thus, while he was reluctant throughout his reign to alienate his Catholic earls, especially his close friend George Gordon, sixth Earl and later first Marquess of Huntly, despite his implication in Catholic conspiracies and the murder of the earl of Moray, James issued proclamations regarding the utter extinction of the MacGregors.[14] This should not be viewed through the lens of a Highland-Lowland divide as James was just as willing to show favour to Gaels as to anyone else (for example, James MacDonnell of Dunluce who he is said to have knighted when MacDonnell visited Scotland in 1596[15]) and just as willing to send Lowlanders such as

12 While James liked to theorise about kingship, as *The Trew Law of Free Monarchies* highlights, in practice he was prepared to compromise to reach a workable solution, as suggested in *Basilicon Doron*. See Jenny Wormald, *Court, Kirk and Community: Scotland, 1470–1625* (Edinburgh, 1981), 148; Jenny Wormald, 'James VI and I, *Basilikon Doron* and the *Trew Law of Free Monarchies*: The Scottish Context and the English Translation', in Linda Levy Peck, ed., *The Mental World of the Jacobean Court* (Cambridge, 1991), 36–54; Jenny Wormald, 'James VI and I (1566–1625)', accessed 26 February 2019; Roger A. Mason, 'Renaissance and Reformation: The Sixteenth Century', in Jenny Wormald, ed., *Scotland: A History* (Oxford, 2005), 138–9.

13 Julian Goodare and Michael Lynch, 'James VI: Universal King?', in Julian Goodare and Michael Lynch, eds, *The Reign of James VI* (East Linton, 2000), 1–31. The king had been the subject of two kidnapping attempts while two of his Regents were victims of assassination.

14 Ruth Grant, 'Brig o'Dee Affair, the sixth Earl of Huntly and the Politics of the Counter-Reformation', in Goodare and Lynch, eds, *The Reign of James VI*, 93–109; Ruth Grant, 'Friendship, Politics and Religion: George Gordon, Sixth Earl of Huntly and King James VI, 1581–1595', in Miles Kerr-Peterson and Steven J. Reid, eds, *James VI and Noble Power in Scotland 1578–1603* (Abingdon, 2017), 57–80. For action against the MacGregors; see *RPCS*, IV, 453–6.

15 Annie I. Cameron, ed., *The Warrender Papers II*, series three, vol. XIX (Edinburgh: Scottish History Society, 1932), 429–30, states MacDonnell appeared at court in April 1596. It is not clear how MacDonnell won James' favour. Donald Gregory, *History of the Western Highlands and Islands of Scotland 1493–1625* (Glasgow, 1881; reprinted Edinburgh, 2009 with an introduction by Martin MacGregor), 266–9, 273–4, asserts that James promised 'high reward' in return for

Andrew Melville or Francis Stewart, Earl of Bothwell, into exile when they crossed him.[16] However, James was also a Renaissance prince, well-educated and well-read on account of his education at the hands of Buchanan. As such he was familiar with the views of his contemporaries' regarding the Highlanders and the wider debates regarding barbaric and uncivilised peoples, whether across the Atlantic in the Americas, across the Irish Sea in Ireland or, perhaps, within his own kingdom.

By the sixteenth century the inhabitants of the Highlands and Isles had been firmly stereotyped as lawless, rebellious subjects. Successive Stewart/Stuart monarchs had made some effort to extend royal authority throughout the west and north of the country in order to bring these subjects into line with the rest of Scottish society.[17] One aspect of the so-called 'Highland problem' in the sixteenth century was the lack of consistency in the governance of the west Highlands and Isles, a result of shortened reigns of monarchs and subsequent long minorities.[18] Not all policy decisions taken

---

assistance 'as should be required' of MacDonnell in the 1596 expedition to the Isles (268); while also adding that MacDonnell was 'described by several Scottish writers of the period as a man of handsome appearance and dignified manners' (273).

16 Alan MacDonald, 'James VI and the General Assembly, 1586–1618', in Goodare and Lynch, eds, *The Reign of James VI*, 180; Ernest R. Holloway, *Andrew Melville and Humanism in Renaissance Scotland, 1545–1622* (Leiden, 2011), 251–77; Rob Macpherson, 'Stewart, Francis, first earl of Bothwell (1562–1612)', *ODNB*, accessed 7 August 2017.

17 Michael Brown, *James I* (Edinburgh, 1994), 93–108; Norman Macdougall, 'Achilles' Heel? The Earldom of Ross, the Lordship of the Isles, and the Stewart Kings, 1449–1507', in Edward J. Cowan and R. A. McDonald, eds, *Alba. Celtic Scotland in the Medieval Era* (East Linton, 2000), 248–75; Jamie Cameron, *James V: The Personal Rule* (East Linton, 1998), 228–54; Alison Cathcart, 'A Spent Force?: The Clan Donald in the Aftermath of 1493', in Richard D. Oram, ed., *The Lordship of the Isles* (Leiden, 2014), 254–70; Pamela E. Ritchie, *Mary of Guise in Scotland, 1548–1560: A Political Career* (East Linton, 2002), 66 n.35, 145–67.

18 Michael Lynch, 'James VI and the 'Highland Problem'', in Goodare and Lynch, eds, *The Reign of James VI*, 208–27, especially 216–25 where Lynch deals with the 'jostling match' (216) of proposed solutions. Nonetheless, too often the 'Highland problem' as it is termed, is viewed from the perspective of the 'centre' with the Highlands being the 'periphery', a framework that is particularly unhelpful and one this study aims to move beyond.

by the crown were wise, effective or even implemented, while the sudden and unexpected deaths of James IV, James V and Mary of Guise, and the interrupted reign of Mary, Queen of Scots, meant any policy initiative of a monarch was not sustained. While Highland matters never featured long or large for a Scottish monarch, they were even less of a priority for a minority government. Only during the regency of Mary of Guise was an effort made to continue with crown policy in all areas of government.[19] Viewed within the wider sixteenth century, one of the reasons the reign of James VI is regarded as such a success is that he ruled in his own right for eighteen years before succeeding to the thrones of Ireland and England as well.[20] This meant a degree of consistency and longevity could be achieved in all areas of policy, including towards the Highlands and Isles of Scotland. Notwithstanding, James' policies have been the subject of debate with some significant disagreement over what the king aimed at and how effective he was.[21] Throughout the sixteenth century Stewart monarchs were primarily

19 Ritchie, *Mary of Guise*, 145–67. Although not without a few flaws, this book provided a nuanced, in-depth study of a hugely important political figure of the sixteenth century. It certainly did not deserve the depth of criticism it received in a review printed in *Scottish Historical Review*, LXXXIII:2 (2004), 235–6.

20 T. B. Macaulay, *The Works of Lord Macaulay: Complete*, ed., Lady Trevelyan, 8 vols (London, 1879), vol. I, 54; Pauline Croft, *King James* (Basingstoke, 2003), 4–9.

21 Julian Goodare, *State and Society in Early Modern Scotland* (Oxford, 1999), 265; Lynch, 'James VI and the 'Highland problem'', 208–27; Julian Goodare, *The Government of Scotland 1560–1625* (Oxford, 2004), 220–45; Allan I. Macinnes, 'Crown, Clan and Fine: The civilising of Scottish Gaeldom, 1587–1603', *Northern Scotland*, 13 (1993), 31–55; Alison Cathcart, *Kinship and Clientage: Highland Clanship 1451–1609* (Leiden, 2006), 50–6, and especially 54 n.79. Some recent debate has centred on the Statutes of Iona; see Maurice Lee, 'The Government of Scotland after 1603', *Scottish Historical Review* LV:159 (1976), 41–53; Maurice Lee, *Government by Pen: Scotland under James VI and I* (Urbana, IL, 1980), 75–82, 136–47; Allan Macinnes, *Clanship, Commerce and the House of Stuart, 1603–1788* (East Linton, 1996), 56–87; Julian Goodare, 'The Statutes of Iona in Context', *Scottish Historical Review* LXXVII:203 (1998), 31–57; Martin MacGregor, 'The Statutes of Iona: Text and Context', *Innes Review* 57/2 (2006), 111–81; Alison Cathcart, 'The Statutes of Iona: The Archipelagic Context', *Journal of British Studies* 49/1 (2010), 4–27. In addition, further scholarship on James VI and his relationship with the Highlanders and Islesmen includes Aonghas MacCoinnich, *Plantation and Civility in the North Atlantic World. The Case of the Northern Hebrides, 1570–1639* (Leiden,

concerned with diplomacy in continental Europe, relations with the church (whether pre- or post-Reformation), and relations with England. James was cut from the same cloth. In domestic matters he wanted to assert his control over the reformed kirk, bring his nobility to heel and find a way to increase crown revenue, none of which entailed much divergence from what had gone before. By the close of the century, however, he had less choice than his predecessors in whether or not to deal fully with the inhabitants of the Highlands and Isles because the context within which he reigned demanded that he would.

James VI ruled during a time when accounts of the Indigenous Peoples encountered across the Atlantic made their way back to the archipelago while the barbarity of the Irish was repeated regularly by the English. Within the context of wider debates regarding the 'other', when James looked at his own kingdom he was well aware of the problem of his cold, dark 'north', inhabited by unintelligent (and unintelligible given their 'Erse' language), barbarous subjects which contrasted sharply with the law-abiding, civil society of south and east Scotland.[22] Like his contemporaries he described the Highlanders and Islesmen as lawless and disobedient but he could not view them as anything other than his own subjects. Herein lay the king's dilemma: James was keen to be seen by his European contemporaries as an effective, authoritative monarch who dealt firmly with lawless subjects but he was not prepared to dismiss the Gaelic origins (and thus the independence) of Scottish kingship. But his Highland subjects

2015); Ross Crawford, 'Noble Power in the West Highlands and Isles. James VI and the end of the mercenary trade with Ireland, 1594–96', in Kerr-Peterson and Reid, eds, *James VI and Noble Power in Scotland*, 117–35.

22 Robert Bartlett, *Gerald of Wales* (Oxford, 1982), 158–77; Debora Shuger, 'Irishmen, Aristocrats, and Other White Barbarians', *Renaissance Quarterly* 50/1 (Spring, 1997), 494–525; David B. Quinn, 'Ireland and Sixteenth Century European Expansion', in T. Desmond Williams, ed., *Historical Studies I* (London, 1958), 20–32; Jane H. Ohlmeyer, "Civilising of those rude parts': Colonisation within Britain and Ireland, 1580s–1640s', in Nicholas Canny, ed., *The Origins of Empire. British Overseas Enterprise to the Close of the Seventeenth Century: The Oxford History of the British Empire I* (Oxford, 1998), 124–47. By the sixteenth century the Gaelic tongue had come to be known as Erse or Irish, a reference 'to language rather than people'; see MacGregor, 'Gaelic Barbarity and Scottish Identity', especially 36–42.

repeatedly flouted his royal authority and, on a European stage, James was not prepared to compromise on this. Over time their behaviour came to be articulated as a threat to civility and, as Elizabeth's death looked increasingly imminent, a threat also to his British 'impyre'.[23] This incivility looked rather different in a Scottish context rather than an Irish one and was, in essence, about the recognition of James as the ultimate source of authority within his kingdom and adherence to his law. Indeed, while James' civilising policy may have had roots in classical antiquity reinforced by Renaissance humanism, it was profoundly shaped by the situation in his west and north.

It has been argued that the emergence of James' Highland policy can be seen in legislation issued on 29 November 1581 on the basis that, prior to this, only 'negligible' attention had been paid to the Highlands.[24] An Act of Parliament passed that year expressed concern regarding the 'monie grevous oppressionis and cruelteis' that had taken place in the region. As a result James' 'peceabill and guid subjectis … findis nathing mair intollerabill nor the deidlie feidis borne by the clannis of theiffis, brokin men and soirnairis upon trew men'.[25] At this time James was heavily influenced by his French, Catholic cousin, Esmé Stewart, who James elevated to duke of Lennox in 1581, but it does emphasise an early effort on the king's part to contain lawlessness in the region.[26] However, it was on 29 July 1587 that, having begun his personal reign, James first gave full expression to any sort of coherent policy for the Highlands if, indeed, such a thing existed. In this year parliament passed an act for 'the quieting and keping in obedience of the

23 *RPCS*, VII, 477–8 (478).

24 Goodare, *State and Society*, 256. Gerald A. Hayes-McCoy, *Scots Mercenary Forces in Ireland (1565–1603)* (Dublin, 1937, reprinted 1996), 193 also asserted that 'from 1581 onwards the general lines of what it must be apparent was his policy emerge'.

25 *RPS*, 1581/10/35, accessed 31 July 2018. The 1581 act was an attempt to limit lawless behaviour in the Highlands but was aimed specifically at 'broken' men, meaning those who were landless or, as they were referred to in the legislation, 'companeis of wikit men'. Such broken men were 'not subjectit to the ordiner cours of justice, nor to onie landislord that will mak thame answerabill to the lawes'.

26 There has not been much attention given to the role of Esmé Stewart in Scotland despite the influence he had on the king, although see Charles Haggerty, '"Unredeemed by any one single virtue"?: Esmé Stuart's political career in Scotland, 1579–1583' (University of Strathclyde, MRes, 2011).

disorderit subjectis, inhabitantis of the bordouris, hielandis and ilis'.[27] This legislation reiterated efforts to make clan chiefs and landlords within the Highland region accountable for the actions of the men, dependants and tenants who inhabited their lands. In order to enforce this, clan chiefs and landlords were required to give surety, a promise of good behaviour on the part of their dependants and tenants, and caution, a monetary payment included in such a pledge. This was not a new tactic, previously James IV had tried to make clan chiefs more accountable, although the addition of surety and caution meant that now clan chiefs and landlords would be penalised financially if they failed in this regard.[28] The legislation had been prompted by the widespread disorder in the region caused by the MacDonald-MacLean feud.[29] On account of close ties of real or fictive kinship and the custom of bonding which created a complex network of alliances, the dispute between these two clans left few in the west unaffected. Nonetheless, legislation passed in Edinburgh, unless thoroughly enacted, did little to bring a greater degree of law and order to the Highlands and James continued to rely on forfeiture as a means of dealing with clans that

27 *RPS*, 1587/7/70, accessed 31 July 2018. James began to assert his authority more forcefully following the execution of his mother in February 1587 which removed any lingering questions over his legitimacy as king of Scotland.

28 For more on the 1587 act see Cathcart, *Kinship and Clientage*, 51–2; Macinnes, 'Crown, Clans and Fine', 31.

29 The MacLeans had long held a claim to land in Islay, and in 1540 received title to lands there although David Caldwell, *Islay: The Land of the Lordship* (Edinburgh, 2008), 85, argues hostilities did not develop until 1561. For further details of the feud between the MacDonalds and the MacLeans see Caldwell, *Islay*, 81–93; Gregory, *History of the Western Highlands and Isles of Scotland*, 217–18, 227–8, 230–44. One version of the story is found in Robert Gordon, *A Genealogical History of the Earldom of Sutherland* (Edinburgh, 1813), 217–22; for the truce reached in April 1587, see *RPCS*, IV, 159–60, and for details of the crimes put to both men when they appeared in Edinburgh in 1591 see Robert Pitcairn, *Ancient Criminal Trials in Scotland: Compiled from the Original Records and Mss., with Historical Illustrations*, 3 vols (Edinburgh: Maitland Club, 1833), vol. I, part II, 224–30. The massacre of the MacLeans by the MacDonalds eventually led to the legislation being passed that sought to eliminate feuding. For more on this and Lachlan MacLean of Duart see Nicholas MacLean-Bristol, *Murder Under Trust: The Crimes and Death of Sir Lachlan Mor Maclean of Duart, 1558–1598* (East Linton, 1995).

continued in their lawlessness. While this was a severe penalty, forcing clans to either take protection from another clan chief or find some other means of employment, it was also counter-productive. It simply served to swell the ranks of 'brokin', or landless, men in the Highlands, men that the earlier legislation had sought to deal with, many of whom would seek employment in Ireland or take to the seas and a life of piracy.

Ongoing unrest was the result of clan feuding in the region. Traditional interpretations tend to rely on political factors to explain the outbreak of feuding in the region. Recent research into climate and its impact on the environment has helped to emphasise socio-economic and environmental factors, suggesting instead that feuding was an expression of resource competition as much as, or instead of, disputed possession of land.[30] Disorder and unrest was further heightened by the murders of James Stewart of Doune, Earl of Moray, and John Campbell of Cawdor, in 1592. The murder of Cawdor was the result of an internal power struggle concerning control of the young Archibald Campbell, seventh Earl of Argyll, and which aimed at the murder of the chief. Coming at the same time as the murder of the earl of Moray, there were severe repercussions for the wider Scottish political community with the potential for disorder throughout the north and west of Scotland.[31] Reluctant to take harsh action against his friend, the earl of Huntly, James sought to contain unrest and returned to tried and tested methods for dealing with lawlessness in the Highlands.

30 Robert A. Dodgshon, 'The Little Ice Age in the Scottish Highlands and Islands: Documenting its Human Impact', *Scottish Geographical Journal* 121/4 (2005), 321–37; Cathcart, *Kinship and Clientage*, 136–44; Richard D. Oram, 'Between a Rock and a Hard Place. Climate, Weather and the Rise of the Lordship of the Isles', in Richard D. Oram, ed., *The Lordship of the Isles* (Leiden, 2014), 40–61; Aonghas MacCoinnich, 'The Maritime Dimension to Scotland's 'Highland Problem', ca.1540–1630', *Maritime Communities of the North Atlantic Arc in the Early Modern Period: Journal of the North Atlantic,* ed., Alison Cathcart, special volume 12 (2019), 44–72.

31 Cathcart, *Kinship and Clientage*, 172–7. Gregory, *History of the Western Highlands and Isles*, 248–56 connects the murder of Moray with the murder of Campbell of Cawdor. For more on the Cawdor murder see E. J. Cowan, 'Kinship, Clanship and the Campbell Acquisition of Islay', *Scottish Historical Review*, LVIII:2 (1979), 132–57; Argyll & Bute Council Archives, Lochgilphead, A:/ARGMSS07, TD 40:1615.

A commission was issued to William Douglas, ninth Earl of Angus, as the king's lieutenant to bring the disobedient inhabitants of the Highlands to order.[32] The commission called for the co-operation of the men of the shires of the north and east to '"convocat thame selffis in armes, ryis and follow the said Lieutennent at sic dayis, placeis, and for sic space as he shall appoint"'. The earl was given '"speciall pouer to intercommoun with the … authouris and movaris of … disordouris and cruelties"' persuading them to refrain from '"armes and hostilite"'. Those Highlanders who did submit were to assist the earl and his forces in pursuing by force '"the uther pairtie that sal happin to shaw himself wilfull or obstinate"'. The most telling aspect of this and similar commissions was 'the usual indemnity' issued to Angus and his men 'for deaths or other injuries inflicted in the execution of his commission'.[33] The wide-ranging powers granted via these commissions effectively legitimised violence against the Highlanders, sending a message that such behaviour was acceptable (even encouraged) as long as it was sanctioned by the crown.[34] It also legitimised the actions of Highlanders who assisted the lieutenant, enabling them to exploit the commission and its indemnity to take revenge on their enemies, doing so under the guise of action against those who opposed the crown. In the 1590s commissions like these were not new.[35] Many were issued throughout the latter years of

32 Angus' commission focused largely on those who claimed to be dependents of George Gordon, sixth Earl of Huntly, who was regarded as responsible for the death of Moray. Along with the commission of 1592, the unrest resulting from the Cawdor-Moray murders led to a Convention of Estates in September 1593 passing twelve acts all aimed at dealing with lawlessness in the Highlands. See *RPS*, A1593/9/2 – A1593/9/13, accessed 31 July 2018; *RPCS*, V, 19–20. These sought to deal with lawlessness in the Borders too.

33 *RPCS*, V, 19–20.

34 Aonghas MacCoinnich, "His spirit was given only to warre': Conflict and Identity in the Scottish *Gàidhealtachd* c.1580–c.1630', in Steve Murdoch and A. Mackillop, eds, *Fighting for Identity. Scottish Military Experience c.1550–1900* (Leiden, 2002), 147–53.

35 One of the most notable had been issued in 1528 to James Stewart, Earl of Moray, as lieutenant-general of Scotland during the minority of James V. Moray had been ordered to take action against the Clan Chattan, 'invaid thame to thair vter destructioun, by slauchtir, byrning, drowning, and vthir wayis; and leif na creatur levand … except preistis, wemen, and barnis'. The women and children were to be

the sixteenth century to individuals across Scotland in an attempt to deal with the rebellious activity of the Highlanders.[36] At the same time, on occasion Highland chiefs sought to exploit these commissions for their own purposes, obtaining them in order to legitimately engage in clan warfare, although this further exacerbated the situation in the Highlands.[37] No doubt such commissions achieved gains, but they were short-term, could be quickly lost, and rarely realised widespread pacification of the region. Unsurprisingly, therefore, in January 1594–5 a Convention of Estates was called specifically for 'repressing of the insolence of the disordourit personis of the Hielandis'.[38]

---

transported 'furth of our realme' to 'Jesland, Zesland, or Norway'. Along with the earl of Moray, this commission had been issued specifically to a number of earls, lairds and chiefs in the region all of whom were close neighbours and kin relations of the Clan Chattan. In doing so, the crown was using local elites to enforce justice as also included in the commission were the earl and master of Sutherland, the earl of Caithness, John, Lord Forbes, Hugh Fraser of Lovat, John Grant of Freuchy, Ewen Allanson, chief of the Camerons, John MacKenzie of Kintail, John MacKay of Strathnaver and William Chisholme, sheriff of Cromarty, along with the sheriffs of Aberdeen, Elgin, Banff, Nairn, Forres, Inverness and all 'frehaldaris, baronis, capitanis of Clannys, and gentilmen' within the said sheriffdoms. Although this commission was not followed through it highlights how lawless activity was acceptable, so long as it was carried out for the benefit of the crown. The Clan Chattan, guilty of 'daly rasing of fire, slauchtir, murthur, heirschippis, and waisting of the cuntre', were to be dealt with by subjecting them to similarly violent behaviour. *The Miscellany of the Spalding Club,* ed., John Stuart (Aberdeen: Spalding Club, 1813–77), II, 83–4; Cathcart, *Kinship and Clientage*, 47–8, 91, 167–8.

36 *RPCS*, V, 19–20; VIII, 507–8; *CSP Scotland*, X, 811–12. At times, specific charges relating to Highlanders were contained within more general commissions aimed at dealing with 'thieves, sorners, masterfull oppressors, "hieland and lauland brokin men" and others', see *RPCS*, V, 49–50 (49). In 1594 a commission granted to Ludovic Stewart, Duke of Lennox, was aimed at the Catholic earls of Huntly, Erroll and Angus along with 'other Jesuits, papists, excommunicates and other treasonable practisers against the true religion'. At the same time, Lennox was to use the powers granted to deal with Highland rebels as circumstances allowed, with the usual indemnity; see *RPCS*, V, 187–8.

37 Such was the case with Kenneth Mackenzie of Kintail in 1594; see *RPCS*, V, 161.

38 This followed legislation passed the previous September; see *RPCS*, V, 94–5, 199.

Unwilling to admit that ongoing unrest was the result of inconsistent or unhelpful crown policy, James turned his attention to another aspect of the so-called 'Highland problem': the economic situation. Underlying his desire to deal with the 'disordourit' Highlanders was James' recognition that crown rentals from the region were 'frustrat' on a regular basis.[39] The inhabitants of the Highlands were regarded as 'avowed enemeis to all lauchfull trade and traffique … sua that the commoditeis of cornis, stoir, and fischeing … doith altogidder perische and vanische away, to the offence of God, dishonnour of the natioun, and hurt of the commounwele'.[40] Such financial concerns regarding the Highland region were not particularly new either. Both James IV and James V had struggled to receive the crown's proper rental from the region, while the 1540 Act of Annexation and the resulting rental increases certainly heightened grievances harboured by the Highlanders and Islesmen towards the crown.[41] Little had changed half a century later in terms of the rents paid by the Highlanders but James VI found himself in a completely different financial situation to that of his predecessors. The rejection of papal authority and abolition of the mass that came with the Reformation of 1560 meant James was no longer able to exploit the finances of the papacy in the way his predecessors had done.[42] The royal purse was noticeably empty and James desperately needed to increase his revenue, especially following his wedding to Anne of Denmark in 1589 and the birth, by 1596, of two children with all the accompanying financial outlay. Debasement of the coinage and inflation exacerbated the lack of finances and, while money was necessary for bestowing patronage, it was also necessary to finance the numerous expeditions to the west Highlands

39 *RPS*, 1597/11/40.

40 *RPCS*, VII, 115.

41 Cathcart, 'The Forgotten '45', 239–41.

42 James IV and James V had exploited loopholes to appoint their preferred candidates to benefices, reaping the revenues while vacant, and appointing family members to the most lucrative positions in the Scottish church. James V was able to capitalise on this fully, given the wider context. Following Henry VIII's break with Rome, the papacy was keen to keep Scotland onside, bestowing on the James the papal cap and sword, a sign of special favour, while also giving James the resources requested to establish and fund his College of Justice although much of the money is said to have been siphoned off to support building projects.

and Isles. Indeed a lack of funds was the reason many were proposed, but few ever followed through with.[43]

Those charged with heading up expeditions, and masters of ships involved, often had to do so at their own cost.[44] In addition, the taxation imposed on Lowland burghs in order to fund these endeavours was unwelcome and, despite the king's proclamations, led to a lack of provisions, whether men, ships, or victuals, a situation not unlike that facing the English in Ireland.[45] Aware of the resentment on the part of the western burghs James tried to alleviate this somewhat in advance of the 1596 expedition.[46] He acknowledged that with 'the harvest now approcheing and the grite derth and scairsitie of victual' in the kingdom, the intended expedition would be a 'grite trouble … baith to burgh and land' so, with the advice of his council, James 'thocht meit to mitigate the rigour' of the obligations placed on shires and burghs. Shires were to provide only twenty horse and thirty foot, furnished with arms and money for the space of forty days or the monetary equivalent; burghs were to provide 500 men, one-third armed with muskets, one-third with pikes and 'corslettis' and one-third

43 Lynch, 'Highland problem', 217.

44 *RPCS*, V, 475. As was the case with the expedition of 1608 led by Andrew Stewart, Lord Ochiltree. See *RPCS*, VIII, 113–14 for the commission and NLS Adv MSS 33.1.1., vol. IV, no. 8 for Ochiltree's later claim that it was this service that led to the 'wraik and rwyne' of his house.

45 *RPCS*, V, 312–13, 313–14. Impositions such as this took its toll on the Lowland burghs, increasing resentment towards their Highland neighbours. This was similar to the growing resentment in England regarding the effort in Ireland and there was a perceptible reluctance by many western shires to provide victuals and other provisions. A decade later, little had changed. James wrote from Whitehall to the council in Edinburgh acknowledging discontent of those charged to assist with an expedition to the Isles planned for 1608, but reiterating the command to assemble on the grounds the venture was 'so necessarie to oure service and so beneficiall to that hole Estate'. See *RPCS*, VII, 92; VIII, 502.

46 Earlier in June 1595 the Privy Council had issued a proclamation forbidding anyone, under pain of treason, to sell or provide any of the Irish with victual or powder and had expressly referred to inhabitants within the burghs of Ayr, Irvine, Dumbarton and Glasgow. This would impact directly on the burgeoning trade of the west coast burghs with the Irish and, no doubt, added to the resentment on their part. See *RPCS*, V, 223–4; and see p.195 n.87, 88.

with hagbuts and head-pieces along with 'three middling shippis furneist with shoit and munitioun'.[47] Shires could compound, paying £24 for each horseman and £12 for each foot, and while most burghs could pay £12 for every man they did not send, there were exceptions. Berwick, Roxburgh and Selkirk were exempted as they were required to provide for service in the Borders; Inverness was exempt entirely but warned to expect similar demands in the spring of the following year; but the sheriffdoms of Tarbert and Bute were not allowed to compound and required to send the full quota of men.[48] The king's subjects were to assemble on 1 August 1596 'at the burgh of Dunbartane … "weill bodin in feir of weir" with ships and boats and provisioned for 40 days service' to assist Sir William Stewart of Houston, Commendator of Pittenweem, who had been granted a commission of lieutenancy for this endeavour on account of the king's continued reluctance to lead personally.[49]

The 1596 expedition, the king declared, was for the 'reduceing the Ilismen to the obediens of God, the Kingis Majestie and his lawis'.[50] Such direct, forceful intervention was necessary to suppress rebellion in order to extract 'payment of the King's rents and duties'.[51] Although articulated in more general terms, the 'interprise' intended to bring to order Angus MacDonald of Dunivaig and take control of his main fortifications. MacDonald and Lauchlan MacLean of Duart had been placed under sentence of forfeiture in 1594 for continuing to refuse to submit to the king on account of the widespread unrest that resulted from their feud. James' proclamation of June 1596 concerning the expedition had brought MacLean to submission but MacDonald held out. With the situation closing in on him, MacDonald made his way to Ireland to seek aid from the earl of Tyrone, in the light of an 'emergency': none was forthcoming.[52] This is

47 The sheriffdoms of Berwick, Roxburgh and Selkirk were exempt as they were needed to 'withstand the insolence of the disordourit personis inhabitantis of the Bordouris'.

48 Gregory, *History of the Western Highlands and Isles*, 266.

49 *RPCS*, V, 296–7, 306–8, 309–10.

50 *RPCS*, V, 306–8 (306).

51 *RPCS*, V, 289.

52 *RPS*, A1596/5/3, accessed 31 July 2018. Hayes-McCoy, *Scots Mercenary Forces in Ireland*, 278–9; Fiona MacDonald, 'MacDonald, Angus, of Dunyvaig and the

unsurprising considering the situation Tyrone was contending with. In the previous year he had been forced to wait for months for a Highland force to reach him, only for a large part of it to be decisively defeated by the English off the Copeland Islands before it retreated back to Scotland.[53] Although MacDonald had not been part of that force, Tyrone was not in a position to send his men to Scotland to support his former Highland allies.[54] Indeed, from Tyrone's perspective, then engaged in war against the English, MacDonald was a burden. Following MacLean's submission to the king in June 1596, and on account of MacDonald's ongoing resistance, the king granted the disputed Rhinns of Islay to MacLean; shortly afterwards, James MacDonnell took forcible possession of the Glens, lands Angus MacDonald held from the queen.[55] Facing opposition or a lack of support from all sides, combined with the prospect of a royal expedition against him and without substantial allies, MacDonald did what rebellious subjects normally did in such circumstances and sought to negotiate, sending his son to offer terms to the king.

Appearing in person before the Privy Council on 8 October 1596 James of Knockrinsay, MacDonald's son, submitted a letter which stated his father

Glens (*c.*1548–1613)', *ODNB*, accessed 12 November 2015, argues that Tyrone refused to give aid because Archibald Campbell, Earl of Argyll, allied to MacLean, controlled the movement of fighting men between Ireland and Scotland. See also Ross Crawford, 'The life of Sir James MacDonald of Knockrinsay', *The Innes Review* 67/2 (2016), 112.

53 See pp. 200–3 above. Not only did the force return quickly to Scotland but a number of the main Highland chiefs offered their services to the English queen which would not have endeared them to Tyrone.

54 *CSP Scotland*, XI, no.609a (655). MacDonald had not joined with the force that went to Ireland in 1595, instead remaining at home in hope of coming to some understanding with MacLean and, no doubt, to ensure his lands were not attacked in his absence.

55 James MacDonnell then wrote to James VI claiming his right to Clan Donald lands in Scotland was 'by tytill of ryghteousnes, and more lawfullie descended and gotten be the act of trew matrimonie'; a right he argued was greater than anyone else's, notably MacDonald's. See *The Spottiswoode Miscellany: A Collection of Original Papers and Tracts, Illustrative Chiefs of the Civil and Ecclesiastical History of Scotland*, ed., James Maidment, 2 vols (Edinburgh: Spottiswoode Society, 1844–5), II, 372–4; Hayes-McCoy, *Scots Mercenary Forces in Ireland*, 279–80.

would willingly submit to the king's '"godlie and princelie will"', and promised that whatever terms Knockrinsay would agree to, MacDonald would accept them. MacDonald went further, promising he would renounce all claim, right and kindness to his estate so that his son would 'receive ... in his own person, such rights and conditions' to be agreed on.[56] Moving from a position of rebellion and resistance to royal authority to that of submission in such a short time highlights the vulnerability and weakness of Angus MacDonald in 1596. He may still have held out hope for assistance from Tyrone but, given the context of war in Ulster, it is unsurprising that Tyrone was otherwise occupied or relatively unconcerned about maintaining an alliance with the Scottish chief. MacDonald was spent: he had no new methods of negotiating with king or government other than to continue the relentless cycle of submission, promises, release, renewed rebellion and crown intervention.

The king was unconvinced that MacDonald could or would fulfil his promises and, having been persuaded that the obedience of the chief and his son, James of Knockrinsay, should be tested, instead imposed a number of his own conditions. Knockrinsay was to remain at court as a pledge, along with MacDonald's illegitimate son, Archibald. The king wanted to determine what lands were in the hands of the crown while MacDonald was to remove himself, his family and dependents who were not tenants out of his lands in Kintyre and the Isle of Gigha. Although he would remain a 'kyndlie tennent and possessour thairof' he would receive a new grant and yearly duty to be paid. As for MacDonald's lands of Islay, Colonsay, Jura and the forty merkland of Kilkerran, the king had 'full libertie' to do as he saw fit for the 'planting of burrow tounis with ciuile people, religioun ... and traffique of merchandice'.[57] These were challenging conditions for MacDonald. Kintyre and Islay were the traditional estates of the clan and Dunivaig Castle its key stronghold in Islay. To accept crown tenants on his

56 *RPCS*, V, 321. The one condition Angus made was that Knockrinsay '"do his honnorable dewitie"' to his parents '"in honnest sustentatioun and obedience, as becumis ane sone to do"'.

57 *The Spottiswoode Miscellany*, II, 374–6; *The Book of Islay. Documents Illustrating the History of the Island*, ed., G. Gregory Smith (Edinburgh, 1895), no. LIII (102–3). Angus was to protect any of the king's new tenants there from attack; see *RPCS*, V, 321.

lands was effectively to co-operate with the king on a policy of plantation but MacDonald had few remaining options. Consequently, he submitted to Sir William Stewart when he arrived at Islay in November that year while Knockrinsay was knighted, remaining in Edinburgh and in relatively close contact with the king. If the king was testing MacDonald's obedience he did not have to wait long. In May 1597 he was denounced a rebel for failing to appear to answer charges relating to the attack on Gilbert Thomson, burgess of Ayr, at Rathlin Island.[58] While MacDonald remained a rebel, the king looked to the son to succeed his father in the hope Knockrinsay would be a more reliable – or pliable – and law-abiding chief who would co-operate fully with plans for plantation.

Despite the king's efforts in 1596 to work with the MacDonalds, the hostility between father and son (Knockrinsay would set fire to the house his parents were sleeping in in 1598) was replicated on a wider scale as the MacDonalds squabbled with dependent kindreds and reignited the feud with the MacLeans of Duart resulting in widespread unrest across the region.[59] During the summer months of 1598 the king declared he was 'fullie resolved' to go personally to the west on account of 'the proude rebellioun, defectioun and disobedience of the inhabitantis of Kintyre and utheris pairtis of the Illis and Hielandis of this realme'.[60] Although not mentioned directly, there is no doubt that as Kintyre was part of his intended itinerary the ongoing rebellious activities of the MacDonalds added to the king's displeasure at the situation in the west. Frustrated by continued lawlessness and flouting of his royal authority, and motivated by economic considerations, James decided to embark on grander, wide-reaching reform for the west Highlands and Isles and moved away from the need to co-operate with the local elites.[61] In taking such action it is hard to ignore the impact events across the North Channel would have had on the king. While James certainly did not toe Elizabeth's line, throughout the 1590s both monarchs were forced to take action in their respective kingdoms. In Ireland the situation was one of rebellion or all-out war; in Scotland it was ongoing lawlessness and disorder.

58 *RPCS*, V, 393; and see pp. 1–2 above.

59 For more on this see Crawford, 'Sir James MacDonald of Knockrinsay', 109–17.

60 *RPCS*, V, 466, 475.

61 Goodare, *Government of Scotland*, 220–45.

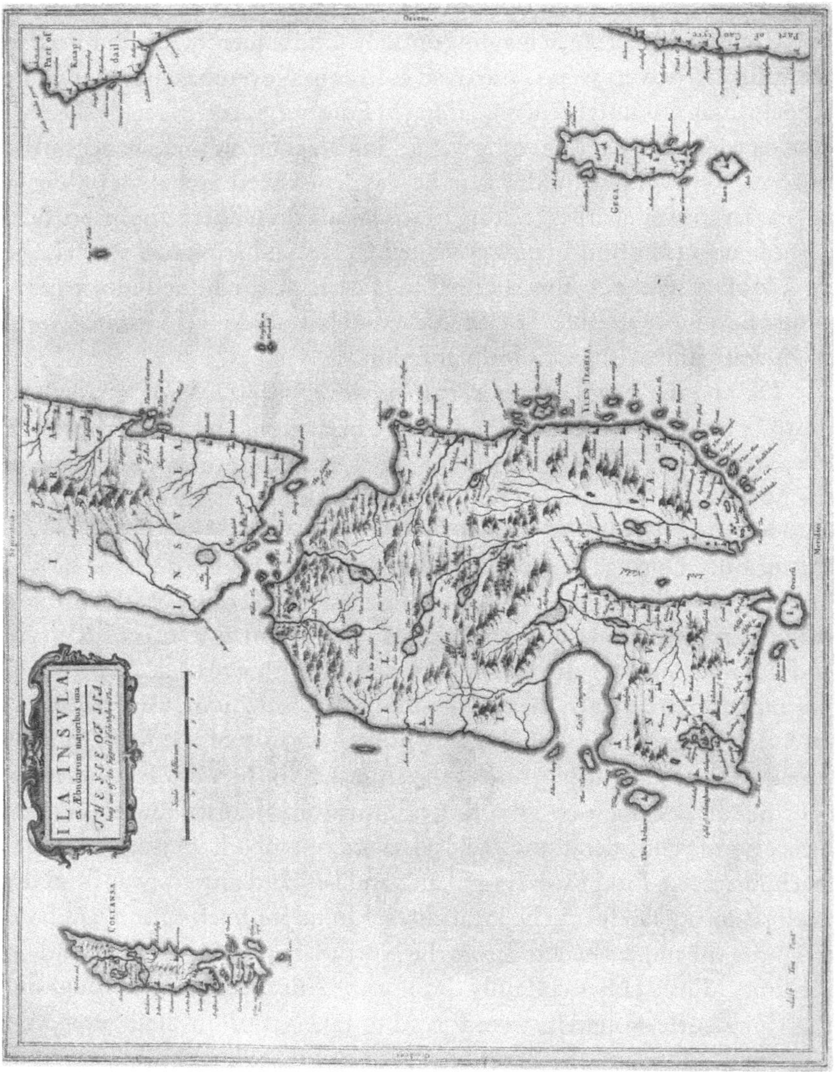

Ila Insula ex Aebudarum majoribus una, The Yle of Ila being one of the biggest of the Western Yles, Timothy Pont, 1560?–1614?, Joan Blaeu, 1596–1673 (ID 481). Reproduced with the permission of the National Library of Scotland.

The desire to deal with the disobedient inhabitants of the west Highlands and Isles, and to curtail the lawlessness of the broken men, had been articulated throughout the sixteenth century by previous Scottish monarchs and their governments, but increasingly during the 1580s and 1590s James spoke of his need to pacify their 'wicked inclinatioun'.[62] By the mid-1590s James had navigated the 'plots' of his Catholic earls and, beyond the odd proclamation, remained relatively undisturbed by the rumoured alliance of the Highlanders with the Irish and Spain.[63] This was not the case for the English who believed that a Spanish invasion via Scotland was imminent: the Spanish would then gather horse and victual in Scotland rather than have to bring such provisions with them. They would sail through the Irish Sea as there were too many obstacles to the west of Ireland and navigating round the north of Ireland into the North Channel was not easy as the Spanish had learned to their cost in 1588.[64] In contrast the Irish Sea afforded a shorter journey, albeit encountering opposing tides at some point, while Milford Haven, along with the Cheshire coast and Isle of Man, were '"infected" with Papists', and would provide protection, refuge and places they could gather additional supplies.[65] Ongoing unrest in the west Highlands and rebellion in Ulster added to the gathering crescendo of English fears about a Catholic, Spanish invasion, forcing James to recognise the reality of the situation and pay it closer attention. Previously prepared to turn a blind eye to the activities of the Highlanders in Ireland, James realised that if the English were to gain the upper hand in a situation that he was unable to contain, this could have severe repercussions for his subjects, his reputation and his aim to succeed to the English and Irish thrones. The question over the English succession remained unanswered but James could not afford to be ambivalent any longer. He may have placated

62 *RPS*, 1587/7/70, accessed 31 July 2018. The sixteenth century is often referred to as the 'age of forays' on account of the level of clan feuding that broke out in the Highlands.

63 *CSP Scotland*, XII, no.98 (104–11).

64 *CSP Scotland*, X, no.694 (688–93)

65 *CSP Scotland*, X, no.694 (690). The Irish Sea was the preferred option for the Spanish, just as it had been for the French during the 1540s; see Cathcart, 'Forgotten '45'.

the fears of English Catholics with his leniency to his own Catholic subjects, but he would not countenance any suggestion that he was an ineffective monarch whose royal authority did not extend through his entire realm. At the same time, if he succeeded Elizabeth, he would inherit a very real law and order problem that existed on either side of the North Channel, adding to his list of concerns.[66]

The movement of the Highlanders into Ulster was a constant source of anxiety for the English but their efforts to make James deal with the situation were futile for he could do little to control it, much in the same way he could do little to resolve the ongoing clan feuding in the west and north of his kingdom. The Irish, for their part, while happy to accept help when it was required, were now ready and willing to repulse opportunistic Highland Scots raiding parties, whose aim was simply to lift cattle, taking hides and tallow back across the sea.[67] In addition, some Irish lords were becoming resentful at the expense involved in maintaining large numbers of Highland Scots but these forces were still a necessity, especially with the heightening of hostilities throughout the later 1590s, and they continued to arrive in Ireland regularly (if not always reliably).[68] While the English would welcome anything that disrupted the flow of either men or provisions into the north of Ireland to bolster the rebellious Irish lords, ongoing disorder on both sides of the North Channel alongside rumours of foreign invasion was concerning for both monarchs. The North Channel was not simply a narrow, turbulent stretch of water separating Ulster from the

66 There has been some excellent recent scholarship on the succession; see Susan Doran and Paulina Kewes, eds, *Doubtful and Dangerous. The Question of Succession in Late Elizabethan England* (Manchester, 2014), and especially Rory Rapple, 'Brinkmanship and Bad Luck: Ireland, the Nine Years' War and the Succession', 236–56; also David Edwards, 'Securing the Jacobean Succession: The Secret Career of James Fullerton of Trinity College, Dublin', in Seán Duffy, ed., *The World of the Galloglass. Kings, Warlords and Warriors in Ireland and Scotland, 1200–1600* (Dublin, 2007), 188–219.

67 SP 63/146, fol.193 mentions how the Scots 'killed to the numbre of 600 cowes fraighting their gallies w[i]th the spoile … taking awaie the hides and tallowe, leaving their carcases on land'. SP 63/181, fol.188v refers to the 600 Scots lately arrived in Ulster. Geoffrey Fenton wrote that they 'come not to abyde but to retorne backe againe w[i]th their spoile of cowes w[hi]ch they haue taken'.

68 Crawford, 'Noble Power in the West Highlands and Isles', 127–8.

western Highlands and Isles of Scotland; it was an international border between Catholic and Protestant Europe, a confessional, territorial, political, economic, cultural, linguistic and legal boundary. For the English, it was a very real threat on various levels.

Plantation in the North Isles of Scotland (1598–1608)

James VI's 'civilising' policy is often looked at in isolation, with a focus on his subjects who inhabited the west Highlands and Isles, or examined alongside his wider policies for Scotland including his efforts to eliminate the bloodfeud amongst his nobility or re-establish control over the kirk. It is more appropriate to place his civilising and plantation policies within a cross-channel context while acknowledging that such a context brought not just an archipelagic, but an international, dimension to the mix. During the closing years of the sixteenth century, as James gradually became more concerned with the activity of his Highland subjects in Ireland, and potentially an alliance with Spain, he realised this was 'ane mater quhilk … concernis his Hienes, in conscience, honnour and proffeit, and tendis alsua to the weilfair of the haill realme'.[69] Thus while his civilising policy aimed at extending his royal authority and securing the obedience of his Highland subjects, by the late 1590s this had evolved to include a policy of plantation that combined these aims with social and economic reform too.

On 16 December 1597 an Act of Parliament was passed that called for the establishment of burghs in the Highlands and Isles. The 'maist convenient and commodious pairtis' where burghs were to be erected, were said to be Kintyre, Lochaber and Lewis.[70] To support this endeavour, James asserted these burghs would have 'all privelegeis … grantit to onie uthair

69 *RPCS*, V, 306–8 (306).

70 *RPS*, 1597/11/41, accessed 31 July 2018; *RPCS*, V, 455. *Collectanea de Rebus Albanicis, Consisting of Original Papers and Documents Relating to the History of the Highlands and Islands of Scotland* (Edinburgh: Iona Club, 1847), 159 states that this eventually led to the establishment of towns in Campbeltown, Fort William and Stornoway.

brughtis' along with such 'land and grund … as may serve to beig the saidis tounis'. The stated intention was 'for the bettir intertening and continuing [of] civilitie and polecie within the hielandis and iles' as, like the English, James believed that commercial activity would contribute to the civilising of his Highland subjects. This act has been interpreted by some as evidence of the lack of commerce in the Highlands, but such a perspective completely overlooks the fact James was well aware his Highland subjects were involved in trade.[71] After all, in June 1593, James had put to the horn one George Smollet, burgess of Dambarton, for his theft of 'guidis, geir and bestiall, clothing and uthiris wairis, brocht be the inhabitantis of the Ilis and uthiris pairtis of the Hielandis to the … burrowis, baith by sey and land' while also imprisoning some of the Highlanders and Islesmen too.[72] If the king had previously sought to protect his Highland subjects as they travelled to the Lowlands to trade, he should not then deny any economic endeavour on their part. He had no intention of doing so; rather James wanted to benefit from their trade. By establishing burghs within the west, Highlanders and Islesmen could no longer complain of attacks on them at the hands of men such as Smollet as they travelled to Lowland burghs. All their trade would now have to take place in burghs within the Highlands and the royal purse would no longer be deprived of its rightful customs and duties from that trade.

There was a clear difference, however, between the situation in Scotland and that in Ireland. Although aware of trading activities of the Irish, the English conveniently ignored it, consciously or unconsciously, because it did not fit with their perception of Irish society. Instead the English preferred to emphasise the lack of economic development which enabled them to declare the land *res nullus*. This provided the legitimacy to undertake plantation, allowing them to argue it was out of duty while also beneficial

71 The extent of trade between the Highlands and the burghs in Scotland was the focus of examination by Katharina Pruente, 'Trade and Commerce in the Western Highlands and Isles of Scotland, *c.*1570–1585. This project was funded by The Carnegie Trust Undergraduate Vacation Scholarship under my supervision at the University of Stirling in summer 2020. We are very appreciative of the financial support provided by The Carnegie Trust to undertake this research.

72 *RPCS*, V, 87.

for both the English and the inhabitants of the land.[73] In Scotland, James did not need to go to such lengths to justify his presence or his policy; it was his kingdom and the Highlanders and Islesmen were his subjects. As a humanist-educated Renaissance prince it could be argued he was fixated with the realisation of a civil society and, like the English, sought to 'civilise' his unruly subjects. His language certainly reflected this as increasingly he described the Highlanders and Islesmen as barbaric and primitive, a terminology shaped both by classical stereotypes of the 'other' and descriptions of the 'barbarous' inhabitants the English encountered in the Americas.[74] No doubt, James articulated his civilising agenda through the rhetoric of reform of his barbaric inhabitants and spreading knowledge of God, but 'civility' was a vehicle, a convenient language to adopt as he was just as much concerned with reaping the rewards of the economic resources of the Highland region. The spread of 'civility' throughout his kingdom would be realised through the development of market centres; settled society and commercial activity would help reform his lawless Gaelic subjects while also contributing to the royal coffers. From James' perspective, this was a beneficial outcome for all concerned.

The king regarded the Highlands as being 'maist commodious … alsweill be the ferteillitie of the ground as be riche fischeingis be sey'.[75] Economic exploitation of the region, both by land and sea, may well have been viewed as the answer to James', and Scotland's, financial difficulties but this was not to be entrusted to the Highlanders themselves.[76] James' outline for what he had in mind for his Highland subjects involved planting

73 See pp. 146–53 above; Alison Cathcart, 'The Maritime Dimension to Plantation in Ulster, ca.1550–ca.1600', *Maritime Communities of the North Atlantic Arc in the Early Modern Period: Journal of the North Atlantic*, ed., Alison Cathcart, special volume 12 (2019), 95–111.

74 These reports would have been circulating widely with the failed Roanoke settlers returning to England in 1586 and individuals like Ralph Lane serving in Ireland thereafter.

75 *RPS*, 1597/11/40, accessed 31 July 2018.

76 James was also attempting to exploit the mineral wealth of Scotland much in the same way the English were attempting to reap the natural resources of Ireland. For more on this see NLS Adv. MS 19.1.24 Papers of John Lindsay, Lord Menmuir,

> Colonies among them of answerable In-lands subiects, that within short time may reforme and ciuilize the best inclined among them; rooting out or transporting the barbarous and stubborne sort, and planting ciuilitie in their roomes.[77]

All he needed to do was to 'root out' the Highlanders. This he did through another act passed on the same day which required all clan chiefs and landowners claiming right and title to land and fishing in the Highlands to appear personally before the council and produce their titles. Clan chiefs held charter from the crown for their lands, giving them legal right to inhabit, 'brukit and ioise', the land which included reaping the economic resources and redistributing them throughout the clan as a whole.[78] However, patterns of landholding and land settlement were not always so easily aligned, with members of one clan living on land belonging to, and paying rent to, another clan chief. In other instances, a clan might 'possess' and claim land as theirs, but legal title could be held by another chief. Thus, legal tenure and claims of customary possession were often out of sync and this was the foundation of many clan feuds in the region as possession of land meant the exploitation of its economic resources regardless of who held legal title. Legal title could be granted on the whim of a monarch but customary claims were based on generations of possession of, and settlement on, land meaning it was regarded as belonging

---

concerning lead and copper mining in Scotland 1567–96; Robert W. Cochran-Patrick, *Early Records Relating to Mining in Scotland* (Edinburgh, 1878).

77 *Basilicon Doron* in Sommerville, ed., *King James VI and I: Political Writings*, 24. This reference to plantation is an indication of James' archipelagic awareness, drawing on Irish precedents to be applied within a Scottish context. Also, it may have been a rather self-conscious attempt to show an English audience that he was capable of dealing effectively with both his own subjects and the Irish situation. This was crucial in the light of the backdrop of Hugh O Neill's rebellion during the 1590s.

78 *The Chiefs of Grant*, ed., William Fraser, 3 vols (Edinburgh, 1883), III, no.140 (143–9). This was a Scots term meaning to enjoy and possess the land. For further explanation see Cathcart, *Kinship and Clientage*, 129–57; Macinnes, *Clanship, Commerce and the House of Stuart*, 5–7, 17–23; for redistribution of resources see Robert A. Dodgshon, 'West Highland Chiefdoms, 1500–1745: A Study in Redistributive Exchange', in Rosalind Mitchison and Peter Roebuck, eds, *Economy and Society in Scotland and Ireland, 1500–1939* (Edinburgh, 1988), 27–37.

to a particular clan. Both claims were recognised in Scots Law and both fiercely fought over. Despite, or perhaps because of, the strength of claims of customary possession, chiefs did not always fully appreciate the importance of keeping the physical, legal charter for future reference.[79] The requirement to appear personally with evidence of the right and title to land may have proved challenging to some and, unfortunately for them, the consequences were severe. If any landholder or chief failed to produce the necessary documents they would be forfeit and their title was 'to be null and of nane avail'.[80]

Perhaps of greater significance, however, was the preamble to the act which most clearly articulated James' agenda behind his plantation policy. The preamble stated that the inhabitants of the Highlands and Isles had 'frustrat his majestie of the yeirlie payment off his proper rentis' and 'throche thair barbarus humanitie ... makis the saidis hielandis and iles ... altogidder unproffitabill baithe to thame selffis and all uthuris'. The description of the Highlanders and Islesmen as 'barbarus' was further reinforced by the lack of 'onie civill or honest societie amangis thame' and their refusal to let Lowland subjects 'trafficque within thair boundis withe saiftie of thair lives and gudes'. Consequently, for 'remeid quhairof' the said inhabitants were to be 'reduced to ane godlie, honest and civill maner of living'.[81] James' plans for plantation, much like those of the English in relation to Ireland, were wrapped up in the rhetoric of civil society and knowledge of God although inextricably connected with the more basic concern that Highlanders pay their rent and behave themselves. Reform of Highland society was essential if James was ever going to reap any profit from the area; profit which was there for the taking. Ultimately, James argued, plantation would be beneficial to the inhabitants of the Highlands and Isles

79 The exception always are the Campbells; see Steve Boardman, 'The Campbells and Charter Lordship in Medieval Argyll', in Steven Boardman and Alasdair Ross, eds, *The Exercise of Power in Medieval Scotland c.1200–1500* (Dublin, 2003), 95–117; Stephen Boardman, *The Campbells, 1250–1513* (Edinburgh, 2006).

80 *RPS*, 1597/11/40, accessed 31 July 2018.

81 *RPS*, 1597/11/40, accessed 31 July 2018.

as well as for the whole realm. It was a policy carefully articulated in acts relating to the plantation of Lewis that commenced in 1598 (see Map 6).[82]

Following the failure of Torquil MacLeod, chief of the MacLeods of Lewis, to present documentation to support his claims to land, he was forfeit of his estates which reverted to the crown. On 28 June 1598 a 'Ratificatioun of the contract of the Lewis' highlighted the desire to bring the inhabitants of the Highlands to order while also making the region 'commodious and profitabill'. After all, 'the saidis landis and iles ar be special providence and blissing of God inrychit with ane incredibill fertilitie of cornis and store of fischeingis and utheris necessairis surpassing far the plentie of ony pairt of the inland'.[83] However, it had been 'the mair difficill' to exploit this potential profit because 'the same ar possest be inhabitantis quha ar voyd of ony knawledge of God or his religioun and naturallie abhoiring all kynd of civilite, quha hes gevin thame selfis over to all kynd of barbarietie and inhumanitie'. Now that the lands of Lewis, Ronalewis, the Shiant Islands,

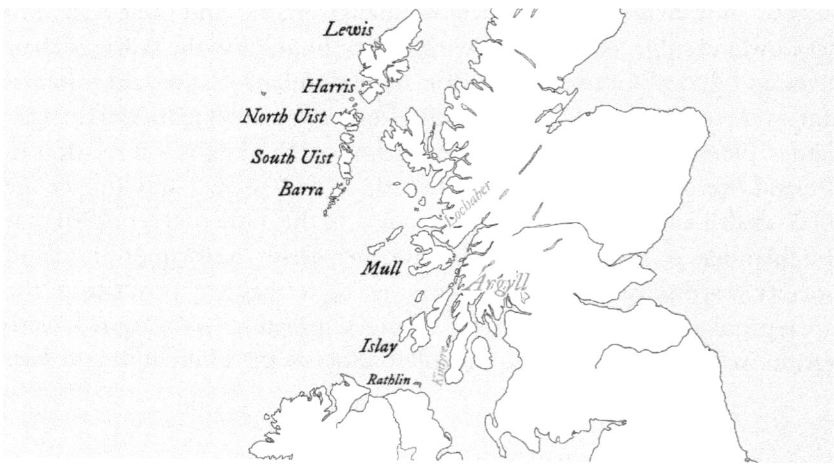

Map 6. The western Isles of Scotland

82 The plantation of Lewis has received full, scholarly attention in MacCoinnich, *Plantation and Civility in the North Atlantic World.*

83 *RPS*, 1598/6/5, accessed 31 July 2018.

and Troutternish in Skye, and everything pertaining to them, belonged to the crown, a number of gentlemen were 'maist willing at the uttermest of thair power to advance and set fordwart the glorie of God, the honour of thair native country' and the king's service. Through 'the planting of kirkis and uther policie' and the erection of 'alsmony burghis of barronie … as they sall think expedient' they would increase the crown's revenue. In addition they had power to 'erect, mak and constitute als mony sey portis and heavinis within the boundis of the foirsaidis landis and iles as they sall think expedient for ressait of schipis, crearis, boittis and utheris veschellis' and to uplift all customs, anchorage dues and other payments accruing. The individuals involved were known as the Gentlemen Adventurers of Fife and had full power to appoint officials, deal with matters of law and order, distribute land and trade freely.[84] In essence, they were to undertake plantation in the Isle of Lewis and establish the infrastructure for ongoing commercial activity, all done through private enterprise.[85]

It was no accident that a number of men from Fife agreed to the Lewis undertaking as, for some time, the Fife merchants and burghs had been complaining of the treatment they received from the locals when fishing off the western Isles. Boats from Crail and Anstruther regularly made the journey to the west in order to exploit the rich and abundant herring fishing to be had there. Like the English in Ireland, James realised the enormous financial potential of fishing rights and was keen to ensure that he would receive his due custom from this activity.[86] Thus, the plantation of Lewis was intimately bound up with James' efforts to exploit

84 The principal men involved were Sir James Anstruther, James Elphinstone, Lord Balmerino, John Forret of Fingask and his son, James Forret, Sir George Hay of Nether Liff, Sir George Hume of Wedderburn and his son and heir apparent, David Hume of Wedderburn, James Learmouth of Balcolmie, Patrick Leslie, commendator of Lindores, Sir Robert Lumsden of Airdrie, Captain William Murray, Sir James Sandilands of Sandilands, Sir James Spens of Wormiston, Colonel William Stewart, commendator of Pittenweem, Ludovick Stewart, Duke of Lennox and Earl of Darnley.

85 MacCoinnich, *Plantation and Civility in the North Atlantic World*, 91–175.

86 This is discussed fully in MacCoinnich, *Plantation and Civility in the North Atlantic World*; Martin Rorke, 'The Scottish Herring Trade, 1470–1600', *Scottish Historical Review* 84 (2005), 149–65.

the economic resources of the region for the benefit of the crown. The right to build harbours and ports was vital, not only for the Adventurers themselves, but also to support trade, especially if burghs were to be established and fairs to be held. As in Ireland, such commercial development went hand-in-hand with the spread of the Protestant religion. Included in the ratification was the provision for six parish kirks to be established throughout Lewis, Ronalewis, and Troutternish so that the Adventurers, and whoever else came to live in the fledgling plantation, would not 'be destitute of the comforte of spirituall pastouris for preicheing to thame of the word of God and administration of the sacramentis'. James hoped that by implanting God-fearing, rent-paying, commercially-minded, Protestant, obedient Lowland subjects, the 'best inclined' Highlanders that remained on Lewis would become imbued with Lowland values and behaviour, resulting in their full assimilation into the Scottish realm.[87]

As both James and the Adventurers were soon to find out, this endeavour would not unfold quite as smoothly as they may have hoped. In July 1599 a commission of lieutenancy over the whole of the Highlands and Isles was granted to Ludovick Stewart, second Duke of Lennox, and George Gordon, sixth Earl of Huntly. In strong language, this commission reiterated the '"barbarous cruelteis"' committed by '"wicked and rebellious inhabitantis"' who lacked any knowledge or fear of God, had no regard for '"Prince, law, and justice"', and withheld '"ane grite parte of the propir rent and patrimonie of the crowne"'.[88] It also made direct reference to the Islesmen who '"hes bandit, conspirit, and dalie practizeis, be force and policie in thair barbarous and rebellious forme, to disappoint his Hienes service in the Lewis"' and who '"spuilyeis the cuntrey of the benefeit quhilk micht redound thairto be the tread of fisheing"'. That neither James nor the Adventurers had anticipated such resistance from the MacLeods of Lewis is surprising, given the unrest that resulted from disputes over possession of land in the Highlands and the long-standing claims to land the Highlands and Islesmen maintained.[89] It suggests either

87 *Basilicon Doron* in Sommerville, ed., *King James VI and I: Political Writings*, 24.

88 *RPCS*, VI, 8–10 (8).

89 They would have been aware of the rebellions of the Irish against English plantation efforts.

a severe underestimation of opposition to this policy or utter contempt for the inhabitants; but as MacConnich has shown, 'even the most consistent rebel … made an accommodation with the incomers'.[90] Such alliances never lasted for long however and, in general, those Islesmen removed from their lands sought to return the favour in due course. The first attempt at plantation in Lewis reached an end in 1602 with the planters defeated, some killed, others dead from disease and a number of hostages taken while others were sent back to Fife in their ships. Nonetheless, not long after the hostages were released the king started gathering support for a second attempt. The reluctance on the part of the Fife Gentlemen to partake in another effort must have frustrated a king who was as concerned about how this looked to external observes, as he was about reaping the economic benefits planation offered.[91]

In July 1602, despite initial setbacks, James was determined to ' "reduce that Ile to obedience and to plant a nowmer of guid and dewtifull subjectis thairin" '.[92] His language did not change following succession to the English and Irish thrones and he continued to refer to ' "the rooting out of all barbaritie" '.[93] This would suppress lawlessness and poverty while trade and profit would increase. On 18 July 1605 he asserted that ' "the interpryse of the conques of Lewis … sal be yit prosequuted" ' while emphasising that ' "the haill remanent Ilis and lands nixt adjacent quha are now disobedient sal be reducit" ' to the king's obedience also.[94] Another expedition to the Isles was duly planned and a commission of lieutenancy was issued on 8 August that year to David Murray, Lord Scone, to lead it; unfortunately for Scone, he was given little authority thus limiting what realistically could be achieved. This expedition was particularly unwelcome by the lords from the southwest of Scotland who regarded it as unnecessary and protested

90 MacCoinnich, *Plantation and Civility in the North Atlantic World*, 106.

91 MacCoinnich, *Plantation and Civility in the North Atlantic World*, 116, 122–3.

92 *RPCS*, VI, 420. In this proclamation James referred to the ' "beistlie and monstrous crueIteis" ' of the inhabitants of Lewis, the extremity of which ' "hes not bene hard of amangis Turkis or Infidellis" '.

93 *RPCS*, VII, 465–66 (466).

94 *RPCS*, VII, 87.

that they were unable to provide the required shipping.[95] Notwithstanding their petitions, they were ordered to serve and the expedition commenced later that month. Various individuals were charged to render their castles to the crown and to deliver all '"limfaddis, boittis, and birlingis"' to Robert Hepburn, lieutenant of the King's Guard, in an effort to curtail the Highlanders' movement, whether in the Isles, to Lewis, to Ireland, or to prevent them engaging in piracy.[96] By this time, Angus MacDonald was barely clinging on to what lands still pertained to him. Direct intervention forced him once more to submit and promise to pay his rents for Kintyre and Islay, but he was the only Highland chief to do and Scone had little authority to take any further action against other, more powerful, individuals.[97] James was far from pleased as his focus had been the North Isles, but he was coming to the realisation that the pattern of behaviour, the relentless cycle of rebellion-forceful intervention-submission, was far from conductive to pacification of the region. The refusal of his Highland subjects to submit to James' royal authority, he reiterated, was '"a matter twitching His Hienes in honour"'.[98] After all, as he told his three estates in Scotland, bringing the Isles to order would benefit the whole nation economically, but it would also increase Scotland's, and no doubt his own, reputation in a wider European context.[99]

In autumn 1605 the Fife Adventurers did return to Lewis, with additional military support, but a siege of the settlement at Stornoway by the MacLeods a year later caused significant demoralisation and the majority of the Fifemen abandoned their project again in early 1607.[100] In the

95 Such resentment at being called upon to provide for expeditions to the Isles was long-standing; see pp. 231–2 and p.231 n.45 above.

96 *RPCS*, VII, 68–9, 69–70. There was also a warrant for 'a sufficient sowmer of gude, able maryneris to serve at his Majesteis charges in the said schip'.

97 This suggests something of the continued vulnerability of Angus and the MacDonalds in general. In the previous year, Angus MacDonald had handed over his son, Sir James of Knockrinsay, to the crown; Crawford, 'Sir James MacDonald of Knockrinsay', 121–2.

98 *RPCS*, VII, 229. By this time, James was king of three kingdoms, not just one.

99 *RPCS*, VII, 465–6.

100 *RPCS*, VII, 256, 430; MacCoinnich, *Plantation and Civility in the North Atlantic World*, 128–32.

intervening period, James had pressed ahead with plans for plantation in the west with a scheme for the North Isles. On 3 December 1606, despite the events at Stornoway, he wrote to his council in Edinburgh that '"having resolved to reduce the North Yllis ... to civilitie and oure obedyence"' he had found '"none so mete to undirtak nor able to perform that service"' as George Gordon, sixth Earl and now Marquess of Huntly.[101] In the previous year the king had turned to Huntly to assist with 'the interpryse of Lewis'.[102] Now, however, he wanted Huntly to undertake plantation of the North Isles, excepting Skye and Lewis.[103] The council and Huntly entered negotiations and by April 1607 most of the details of the plan had been agreed. In contrast to the Lewis plantation which had made little specific mention of the inhabitants of the Isles, Huntly was to follow through with the 'extirpatioun of the barbarous people of the Yllis within a yeare'.[104] Clearly James sought to learn the lessons of the Lewis endeavour and surmised that the 'rooting out' of the MacLeods of Lewis had not been thorough enough. Hence he specified that Huntly was to '"extirpat and

101 *RCPS*, VII, 504. Huntly was created first Marquess in April 1599. Throughout the sixteenth century, successive Scottish monarchs had delegated responsibility for law and order in the Highlands and Isles to the Gordons of Huntly in the North Isles and the Campbells of Argyll in the South Isles; see Cathcart, 'A Spent Force?', 261–4.

102 *RPCS*, VII, 92.

103 *RPCS*, VII, 341–2, 360–2, 524–5; *Highland Papers III*, ed., J. R. N. MacPhail, second series, vol. XII (Edinburgh: Scottish History Society, 1920), 100–05; Barry Robertson, *Lordship and Power in the North of Scotland. The Noble House of Huntly, 1603–1690* (Edinburgh, 2011), 37–43.

104 *RPCS*, VII, 360–2. There had been reluctance to deal with Huntly concerning the pacification of the North Isles. For some time the council had tried to get James to deal with Huntly on account of his Catholicism (*RPCS*, VII, 516) but James, 'while reproachful of' Huntly's 'unenthusiastic backing of the Protestant faith' did not concede (Robertson, *Lordship and Power in the North of Scotland*, 55; *RPCS*, VII, 462). He admonished the council for its delay and made it clear that any charges against the Marquess were to be suspended until after his enterprise in the Isles (*RPCS*, VII, 516–17). James wrote again to the council in early April, the tone of which was much more appeasing, ensuring the council that if Huntly did not undertake this enterprise, they could continue in their action against him (*RPCS*, VII, 520–1).

rute out" ' the captain of the Clanrannald and the entire clan within the Isles, Moidart and Knoydart, the McNeills of Barra and the whole Clan Donald North, and was to assist those involved in the plantation of Lewis ' "aganis thair enemeyis whatsomevir" '. In addition, before the end of the year Huntly was to plant the North Isles with ' "civile people" '.[105] This was quite an agenda, but it signified the king's growing frustration with his Highland subjects and the ongoing lawlessness in the west. Consequently, Huntly was granted a commission of lieutenancy and justiciary over the Isles, power to prohibit the reset of the inhabitants of the Isles and 'a special justiciarie aganis the resettaris whatsomevir of the saidis barbarous people'. While both parties agreed that he would be exempt from paying any duty for the North Isles for the space of one year, there was disagreement over the amount of annual duty to be paid thereafter. Huntly offered the sum of £400; £300 for the Uists and £100 for the rest of the North Isles. The council thought this 'a very meane dewytie for the haill North Yllis', and later suggested an alternative duty of £5,000.[106] It was on this issue of annual duty that the project stalled.

One explanation as to why the endeavour was never put into execution was on account of this disagreement over the annual duty to be paid.[107] However, it is questionable how much Huntly wanted to be involved in the pacification of the North Isles. The Gordons of Huntly had risen to prominence in Scotland throughout the sixteenth century on the basis of loyal and effective service to the crown. Although a close friend of the king's, and despite granted the authority to forcibly remove the Clan Donald, a commission the marquess would have relished, it is doubtful Huntly wanted anything to do with this scheme.[108] Aware of the failure of the first two attempts at plantation of Lewis by the Fife Adventurers, he also would have known of the extent of the king's displeasure that was directed at the

105 *RPCS*, VII, 524–5. Huntly was not to plant the North Isles with men from Badenoch or Lochaber and, while Skye and Lewis were excepted, so too was Harris and the small Isles belonging to Skye and Lewis.

106 *RPCS*, VII, 361, 523.

107 *RPCS*, VII, 528; Goodare, 'The Statutes of Iona', 33.

108 MacCoinnich, *Plantation and Civility in the North Atlantic World*, 180.

unsuccessful planters.[109] Huntly had little desire to see such an eventuality played out in the North Isles under his watch, especially if he was to be held responsible for success or failure of the venture. Fortunately for the marquess, the main opposition to his involvement in the North Isles was not on account of the amount of annual duty to be paid but was a result of sustained pressure on the king from both the kirk and the Privy Council who complained that Huntly 'nawyse repairis to the kirk and … abstenis frome the communion'.[110] The marquess was a committed Catholic and, in recent decades, had been implicated in more than one Catholic conspiracy, was widely regarded as being responsible for the death of James Stewart, Earl of Moray, at Donibristle, Fife, in 1592, and had opposed and defeated crown forces sent against him at Glenlivet in 1594. He was ordered to be confined to the burgh of Elgin.[111]

James was aware he had to be seen to take a strong stand against Catholicism, both in order to placate his subjects in Scotland, and to satisfy wider Protestant opinion throughout his, now three, kingdoms in the wake of the rehabilitation of the earls of Tyrone and Tyrconnell in Ireland in 1603, peace with Spain in 1604, and the failed gunpowder plot in England in 1605.[112] The king tried to calm the troubled waters in his council in Edinburgh by stating he had never intended to prefer the marquess over any of his other subjects in this proposed plantation, but he did not want to further delay the enterprise at this stage. This did little to allay the fears of the council or the kirk; if Huntly was responsible for planting the North Isles, the fear was that this would result in the spread of

109 MacCoinnich, *Plantation and Civility in the North Atlantic World*, 136.

110 *RPCS*, VII, 395–6.

111 *RPCS*, VIII, 9, 139–42 n.1 (140), 487, 505; Robertson, *Lordship and Power in the North of Scotland*, 55–56. But this was after the Flight of the Earls and the rebellion of Sir Cahir O'Doherty and James had less reason then to continue to support Huntly in any plans for the North Isles.

112 *RPCS*, VII, 476–7; Gordon Donaldson, *Scotland, James V – James VII* (Edinburgh, 1965), 186–96; Roger A. Mason, 'Renaissance and Reformation', in Jenny Wormald, ed., *Scotland, A History* (Oxford, 2005), 136–42; Jenny Wormald, 'Confidence and Perplexity: The Seventeenth Century', in Wormald, ed., *Scotland*, 145–53.

Catholicism, not Protestantism, in the region.[113] For a man who previously had endured years of exile, confinement in Elgin, and later Aberdeen, was a much more attractive proposition than an expensive and dangerous enterprise in the North Isles, one that did not offer much reward or much hope of success. By the end of 1607 James VI and I's plans for plantation in the western Highlands and Isles appeared to be coming to a rather wretched end. For members of his councils in both Edinburgh and London, the real threat appeared to be Catholicism. James' rehabilitation of O'Neill of Tyrone and O'Donnell of Tyrconnell appalled many in England but James appeared committed to working with them. In Scotland, despite Huntly's confinement, it was by no means clear what the resolution in the North Isles would be.

The solution to the North Isles would not become clear until the end of the first decade of the seventeenth century. There is circumstantial evidence for collusion with the Mackenzies of Kintail in the final efforts by the Fife Adventurers in the plantation of Lewis.[114] But the conclusion of the last attempt at plantation in 1609, and the embarrassment of that failure, was offset by the wider agreement reached with Highland and Hebridean chiefs in 1609 known as the Statutes of Iona which compounded the events that occurred in Ulster in 1607 and 1608. For Lewis, however, it would be the Mackenzies of Kintail who stepped in to provide an agreeable solution to the situation. In November 1609 Kenneth Mackenzie of Kintail was granted a parliamentary lordship, the details of which specified that the newly created Lord Kintail would 'civilise the Isle of Lewis and reduce the inhabitants to obedience'.[115] The king was now looking to private individuals to undertake plantation in the western Highlands and Isles of Scotland, and also in Ulster.

113 After all, many of the arguments that had been used in an attempt to persuade Elizabeth to engage more fully in 'western planting' across the Atlantic earlier in the sixteenth century were based on confessionalism. Where the Spanish extended their territory, they took Catholicism with them.

114 MacCoinnich, *Plantation and Civility in the North Atlantic World*, 140–1.

115 MacCoinnich, *Plantation and Civility in the North Atlantic World*, 181 and n.21; *RMS*, VII, nos 167, 168; *RPCS*, VIII, 470. The rather meteoric rise to power of this kindred that followed was a result of ongoing service to the crown.

CHAPTER 7

James VI and I, Ulster and the South Isles

In his 1604 *Discourse touching Ireland*, the English lawyer Richard Hadsor referred to a late-sixteenth century tract that advocated colonisation on the shores of Lough Foyle for the purposes of fishing. Hadsor reiterated this, advising

> that the offer made by Dutchmen to the late Queene to inhabitt Loghfoile upon the borders of the country of the Earle of Tyrone upon such condi[ti]ons as … shalbe thought fytt, be accepted, and certen … cyvile subiects ioyned w[i]th them, whose trades & example may drawe the people [i.e. the Irish] to growe civil. And colonies … likewise planted at … such other uncivill place of the realme.[1]

Indeed, the 1598 *Discourse* Hadsor referred to argued that the Dutch were 'the most ready and perfecte Arteistes that be hauing the greatest store of shippes of any men wherew[i]th they can w[i]th great facility carrie frames of Tymber and lyme w[i]th them thether, where they shall finde stores in great plenty to build howses'. The Dutch would also do this 'willingly' in return for 'large Immunities, previledges, and liberties, w[i]th some good proportion of landes and freedome of fishing in Ouchfoyle, the Bande, and such lyke'.[2] The suggestion of using the Dutch in efforts to develop plantation and commercial fishing in Ireland should not be too surprising. There had been instances of Dutchmen in Ireland during the sixteenth century involved in economic activities and in 1609

1 SP 63/216, fols 180–1 (181r); Joseph McLaughlin and Richard Hadsor, 'Select Documents XLVII: Richard Hadsor's 'Discourse' on the Irish State, 1604', *Irish Historical Studies* 30/119 (1997), 337–53.

2 SP 63/202/4, fols 232–6, at fol.233v. Hadsor was also involved in the 1622 Commission. For more on Hadsor and his later role in Ulster; see Victor Treadwell, 'Richard Hadsor and the Authorship of 'Advertisements for Ireland', 1622/3', *Irish Historical Studies* 30/119 (1997), 305–36.

Maximillian Vanderlere, 'who, like the rest of his nation is diligent & industrious' submitted proposals to plant 'a colony of Hollanders … in the Ilands of Lough Erne'.[3] Sir Henry Docwra had been forced to trade with Dutch merchants in order to maintain his garrison at Derry, evidence of their maritime and trading strength.[4] The Dutch had gradually extended their monopoly over the fishing trade throughout the sixteenth century to the extent that, during the reigns of both Edward VI and Elizabeth, William Cecil had often complained of the demise of English fisheries. In previous centuries English monarchs had actively encouraged foreign fishing in waters around the English coasts but given the heightened security risks following the Reformation there was a distinct change in attitude. Decline of English fisheries also meant a decline in seamanship; those who spent a lifetime at sea fishing were those who knew the coasts and tides and could be called upon, when required, for the naval defence of the country.[5] Neither Cecil nor Elizabeth suggested interfering with foreign fishing in English coastal waters but others, like John Dee, certainly did: so too did the Scots who were 'particularly jealous' about

3 TNA AO 1/290/1090 Government Accounts 1 October 1611–30 September 1613 Vanderlere's occupation was noted as 'salvager of wrecks'. Sir John Davies asserted this would be 'a great incouragement & benefitt to the undertakers'; SP 63/227, fol.110. For another Dutchman involved in salvaging wrecks from the coast of England and Ireland see Alan Roddie, 'Jacob, the Diver', *The Mariner's Mirror* 62/3 (1976), 253–69; see also Rolf Loeber, 'English and Irish Sources for the History of Dutch Economic Activity in Ireland, 1600–89', *Irish Economic and Social History* 8 (1981), 70–85. My thanks to Professor Rolf Loeber for these references and discussing this with me. A Maximillian Vanderlere is also noted in the port customs of the Isle of Man in 1604; see MNH MS 10058: Accounts of Water Bailiff … Ingates and Outgates 1604.

4 Amongst an ocean of literature on this topic see A. Calder, *Revolutionary Empire: The Rise of the English-Speaking Empires from the Fifteenth Century to the 1780s* (London, 1981); Jan De Vries and Ad Van Der Woude, *The First Modern Economy: Success, Failure, and Perseverance of the Dutch Economy, 1500–1815* (Cambridge, 1997).

5 T. W. Fulton, *The Sovereignty of the Sea. An Historical Account of the Claims of England to the Dominions of the British Seas, and of the Evolution of the Territorial Waters: with Special Reference to the Rights of Fishing and the Naval Salute* (London and Edinburgh, 1911), 75, 86–95.

foreigners fishing in their waters.[6] While English fisheries had gone into decline during the sixteenth century, the Dutch had expanded theirs, regarding the fisheries as the foundation of commerce and of their shipping and maritime power in general.[7] Indeed, by the turn of the seventeenth century they had largely monopolised the fishing trade, had the vessels, equipment and skill to maintain this, were active in the waters off the west and north of Scotland and Ireland, and were regarded as an economic power in Europe at this time. The proposal to allow the Dutch to establish a colony at Derry in order to exploit the fishing of the Foyle was a forerunner of their efforts to gain access to the fisheries of the western Isles of Scotland; it was also a proposal that would have relied on private enterprise, albeit out-sourced to foreigners.[8]

Hadsor's arguments, like the proposal of Maximillian, held little attraction for James. Although the king acknowledged that certain Dutchmen had been allowed to plant in Ulster, the intention had been to 'impose uppon them greater customes then to the natives' while limiting their trade so it was 'onlie betweene England and Ireland, lest otherwise they would by their extraordenarie industrie exhaust the treasure from both kingdomes'.[9] He certainly did not want the Dutch enriching themselves at the expense of his own realm thus preventing him from reaping the economic resources of his three kingdoms and he did not want to see them fishing in the rich waters around Scotland and Ireland. Unlike Elizabeth, who had made no claim for dominance of the English seas, James was increasingly hostile to any foreign intervention in the waters around Scotland and, post-1603, moved into a position where he advocated *mare clausum* or 'closed seas'

6 John Dee, *General and Rare Memorials pertaining to the Perfect Arts of Navigation …* (1577). Quoted in, and for more on Dee's arguments regarding the boundaries of the British seas, see Fulton, *Sovereignty of the Sea*, 100–5; for the Scots see 75–86.

7 Fulton, *Sovereignty of the Sea*, 134–5.

8 Aonghas MacCoinnich, *Plantation and Civility in the North Atlantic World. The Case of the Northern Hebrides, 1570–1639* (Leiden, 2015), 258–89.

9 *A Repertory of the Inrolments of the Patent Rolls of Chancery, in Ireland; Commencing with the Reign of King James I*, ed., John Caillard Erek, vol. I, part I (Dublin, 1846), 14 (20).

around his British empire.[10] Just as the Dutch were not to be permitted to fish in James' waters, their proposal to establish a colony at Derry found little favour with the king. He did not want to give them any foothold as, having recently established peace with Spain, sanctioning Dutch settlements in Ireland would not have helped the situation. Regardless of arguments advocating Dutch plantations, James needed to consider the wider international dimension as well as the local one. The changed circumstances

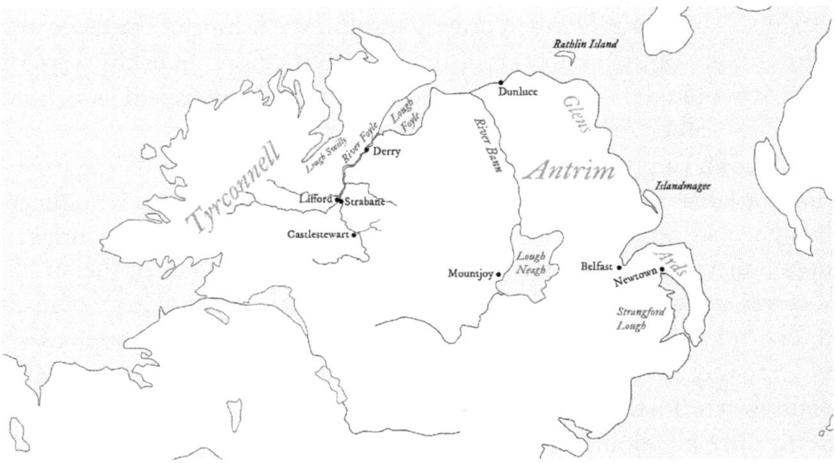

Map 7. Locations in Ulster post-plantation

10 For more on this see Fulton, *Sovereignty of the Sea*, 118–209; for the wider debate involving Hugo Grotius and William Welwood see M. J. Van Ittersum, 'Mare Liberum versus the Propriety of the Seas? The debate between Hugo Grotius (1583–1645) and William Welwood (1552–1624) and its impact on Anglo-Scottish-Dutch fishery disputes in the second decade of the seventeenth century', *Edinburgh Law Review* 10 (2006), 239–76; Helen Thornton, 'Hugo Grotius and the Freedom of the Seas', *International Journal of Maritime History* 16/2 (2004), 17–38. James' eventual execution of Patrick Stewart, Earl of Orkney, in 1615 may well have been connected to efforts to suppress ongoing rebellion in the Isles, following the outbreak of the Islay rebellion in 1614, but Stewart had long tested the king's patience. The decision to execute the earl of Orkney is more likely to have been linked to James' arguments of closed, 'British' seas and the need for a more compliant and obedient magnate in the northern Isles.

in the years of his reign as king of three kingdoms enabled James to contemplate a different course of action for Ulster. While James would not countenance the Dutch establishing a plantation in west Ulster, the proposal for plantation in the east of the province put forward by two Scots in 1605 was viewed much more favourably by the king.

The Hamilton-Montgomery plantation

In the plantations that developed in Ulster and the South Isles in the early seventeenth century, James appears to have followed the precedent of Sir Thomas Smith by out-sourcing to private individuals who undertook these endeavours at their own expense. This relatively hands-off attitude of the king, devolving responsibility to private individuals, was evident in the early seventeenth-century plantation in the east of Ulster, known as the Hamilton-Montgomery plantation. In April 1605 an agreement was reached whereby the lands of Upper Clandeboy and the Great Ards in County Down formerly belonging to Con O'Neill were divided into three portions.[11] One-third was passed to Hugh Montgomery, sixth Laird of Braidstane; another third to James Hamilton, a former schoolmaster in Glasgow and son of Hans Hamilton, a minister in Dunlop, Ayrshire; and the final third remained in the possession of Con himself.[12] The details of

11 BL Add MS 36775: Copies of … documents … connected with Ireland during the reign of James I … : 1603–25, fol.137v; SP 63/217, fols 112v–13r. Con O'Neill was the grandson of Sir Brian Phelim O'Neill who had so strenuously opposed Sir Thomas Smith's endeavour to plant English colonies in the Ards.

12 Hamilton had become an agent for the king in Ireland and, along with fellow Scot, James Fullerton, was instrumental in the establishment of Trinity College Dublin while Fullerton later played a crucial role in securing James VI's succession to the English and Irish thrones. See Michael Perceval-Maxwell, *Scottish Migration to Ulster in the Reign of James I* (London, 1973), 50–1; Philip Robinson, *The Plantation of Ulster: British Settlement in an Irish Landscape, 1600–1670* (Belfast, 1994; reprinted 2000), 52–4; David Edwards, 'Securing the Jacobean Succession: The Secret Career of James Fullerton of Trinity College, Dublin', in Seán Duffy, ed.,

how this settlement was concluded are rather confused, but both Scots exploited their previous and existing connections with James VI.[13] This led to the decision whereby the lands were divided between the three men.[14] While this was a result of the private initiatives of Montgomery and Hamilton, the terms of the grant suggest James' own agenda too.[15]

Half of Upper Clandeboy plus the whole of the Ards was divided between Hamilton and Montgomery while Con received the other half of Upper Clandeboy. In terms of location this meant O'Neill's holdings

---

The World of the Galloglass. Kings, Warlords and Warriors in Ireland and Scotland, 1200–1600 (Dublin, 2007), 188–219. Fullerton was also granted land in Ireland worth an annual amount of £50, see BL Add MS 36775, fol.6v. Therefore, although very much a private enterprise, as with his attitude towards his Scottish Catholic earls, James was willing to give approval to this scheme because both men, or their close kin relations, had a record of loyalty and service to the crown.

13 For a more detailed account of this see *Irish Patent Rolls of James I. Facsimile of the Irish Record Commission's Calendar prepared prior to 1830*, foreward by M. C. Griffith, Irish Manuscripts Commission (Dublin, 1966), 72–4, nos xlix, l; 84, nos xxxiii, li; *A Repertory of the Inrolments on the Patent Rolls of Chancery, in Ireland: Commencing with the Reign of King James I* (Dublin, 1846), 194 (48); 194–6 (49); 196–201 (50); *CSP Scotland*, XII, 163; George Hill, ed., *Montgomery Manuscripts (1603–1706) Compiled from Family Papers by William Montgomery of Rosemount, Esquire* (Belfast, 1869), vol. I, 9–20; T. K. Lowry, ed., *The Hamilton Manuscripts: Containing Some Account of the Settlement of the Territories of the Upper Clandeboye, Great Ardes, and Dufferin, in the County of Down by Sir James Hamilton, Knight* (Belfast, 1867), 1–10; Perceval-Maxwell, *Scottish Migration to Ulster*, 49–53.

14 The lands were said to be in crown hands because of the attainder of Shane O'Neill, not Con's rebellion. See *Calendar of the Patent and Close Rolls of Chancery in Ireland of the Reign of Charles the First*, ed., James Morrin (Dublin and London, 1863), 230–3; *Montgomery Manuscripts*, 43–4, 43 n.43; Perceval-Maxwell, *Scottish Migration to Ulster*, 52 n.17; Ciaran Brady, 'The Attainder of Shane O'Neill, Sir Henry Sidney and the Problems of Tudor State-Building in Ireland', in Ciaran Brady and Jane Ohlmeyer, eds, *British Interventions in Early Modern Ireland* (Cambridge, 2005), 28–48.

15 *Montgomery Manuscripts*, 21–33. For the wider background to these developments and plantation in east Ulster and across Ulster respectively, essential reading includes Raymond Gillespie, *Colonial Ulster. The Settlement of East Ulster, 1600–1641* (Cork, 1985), 9; Robinson, *Plantation of Ulster*, 52–5.

were situated inland in the northwest of Down, thus ensuring 'the sea coasts … be possessed by Scottish men, who would be traders … for his Majestie's future advantage'.[16] No doubt this was partly to do with securing the plantation, making it accessible by sea and thereby also protected by the sea (just as Sir Thomas Smith and Richard Hakluyt the elder had advocated), but it also ensured the new settlers had ready access to their lands while merchants would be encouraged to trade with the new plantation.[17] Incentives were provided. Hamilton was given one day's free fishing rights in the River Bann and all fishing rights to the Laggan river, along with all woods, mills, houses, tithes and other appurtenances pertaining to his lands; the right to import and export grain and other commodities (linen yarn excepted) unless the council felt the need to prohibit this; the right to hold markets and fairs; and the right to import cattle, grain, commodities and men freely for the establishment of his settlement.[18] The king also imposed conditions: regular courts were to be held for hearing pleas and dealing with matters arising; neither Hamilton nor Montgomery were to alienate the land 'to anie of the mere Irish'; and, as well as settling tenants on their own lands they were to supply Scottish and English tenants to populate one-third of O'Neill's lands too.[19] Although it would find fuller

16 BL Add MS 36775, fol.137v; *Hamilton Manuscripts*, i–x, general appendix no.1; *Montgomery Manuscripts*, 32–3, 32 n.7; Gillespie, *Colonial Ulster*, 9; Robinson, *Plantation of Ulster*, 52–5. Montgomery's portion consisted of the southern part of these lands, the area at the head of Strangford Lough around Comber, Newtownards and Grey Abbey; Hamilton's lands lay further to the north, along the southern shore of Belfast Lough from Holywood to Bangor and Groomsport.

17 Like Sir Thomas Smith's plantation, these lands had been targeted on account of their fertility as well as their location. See Richard Hakluyt, 'Notes on Colonisation', in D. B. Quinn, ed., *The Voyages and Colonising Enterprises of Sir Humphrey Gilbert*, 2 vols (London: Hakluyt Society, 1940), I, 181–6; Alison Cathcart, 'The Maritime Dimension to Plantation in Ulster, ca.1550–ca.1600', *Maritime Communities of the North Atlantic Arc in the Early Modern Period: Journal of the North Atlantic*, ed., Alison Cathcart, special volume 12 (2019), 102; see pp. 161–3, 161–2 n.147 above.

18 *A repertory of the inrolments of the Patent Rolls of Chancery, in Ireland*, 196–201 (50). He was to have a weekly market and annual fair at Castlereagh, Bangor and Holywood.

19 BL Add MS 36775, fol.137v; Perceval-Maxwell, *Scottish Migration to Ulster*, 52.

expression in the Plantation of Ulster that would follow a few years later, James was aiming for an outworking of his 'British' agenda by integrating Ireland more fully into British society, an initiative that involved all three of his kingdoms, by which means he would also assert his royal authority throughout those three kingdoms. More importantly perhaps, this endeavour highlighted the realities of regnal union. Scottish settlers were actively encouraged, a complete volte-face from policy under the Tudor monarchs who had sought to expel Highland Scots from Ulster. Elizabeth may have looked more favourably on James' Lowland subjects than his Highland Gaels but they were still Scots and not perceived to be suitable for such endeavours. In the changed context of the early seventeenth century, the 'civilised', acceptable Scots, were regarded as suitable undertakers and tenants by a Scottish king.[20] As a result, a number of Lowland Scots, many from the southwest, became heavily involved in these early seventeenth-century plantations in Ulster.[21]

The first of these plantations, that of Hamilton and Montgomery, began in earnest in 1606 and in the early years tenants were attracted by the availability of relatively cheap land of good quality, low rents and long leases. Ards was a well-drained fertile region, suitable for arable farming with plenty of opportunities for the exploitation of natural resources and,

20 Just as men like Thomas Radcliffe, Earl of Sussex, and Captain William Piers, commander of Carrickfergus Castle, were unable to countenance Scottish involvement in Ulster in the early 1560s, so in the early seventeenth century men like Sir John Davies were reluctant to see Scottish involvement in the Ulster plantations. The accession of a Scottish king to the thrones of England and Ireland, which no doubt caused Davies to change his opinion, at least publicly, would ensure the participation of Scots in the Ulster Plantation. See Jane E. A. Dawson, *Politics of Religion in the Age of Mary, Queen of Scots. The Fifth Earl of Argyll and the Struggle for Britain and Ireland* (Cambridge, 2002), 126–37; Sir John Davies, *A Discovery of the True Causes why Ireland was never entirely Subdued* (1612) stated that 'a mixed plantation of British and Irish' would 'secure the peace of Ireland, assure it to the Crown of England for ever; and … make it a civil and a rich … Kingdom'; quoted in C. Maxwell, ed., *Irish History from Contemporary Sources, 1509–1610* (London, 1923), 292–3.

21 LPL MS 630: Carew Manuscripts, fol.2r. The 'Englishe and Scottishe undertakers … are to make plantation with Englishe or Inland Scottishe tenants'.

although in 1575 it had been described as 'depopulated and wasted', in 1586 Marshal Bagenal described the Great Ards as 'a champion and fertile land'.[22] Such contrasting descriptions of the region were the result of sixteenth-century cartographic efforts to justify English colonising efforts in Ireland. Elizabeth could not use the argument of *res nullus* if the land was well populated, cultivated and fruitful so it became common for the land to be described as empty and vacant. Indeed in 1586 Lord Deputy Sir John Perrot justified the grant of the Route to the MacDonalds by asserting that local Irish lords did not have sufficient dependents to populate the land.[23] To be fair, the description of a 1604 patent which referred to the 'whole region of the county Antrim' as 'wasted by rebellion' was probably more or less accurate.[24] Decades of sporadic warfare and outbreaks of plague combined with Tyrone's rebellion and famine in the 1590s, had ravaged the landscape and caused depopulation but it was neither empty nor barren as so often described. Such terminology was used deliberately to account for English attempts to colonise the region but it was far from accurate. That the early English efforts at plantation, such as those by Sir Thomas Smith and Walter Devereux, Earl of Essex, met with violent resistance from the Irish highlights that the land certainly was inhabited albeit with a lower population density than in England.[25] In Clandeboy and the Ards, the availability of good quality land attracted settlers from across the water and the incorporation of the local elite (Con O'Neill) into the settlement, thereby offering some degree of validity to his claims to land, reduced the likelihood of rebellion by the Irish. That said, the events of the preceding years including the defeat at Kinsale and Tyrone's submission also reduced

22 *Patent Rolls of Chancery, in Ireland*, 196–201 (50) at 197; Robinson, *Plantation of Ulster*, 48 where it is described as 'desolate and waste'; Marshal Bagenal, Herbert F. Hore and Lord Burghley, 'Marshal Bagenal's Description of Ulster, Anno 1586', *Ulster Journal of Archaeology*, first series 2 (1854), 154. See also Gillespie, *Colonial Ulster*, 7–27, especially 12.

23 *Acts of the Privy Council of England. New Series*, ed., John Roche Dasent, 46 vols (London, 1890–1964), vol. XIX (1590), 50–1 states that part of the reasoning for the grant to Sorley Boy was that McQuillan 'was not able to inhabite his whole countrey nor to defende it from the Scottes'; Gillespie, *Colonial Ulster*, 8–10; 47–9.

24 *Patent Rolls of Chancery, in Ireland*, 137 (57).

25 For these earlier plantation efforts see Robinson, *Plantation of Ulster*, 46–8.

the likelihood of Irish rebellion although concern over future unrest lingered.[26] The peaceful, more settled conditions in Ireland post-1603 most likely contributed to the 'stream of emigrants' Sir Thomas Craig observed passing from Scotland to Ulster in 1606 and 1607.[27]

As well as bringing over appropriate numbers of tenants who would undertake plantation in County Down, Hamilton and Montgomery were keen to develop economic activity in their lands and exploit natural resources whether fishing, timber, or mineral deposits.[28] From the very outset James encouraged both men to develop internal and external trading links, granting them rights to import and export goods and hold weekly markets and annual fairs on their plantations.[29] There is no doubt that Hamilton was an ambitious, entrepreneurially-minded individual as he quickly acquired title to lands elsewhere in Ulster including the abbey lands of Coleraine, later granted to Sir Thomas Phillips, and the fishing of

26 T. W. Moody, 'The revised Articles of the Ulster Plantation, 1610', *Bulletin of the Institute of Historical Research* 12 (1934–35), 178–83; Thomas Blennerhasset, *A Direction for the Plantation in Ulster* (London, 1610).

27 Thomas Craig, *De unione regnorum Britanniae tractatus,* ed., Charles Sanford Terry, first series, vol. LX (Edinburgh: Scottish History Society, 1909), 446–7. When Craig's 'stream of emigrants' is placed in context, however, it is clear he was not referring to those participating in the Hamilton-Montgomery plantation. Craig emphasised the crucial role of Scotland in pacifying Ireland but the movement to Ulster was a result of the Scots who had 'long since settled themselves by force of arms in that part of the island nearest to their country', a reference to the MacDonalds.

28 Gillespie, *Colonial Ulster*, 11–18; 131–2. Indeed, James VI and I was granting rights of land and fishing across Ireland to various individuals although rights to woods and mineral deposits were more often retained by the crown or granted to individuals with considerable standing, such as Sir Arthur Chichester; see, for example, *Patent Rolls of Chancery, in Ireland*, 61 (79); 64–5 (88); 69 (94); 70–1 (97); 189 (28). At the same time, James ordered a stop on the import and export of all grain, silver and gold in an effort to stimulate the economy there; ibid, 73 (36). For the rights to fishing and woods allocated in the Plantation of Ulster see LPL MS 630, fols 3v, 4v–5r, 8v, 10r.

29 BL Add MS 4794: Milles Collection, Clarendon Mss vol. XLVIII, fols 56v–7v; BL Add MS 36775, fols 158v–9v. The king continued to protect Hamilton's efforts in east Ulster.

the River Bann from Lough Neagh to the salmon leap, the cause of a later dispute with Sir Randal MacDonnell, along with other lands in Down.[30] The surviving evidence for the plantation of Hugh Montgomery likewise says a great deal about the energy and effort required in establishing a thriving settlement.[31] Like Hamilton, Montgomery utilised kinship and clientage ties within his community back in Scotland to find willing settlers and, although land was offered at relatively cheap rents, Montgomery is said to have brought over 'divers wealthy able men' who had the financial means to undertake plantation. They capitalised on the natural resources of the region, as well as existing structures and buildings, to begin their settlement, cutting down wood for temporary dwellings, utilising waterways and inland communication routes for transport. They also brought with them 'smiths, masons, carpenters' and other skilled workmen to build stone houses in Grey Abbey, Newtown (Newtownards as it is now known) and Donaghadee, the main market centres of Montgomery's plantation, and they built water mills to support both arable and pastoral farming.[32] While trade was encouraged the close proximity to Scotland ensured that provisions were obtained with relative ease as Donaghadee was 'but three hours' sail from Port Patrick'.[33] The progress is evident in the 1611 plantation survey undertaken by George Carew where he described eighty new houses on Hamilton's estate at Bangor, all inhabited by English and Scots, plus a

30 *Patent Rolls of Chancery, in Ireland*, 189 (28); Perceval-Maxwell, *Scottish Migration to Ulster*, 51–8; Gillespie, *Colonial Ulster*, 13, 15–16, 67. Hamilton was also granted the 'the fee simple of the late dissolved monastery of the Blessed Virgin Mary in Dublin and St Mary Abbey' with all land and tithes pertaining, see BL Add 36775, fol.43v. See also P. Roebuck, 'The Making of an Ulster Great Estate: the Chichesters, Barons of Belfast and Viscounts of Carrickfergus, 1599–1648', *Proceedings of the Royal Irish Academy. Section C: Archaeology, Celtic Studies, History, Linguistics, Literature* 79 (1970), 1–25.

31 *Montgomery Manuscripts*, 51–68; Perceval-Maxwell, *Scottish Migration to Ulster*, 57–60; Raymond Gillespie, 'The Making of the Montgomery Manuscripts', *Familia* 2/2 (1986), 23–9.

32 *Montgomery's Manuscripts*, 59.

33 *Montgomery's Manuscripts*, 60. Constraints on shipping, however, did present difficulties for the planters; see pp. 291–5 below.

further twenty houses at Holywood.[34] He also noted that Montgomery's lands were well-settled, but more so with Scots than with English tenants.[35] Nonetheless, Newtown(ards) had 100 houses while Hugh Montgomery had purchased mining rights with an aim to further develop commercial activity where and when he could.[36]

If socio-economic advancement had been the aim of both James Hamilton and Hugh Montgomery at the outset of this endeavour they were not to be disappointed.[37] The Scotsmen quickly climbed the social hierarchy in a country where, from a Lowland or English perspective, there was little, if any, existing nobility at all, although a clearly recognisable social order.[38] In contrast the Irish suffered the most from plantation. Unable to

34 Hamilton initially made Bangor his main residence before moving to Killyleagh where he built a castle; see Rowan McLaughlin and James Lyttleton, eds, *An Archaeology of Northern Ireland 1600–1650* (Belfast, 2017), 97–103, 125, 353–4. Carew does not distinguish between what buildings may have already existed and were simply repurposed by the incomers.

35 McLaughlin and Lyttleton, eds, *An Archaeology of Northern Ireland*, 103–15, 117.

36 LPL MS 630, fol.144.

37 Hamilton was probably knighted some time in 1608 but was created Viscount Clandeboy on 4 May 1622 on account of 'his great labour and expence' and, having 'brought a plantation of British subjects … into Ireland', Hamilton had 'procured the tranquillity of the Province of Ulster'. Hugh Montgomery was created Lord Viscount Montgomery on 3 May 1622 'on account of his many and great deserts'. See *Hamilton Manuscripts*, 10–11 n.i; *Irish Patent Rolls of James I*, 552, nos v, xi; *Montgomery Manuscripts*, 77 n.31. For more on the wider social-economic status of planters and Irish see Gillespie, *Colonial Ulster*, 113–42, 152–66, 195–206. The reaction of and consequences for the Irish has received some recent, significant attention; see Raymond Gillespie, 'Success and Failure in the Ulster Plantation', in Éamonn Ó Ciardha and Micheál Ó Siochrú, eds, *The Plantation of Ulster: Ideology and Practice* (Manchester, 2012), 98–115; Marc Caball, 'Responses to Transformation: Gaelic Poets and the Plantation of Ulster', in Ó Ciardhá and Ó Siochrú, eds, *The Plantation of Ulster*, 176–97; Diarmaid Ó Doibhlin, 'The Plantation of Ulster: Aspects of Gaelic Letters', in Ó Ciardhá and Ó Siochrú, eds, *The Plantation of Ulster*, 198–217.

38 James also sought to realise reform of the church in Ireland, clawing back lands from the Irish and securing Protestantism. In February 1605 George Montgomery, brother to Hugh, was appointed Bishop of Derry, Raphoe and Clogher and was important in establishing the basis for the new Protestant Church of Ireland. Montgomery was moved to Meath in 1609 and replaced in Derry and Raphoe

come to terms with new forms of landholding that were based on economic, rather than symbolic, values of the land, the Irish who did receive lands could become indebted quickly. Even Con O'Neill struggled to adjust to the new economic reality and soon sold on his lands to the two Scots.[39] The declining fortunes of the Irish inhabitants during these early years mirrored the plantation which thrived, assisted considerably by good harvests but also facilitated by the commitment of the planters themselves, the exploitation of their connections across the North Channel, and the relative freedom to develop their new estates as they wished.[40] The beginning of trade and the growth of market centres fostered the commercial activity that James VI and I wanted to see in Ireland.[41] This internal economic activity, along with pastoral and arable farming, fed into the expanding trade networks between Ireland and southwest Scotland, networks encouraged by the changed circumstances of the North Channel region.

---

with Andrew Knox, formerly Bishop of the Isles. See H. A. Jefferies, 'George Montgomery, First Protestant Bishop of Clogher (1605–1621)', *Clogher Record* 16/3 (1999), 127–9; H. A. Jefferies, 'George Montgomery, First Protestant Bishop of Derry, Raphoe and Clogher (1605–1610)', in H. A. Jefferies and Ciaran Devlin, eds, *History of the Diocese of Derry* (Dublin, 2000), 140–66; Henry A. Jefferies, 'Montgomery, George (1569–70–1621), Church of Ireland bishop of Meath and Clogher', *ODNB*, accessed 29 July 2020; Fiona A. MacDonald, *Mission to the Gaels. Reformation and Counter-Reformation in Ulster and the Highlands and Islands of Scotland, 1560–1760* (Edinburgh, 2006), 33–6.

39 Gillespie, *Colonial Ulster*, 123, 140–2.

40 Numerous families were encouraged to settle in east Ulster and the plantation flourished quickly as, in July 1607, James wrote to Chichester following a request from Hamilton himself. The king stated he had decided to issue charters of incorporation and other privileges to Belfast, Coleraine and Bangor 'for the better setling and incouraging of the new Colonies of English and Scotish which do daylie indeavour to make Civill plantacion with in our Counties of Downe and Antryme'; quoted in Perceval-Maxwell, *Scottish Migration to Ulster*, 57. These towns did not receive their charters until 1613, see SP 63/232, fols 83–7 (84v); T. W. Moody, *The Londonderry Plantation, 1609–41. The City of London and the plantation in Ulster* (Belfast, 1939), 122–42.

41 Gillespie, *Colonial Ulster*, 64–83; 113–94. Overall although both agriculture and industry remained out of step with that of either England or Lowland Scotland, the plantation in County Down did bring about significant change.

With James VI's succession, as James I to the thrones of England and Ireland in 1603, the significance of the waters of the North Channel had changed completely. The North Channel and the Irish Sea were part of the 'one Sea' that, according to James, 'made vs all in one Island'.[42] In October 1604 James declared his intention to use the title 'King of Great Brittaine, France, and Ireland' although aware his wider British empire consisted of 'an aggregation of dominions under' his monarchy.[43] Both the English and Scottish parliaments rejected the king's calls for closer union, but this did not prevent James from adopting an archipelagic perspective. Members of his nobility might have paid lip-service to James' concept of British union, but the king himself regarded them as a related whole. The Hamilton-Montgomery plantation became a tangible expression of James' vision of empire. The plantation of English and Scottish subjects into Ireland would reform Irish society, bringing it into line with civil society in England and Lowland Scotland and thereby realising a more 'perfect Vnion', all of which would facilitate the extension of his royal authority.[44]

At this stage, James was not contemplating any wider plantation projects for Ulster, although immediately following his succession he sought to ascertain what lands in Ulster were now in his hands on account of forfeiture of those who rebelled.[45] In 1607 the Jamestown plantation was just commencing and would not be confident of its success for a decade, too often nearing a similar fate to the earlier sixteenth-century effort to

42 James VI, Speech to parliament of 19 March 1604 in Johann P. Sommerville, ed., *King James VI and I: Political Writings* (Cambridge, 1994), 135. In this context, however, he was referring to the landmass of England and Scotland, while viewing Ireland as a dependant kingdom.

43 James Francis Larkin and Paul L. Hughes, eds, *Stuart Royal Proclamations. Royal Proclamations of King James I, 1603–1625* (Oxford, 1973), 94–8 no.45; Brian P. Levack, *The Formation of the British State. England, Scotland and the Union 1603–1707* (Oxford, 1987), 2. James' 'aggregation of dominions' is the focus of my next monograph, exploring the outlying island communities within the wider 'empire' that James ruled over.

44 James VI, Speech to parliament of 31 March 1607 in Sommerville, ed., *King James VI and I: Political Writings*, 161, although admittedly in this specific context James was again referring to closer union between Scotland and England.

45 *Patent Rolls of Chancery, in Ireland*, 12, no.20, pt 5.

plant in Roanoke, North Carolina.[46] Closer to home, the second attempt at the Lewis enterprise had reached an embarrassingly, and frustratingly, similar conclusion to the initial effort, while plans for plantation in the North Isles had reached an impasse. The early successes of the Hamilton-Montgomery plantation, too often overlooked, were significant in shaping the king's perspective, ensuring plantation took central place in James' civilising agenda for the North Channel context with the aim of benefiting his entire three kingdoms. This was an endeavour undertaken by private individuals, albeit with crown support, and the initial years looked promising for what might follow.

The early successes of the Hamilton-Montgomery plantation also shaped the perspective of future potential undertakers and tenants, many of whom came from the southwest of Scotland. Too often the reasons for Scottish planters settling in Ulster have been summarised as available arable land at low rent, reasons that are also said to have contributed to the response of Scots to the official Plantation of Ulster in 1610.[47] More recently it has been argued that the men of the southwest were 'geographically and physically preconditioned to live where English' and other Lowland Scots, from further east and north, could not.[48] This predisposition for men from the west to engage more readily with the concept of plantation is a rather environmentally-deterministic perspective. Undoubtedly there were similarities in climatic and agricultural conditions between Ulster and southwest Scotland but other factors also deserve fuller consideration such as opportunities for trade and commerce, the changed North Channel context

46 Karen O. Kupperman, *The Jamestown Project* (Cambridge, MA, 2007), 1–7.

47 Perceval-Maxwell, *Scottish Migration to Ulster*, 91–106; 327–61; Robinson, *Plantation of Ulster*, 79–80. When the plantation of Ulster proposal was put forward the Scottish response was considerable. It attracted potential planters from across the country, including Haddington, Fife and Caithness. However, the most substantial number of planters came from the southwest of Scotland and the regions of Ayrshire and Galloway, as well as from Lanark and around the Clyde valley.

48 J. Michael Hill, 'The Origins of the Scottish Plantations in Ulster to 1625: A Reinterpretation', *Journal of British Studies* 32/1 (1993), 24–43 at 37; Robinson, *Plantation of Ulster*, 78–9.

and geographic proximity.[49] A cursory consideration of geography explains the attractions for the settlers who came to Ulster post-1608 and who predominantly were from Ayrshire, Lanarkshire, Renfrewshire, Argyllshire, Bute, Arran, Kirkcudbrightshire and Dumfries. Ulster was not *terra incognita* like Lewis or the Americas; only a short sea-crossing separated the two regions, making settlement there a much more attractive option.[50] Nonetheless, while external, contributing factors can be highlighted, much of the success of these early plantations is due to the energy and efforts of the individual planters themselves. Another plantation that encouraged subsequent migration from Scotland into Ulster, and which pre-dated the official Planation of Ulster, was also undertaken by a private individual. In this case, also facilitated by land grants from the crown, the endeavour was entirely due to one man: Randal MacDonnell.

Randal MacDonnell and plantation in Antrim

James MacDonnell of Dunluce, who had made such an impression on James VI during his visit to Scotland in 1596, died in 1601 and was

49 Hill, 'The Origins of the Scottish Plantations in Ulster', 38. The men from southwest Scotland did not exhibit a 'typically lax Celtic attitude toward general economic development'. Nor did the chief undertakers lack 'the resources (as well as the skill and inclination) to engage in any sort of commercial or trading activity that would significantly increase their wealth'. As it was mostly men from Devonshire in the southwest of England that embarked on plantation in Munster this perhaps points to geographic proximity as a driver rather than environmental determinism.

50 The Montgomeries were familiar with this short stretch of water. On 21 May 1586 the Privy Council of Scotland heard a complaint from Thomas Copran, a Dublin merchant. Copran claimed he had been at 'his lauchfull trade of merchandice at the north pairtis of Irland' when 'Adam Montgomerie of Braidstane, with uthiris his complices, all rubbaris and pyratis … rubbis and spuilzeit' him of his ship and goods. Adam, the fifth Laird of Braidstane and father to Hugh, failed to appear and was denounced a rebel. See *RPCS*, IV, 72. My thanks to Scott Carballo for this reference.

succeeded by his younger brother, Randal.[51] The fourth of five sons of Sorley Boy MacDonnell, Randal had been fostered by the Stewart family on the island of Arran, an upbringing that provided a keen sense of the cross-channel context within which he would spend his entire life. Following the death of his elder brother, Randal became head of the MacDonnells of Antrim and later that year joined Hugh O'Neill, Earl of Tyrone, and his forces at Kinsale. Surviving defeat there, shortly afterwards he submitted to Lord Lieutenant Mountjoy, offering to serve against Tyrone at his own expense and was knighted in return. Having realised what way the political winds were blowing in Ireland, Randal would reap the full rewards of his submission after Elizabeth's death. One of the first grants made by the new king of Ireland was the lands of the Route and the Glens in Antrim to Randal while the following year a regrant was issued which confirmed Randal in these lands but importantly included Rathlin Island.[52] Perhaps what was most interesting about the 1603 grant was that it gave Randal the power to divide his estates into precincts of 2,000 acres and to build a castle or manor in each. As Michael Perceval-Maxwell noted this was, 'in tentative outline, … a design for plantation which was later to be applied throughout the province'.[53] The same year Randal married Alice, daughter of Tyrone, by his second wife, thereby re-aligning himself with the Irish earl following the latter's submission to the king. Thus, within a few short years, Randal had moved from a position of rebellion against the English crown, to that of supporter of the new Stuart monarchy and allied with those in Ulster who were now in favour with the new monarch.[54] Much like the widespread revulsion in England that resulted from James VI and I's favour to Tyrone, Randal's position drew

51 Randal is said to have been in Scotland with his brother to meet the king in 1598; see SP 52/62, fols 66v, 70r; Terry Clavin, 'MacDonnell, Sir Randal mac Sorley', in James McGuire and James Quinn, eds, *Dictionary of Irish Biography* (Cambridge, 2009), <dib.ie>, accessed 10 February 2020.

52 PRONI, Earl of Antrim Papers: D2977/5/1/1/1; D2977/5/1/1/2/2.

53 Perceval-Maxwell, *Scottish Migration to Ulster*, 49.

54 Breandán O Buachalla, 'James Our True King: The Ideology of Irish Royalism in the Seventeenth Century', in D. G. Boyce, ed., *Political Thought in Ireland since the Seventeenth Century* (London, 1993), 7–35.

criticism and opposition, notably from the new Lord Deputy of Ireland, Sir Arthur Chichester, who had an abiding hatred of the MacDonnells. In 1597 Randal had assisted his brother Sir James in defeating an expedition by the English, during which Arthur's brother, Sir John Chichester, Governor of Carrickfergus Castle, was killed. Chichester disliked the Highland Scots in general but, following the murder of his brother, it became personal and he remained an enemy of MacDonnell.[55]

Much like the new king's attitude towards Tyrone and Rory O'Donnell, Earl of Tyrconnell, it was clear James sought to work with MacDonnell, another local chief, in furthering his policy for Ulster.[56] The family had long-standing connections in the area and were already known to the king, on account of his relationship with Randal's brother, Sir James. These grants of lands in Antrim to Randal may have been a reward for 'friendship and ancestry' but they were also an incentive, encouraging loyalty and co-operation with the king's policy for Ireland.[57] In the early years of the seventeenth century James VI and I's experience of plantation in Scotland was not a positive one and, as yet, it was not clear how the Lewis project might be resolved successfully. At the same time, the king was encouraging George Gordon, Marquess of Huntly, to undertake plantation in the North Isles, and had granted him the authority to extirpate the inhabitants. Thus,

55 SP 63/201, fols 132–3. Arthur Chichester's brother, Sir John Chichester, governor of Carrickfergus Castle, was defeated and killed in Antrim fighting against James MacDonnell. According to SP 63/201, fol.234 MacDonnell sent the governor's severed head to the earl of Tyrone. It is rumoured that Tyrone and his troops played a game of football with the said severed head. See H. Pawlisch, *Sir John Davies and the Conquest of Ireland* (Cambridge, 1985), 86 quoted in David Finnegan, 'Why Did the Earl of Tyrone Join the Flight?', in David Finnegan, Éamonn Ó Ciardha, and Marie-Claire Peters, eds, *The Flight of the Earls: Imeacht na nIarlaí* (Derry, 2010), 11 n.25.

56 There are differing views on this, although often expressed in the wider context of the causes of the flight, see N. P. Canny, 'The Flight of the Earls, 1607', *Irish Historical Studies* XVI (1971), 380–99; M. Kerney Walsh, *'Destruction by peace': Hugh O'Neill after Kinsale* (Armagh, 1986); J. McCavitt, 'The Flight of the Earls', *Irish Historical Studies* XXIX (1994), 159–73; John McCavitt, *The Flight of the Earls* (Dublin, 2002); Finnegan, 'Why Did the Earl of Tyrone Join the Flight?', 2–12.

57 Colin Breen, *Dunluce Castle: History and Archaeology* (Dublin, 2012), 96.

while in Scotland the king was still working towards removal, primarily of the MacDonalds, in Ireland he was seeking to work with the elite on the ground, including the MacDonnells. Although in 1606 some lands and property were removed from MacDonnell's grant, he still held 333,907 acres in an area that stretched from Larne on the east coast to Coleraine at the mouth of the Bann.[58] With land grants from the king, he became one of the largest landowners in Ireland, and he was both a Highland/Irish Gael and a Catholic. If James had used these grants to reward Randal for loyalty, he was to reap enormous returns over the next twenty years. Antrim was not one of the six escheated counties where land was allocated as part of the Plantation of Ulster, so there were no obligations placed on MacDonnell like those placed on the undertakers in that plantation; he was free to develop his own estates in his own way. His actions in this regard are evidence of MacDonnell's political awareness. Much in the same way as he had appreciated the need to submit to English authority after the defeat at Kinsale, in the early seventeenth century he was aware that co-operation with the new Stuart monarchy was the most advantageous means of self-preservation and self-promotion. As Colin Breen has argued, in undertaking a civilising programme on his Antrim lands, MacDonnell 'demonstrated a particular talent for survival', a trait exhibited by family members over the preceding half century.[59]

Like other Scottish undertakers in Ulster, for example, James Hamilton, Earl of Abercorn, who was granted the lands of Strabane in county Tyrone, MacDonnell was an enthusiastic and energetic planter.[60]

58 Hector McDonnell, 'MacDonnell, Randal, first earl of Antrim (*d.* 1636)', *ODNB*, accessed 4 May 2019; Breen, *Dunluce Castle*, 97 for a full breakdown of these lands. Dunluce, Olderfleet Castle at Larne, three-quarters of the fishing rights of the Bann and church lands including the priory of Coleraine were removed from Randal, although Dunluce was returned to him in 1615. In 1610 Randal also surrendered nine townlands adjacent to Coleraine for the City of Londonderry plantation there, in return he was regranted the rest of his lands for half the original rental; see PRONI D2977/5/1/1/4/1; D2977/5/1/1/4/2.

59 Breen, *Dunluce Castle*, 99.

60 For the Hamilton plantation at Strabane see Patrick Fitzgerald, 'Scottish Migration to Ireland in the Seventeenth Century', in Alexia Grosjean and Steve Murdoch, eds, *Scottish Communities Abroad in the Early Modern Period* (Leiden, 2005), 27–52;

Almost immediately after receiving charter for his lands Randal divided his estates and began preparations for building a castle or some sort of dwelling on each precinct, in most cases reworking existing structures to his advantage, as both Hamilton and Montgomery had done on their lands. MacDonnell set about establishing a network of settlements across his estates which were to act as centres of trade and small-scale industrial activity and, as early as 1606, just as the Hamilton-Montgomery plantation was getting off the ground, he gained the right to hold fairs and markets at a number of settlements.[61] In order to support these fledgling market centres MacDonnell encouraged agricultural and industrial development on his estates. He introduced the horse collar and heavy plough, so favoured by the English but not used widely in Irish society in Ulster, as opposed to ploughing by the tail which was regarded as a 'barbarous custome'.[62] Although ploughing by the tail was more suited to the landscape and rocky soils of various localities, MacDonnell was aware the English regarded this as a sign of progressive farming methods and was keen to construct the

---

Robert J. Hunter, ed., *Strabane Barony during the Ulster Plantation 1607–1641* (Belfast, 2011); William Roulston, 'Scottish Settlement and Society in Plantation Ulster, 1610–40', in David Edwards with Simon Egan, eds, *The Scots in Early Stuart Ireland. Union and Separation in Two Kingdoms* (Manchester, 2016), 95–115. For details of Abercorn's settlement in the various plantation surveys see as follows: Carew 1611: LPL MS 630, fols 42–71, 96–105; *CCM*, V, no.58 (77), 130 (232). Josias Bodley 1613: *Historic Manuscripts Commission 78. Report on the Manuscripts of the late Reginald Rawdon Hastings* 4, ed., Francis Bickley (London, 1947), 159–82 at 181–2. Nicholas Pynnar 1619: *CCM*, V, no.211 (392–422, at 409–10); LPL MS 630, fol.100v. For the 1622 commission see Victor Treadwell, 'The Survey of Armagh and Tyrone, 1622', *Ulster Journal of Archaeology*, third series XXIII (1960), 126–37 and 'The Survey of Armagh and Tyrone, 1622 (continued)', *Ulster Journal of Archaeology*, third series XXVII (1964), 140–54. For the information on Abercorn's plantation see vol. XXVII (1964), 140–2; Victor Treadwell, ed., *The Irish Commission of 1622: An Investigation of the Irish Administration, 1615–1622, and Its Consequences, 1623–1624* (Dublin: Irish Manuscripts Commission, 2006), 588–9, 592–4.

61 Breen, *Dunluce Castle*, 100. Fairs were to be held at Clough (24 June, feast of St John the Baptist) and Dunkerd (29 September, feast of St Michael); and markets at Dunluce (Saturday), Dunieney (Tuesday) and Glenarm (Thursday).

62 BL Add MS 4756, Reports of the Irish Commission 1622, fol.62r.

image of a land-owner seeking to realise the economic potential of his estates.[63] In time he also developed rabbit warrens, deer parks, quarries and a salt pans near Ballycastle.[64] Alongside these efforts at economic development there was considerable building work undertaken: manor courts, imposing residences at Dunluce and Glenarm, roads, bridges, mills and townships, often in a distinctive Scottish style. This internal infrastructure was crucial for transportation of goods and people around his estates and for the success of his settlements.

In developing settlements across his estates MacDonnell utilised his North Channel connections, establishing both Irish and Scottish tenants on his lands; he was free to do so as he was not bound by the 'Conditions' that applied to undertakers in the official Plantation of Ulster.[65] In the early years his plantation in Antrim acted as a welcome safety-value for the inhabitants of Kintyre. Some faced forced removal from their lands by the earl of Argyll, who had recently acquired the lands, but it was the wider outbreak of unrest led by Angus MacDonald in 1607 that caused the most difficulty, while also resulting in the displacement of the McPhees of Colonsay. Kintyre was a former MacDonald stronghold and customary claims of possession of land remained strong. Although some accepted Campbell lordship and remained on their estates, those who rebelled against the new regime fled the unrest and many made the short passage across to Antrim, attracted by the availability of good land, at low rents and with long leases, and landlord toleration of confessional allegiances. The Irish and Highland Scots took advantage of the opportunity of settlement in MacDonnell's plantations in the wake of the unrest in Kintyre. It is likely that the rhetoric of civility and Protestantism contributed to the 'probable

63 BL Add MS 4756, fol.68v. Willy Maley, 'Barbarisme and obdurate wilfulnesse'. Agricultural materialism, animal welfare, and Irish studies' in Sarah Covington, Vincent P. Carey, and Valerie McGowan-Doyle, eds, *Early Modern Ireland. New Sources, Methods and Perspectives* (London, 2019), 233–53. The agricultural dimension to English policy in Ireland is the subject of a University of Strathclyde PhD thesis; see Lauren McDougall, 'Civility, Agriculture, and the 1641 rebellion' (in progress).

64 See p.160 and n.141 above.

65 Moody, 'Revised Articles of the Ulster Plantation', 181–2.

underestimation of the extent of Highland emigration to Ulster during the plantation' both at the time and in the subsequent historiography.[66] The MacDonnell plantation, therefore, challenges the generalised assumption of plantation as undertaken by civilised, Lowland Scots and English undertakers. Nonetheless, despite MacDonnell's Gaelic connections and adherence to Catholicism, there was a significant number of Lowland Scots who settled on the fertile land of the Route in the north of Antrim. Many of these Lowland settlers, along with some Highland tenants too, were of a Protestant persuasion and regarded as more suitable tenants.[67]

MacDonnell's agenda and entirety of the improvements carried out on his estates have recently come to light thanks to archaeological research undertaken by Dr Colin Breen, Centre for Maritime Archaeology, University of Ulster, alongside the Centre for Archaeological Fieldwork and archaeology students from Queen's University Belfast, as part of a project supported by the Northern Ireland Environment Agency.[68] The settlement at Dunluce went into decline following the earl's death in 1636 only to be abandoned later in the seventeenth century after the 1641 rebellion and the

66 MacDonald, *Mission to the Gaels*, 58, 113 argues there was an official reluctance to grant denization to Highland settlers. Utilising various sources MacDonald argues that many names assumed to be Irish were Gaelic Scot patronymics. For more on the use of surnames and patronymics by Scottish Gaelic clans in Scotland and Ulster see Allan I. Macinnes, 'Social Mobility in Medieval and Early Modern Scottish Gaeldom: the controvertible evidence', *Transactions of the Gaelic Society of Inverness*, 58 (1993–94), 371–405 at 398 concerning the Munros from Easter Ross.

67 A. F. Scott Pearson, 'Alumni of St Andrews and the Settlement of Ulster', *Ulster Journal of Archaeology*, third series 14 (1951), 7–14 at 7–8 highlights how many of the early ministers to settle in the diocese of Down and Connor, mostly graduates of the University of St Andrews, were 'Prescopalian', men who were comfortable with a hybrid church structure that incorporated elements of, what would become known as, Presbyterianism and Episcopalianism. The diocese of Derry, Clogher and Raphoe attracted graduates of the University of Glasgow; see MacDonald, *Mission to the Gaels*, 33–6, 117.

68 I was fortunate enough to be able to visit Dunluce Castle in 2010 while the archaeological dig was underway. My thanks to Dr Colin Breen for the opportunity and showing us around, and to Professors Rolf and Magna Loeber, Hector McDonnell and Professor Jane Ohlmeyer for the company.

upheavals of civil war and restoration.[69] The land around Dunluce Castle has lain undeveloped thanks to the fact that it remained in the hands of the MacDonnell family until 1928 when it was passed into state care. The dig that took place at Dunluce between 2008 and 2011 uncovered the full extent of MacDonnell's energy in relation to his plantation and his efforts to align with James VI and I's civilising agenda. In the castle grounds Randal developed a 'garden complex, including a possible bowling green' and an orchard, as well as making improvements to the castle itself, incorporating both Scottish and European architectural trends. He also added new lodgings, stables and a brew-house. Beyond the castle was the developing town, including a church and several houses, and the excavations point to the trading activity that went on at Dunluce.[70]

Regardless of his civilising, commercialising outlook which suggested that, at least outwardly, he was fully on board with the king's agenda for Ireland, Randal remained a traditional Gaelic lord and a committed Catholic. The family had patronised the Francisan friary at Bonamargy where Randal and his son would be buried.[71] Nonetheless, while bringing both Catholic and Protestant Scottish and Irish settlers onto his lands and developing his estates in line with the official Plantation of Ulster, Randal's own confessional stance was overlooked, at least by a king (if not by his councillors) who prioritised recognition of his royal authority over adherence to the Catholic faith. Consequently, Randal's loyalty, his energy and his political astuteness were recognised and richly rewarded; he was created Lord Viscount Dunluce in 1618 on account of the 'many … faithfull services' he had performed 'as a valiant gentleman … aswell for the settling of a general peace … in reducing to civility the barbarous people' of the north of Ireland.[72] In 1620 he was made earl of Antrim. That he died in

69 Breen, *Dunluce Castle*, 164–80. For more on the upheavals of the seventeenth century and the role of Randal MacDonnell, second earl and first marquis of Antrim, see Ohlmeyer, *Civil War and Restoration*.

70 For more details see Breen, *Dunluce Castle*, 95–163.

71 Ohlmeyer, *Civil War and Restoration*, 27, 47, 75. Bonamargy was a vital base for the Franciscan missions to the western Isles in the 1620s and 1630s and received many Scots who attended mass there.

72 BL Add MS 36775, fol.260v.

1636 with Dunluce still a thriving settlement and, it is said, without any debt suggests something of the success of all his efforts.[73]

Within a century, the MacDonnells had moved from being unwanted migrants habitually moving between estates in Ireland and Scotland and regarded as the source of Ulster's problems, to being part of the political establishment, members of the Irish peerage, and a crucial part of the crown's answer to the perceived problem in the north of Ireland. This ability to survive and adapt to the political, social, economic and confessional changes of the time was remarkable and in doing so they had exploited the North Channel context expertly. The MacDonalds had moved swiftly back and forth across the water during the sixteenth century in their efforts to retain their hold on lands both in Ireland and Scotland; the MacDonnells had fully integrated themselves into Irish society, and gained recognition as subjects of the English queen while still utilising their connections across the water to consolidate and expand their estates. In the context of post-1603 regnal union, Randal once more exploited the cross-channel connections and events to build, fortify and maintain thriving plantation settlements in his Ulster estates. The MacDonnells of Antrim had navigated the turbulent times and waters of the archipelago. Their resistance to earlier English attempts to extend authority in Ulster contributed to the development of a policy that evolved into calls for plantation, and they helped to thwart early English efforts in that regard. In the changed circumstances of the seventeenth century they contributed to the success of James' wider civilising policy and themselves realised one of the most successful plantations of the time. Their fortunes in the early seventeenth century stood in marked contrast to those of their kin across the North Channel. The MacDonalds of Dunviaig were in gradual and terminal decline, a process shaped by and inextricably connected to, the actions of the Campbells of Argyll.

73 Hector McDonnell, 'MacDonnell, Randal, first earl of Antrim (*d.* 1636)'.

Rooting out of the barbarous sort and planting civility in their rooms

The Campbells of Argyll had survived the possibility of internal fracturing during the early 1590s and were once again dominant in the western Highlands and Isles. After 1603, Archibald Campbell, seventh Earl of Argyll, committed fully to the king's British agenda, even using the terminology of 'North British' for Scotland and 'British' for the planters in Ulster.[74] It is unlikely that Argyll himself ever harboured any serious ambition to undertake plantation, at least not on an Ulster or Lewis model, but he was aware the 'civilising' agenda in Scotland was concerned with establishing law and order, ensuring James' royal authority was respected, and developing commercial endeavour in order to integrate the region more fully into Scottish society and economy. Argyll wanted to secure Campbell influence in the region and nationally and this meant retaining the king's favour. Consequently, the 'civilising' agenda was a means to an end: the end that emerged gradually was the complete removal of the troublesome Clan Donald while extending Campbell dominance. In doing so, whether consciously or not, he was following the advice of James VI in *Basilicon Doran* when he advocated 'rooting out … the barbarous … sort, and planting ciuilitie in their roomes'.[75]

From the mid-1590s onwards the MacDonalds of Dunivaig continued to fall foul of the crown while the effects of the royal expeditions of 1605 and 1608, aimed at bringing them to order, were short-lived. The decade between 1596 and 1606 was pivotal. During this time the MacDonalds went from a clan James thought he would work with, to one he had no intention of working with, while the Campbells moved from ambivalence to outright hostility towards the MacDonalds. Ongoing discord between Angus MacDonald of Dunivaig and his son, Sir James of Knockrinsay, did little to alleviate the clan's reputation for lawlessness and sustained flouting

74 Allan I. Macinnes, *Clanship, Commerce, and the House of Stuart, 1602–1788* (East Linton, 1996), 60.

75 Sommerville, ed., *King James VI and I. Political Writings*, 24.

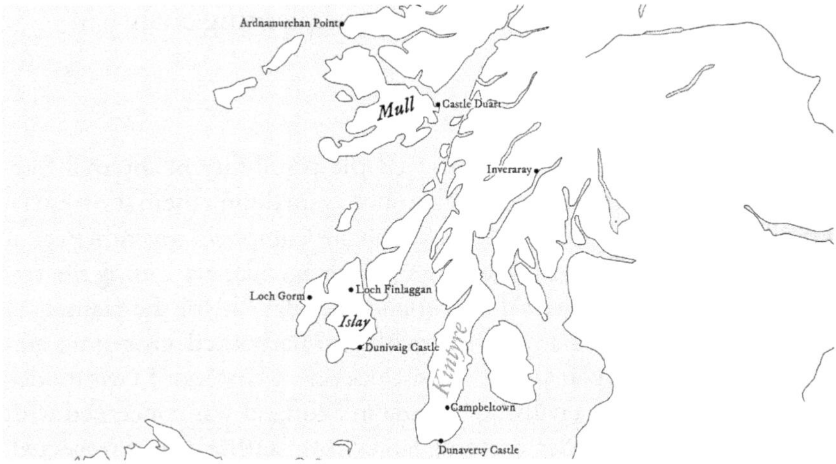

Map 8. South Isles

of royal authority. Nonetheless, on 8 September 1606 MacDonald wrote to the king in an attempt to regain favour and submitted offers to the king concerning Islay and Kintyre.[76] Two days later he wrote another letter from Islay to the king and council, hoping to inform them 'quhat hes bene my behaviour evir sen your Hienes past out of thir North pairtis of your Maiesteis dominionis'.[77] He explained he had written to the council that sat in Glasgow in 1605 and had made several offers but, having 'reseavit na ansuer nor quhat your Ma[ies]tie resoluis and derectis me to do; and being refusit of Licence to haif cum and presentit my self personalie befoir your hienes', he was feeling rather frustrated. As the council explained to the king in a letter dated 19 June 1607, although 'cautioun wes promeist for performaunce of … offeris' made by both MacDonald and Knockrinsay,

76 *The Book of Islay. Documents Illustrating the History of the Island*, ed., G. G. Smith (Edinburgh, 1895), no. LXII (118–19); Robert Pitcairn, *Ancient Criminal Trials in Scotland: Compiled from the Original Records and mss., with Historical Illustrations* (Edinburgh: Maitland Club, 1833), vol. III, part I, 365–6.

77 *Book of Islay*, no. LXIII (119–20). In this letter Angus deliberately refers to the king's 'realme of North Britane'.

'they failyeit in that poynt sua that no certane conclusion could be tane w[i]t[h] [th]ame'.[78] MacDonald's offers had been rejected.

Many on the council had a deep distrust of the MacDonalds and would oppose any move to see them rehabilitated in the same way as the earls of Tyrone and Tyrconnell had been in Ireland. Scholarship is largely united on the likelihood of Argyll manipulating the council to suit his agenda.[79] David Caldwell suggests Argyll had been supporting MacDonald against both his son, Knockrinsay, and Sir James of Dunluce, and was reluctant to see the MacDonnells in Antrim gain title to Islay and Kintyre. While Caldwell argues that in 1597 there was 'no evidence of any conspiracy ... to oust the MacDonalds in favour of the Campbells', by 1610 it was 'possible that Argyll was already scheming to acquire Islay'.[80] No doubt the seventh earl became increasingly acquisitive and aggressive in taking action against clans that continued to rebel against royal authority. It is likely that in the crucial decade between 1596 and 1606 Argyll ensured MacDonald remained as chief, while extinguishing any threats from Dunluce or Knockrinsay, only to later undermine the chief's position in Islay and Kintyre. To be sure, however, events in Ireland from 1602 onwards must have pushed Argyll down a particular path, one where Campbell interests were served at the expense of their former MacDonald allies. As well as seeing Tyrone and Tyrconnell receive the king's favour, Argyll also saw Randal MacDonnell

78 NLS Denmilne MSS, Adv MSS 33.1.1., vol. II, no.30.

79 Donald Gregory, *History of the Western Highlands and Isles of Scotland, from AD 1493 to AD 1625: With a Brief Introductory Sketch, from AD 80 to AD 1493* (Edinburgh, 1836; reprinted Edinburgh, 2009 with an introduction by Martin MacGregor), 310–13.

80 Caldwell, *Islay*, quotations on 92, 95. Caldwell is relatively even-handed, only suggesting that Argyll was angry with Sir James on account of his murder of Argyll's ally, Lauchlan MacLean of Duart in 1598. Martin MacGregor, 'The Statutes of Iona: Text and Context', *Scottish Historical Review* LVII/2 (2006), 163–70 argues that Bishop Knox and an anti-Campbell element in the council sought to 'roll back the tide of Campbell influence' in the early seventeenth century (168). See also Allan I. Macinnes, *The British Confederate. Archibald Campbell, marquess of Argyll, c.1607–1661* (Edinburgh, 2011), 54–5; E. J. Cowan, 'Fishers in Drumlie Waters: Clanship and Campbell Expansion in the time of Gilleasbuig Gruamach', *Transactions of the Gaelic Society of Inverness* 54 (1984–86), 269–312.

confirmed in his lands in Antrim. Any such rehabilitation of the main Highland chiefs in Scotland would have curtailed Argyll's own influence and ambition. In the end, though, it was a general unwillingness by the Privy Council to support Angus MacDonald's proposals for Islay and Kintyre that presented Argyll with the perfect opportunity.

Argyll requested a gift of lands in Kintyre in recompense for the services performed against the MacGregors and the council supported it.[81] The council wrote to James, persuading him of the benefits of such a grant, subsequently confirmed on 30 May 1607.[82] While Argyll may have sought to manipulate the Privy Council to suit his own agenda, like the earl himself, the council also had an eye on developments in Ireland. As with Argyll, James' policy of co-operation with Tyrone and Tyrconnell, alongside the extensive grants made to Randal MacDonnell, made council wary of how a similar policy towards formerly rebellious Gaelic lords would play out in Scotland.[83] While the king himself was somewhat hesitant to encourage further Campbell dominance in the west, plans for the North Isles were not promising while Lewis was not working out as he had hoped. In the South Isles, James could use Argyll to bring order and stability while working with the local elite who held sway in the region. And, after all, the Campbells were the acceptable face of Scottish Gaeldom and this was more palatable to the council in Edinburgh.[84] There were those who, like James, were

81 For some years the MacGregors had been regarded as lawless and rebellious, but their brutal murder of most of the Clan Colquhoun in early 1603 resulted in a campaign to hunt them down over the next few years and, in so doing, abolish the MacGregor name.

82 *RPCS*, VII, 528–9, 749, 750, 750 n.1; ICA Argyll Transcripts post-1600.

83 How the council would have responded had negotiations for a marriage between Tyrone's son and Argyll's daughter gone ahead is interesting; it is likely they would have had a similar reaction to their English counterparts. See ICA A36 Argyll personal letters, 1602–1638. But this was not simply Argyll allying with those close to the king for there was never any suggestion of an alliance with the MacDonnells of Antrim, despite the favour shown to Randal by James VI and I.

84 SP 52/58, fol.72: 'Observations of [th]e D[ean] of Lymerick for [th]e owt Iles of Scotland' which states that 'the better sorte of the Cambells are of an hono[ur]able disposition, favo[ur]ers of religion, trustie, valiant and civillye inclined'. The quotation comes at the top of the ninth side of this report.

somewhat reluctant to see Argyll's influence and authority in the west spread further, but it was preferable to ongoing Clan Donald dominance. Indeed, the spectre of a revived and reinvigorated Clan Donald in the west had been highlighted with the (albeit failed) attempts of Sir James of Knockrinsay to escape his captivity, firstly from Blackness in 1604, and secondly, from Edinburgh in 1606; and the escape of Archibald MacDonald from Dumbarton in March 1607.[85] In addition, there was a widespread appreciation of the need for economic development in the region. With the Hamilton-Montgomery plantation underway in Ulster, efforts to exploit commercial opportunities in Ulster were evident and many in the council would have been keen to realise the economic potential of a region long since regarded as fertile of soil and rich in fishings.[86] From a Lowland perspective, as the region's Gaelic inhabitants were lawless and disobedient, with events on Lewis reinforcing such views, it would be advantageous for the Highland chiefs to be at least curtailed, if not removed entirely, so that economic exploitation could begin in earnest. Consequently, the council argued that granting lands in Kintyre to Argyll would benefit not only Scotland, but the entire archipelago, while also repressing the Clan Donald who were 'the scoolemaisteris and fosteraris of all barbaritie, savaignes, and crueltye'. As such 'thair utter extirpatioun and ruitteing out' was essential.[87]

Once Argyll received his grant of lands in Kintyre he wasted little time in taking steps to assert Campbell lordship. The earl knew of the non-payment of rental by MacDonald and the recent surveys of Kintyre in which many areas were regarded as 'waist'.[88] The devastation of famine and harvest

85 Pitcairn, *Ancient Criminal Trials in Scotland*, 7; NLS Denmilne MSS, Adv. MSS 33.1.1., vol. II, no.17; Crawford, 'Sir James of Knockrinsay', 122.

86 Much as the Fife lords sought to do in their exploitation of the 'plentis of fischeis' around Lewis that '"wald rander maist inestemable commoditeis"'; see *RPCS*, VI, 420.

87 *RPCS*, VII, 749–50.

88 *Highland Papers volume III*, ed., J. R. N. MacPhail, second series, vol. XX (Edinburgh: Scottish History Society, 1920), 66–85. In 1605 'out of 161.5 merklands, 62 lay 'waist' in north Kintyre'; in south Kintyre 51 out of 203 merklands were likewise described as 'waist'; see Robert A. Dodgshon, 'The Little Ice Age in the Scottish Highlands and Islands: Documenting its Human Impact', *Scottish Geographical Journal* 121/4 (2005), 328.

failures during the 1590s had taken its toll but the early years of the seventeenth century had brought more stable conditions. With one eye on the emerging plantations across the North Channel and another on the king's proposals for the North Isles, Argyll sought to maintain and increase royal favour by taking steps to implement his own 'civilising' agenda in his newly acquired lands of Kintyre just as, across the water, MacDonnell sought to ingratiate himself with the king by developing his estates along plantation lines. After all, as the charter to Argyll stated, Kintyre 'had been possessed for a long time by rude and barbarous people destitute of all fear of God and respect to their Prince'.[89]

On 4 March 1609 Argyll entered into a bond with Sir Colin Campbell of Lundy and Sir John Campbell of Cawdor as cautioners by which he was obliged 'for the biging and planting of ane town within the saidis landis [and] lordschip of Kyntyre to be erectit be His Ma[ies]tie withe all frie previlegis and immuniteis pertein[in]g to a burgh royall'. He was discharged of the rents and duties for the space of five years on the grounds that he would plant a burgh to be inhabited by 'lawland men and traffiquing burgesses' within the bounds of Kintyre 'quhair thair is ane verie guid commoditie of ane choiss convenient harborie for schippis'.[90] If the earl failed to establish the burgh he would be held liable for the payment of rents for the said five years. Almost immediately Argyll began issuing orders to Duncan McDougall of Dunollie and others, 'pretended tenants' on the island of Luing, 'to flit and remove', and also the tenants of the barony of Lochhead in south Kintyre.[91] Having taken the necessary steps to remove unwanted, or rather, uncivil tenants, it was at Campbeltown that Argyll

89 ICA Argyll Transcripts post-1600; dated 30 May 1607.

90 Even before he received the grant of Kintyre he began warning 'pretended tenants' inhabiting lands on the island of Luing 'to flit and remove' with forty days' notice. These early efforts were ineffective as letters of horning were later issued by the earl at Inveraray against the same tenants, charging them to move from their lands; see ICA Argyll Transcripts post-1600; dated 14 February 1607; [undated] 1607. ICA Argyll Chartulary, 1600–1700, 4 March 1609; ICA Inveraray bundle no.1116; *Fourth Report of the Royal Commission on Historic Manuscripts* (London, 1874), I, 475, Argyll Charters no. 23.

91 ICA Argyll Transcripts, 1600–1700; dated 7 June 1609, and 28 June 1609.

began to build his new burgh.[92] A week later Argyll received confirmation from the king of the lands, woods, fishings, manors and other appurtenances, which previously had been in the possession of Hector MacLean of Lochbuie but since resigned to the king; on account of the earl's 'good faithful and thankful service' these lands were to be known as the Barony of Lochhead.[93]

Having begun the process of removing tenants, Argyll made his first grant of lands to new tenants for his burgh on 31 August the same year. At Inveraray, Argyll granted a charter of the lands of Askomilbeg to John Boyle, younger of Ballochmartin, his heirs and assignees on condition it was not sublet to any MacDonald, MacLean, MacAlister or MacNeil.[94] This was followed on 5 September with a grant to Boyle of three acres of land 'where it shall seem best to John on the north part of the river' and another acre to be 'built and planted with houses from of old about those formerly built excepting the house and gardens formerly possessed by MacConill of Dounnavig'. He was granted the right to graze six horses, to make and sell whisky, and cut peat. He was required to build 'a good and sufficient house of 3 houses height of lime and stone and slated within 3 years' at his own charges. In return Boyle and his heirs would be free burgesses of Campbeltown.[95]

There is not much more to say about Argyll's efforts at plantation in the South Isles. He removed some of the main sitting tenants and made a few grants to Lowlanders that were similar to inducements to plantation but, beyond that, the earl seems to have had little enthusiasm for the endeavour. There was some resettlement of Campbells from Knapdale into Kintyre, but it was not until much later in the seventeenth century that Campbeltown was established as a burgh of Barony. No doubt Argyll was dealing with residual unrest while asserting Campbell authority throughout Kintyre, but by 1610 plantation was no longer a policy being pursued in the west Highlands and Isles of Scotland.[96] The plantation of Lewis and

92 Macinnes, *Clanship, Commerce*, 74.

93 ICA Argyll Transcripts, 1600–1700; dated 4 July 1609.

94 Alastair Campbell of Airds, *A History of Clan Campbell, Volume II: From Flodden to the Restoration* (Edinburgh, 2002), 151.

95 ICA Argyll Transcripts, 1600–1700; dated at Inveraray 5 September 1609.

96 Macinnes, *Clanship, Commerce*, 63.

efforts to establish a burgh at Stornoway were concluded in 1609 while the Statutes of Iona, agreed that year, had brought about a negotiated agreement between the king and his Highland and Hebridean elite that aimed at integrating them more fully into wider Scottish social, political and economic society.[97] James then turned to the MacKenzies of Kintail in the North Isles and the Campbells of Argyll in the South Isles which enabled the king to devote his energies elsewhere. Following this, plantation, as it would develop in Ireland, was not so high on the agenda in Scotland. Keen to realise economic development and commercialisation, James would have encouraged any efforts by Argyll and MacKenzie to develop the market centres necessary for reaping the full economic benefits of the western Highlands and Isles while the more settled circumstances across the region enabled the king to give fuller attention to the official Plantation of Ulster soon to be underway across the North Channel.[98]

By 1610 Argyll's attention was focused elsewhere. In November 1609 he remarried to the English Catholic, Anne, daughter of Sir William Cornwallis of Brome, in London which served to increase his absenteeism from his estates in Scotland.[99] This did not bring an end to further Campbell expansion in the southern Highlands and Isles, their role as agents of the crown, their efforts to suppress ongoing rebellious activity, or their commercial endeavours but the ability to expand further came about largely through the actions of Angus MacDonald. When MacDonald submitted

97 Macinnes, *Clanship, Commerce*, 65–71; MacGregor, 'The Statutes of Iona', 138–50.

98 Throughout the previous two centuries the Campbells of Argyll had been exploiting the fishing of the Firth of Clyde and wider Argyll region, and the export of hides, to engage in international trade alongside their utilisation of surpluses within the locality to consolidate clan cohesion. Their efforts to do so point to much earlier attempts to develop commercial opportunities and fully exploit the economic resources of their estates than has been, and continues to be, fully appreciated. See Boardman, *The Campbells*, 291–310. The earl also had the assize herring of the western seas; see ICA Argyll Chartulary 1600–1700; dated 20 December 1607; *Fourth Report of HMC*, I, 481, Argyll Charters no. 149.

99 Campbell of Airds, *History of Clan Campbell*, 151.

in 1608 he had agreed to a payment of rental arrears.[100] Given his loss of lands and the repercussions of years of famine and harvest failure during the 1590s, repayment presented a significant obstacle as did the obligation to adhere to the Statutes and appear annually before the Privy Council in Edinburgh. Already an old man and struggling to adjust to a new political landscape in which his lands and influence were diminishing, while facing greater accountability for himself and his dependents, he could see no other way out. Consequently, in January 1612, for the sum of 6,000 merks MacDonald 'renuncit, discharget, and overgevin … all richt, tytil, propertie, and possessioun' which he had to the island of Islay in favour of John Campbell of Cawdor, also promising 'neuir to trubil, inquyet, nor molest the said Sir John nor na utheris his tenentis'.[101] How MacDonald felt, nine months later, when Randal MacDonnell bought outright Cawdor's claim to Islay, is unclear.[102] There was little love left between the two families and MacDonald may even have preferred to see Campbell rather than MacDonnell overlordship of Islay. Either way, it was the Islay tenants themselves who, in 1613, complained of 'the forme and custome of Yreland' that

100 F. A. Macdonald, 'MacDonald, Angus, of Dunyvaig and the Glens (c.1548–1613), chief of Clan Iain Mhòr or Clan Donald South', *ODNB*, accessed 17 April 2019, states he agreed to pay £3000 arrears of rent.

101 *Book of Islay*, no. LXXXl (148–49); *The Book of the Thanes of Cawdor: A Series of Papers Selected from the Charter Room at Cawdor 1236–1742*, ed., Cosmo Innes (Edinburgh: Spalding Club, 1859), 226–7. Angus' son, Sir James of Knockrinsay, was married to Margaret, sister of Cawdor. Edward J. Cowan, 'Clanship, Kinship and the Campbell Acquisition of Islay', *Scottish Historical Review* LVIII:2/166 (1973), 154 notes that Sir James had been communicating with Cawdor over a possible exchange of lands between the two men, of lands in Islay for Cawdor's lands in the north. Given Sir James' later actions concerning Islay his agenda is questionable.

102 *Book of Islay*, no. LXXXIII (152–3). David Stevenson, *Highland Warrior. Alasdair MacColla and the Civil Wars* (Edinburgh, 1980; reprinted 2003), 30–1 argues MacDonald and MacDonnell came to an agreement that MacDonnell and not Cawdor should take over the island. In the light of the relationship between these men and their kindreds it is hard to agree with Stevenson's view here.

MacDonnell imposed on them, thus paving the way for Cawdor to acquire the island.[103]

This Campbell acquisition of Islay, the core of the MacDonald estate in Scotland for centuries, was further facilitated by rebellion as, throughout 1614 and 1615, Dunivaig Castle, the former stronghold of the chiefs of Clan Donald South, was besieged a number of times by both members of the clan and by forces of the crown. The transfer of the island into MacDonnell hands combined with the death of Angus MacDonald in 1613 is said to have encouraged Ranald Og, illegitimate son of Angus MacDonald to rebel, taking possession of Dunivaig Castle. Sir James' younger brother (and thus younger son of Angus), Angus Og then expelled his half-brother and claimed to hold the castle on behalf of the crown. The king gathered men and cannon from Ireland to join royal forces in suppressing the rebellion and commission was granted to Sir John Campbell of Cawdor to lead them.[104] A detailed discussion of the rebellion, that subsequently saw Sir James of Knockrinsay escape from Edinburgh and make his way to Islay to recapture Dunivaig Castle, is not needed here.[105] The outcome was that Islay passed from MacDonnell to Campbell possession when, in November 1614, Cawdor was persuaded to accept a feu of Islay for 9,000 merks, a sum far above what he was able to pay.[106] Residual MacDonald influence in and possession of the island was picked apart as Cawdor banded with the

103 *RPCS*, X, 13–14; *Book of Islay*, no. LXXXIV (153–5). However, see Crawford, 'Sir James of Knockrinsay', 116–17 and 117 n.67 where Crawford suggests that it was in 1610 that the tenants of Islay petitioned the Privy Council in favour of MacDonald and Knockrinsay.

104 *RPCS*, X, 716–20, 720–2; *Book of Islay*, nos CI (179–82), CII (182–3), CIII (183–6), CIV (186–8); *Book of the Thanes of Cawdor*, 231–3.

105 See Gregory, *History of Western Highlands and Isles*, 349–90; Cowan, 'Campbell acquisition of Islay', 132–57; Stevenson, *Highland Warrior*, 30–1, 34–47; Caldwell, *Islay*, 96–103; and more recently Ross Crawford, 'Warfare in the West Highlands and Isles of Scotland, *c.*1544–1615' (University of Glasgow, PhD, 2016), 207–28.

106 *Book of Islay*, nos CXIV (199–230), CLXIX (333–4); *Book of the Thanes of Cawdor*, 237–8. Cawdor would later petition the Privy Council in January 1618 arguing that, as he was subject to 'a grite yeirlie dewytie', he needed protection against the 'maisterles and lawless personis' that came to Islay and spoiled his tenants who then were unable to pay their rents; see *RPCS*, XI, 624–5.

inhabitants, thus gradually replacing MacDonald lordship with Campbell lordship.[107] In 1619 Cawdor tried to alleviate his financial burden with an exploration of lead mines and consideration of exploitation of the fishing to be had. In these endeavours he was encouraged to 'drawe in Inglische men to Ila' as there was a 'great mony in Ingland who wold be glad to imbrace that bussines'. Later, in 1621, Cawdor's 1614 grant was ratified by parliament in which the lands were erected into the Barony of Islay.[108] The ratification also referred to 'ane burgh of baronye to be biggit … with all priuiledgis, liberties, and immunities of ane frie burgh of baronie'. Such inducements resulted in neither plantation nor profit and in 1623 Cawdor considered selling the island. A few years later, in 1626, he resigned it in favour of his eldest son, John Campbell.[109]

Campbell lordship, and economic exploitation, of the island would continue.[110] So too would their role as law enforcers and agents of the crown in the region. Archibald, Lord Lorne, eldest son of the earl of Argyll, took over effective management of his father's inheritance after the earl converted to Catholicism in 1617–18 and entered the service of Spain, for which he was proclaimed a traitor.[111] In doing so Lorne took on the mantle of extending royal authority while simultaneously ensuring expansion of

107 *Book of Islay*, no. CLXXXIV (364); *Book of the Thanes of Cawdor*, 242–3.

108 *Book of Islay*, no. CLXXXIX (369–70).

109 *Book of Islay*, no. CXCII (372–3).

110 The MacDonalds continued to lay claim to the island. Randal MacDonnell tried to buy Islay in 1627 and again in 1635 but was unsuccessful while in 1647 Coll Ciotach established a garrison at Dunivaig Castle during the summer of 1647; see Stevenson, *Highland Warrior*, 49–50, 230–1. Archibald, Lord Lorne, later brought over skilled men from Ulster to construct a salt-pans that would be fuelled by coal from Kintyre; see Macinnes, *Clanship, Commerce*, 75.

111 J. Callow, 'Campbell, Archibald, seventh earl of Argyll (1575/6–1638), magnate and politician', *ODNB*, accessed 18 April 2019; David Stevenson, 'Campbell, Archibald, marquess of Argyll (1605x7–1661), nobleman and politician', *ODNB*, accessed 18 April 2019; Campbell of the Airds, *History of Clan Campbell*, 152; Stevenson, *Highland Warrior*, 49–50. In 1611 Argyll resigned all his lands and offices into the hands of the king with a regrant to himself in liferent and to his son, Archibald. However, in 1617 Argyll divided his estates between Lorne and James, son of his second marriage, who was created Lord Kintyre in 1622.

Campbell overlordship and influence in the west. Following the reinforcement of the Statutes of Iona in 1616, the situation in the western Highlands and Isles was relatively more settled as various clan chiefs slowly integrated more fully into commercial society with extended stays in Edinburgh while they appeared before the Privy Council.[112] The king, largely absent from Scotland and realising some thriving plantation settlements in Ulster, was content to rely on Lorne to maintain law and order in the region.

By the 1620s there was one last rebellious clan to contend with: the MacIans of Ardnamurchan. Lorne's predecessors had gained title to the lands of Ardnamurchan and Sunart in the mid-sixteenth century but it was not until the early seventeenth century that Argyll began to assert his superiority. This caused internal unrest, heightened on account of the minority of the then chief, Allaster, so Argyll delegated to a kinsman, Donald Campbell of Barbreck-Lochow, to take custody of Mingarry Castle, collect rents and punish wrong-doers. Such interference was not welcomed by the MacIans who requested that Campbell of Barbreak-Lochow gain the obedience of the people 'with [kindness] rather nor extermitie'.[113] This advice was evidently ignored and eventually the MacIans were in open rebellion. They were called to appear to give answer for their crimes in 1619 but 'thay absentit thameselffis and compeirit not … for the whilk thay wer declairit fugitives and rebels'. Consequently, many of the clan resorted to piracy and general lawlessness as there were few other options open to them given the extent of Campbell influence in the region. In April 1625 a commission was issued to Lord Lorne to go against 'the rebellious theeves and lymmars of the Clan Eane'. The commission stated that they 'meddlit with the shippis and goodes not onlie of some honest trafficquaris' but also 'with all hostilitie persewit his Majesties awne peacablle and goode subiects travelling about the isles in thair lauchfull trade'. While the commission

112 Robert A. Dodgshon, *From Chiefs to Landlords. Social and Economic Change in the Western Highlanders and Islands, c.1493–1820* (Edinburgh, 1998), 114–16; Stana Nenadic, *Lairds and Luxury. The Highland Gentry in Eighteenth Century Scotland* (Edinburgh, 2007); Jean Munro, 'When Island Chiefs Came to Town', *Notes & Queries of the Society of the West Highlands and Island Historical Research* XIX (1982), 11–19.

113 Gregory, *History of the Western Highlands and Isles*, 405–12 at 409.

did refer to the MacIans having 'barbarouslie and inhumanelie murdresit and slayne some of' the king's subjects, there was little pandering to the rhetoric of civility; the issue was simply one of law and order. The MacIans were 'rebellious theeves', 'insolent and lawless', aiming at 'universall defection and rebellious in the ills'. They were to be pursued by fire and sword and to be apprehended on land or at sea.[114]

Having gained title to MacIan lands, Lorne was given commission to remove the clan, paving the way for further Campbell expansion. While the king had abandoned plantation efforts in the western Highlands and Isles after Lewis, he still willing to 'root out' the rebellious inhabitants as a means of extending royal authority, law and order. Lawlessness, and the flouting of his royal authority, was one matter but the interference with trade on the part of the MacIans also caused significant concern as this threatened the growing cross-channel trade and the supply to and from the plantations in Ulster. The requests of merchants, engaged in lawful trade, to deal with this piratical behaviour was responded to by the government of Charles I who had recently succeeded his father. With less tolerance for Highland disorder the treatment meted out to the MacIans was swift and brutal: a clear sign, if it were needed at this stage, of the consequences of ongoing opposition to processes of reform and integration in the western Highlands and Isles, especially if it had the potential to interfere with such policies elsewhere.

North Channel commerce

Cross-channel shipping was fundamental to the successful establishment of the early seventeenth-century plantations in Ulster, whether part of the official plantation or not. By the 1620s the Hamilton-Montgomery plantation was well underway, as too were settlements elsewhere, established by Scottish undertakers as part of the Plantation of Ulster. The new settlers in Ulster needed foodstuffs, tools, agricultural and building

114 ICA Inveraray bundles, no.47; Macinnes, *Clanship, Commerce*, 63–5.

material, livestock, clothing and all other necessaries not readily available within Ireland, as well as tenants, labourers and craftsmen. This demand put a strain on the supply of cross-channel shipping, in terms of available vessels and the cost of carriage.[115] James Hamilton, first Earl of Abercorn, one of the undertakers in the Plantation of Ulster, had been personally encouraged by the king to become involved in the endeavour. Despite some initial reluctance, Abercorn soon responded with vigour but quickly realised the dangers of shipping in the North Channel.[116] However, if his settlement was to succeed he needed regular and safe transportation for himself; his tenants; and any goods, building materials or livestock he required. In February 1612, the Privy Council in Edinburgh gave permission for Abercorn, to '"presse ony ship … on the west coast"' of Scotland '"for transporting of him to and fra Yreland at all suche tymes and occasionis as the necessitie of going thair sall requyre"', although Abercorn was always to pay '"the freight of the ship"'.[117] This appears to have helped as Abercorn was able to establish a regular trade connection between Derry and the southwest of Scotland. The *Gift of God*, like Abercorn himself, is said to have journeyed regularly across the North Channel. It was a transport route that also gave easy, albeit increasingly expensive, passage to the tenants Abercorn and other undertakers brought over to populate their estates with.[118] Indeed, the expense

115 *RPCS*, IX, 478–9; Gillespie, *Colonial Ulster*, 25, 51.

116 NLS Denmilne MSS, Adv. MSS 33.1.1., vol III, no.45, dated 12 April 1610. Abercorn received the lands of Strabane which initially had not been allocated for plantation. The land had been granted already to the sons of Sir Art Og O'Neill, son of Turlough Luineach O'Neill, while the decision to establish a town at Lifford, a short distance across the River Foyle, may have minimised the perceived need for a town at Strabane; see LPL, MS 630, fol.2v. Given the location of Strabane, on the river with direct access to Lough Foyle and the open sea, shipping was vital to the success of the settlement.

117 *RPCS*, IX, 327.

118 *RPCS*, IX, 478–9; Perceval-Maxwell, *Scottish Migration to Ulster*, 123, 147, 151; Hunter, ed., *Strabane Barony*, 58–9; Gillespie, *Colonial Ulster*, 12–14, 21–7, 47–52; Fitzgerald, 'Scottish Migration to Ireland in the Seventeenth Century', 39–43. The traffic between Scotland and Ireland was such that very quickly '"passage is now become a common and ane ordinarie ferrie"' and was soon being exploited.

soon became burdensome and in October 1612 Abercorn was among those who petitioned the Privy Council in Edinburgh on behalf of the Scottish undertakers in Ulster regarding the state of shipping. The petition stated that the undertakers were '"compellit to transporte … verie frequentlie"' from Scotland into Ireland '"nomberis of men for labouring of the ground, and mony bestiall and cattell for plenischeing of the same"'. While '"daylie passage"' was necessary they argued that '"the seafaren and boitmen of the west coast … exactis, extortis, and will ather haif suche extraordinair frauchtis … as thay think good to uplift, or … will altogidder refuise to transporte thame"'. Consequently, '"the saidis frauchtis ar rissin to suche ane extraordinair heicht as no man salbe able to travell betuix the saidis cuntreyis"'. Not only would this frustrate and obstruct the intended plantation, but it would hinder potential tenants. The council agreed to look into the matter and, if need be, would attempt to address it by establishing '"reasounable and moderat frauchtis to be tane for the transporte of men, bestiall, and goodis"' across the channel.[119] But alongside regular passage and reasonable costs, the council also had to try to contend with the increase in piracy in the North Channel as they received regular complaints regarding the '"pyrotes of divers nationis whiche frequent the coast of Yreland"'.[120]

Maritime predation in the North Channel was opportunistic, exploiting the burgeoning cross-channel trade. Evidence for the trade to and from Ulster is found in surviving port books, extant only for the period from 1612 to 1615. These highlight the natural, raw materials that were exported from Ireland, primarily beef, skins, oats and salmon. At the same time, they also point to the luxury, manufactured goods being imported. Along with the tools and household items necessary to establish a new society, goods such as wine, raisins, almonds, prunes, aniseed, ribbons, glasses, silk, lace and playing cards were imported to Ulster, with the bulk of the trade occurring at Carrickfergus and the new port of Derry.[121] In its initial

119 *RPCS*, IX, 478–9.

120 *RPCS*, IX, 327; and see Gillespie, *Colonial Ulster*, 25 on the problems of piracy in the North Channel.

121 West Yorkshire Archive Service, Port books of Ulster: WYL 100/PO/7/I/1–4. Having made the trip to Leeds to transcribe these I subsequently found this task

stages the planters would need regular supplies and as time went on both English and Scottish settlers sought to replicate their former life in new surroundings and develop new markets. Cross-channel traffic increased while ongoing engagement of merchants and traders from the southwest of Scotland would be fundamentally important if the economic potential of Ulster was to be realised. This trade, in turn, was also important for the growing Scottish economy.

Burghs in the southwest of Scotland would develop significantly in the seventeenth century as these locations became the key trading ports for the new colonies across the Atlantic, but in the late sixteenth and early seventeenth century, the new markets that offered opportunities for trade lay across a narrower body of water, in lands much closer to home.[122] There

---

had already been done and published (by the late, great, Bob Hunter) with a useful introduction; see R. J. Hunter, ed., *The Ulster Port Books 1612–15* (Belfast, 2012).

122 As well as evidence from custom books concerning the growth of trade at this time, the expansion of burghs like Ayr, Irvine and Kirkcudbright at this time also points to an increase in commercial activity. In February 1610 the Privy Council wrote to the king concerning the 'necessitie of the upholding of the harborie of yo[u]r maiesteis burgh of Air' and 'the harme that may ensew by decay thairof' arguing that 'the reparatioun of the said harborie is most necessair and expedyent for the honnour creditte and benefeit of the whole cuntrey'. The council continued, emphasising the importance of Ayr, 'being the onlie sey poirt upoun that haill coast whair the ressett and dispatche of goodis is most ordinar and frequent and quhar the trade of navigatioun is alwayes in practise And for nomber of goode schippis and skilfull and able marinaris it is the best in this yo[u]r maiesteis kingdome, leyth and dundee onlie except And besydis the commodiousnes of the place the nomber of schipping and marynairs and the frequent importatioun and exportatioun of commodityis at that poirt, it lyis oppin to Yrland within twelff houris sailling to the north pairtis, [th]airof whair the seid of all the rebellioun of that kingdome tooke roote, unto the w[hi]lkis partis yo[u]r maiestie at everey occasioun may half the commoditie of transportatioun whatever yo[u]r maiestie sall think goode And yf this intendit worke be not finished thair wilbe no commodious nor saulff ressett for schipping thair, and in schorte tyme the haill schipping of that towne w[hi]che wold serve for a bulwarke to that haill coast incaise of foreyne troublis will decay and consequentlie the towne w[hi]che is so antient and for civilitie bewtye buildingis and goode gouernament may be rekyuned amangis the best and worthiest of this kingdome will come to noght whairby the haill trade of the west cuntrey w[hi]che was interteinyed be the schipping of Air will ceise to the impoverisheing

was a growing community of merchants and traders who operated in the waters of the Irish Sea and the North Channel, trading between the Isle of Man, Liverpool, Ulster and the southwest of Scotland. This trade had benefitted not only the near-desperate English forces in Ireland during the latter decades of the sixteenth century, but also the merchants, traders and inhabitants of burghs in the southwest of Scotland.[123] Even before plantation commenced in Ulster Scottish merchants and local traders were travelling to Derry and developing a regular trade across the channel. For men from the southwest of Scotland, burghs like Ayr, Irvine, Kirkcudbright, Wigton and elsewhere, the developing trade with Ireland was crucial. While there were steady markets for salt, herring and other goods in the Isle of Man and English ports like Liverpool and Chester, the close proximity of Ulster to southwest Scotland made it a preferred destination for merchants with a boat, or at least a share of one, albeit not of a grand scale, but one that could carry a cargo of, usually, around twenty to forty tons.[124] Some vessels could carry only up to ten tons, but other vessels were larger and could accommodate a more significant cargo. Regardless, the development of towns (outwith the garrisons) at places like Carrickfergus and Coleraine, plus the establishment of a garrison at Derry in 1600, meant secure markets within easy reach of southwest Scotland.

It was these markets that Gilbert Thomson, burgess of Ayr, one of the merchant traders, sought to capitalise on in the late sixteenth century.[125]

---

of that nuke of yo[u]r maiesteis kingdome, wheras yf this worke be haldin hand to and perfytit, that towne will daylie floorishe in schipping traffic[ue] policye and strenth, and yo[u]r maiestie may rest assured at everie interuening occasioun of yo[u]r maiesteis seruice to be furnist with a nomber of goode schippis and able fellowis frome that pairt'; see NLS Denmilne MSS, Adv. MSS 33.1.1., vol III, no.37.

123 SP 63/170, fol.142. On 8 July 1593 Captain Charles Eggarton wrote to the Lord Deputy from Carrickfergus with information obtained from 'John Stevenson a Skottishe marchande who useth muche to trade unto this towne.' See pp. 195–6 above.

124 MNH, MS 10058: Custom Book 1594, Ingates and Outgates, 1611; *Ayr Burgh Accounts, 1534–1624*, ed., George S. Pryde, third series, vol. XXVIII (Edinburgh: Scottish History Society, 1937), 234.

125 Much like the attack on Thomson in 1586, in August 1583 a William Sommerville, burgess of Renfrew, with two other merchants, 'in ane bark of Renfrew purposit to the fischeing of Lochefewle' were attacked by a number of men refered to as

As he discovered to his cost, however, the North Channel was not always a safe place for merchants.[126] Thomson was the victim of an opportunistic piratical attack at a time when the Highlanders dominated the waters between Ireland and Scotland. In the early seventeenth century the context had changed and while the warfare in Ireland was at an end and the mercenary trade finally over, it is too easy to assume that the waters were safer now for merchants and planters crossing the narrow channel. A closer look at the sources suggests the opposite and, as trade increased, so too did piracy. Although the mercenary trade had ended there was no way of facilitating an easy transition from fighting men to a settled life of farming, whether arable or pastoral. Evidence shows that rents were being converted to cash from the late sixteenth and early seventeenth century, a result of the increased demands for payments in cash placed on chiefs, which in turn placed a burden on clansmen or tenants to convert produce to cash. Increasingly both chiefs and tenants were orientated towards the market and while arable farming continued, more emphasis was placed on cattle as part of the economic system. Cultivation of further upland areas did not commence until later, corroborating the difficulty in moving from a military economy to an agrarian one.[127] In addition, although the Statutes

'notorious clannis of robberis, brokin men, and sornaris' who lived on the lands of Angus MacDonald of Dunivaig. They came 'bodin in veirlyk maner … in ane birling and ane grite boit'. Sommerville and his companions had their cargo taken from them; this included wine, whisky, powder and bullets, swords, beer, salt and cash along with some other items; see *Extracts from the Records of the Burgh of Glasgow*, eds, James D. Marwick and Robert Renwick, 7 vols (Glasgow: Scottish Burgh Records Society, 1876), I, 103–5. There are numerous, albeit scattered, references to the level of piracy in the North Channel; see BL Add MS 4819: Pococke Collection: Collections relating to Irish history of the 16th–17th century, Collectanea de Rebus Hibernicis, fol.190r; SP 63/217, fol.114v; SP 63/222, fols 21–3; T. W. Moody, 'Sir Thomas Phillips of Limavady, Servitor', *Irish Historical Studies* I/3 (1939), 261 gives a 1616 example of piratical behaviour on the part of Scottish Highlanders.

126 Thomson appears not to have recovered at all from this attack as he received 'alms' from Ayr burgh council during the 1590s; see *Ayr Burgh Accounts*, ed., Pryde, 187, 197.

127 Dodgshon, *From Chiefs to Landlords*, especially 102–22.

of Iona encouraged the establishment of inns as a means of stimulating a growing economy (as well as eliminating sorning), they also sought to prevent landless or 'broken' men, those without employment, remaining in the region and ended the custom of *cuid-oidhche* or provision of hospitality. Added to this was the acquisition of land in the west by lords like Campbell of Cawdor. Land in the western Highlands and Isles remained an economic resource but, while several factors encouraged commercial activity, clans like the MacDonalds and MacIans faced displacement or dislocation. Without recourse to employment in Ireland or acquisition of land in Scotland, where they also faced increased royal intervention, piracy was an attractive alternative for many Highlanders who could exploit their knowledge of the tides and coastline, capitalise on the greater number of merchant vessels now traversing the North Channel, and take to the seas to find a living.[128] The policy of plantation aimed at extending royal authority, civilising the inhabitants, developing economic activity and pacifying the cross-channel region. Despite all his efforts to realise the success of his policy of plantation on land, James had not paid enough attention to the need to secure the seas, nor to the inhabitants who lived at the interface of land and sea, for whom plantation brought both obstacles and opportunities.

128 Scott Carballo, 'Piracy in the Irish Sea: Sovereignty, Economy and the Scottish Western Burghs, 1560–1630', University of Stirling ESRC-funded PhD (in progress). Indeed, Highlanders were not the only parties guilty of engaging in maritime violence and opportunistic piracy in these waters. *Ayr Burgh Accounts*, ed., Pryde, 163, 241, 243 refers to both English and Irish pirates.

Conclusion

Within less than a century, the communities of the North Channel had experienced significant changes. In wider national and archipelagic terms, the decades of the mid-sixteenth century were characterised by a rapid change of monarchs both in England and Scotland along with years of minority government (at least in Scotland); warfare, as Henry VIII embarked on his 'rough wooing' of Scotland along with Border campaigns in the 1550s; and, perhaps above all, religious change as England followed through with more meaningful Protestant reform while Scotland also officially adopted Protestantism in 1560. In Ireland the Reformation failed to take root and, while the Irish continued to oppose the so-called Tudor reconquest, Highland Scots established a settlement in the north of the country, and English efforts at plantation commenced in Laois and Offaly. For the communities of the North Channel, who were somewhat geographically peripheral to the main centres of government in Dublin, Edinburgh and London, these wider processes were keenly felt at a local level. This lack of geographic proximity to the centre did not mean they were cut off from wider events and, at the same time, local and regional events occurring in the North Channel hinterland likewise influenced policy and decisions made in Dublin, Edinburgh and London. Thus, the processes of change were shaped by both central government and the local communities that existed at the fringes of national and territorial boundaries.

Having established a branch of their clan in Antrim in earlier centuries, the MacDonalds utilised this settlement in various ways, whether as a refuge in times of trouble and unrest in Scotland, as a means of sustaining their fighting force when not required, or as a source of economic wealth to be redistributed in times of hardship. Despite consistent efforts by the English to expel them, they maintained a presence in the north of

Ireland because of their maritime dominance which afforded the ability to cross the North Channel with relative ease. Eventually in the 1580s the MacDonnells, as they became known, gained recognition from the English crown of their lands and a charter of denization. Despite siding with Hugh O'Neill, second Earl of Tyrone, at Kinsale, Randal MacDonnell quickly submitted following defeat by the English and, after the succession of James VI to the thrones of England and Ireland, found himself in favour with the new regime and one of the largest landowners in Ireland. In the transition from economic migrants and an unwanted presence in Ulster to becoming part of the establishment, MacDonnell fortunes contrast sharply with that of their kinsmen across the North Channel. For their part, the MacDonalds had remained important players in west Highland and Island affairs throughout the sixteenth century and, despite sporadic instances of disagreement, were closely aligned to the Campbell earls of Argyll, increasingly the source of extensive jurisdiction within the west Highlands and Isles. But the MacDonald-MacLean feud that broke out in the latter decades of the sixteenth century threatened the MacDonald hold on their traditional clan lands of Islay, while the repercussions of the feud were felt throughout western Scotland. Familial discord between Angus MacDonald and his son, Sir James of Knockrinsay, and repeated instances of lawlessness, was far from welcome by a monarch intent on asserting his royal authority and ensuring obedience on the part of the clans.

The murder of Lauchlan MacLean of Duart by Sir James of Knockrinsay in 1598 is often suggested as the point at which Campbell support for the MacDonalds ended but this is not quite so clear cut. The Campbells themselves were focused on re-affirming clan solidarity following the internal unrest caused by the murder of John Campbell of Cawdor in 1592 and, at the same time, young Archibald, seventh Earl of Argyll, was re-establishing Campbell dominance at local, regional and national levels. Argyll delicately balanced all his interests, appearing loyal to his monarch, while also useful to Elizabeth as a means of countering (or controlling) the mercenary trade to Ireland. His ability to delegate meant he was often conveniently distant from the action and it is probable Argyll was biding his time to see how events would unfold across the archipelago. After all, in 1598 it was by no means clear that Elizabeth would suppress the Tyrone rebellion, nor was it inevitable that James would succeed to the English throne.[1] Nonetheless, the end of war in Ireland was followed quickly by James' succession and Argyll acted immediately. Campbell support for the persistently lawless MacDonalds may have been on the wane, but the events of the early years of the seventeenth century ensured that support evaporated as quickly as Argyll adopted a 'British' perspective, and the earl again reinforced his worth as a loyal agent of royal authority.[2] Argyll's adoption of the king's 'British' rhetoric highlights his pragmatism, while the consolidation of his extensive jurisdiction in the west Highland and Isles meant that he was able to spread Campbell lordship and influence throughout the west. He bought fully into James' civilising policy for the Highlands, establishing law and order and ensuring obedience to royal authority. Initially Argyll had given the outward of appearance of adhering to the king's policy of plantation when James sought to implement it in the South Isles but, while he removed some sitting tenants and granted lands in Kintyre to outsiders, this was more about removing lawless inhabitants and developing a burgh at Campbeltown than embarking on plantation along the lines of the Ulster model. The negotiated settlement agreed between the king and the main Highland and Hebridean chiefs in 1609, the Statutes of Iona, saw a return to conciliation and co-operation, although Argyll himself played little part in reaching that end.[3] It meant the earl, who in 1610 remarried and spent the majority of his time down south, could remain the enforcer of crown policy in the west and delegate to trusted kinsmen. Argyll continued to deal with law and order in the Highlands when necessary, but gradually clan chiefs were accepting the benefits of co-operation and economic development

1 David Edwards, 'Securing the Jacobean Succession: The Secret Career of James Fullerton of Trinity College, Dublin', in Seán Duffy, ed., *The World of the Galloglass. Kings, Warlords and Warriors in Ireland and Scotland, 1200–1600* (Dublin, 2007), 188–219 at 188–96.

2 Martin MacGregor, 'The Genealogical Histories of Gaelic Scotland', in Adam Fox and Daniel Woold, eds, *The Spoken Word: Oral Culture in Britain, 1500–1850* (Manchester, 2003), 196–239 at 221–2; W. D. H. Sellar, 'The earliest Campbells – Norman, Briton or Gael?', *Scottish Studies XVII* (1977), 109–25.

3 Martin MacGregor, 'The Statutes of Iona: Text and Context', *Innes Review* 57/2 (2006), 111–81, especially 163–70 for efforts to see 'the Campbells reined in by the Iona settlement'.

with James as opposed to continued resistance despite the economic burden that entailed. In Scotland civility meant the extension of law and order and royal authority, alongside economic development.

Civility in an Irish context had meant something rather different. Throughout the sixteenth century the Irish had experienced increasing efforts by Tudor monarchs to spread reform to Ireland; part of this was the constitutional shift of Ireland from lordship to kingdom in 1541 but it did not bring the anticipated results. Indeed, the accompanying policy of surrender and regrant, which saw Irish lords surrender their lands only to have them regranted with an English title by the king of England, was fundamentally incompatible with Irish society and custom and ultimately laid the foundations for even greater unrest to erupt during Elizabeth's reign. The Irish experience of the 'civilising' process, therefore, was entirely different. It was one imposed by an external, and unwanted, regime; the imposition of English law, governance, custom and language went hand-in-hand with efforts to eradicate the society, culture and language of the Irish themselves, articulated as primitive and uncivilised. Efforts to extend Protestantism into Ireland also failed. The plantation into Ireland of English-born Englishmen came to be regarded as the best way to reform the country although, after a few failed attempts and with the outbreak of Tyrone's rebellion, many would have agreed with Edmund Spenser's assessment that the land needed first to be conquered before reform could take place, and indeed had advocated that for some time.[4] Such a conquest was

4 There is a wealth of literature on Spenser but see Ciaran Brady, 'Spenser's Irish Crisis: humanism and experience in the 1590s', *Past and Present* 111 (1986), 17–49; Nicholas P. Canny, 'Edmund Spenser and the development of an Anglo-Irish identity', *Yearbook of English Studies: Colonial and Imperial Themes*, 13 (1985), 1–19; Nicholas P. Canny, "Spenser's Irish Crisis': A Comment', *Past and Present* 120 (1988), 201–09; David Edwards, 'Ideology and Experience: Spenser's *View* and Martial Law in Ireland', in Hiram Morgan, ed., *Political Ideology in Ireland, 1541–1641* (Dublin, 1991), 127–57; Andrew Hadfield and Willy Maley, eds, *Edmund Spenser. A View of the State of Ireland* (Oxford, 1997); Andrew Hadfield, 'Educating the Colonial Mind: Spenser and the Plantation', in Éamonn Ó Ciardha and Micheál Ó Siochrú, eds, *The Plantation of Ulster. Ideology and Practice* (Manchester, 2012), 158–75; D. B. Quinn, *'A Vewe of the Present State of Ireland',* in A. C. Hamilton, ed., *The Spenser Encyclopaedia* (London, 1990), 713–15.

only realised in the final days of Elizabeth's life, by which time attempts to plant and exploit the raw materials had been tried and found wanting.

It was the new King James VI and I that would oversee plantation on a grand scale across much of Ulster but such plans could only begin to be developed after the unexpected events of 1607 and 1608.[5] Consequently, it is difficult to accept that James introduced plantation in order to place 'a permanent wedge between the Gaels of Ireland and of Scotland'.[6] There was as much cross-channel conflict and hostility as there was integration and co-operation. Nonetheless, as James continued his plantation plans for large parts of Ulster he was able to reconsider policy for Gaelic Scotland and move towards conciliation with his Highland subjects.[7] The Statutes of Iona enabled James to abandon his failing efforts at plantation in the Isles; he turned to the Mackenzies of Kintail to mop up the Lewis mess, while in the South Isles he allowed Argyll to deal with ongoing unrest. Those who did not work with him would face dispossession and extirpation: the fate of both the MacDonalds of Islay (or the Clan Donald South as they became known) and the MacIans of Ardnamurchan. At the same time, he encouraged his Lowland Scottish subjects to partake in the opportunities of plantation across the North Channel in Ulster.

Scottish plantation in Ulster had begun earlier as a private enterprise by James Hamilton and Hugh Montgomery of Braidstane. They established settlements in Down and the Ards, the same area that Sir Thomas Smith had chosen for his planation in the 1570s, which thrived: a combination of personal enthusiasm and a requisite number of suitable tenants; good quality land, long leases and low rents; no resistance from the Irish; and

5 For Irish response to James as king see Breandán Ó Buachalla, 'James Our True King. The Ideology of Irish Royalism in the Seventeenth Century', in D. G. Boyce, Robert Eccleshall and Vincent Geoghegan, eds, *Political Thought in Ireland since the Seventeenth Century* (London and New York, 1993), 7–35.

6 Allan I. Macinnes, *Clanship, Commerce and the House of Stuart, 1603–1788* (East Linton, 1996), 58.

7 As Macinnes goes on to argue, 'action on the part of the Crown did not require a uniform policy for 'civilising' the Gael', see *Clanship, Commerce*, 58; Alison Cathcart, 'The Statutes of Iona: An Archipelagic Perspective', *Journal of British Studies* 49/1 (2009), 4–27, at 22–7.

calmer, more settled environmental conditions. While Scots petitioned to be undertakers in the king's 'British' project for plantation, the majority of them came from the southwest of the kingdom.[8] Caution is needed in relation to arguments of environmental determinism but certainly geographic proximity and familiarity of the inhabitants of the southwest with the north of Ireland played a role. So too did peace in Ulster and James' succession as king of England and Ireland, and this, combined with his support for Randal MacDonnell from the very beginning of his reign, highlights the distinction between rhetoric and reality.[9] While James utilised much of the same terminology as the English had when advocating plantation, emphasising the spread of the true religion, reform of the barbarous inhabitants and developing agriculture and economy as a marker of civility; in truth James was more concerned with the spread of his royal authority. He was unconcerned with the participation of Catholics, so long as they recognised his, and not papal, supremacy and engaged in economic development; he actively promoted and favoured Randal MacDonnell, an Irish/Highland Gael; and he gave over County Derry to the City of London. As such, plantation developed in different ways across the north of Ireland.

Plantation as a policy is more often considered as part of wider processes of state formation, and such arguments have come to dominate the historiography of early modern British and Irish history. For too long, there has been a lack of clarity of what is meant by 'state formation' while reference to Max Weber's definition, perhaps useful for later centuries, is unhelpful for this period. Thankfully, J. H. Elliot has defined it in a more meaningful way.[10] Steve Hindle has added further nuance to this by presenting a different perspective of state formation, arguing that local elites played a crucial role in these processes by opting-in to the aims of central

8 James also personally encouraged some individuals to get involved as undertakers.

9 J. Michael Hill, 'The Origins of the Scottish Plantations in Ulster to 1625: A Reinterpretation', *Journal of British Studies* 32/1 (1993), 24–43 at 37–8, 41–3.

10 J. H. Elliott, 'Atlantic History: A Circumnavigation', in David Armitage and Michael J. Braddick, eds, *The British Atlantic World, 1500–1800* (Basingstoke, 2009), 260–1; J. H. Elliott 'A Europe of Composite Monarchies', *Past & Present* 137/1 (1992), 48–71.

government.[11] Yet this still tends towards a reading of the past where policy was formulated at the centre and imposed onto the periphery. It presents governance as one-way when, in practice, it was a dialogue. Both centre and periphery played their part, interacted, conflicted and co-operated. The 'winners' in this situation were those who co-operated: the MacDonnells and the Campbells, both of whom outwardly aligned with crown agenda while inwardly preserving personal and family interests; the undertakers who fulfilled the obligations required and established thriving settlements in Ulster; and the merchants of the southwest who exploited the emerging communities in the north of Ireland to establish effective and increasingly lucrative trade routes. The 'losers' undoubtedly were the Irish who were forcibly displaced from their lands or who became heavily indebted by new economic forces; as well as those like the MacDonalds of Islay who continued to oppose greater royal intervention and changed political realities, and who could not adapt to different economic and environmental conditions.

To observe winners or losers (or success and failure), however, results in a focus on the outcome and ignores the processes involved. Indeed, to view the MacDonnells as 'winners' is to take but a snap-shot of the North Channel communities in the early seventeenth century and it glosses over the nuance of the situation. For the duration of the sixteenth century the MacDonnells in Ulster were very much in opposition to the English crown and government policy, which sought to expel the Highland Scots, and that opposition in turn significantly shaped English policy. Indeed, the initial policy of coastal garrisons which developed into the policy of plantation was proposed as a means of keeping out the Highland Scots once they had been repulsed. When the English finally recognised the claims of the MacDonnells to their lands in 1586 it was an acceptance of a status quo that, no matter how hard they tried, they could not change. The Campbells of Argyll, much like the Mackenzies of Kintail in the North Isles, benefited greatly from their position as enforcers of royal policy, but by this stage

11 Steve Hindle, *The State and Social Change in Early Modern England, 1550–1640* (Basingstoke, 2000); and see Allan Kennedy, *Governing Gaeldom: The Scottish Highlands and the Restoration State, 1660–1688* (Leiden, 2014), especially 1–14 for a discussion of 'imperial' and 'collaborative' approaches towards integration.

they had mastered the ability to align crown agenda with kindred and personal agenda. At the same time, because of events in Ireland crown policy in Scotland had shifted from one of coercion, forfeiture and 'rooting out', to one of co-operation and integration; this was a policy both Argyll and Kintail could work with and exploit for their own ends. In contrast, the MacDonalds of Islay, with whom the crown had repeatedly tried to work throughout the sixteenth century, fell out of royal favour and patience. The relentless cycle of ongoing resistance to the crown followed by submission, promises of good behaviour and payment of rent served no one's best interest and James became frustrated. It was a pattern of behaviour borne out of bitter conflict between father and son (Angus MacDonald and Sir James of Knockrinsay) regarding the clan lands of Kintyre and Islay; of differences in opinion as to how best to deal with an increasingly interventionist king; and of ongoing unrest with neighbouring clans and former allies. Such conflict combined with ever-amounting arrears of rent caused by unrest, harsh climatic conditions, and harvest failures, forced the clan into a position where they saw no alternative course of action. Unable to adapt to a new political situation in the west the clan gradually disintegrated, losing out to their neighbours, the Campbells of Argyll and Campbells of Cawdor, and to their kinsmen, the MacDonnells, across the North Channel.

To view plantation as a tool of government, whether to drive a wedge between the problematic areas of Gaelic Ireland and Gaelic Scotland or as a tool of state formation, a means by which to impose royal authority onto outlying regions, is problematic.[12] Such interpretations continue to

12 Macinnes, *Clanship, Commerce*, 58; Martin MacGregor, 'Civilising Gaelic Scotland: The Scottish Isles and the Stewart Empire', in Ó Ciardha and Ó Siochrú, eds, *The Plantation of Ulster*, 33–54, especially 37–9. Plantation was a tool of state formation used elsewhere in Europe at this time too; see Thomas Brochard, 'Plantation: its process in relation to Scotland's Atlantic communities, 1590s–1630s' *Maritime Communities of the North Atlantic Arc in the Early Modern Period: Journal of the North Atlantic*, ed., Alison Cathcart, special volume 12 (2019), 73–94. For arguments concerning state formation see Michael Hechter, *Internal Colonisation: The Celtic Fringe in British National Development, 1536–1966* (London, 1975).

perpetuate political development as a one-way process whereby change was the result of events that occurred at the centre and imposed onto the locality. To argue plantation was a tool of state formation also implies a degree of premeditation and planning that simply did not happen. Admittedly James' policies achieved the integration of his unruly, barbarous periphery into Scottish society (or his wider British empire) because, as a pragmatist, he continued to try to find a workable solution in order to realise change on the ground. This was true also in Ulster. No doubt regnal union had removed national borders, while the war in Ulster ended before James succeeded to the English and Irish thrones. These events shaped the development of the archipelago in the seventeenth century, but James still had to deal with local communities and their reactions to policy implemented from the centre much in the same way previous Tudor and Stewart monarchs had done. These communities, and their response to interventionist crown policy, in turn shaped the policy that was formulated at the centre. Thus, policy was the result of an evolving process between centre and periphery, not one imposed by the centre onto the periphery. While local elites may have co-opted with crown policy this was the result of a long-negotiated process or dialogue, and changing perspectives and priorities of those involved. In the early seventeenth century, wider events ensured that accommodation and co-operation came to the fore in Scotland, while in Ireland James was more than happy to allow for divergence and difference so long as his royal authority was recognised.

A focus on these local communities, their interactions with each other, and with crown and government, emphasises that arguments of state formation need much greater nuance. As far as the policy and processes of plantation are concerned, there is no simple cause and effect. When placed within a wider archipelagic context, plantation as both policy and process on one side of the North Channel influenced that on the other, and the wider effects of the impact of plantation on these marginal communities needs greater recognition. Indeed, to realise a deeper understanding of the communities of the North Channel points to the need for different historiographical approaches; to incorporate yet move beyond both national and local history to consider transnational approaches to a region bounded by sea rather than land. Like the tides that carried English, Irish and Scottish communities back and forth across the North Channel and through the Irish Sea, their authority, power and influence ebbed and flowed, while policy and process was victim to 'contrary winds' at every turn.

Bibliography

This bibliography is not exhaustive but contains all works cited.

Archival sources

Belfast, N. Ireland – Public Record Office of Northern Ireland

D 2977: Earl of Antrim Papers

D 623: Abercorn Papers

D 3077: Hart Papers

D 4216: Ward Papers

Douglas, Isle of Man – Manx National Heritage

MS 10057: Historical land holding records known as the 'manorial rolls' documenting 'Lord's rent' payments (payments to the Lord of Mann) and other transactions

MS 10058: Accounts of Water Bailiff relating to fiscal customs, in particular ingates and outgates 1579–1755

MS 10071: Judicial records containing historical records of the courts of civil jurisdiction (courts of chancery and exchequer etc.)

Dublin, Ireland – Trinity College Dublin

MS 1209: Hardiman Collection

MS 743: Account of Ireland (with maps) c.1590

Edinburgh, Scotland – National Library of Scotland

Adv. MS 33.1.1.: Denmilne MSS

Adv. MS 19.1.24: Papers of John Lindsay, Lord Menmuir, concerning lead and copper mining in Scotland 1567–96

Edinburgh, Scotland – National Records of Scotland

GD 25: Ailsa Muniments

Greenwich, England – National Maritime Museum

P 49: Dartmouth Collection

Inveraray, Scotland – Inveraray Castle Archives

Argyll Transcripts pre 1600

Argyll Transcripts post 1600

Argyll Transcripts, 1600–1700

Argyll Letters, A36 Personal Letters, 1602–38
Argyll Chartulary, 1600–1700
Inveraray bundles

Leeds, England – West Yorkshire Archive Service
WYL 100/PO/7/I/1–4: Port books for Coleraine; Strangford, Ardglasse, Killough and Dundrum; Karickefergus [Carrickfergus]; and Londonderry

Lochgilphead, Scotland – Argyll & Bute Council Archives
A:/ARGMSS07
Argyll Papers

London, England – British Library
Add MS 4756: Milles Collection: Entry book of the reports of the Commissioners for Ireland, appointed by James I in 1622 …
Add MS 4794: Milles Collection: Letters from James I and his Council to the government of Ireland: 27 May 1603–10 September 1623
Add MS 4819: Pococke Collection: Collections relating to Irish history of the sixteenth to seventeenth century
Add MS 36775: Copies of royal warrants, instructions and other documents … connected with Ireland during the reign of James I … : 1603–25
Add MS 48015: Papers relating to Ireland, 1538–1600
Cotton MS Augustus I: Maps and plans
Cotton MS Titus B XIII: Ireland, Sussex correspondence

London, England – Lambeth Palace Library
MS 630: Carew Manuscripts

London, England – The National Archives
HCA 13: Admiralty Court Records: examinations
MPF 1: Irish Maps c.1558–c.1610
SP 52: Secretaries of State: State Papers Scotland Series I, Elizabeth I, 1558–1603
SP 60: State Papers, Henry VIII: Ireland Series, 1509–46
SP 61: Secretaries of State: State Papers Ireland, Edward VI, 1547–53
SP 62: Secretaries of State: State Papers Ireland, Mary 1, 1553–58
SP 63: State Paper Office: State Papers Ireland, Elizabeth I to George III, 1558–1782
AO 1/290/1090: T. Lord Ridgeway (Baron of Gallen) Treasurer at War in Ireland

San Marino, CA, USA – Huntington Library
Ellesmere and Bridgewater Collection
Hastings Irish Papers

Printed primary

Accounts of the Lord High Treasurer of Scotland, 1473–1580: Compota Thesaurariorum Regus Scotorum, eds, T. Dickson, J. B. Paul and C. T. Innes, 13 vols (Edinburgh: General Register Office, 1877–1978)

Acts of the Lords of Council in Public Affairs, 1501–1554: Selections from the Acta Dominorum Concilii Introductory to the Register of the Privy Council of Scotland, ed., R. K. Hannay (Edinburgh: General Register Office, 1932)

The Acts of the Lords of the Isles, eds, Jean Munro and R. W. Munro, series four, vol. XXII (Edinburgh: Scottish History Society, 1986)

The Acts of the Parliaments of Scotland, eds, T. Thomason and C. Innes, 12 vols (Edinburgh: Record Commission, 1814–75)

Acts of the Privy Council of England. New Series, ed., John Roche Dasent, 46 vols (London: Public Record Office, 1890–1964)

'A Description of Ireland by Fynes Moryson, Secretary to the Lord Mountjoy, then Lord Deputy. 1600–1603', in *Ireland under Elizabeth and James the First, Described by Edmund Spenser, Sir John Davies and Fynes Moryson,* ed., Henry Morley (London: G. Routledge and sons, 1890)

A Discourse Concerning Western Planting Written in the Year 1584 by Richard Hakluyt, ed. and intro., Charles Deane and Leonard Woods (Cambridge, MA: Press of John Wilson and son, 1877)

Annála Rioghachta Éireann: Annals of the Kingdom of Ireland by the Four Masters, from the Earliest Period to the Year 1616, ed. and trans., J. O'Donovan, 7 vols (Dublin: Hodges, Smith and Co., second edn, 1856), accessed online via Internet Archive

Annals of Ulster, ed. and trans., W. M. Hennessy and B. MacCarthy; new edn to A.D. 1131 by S. MacAirt and G. MacNiocaill, 4 vols (Dublin: A. Thom & Co. (Ltd), 1887–1901)

Anon., *A Letter Sent by I. B. Gentleman unto His Very Frende Mayster R. C. Esquire, Wherein Is Conteined a Large Discourse of the Peopling & Inhabiting the Cuntrie Called the Ardes, and Other Adiacent in the North of Ireland, and Taken in Hand by Sir Thomas Smith, One of the Queenes Majesties priuie Counsel, and Thomas Smith Esquire, His Sonne* (London, 1572), accessed online via Early English Books Online

A Repertory of the Inrolments of the Patent Rolls of Chancery, in Ireland; Commencing with the Reign of King James I, ed., John Caillard Erek (Dublin: J. M'Glashan, 1846)

Ayr Burgh Accounts, 1534–1624, ed., George S. Pryde, Scottish History Society, series three, vol. XXVIII (Edinburgh, 1937)

Bagenal, Marshall, Herbert F. Hore, and Lord Burghley, 'Marshal Bagenal's Description of Ulster, Anno 1586', *Ulster Journal of Archaeology*, first series 2 (1854), 137–60

Blennerhasset, Thomas, *A Direction for the Plantation in Ulster* (London, 1610), accessed online via Early English Books Online

'Bodley's Visit to Lecale, County of Down, A.D. 1602–3', *Ulster Journal of Archaeology*, first series 2 (1854), 73–95

The Book of Islay. Documents Illustrating the History of the Island, ed., G. Gregory Smith (Edinburgh: privately printed, 1895)

The Book of the Thanes of Cawdor: A Series of Papers Selected from the Charter Room at Cawdor 1236–1742, ed., Cosmo Innes (Edinburgh: Spalding Club, 1859)

Bourchier, Walter, *Lives and Letters of the Devereux, Earls of Essex: In the Reigns of Elizabeth, James I, and Charles I, 1540–1646*, 2 vols (London: J. Murray, 1853)

Calendar of Carew Manuscripts, Preserved in the Archiepiscopal Library at Lambeth, 1515–1624, eds, J. S. Brewer and William Bullen, 6 vols (London: Public Record Office, 1867–73)

Calendar of Letters and State Papers Relating to English Affairs Preserved in, or Originally Belonging to, the Archives of Simancas, ed., Martin A. S. Hume, vol. IV (London: Public Record Office, 1899)

Calendar of the Patent and Close Rolls of Chancery in Ireland of the Reign of Charles the First, ed., James Morrin (Dublin and London: A. Thom & Co. (Ltd), 1863)

Calendar of State Papers Relating to Ireland of the Reigns of Henry VIII, Edward VI, Mary and Elizabeth, eds, H. C. Hamilton et al., 11 vols (London: Public Record Office, 1860–1912)

Calendar of State Papers Relating to Scotland and Mary, Queen of Scots, 1547–1603, eds, J. Bain et al., 13 vols (Edinburgh: General Register House, 1898–1969)

Cambrensis, Giraldus, *The History and Topography of Ireland*, ed. & trans., J. J. O'Meara (London: Penguin, 1982)

The Chiefs of Grant, ed., William Fraser, 3 vols (Edinburgh: Clan Grant Centre Trust Ltd, 1883)

Collectanea de Rebus Albanicis, Consisting of Original Papers and Documents Relating to the History of the Highlands and Islands of Scotland (Edinburgh: Iona Club, 1847)

Craig, Thomas, *De unione regnorum Britanniae tractatus*, ed., Charles Sanford Terry, first series, vol. LX (Edinburgh: Scottish History Society, 1909)

Davies, Sir John, *A Discovery of the True Causes Why Ireland Was Never Entirely Subdued* (1612), accessed online via Early English Books Online

Dee, John, *General and Rare Memorials Pertaining to the Perfect Arts of Navigation* ... (1577), accessed online via Early English Books Online

Docwra's Derry: A Narration of Events in North-West Ulster 1600–1604: The 1849 O'Donovan Edition, ed., William P. Kelly (Belfast: Ulster Historical Foundation, 2003)

'Docwra's Tracts', in *Miscellany of the Celtic* Society, ed., J. O'Donovan (Dublin: Printed for the Celtic Society, 1849), 187–325, accessed online via Internet Archive

Early Records Relating to Mining in Scotland, ed., Robert Cochran-Patrick (Edinburgh: David Douglas, 1878)

'Epitome of the Origin and Increase of the Mackintoshes', in J. T. Clark, ed., *Genealogical Collections Concerning Families in Scotland, Made by Walter Macfarlane 1750–51,* series one, vol. XXXIII (Edinburgh: Scottish History Society, 1900), 144–404

The Exchequer Rolls of Scotland 1264–1600: Rotuli Scaccarii Regum Scotorum 1264–1600, eds., George Burnett and John Stuart, 23 vols (Edinburgh: Court of Exchequer, 1878–1908)

'Extracts from the collection of State Papers in the Advocates' Library Known as the Denmylne MSS', in J. R. N. MacPhail, ed., *Highland Papers III,* series two, vol. XX (Edinburgh: Scottish History Society, 1920), 90–320

Extracts from the Records of the Burgh of Glasgow, eds, James D. Marwick and Robert Renwick, 7 vols (Glasgow: Scottish Burgh Records Society, 1876)

Fordun, John of, *Chronicle of the Scottish Nation,* ed., W. F. Skene, 2 vols (Edinburgh: Edmonston and Douglas, 1872)

Fourth Report of the Royal Commission on Historic Manuscripts (London: Historic Manuscripts Commission, 1874)

Gordon, Robert, *A Genealogical History of the Earldom of Sutherland* (Edinburgh, 1813)

The Hamilton Manuscripts: Containing Some Account of the Settlement of the Territories of the Upper Clandeboye, Great Ardes, and Dufferin, in the County of Down by Sir James Hamilton, Knight, ed., T. K. Lowry (Belfast, 1867)

The Hamilton Papers: Letters and Papers Illustrating the Political Relations of England and Scotland in the Sixteenth Century, ed., Joseph Bain, 2 vols (Edinburgh: General Register House, 1890–92)

Historic Manuscripts Commission 78. Report on the Manuscripts of the late Reginald Rawdon Hastings 4, ed., Francis Bickley (London: HMC, 1947)

History of Scotland, George Buchanan trans., J. Aikman, 4 vols (Glasgow, 1827)

'History of the MacDonalds', in J. R. N. MacPhail, ed., *Highland Papers I,* series two, vol. V (Edinburgh: Scottish History Society, 1914), 5–72

The Irish Commission of 1622: An Investigation of the Irish Administration, 1615–1622, and Its Consequences, 1623–1624, ed., Victor Treadwell (Dublin: Irish Manuscripts Commission, 2006)

The Irish Fiants of the Tudor Sovereigns during the Reigns of Henry VIII, Edward VI, Philip and Mary, and Elizabeth I, III, 1585–1603 (Dublin: Éamonn de Búrca for Edmund Burke, 1875, reprinted 1994)

Irish Patent Rolls of James I. Facsimile of the Irish Record Commission's Calendar Prepared Prior to 1830, Foreward by M. C. Griffith (Dublin: Irish Manuscripts Commission, 1966)

The Irish Sections of Fynes Moryson's Unpublished Itinerary, ed., Graham Kew (Dublin: Irish Manuscripts Commission, 1998)

King James VI and I: Political Writings, ed., Johann P. Sommerville (Cambridge: Cambridge University Press, 1994)

Kirkcudbright Town Council Records 1576–1604, trans., M. B. Johnston and C. M. Armet at the instance of John, Marquis of Bute (Edinburgh: privately printed, 1939)

Kirkcudbright Town Council Records 1606–1658, trans., John, IV Marquis of Bute and C. M. Armet, vol. I (Edinburgh and London: privately printed, 1958)

Letters and Papers, Foreign and Domestic, of the Reign of Henry VIII, eds, J. S. Brewer et al., 21 vols (London: Public Record Office, 1862–1910, 1929–32)

The Letters of James the Fourth, 1505–1513, eds, R. K. Hannay and R. L. Mackie, series four, vol. XLV (Edinburgh: Scottish History Society, 1953)

The Letters of James V, eds, R. K. Hannay and D. Hays (Edinburgh: Scottish Office, 1954)

Lindsay, Alexander, *A Rutter of the Scottish Seas (ca. 1540)*, eds, I. H. Adams and G. Fortune (Greenwich: National Maritime Museum, 1980)

The Miscellany of the Spalding Club, ed., John Stuart (Aberdeen: Spalding Club, 1813–77)

Monmouth, Geoffrey of, *The History of the Kings of Britain*, trans., Lewis Thorpe (London: Penguin, 1964)

Montgomery Manuscripts (1603–1706) Compiled from Family Papers by William Montgomery of Rosemount, Esquire, ed., George Hill (Belfast, 1869)

Ó Cléirigh, L., *The Life of Aodh Ruadh Ó Domhnaill*, ed., P. Walsh and C. Ó Lochlainn, 2 vols (Dublin: Irish Text Society, 1948–57), accessed online via Internet Archive

'Papers relating to Kintyre', in J. R. N. MacPhail, ed., *Highland Papers III*, series two, vol. XX (Edinburgh: Scottish History Society, 1920), 66–88

Perrot, Sir James, *Chronicle of Ireland, 1584–1608*, ed., H. Wood (Dublin: Irish Manuscripts Commission, 1933)

Pitcairn, Robert, *Ancient Criminal Trials in Scotland: Compiled from the Original Records and Mss., with Historical Illustrations*, 3 vols (Edinburgh: Maitland Club, 1833)

Register of the Privy Council of Scotland, 1545–1625, eds, R. K. Hannay and John Hill Burton, 14 vols (Edinburgh: General Register House, 1877–98)

Registrum Magni Sigilli Regum Scotorum/The Register of the Great Seal of Scotland, A.D. 1306–1688, eds, J. M. Thomson et al., 11 vols (Edinburgh: General Register House, 1882–1914)

Registrum Secreti Sigilli Regum Scotorum/The Register of the Privy Seal of Scotland, 1488–1580, eds, M. Livingstone et al., 8 vols (Edinburgh: General Register House, 1908–66)

Report on the Present State of the Agriculture in Scotland, Arranged under the Auspices of the Highland Agricultural Society (Edinburgh: Neill & Co., 1878)

The Scottish Correspondence of Mary of Lorraine Including Some Three Hundred Letters from 20 February 1542–3 to 15 May 1560, ed., A. I. Cameron, series three, vol. X (Edinburgh: Scottish History Society, 1927)

Selections from Unpublished Manuscripts in the College of Arms and the British Museum Illustrating the Reign of Mary Queen of Scots MDXLIII-MDLXVIII (Glasgow: Maitland Club, 1837)

Smith, Adam, *An Inquiry into the Nature and Causes of the Wealth of Nations* (1776), accessed online via Eighteenth Century Collections Online

The Spottiswoode Miscellany: A Collection of Original Papers and Tracts, Illustrative Chiefs of the Civil and Ecclesiastical History of Scotland, ed., James Maidment, 2 vols (Edinburgh: Spottiswoode Society, 1844–45)

State Papers Published under the Authority of His Majesty's Commission, 11 vols (London: Public Record Office, 1830–52)

Stuart Royal Proclamations. Royal proclamations of King James I, 1603–1625, eds, James Francis Larkin and Paul L. Hughes (Oxford: Oxford University Press, 1973)

Two Missions of Jacques de le Brosse: An Account of the Affairs of Scotland in the Year 1543 and the Journal of the Siege of Leith, 1560, ed., Gladys Dickinson, series three, vol. XXXVI (Edinburgh: Scottish History Society, 1942)

Ulster and other Irish Maps, c.1600, ed., G. A. Hayes-McCoy (Dublin: Irish Manuscripts Commission, 1964)

'Ulster Plantation Papers', ed., T. W. Moody, *Analecta Hibernica* 8 (1938), 179, 181–7, 189–297

The Virginia voyages of Hakluyt, eds, D. B. Quinn and A. Quinn (Oxford: Oxford University Press, 1973)

The Voyages and Colonising Enterprises of Sir Humphrey Gilbert: Volume I (ed.), David Beers Quinn (London: The Hakluyt Society, 1940)

The Warrender Papers II (ed.), Annie I. Cameron, third series, vol. XIX (Edinburgh: Scottish History Society, 1932)

Online resources

Dictionary of Irish Biography, published online by the Royal Irish Academy (2009–) at <dib.ie>; <https://creativecommons.org/licenses/by/4.0/legalcode>

Medieval and Early Modern Sources Online [MEMSO] (TannerRitchie Publishing, 2003–21)

Oxford Dictionary of National Biography (Oxford: Oxford University Press, 2004; online edition 2008–14), <www.oxforddnb.com>

Records of the Parliaments of Scotland, eds, Keith Brown, et al., published online by the University of St Andrews (2007–21) at <www.rps.ac.uk>

State Papers Online, 1509–1714: Part II: The Tudors: Henry VIII to Elizabeth I, 1509–1603: State Papers Foreign: Ireland, Scotland, Borders and Registers of the Privy Council. The National Archives of the UK from *State Papers Online* available via Gale: A Cengage Company

Secondary sources

Adams, Simon, *The Armada Campaign of 1588* (London: Historical Association, 1988)

——, 'The Outbreak of the Elizabethan Naval War against the Spanish Empire: The Embargo of May 185 and Sir Francis Drake's West Indies Voyage', in M. J. Rodríguez-Salgado and Simon Adams, eds, *England, Spain and the Gran Armada, 1585–1604* (Edinburgh: John Donald, 1991), 173–96

Anderson, R. C., 'Henry VIII's "Great Galley"', *The Mariner's Mirror* 6/9 (1920), 274–81

Anderson, Sue, Rees, Alastair Roy, Dunne, Catherine M., Gormley, Sarah, Hamilton-Dyer, Shelia, Murphy, Eileen M., Nelis, Eiméar L., and Noel, Mark, 'The Excavation of a Medieval Rural Settlement at Portmuck, Islandmagee, County Antrim', *Ulster Journal of Archaeology*, third series 63 (2004), 76–113

Andrews, J. H., 'The Irish Surveys of Robert Lythe', *Imago Mundi*, 19 (1965), 22–31

——, 'Geography and Government in Elizabethan Ireland', in N. Stephens and R. E. Glasscock, eds, *Irish Geographical Studies in Honour of E. Estyn Evans* (Belfast: Queen's University Belfast, 1970), 178–91

——, 'The Maps of the Escheated Counties of Ulster, 1609–10', *Proceedings of the Royal Irish Academy. Section C: Archaeology, Celtic Studies, History, Linguistics, Literature* 74 (1974), 113–70

——, *Shapes of Ireland: Maps and Their Makers 1564–1839* (Dublin: Geography Publications, 1997)

——, 'Sir Richard Bingham and the Mapping of Western Ireland', *Proceedings of the Royal Irish Academy. Section C: Archaeology, Celtic Studies, History, Linguistics, Literature* 103 (2003), 61–95

——, 'The Mapping of Ireland's Cultural Landscape, 1550–1630', in Patrick J. Duffy, David Edwards, and Elizabeth Fitzpatrick, eds, *Gaelic Ireland, c.1250–c.1650: Land, Lordship and Settlement* (Dublin: Four Courts Press, 2004), 153–80

——, *The Queen's Last Map-Maker: Richard Bartlett in Ireland, 1600–03* (Dublin: Geography Publications, 2008)

Andrews, Kenneth R., *Elizabethan Privateering: English Privateering during the Spanish War 1585–1603* (Cambridge: Cambridge University Press, 1964)

——, N. P. Canny, and P. E. H. Hair, eds, *The Westward Enterprise: English Activities in Ireland, the Atlantic and America, 1480–1650* (Liverpool: Liverpool University Press, 1978)

——, *Trade, Plunder and Settlement: Maritime Enterprise and the Genesis of the British Empire, 1480–1630* (Cambridge: Cambridge University Press, 1984)

Appleby, J. C., 'A Nursery of Pirates: The English Pirate Community in Ireland in the Early Seventeenth Century', *International Journal of Maritime History* II/1 (1990), 1–27

——, 'Women and Piracy in Ireland: From Gráinne O'Malley to Anne Bonny', in M. MacCurtain and M. O'Dowd, eds, *Women in Early Modern Ireland* (Edinburgh: Edinburgh University Press, 1991), 53–68

——, 'War, Politics, and Colonization, 1558–1625', in Nicholas Canny, ed., *The Origins of Empire. British Overseas Enterprise to the Close of the Seventeenth Century: The Oxford History of the British Empire I* (Oxford: Oxford University Press, 1998), 55–78

——, 'The Problem of Piracy in Ireland, 1570–1630', in Claire Jowitt, ed., *Pirates? The Politics of Plunder 1550–1650* (Basingstoke: Palgrave Macmillan, 2007), 41–55

——, *Under the Bloody Flag: Pirates of the Tudor Age* (Stroud: Tempus, 2009)

Archer, Ian W., 'Smith, Sir Thomas (1513–1577), *Scholar, Diplomat and Political theorist*', *Oxford Dictionary of National Biography* (Oxford: Oxford University Press, 2004; online edition 2008–14), <www.oxforddnb.com/>

Armitage, David, 'Making the Empire British: Scotland in the Atlantic World, 1542–1707', *Past and Present* 155 (1997), 34–63

——, ed., *Theories of Empire, 1450–1800* (Aldershot: Ashgate, 1998)

——, 'Literature and Empire', in Nicholas Canny, ed., *The Origins of Empire. British Overseas Enterprise to the Close of the Seventeenth Century: The Oxford History of the British Empire I* (Oxford: Oxford University Press, 1998), 99–123

——, 'Greater Britain: A Useful Category of Historical Analysis?', *American Historical Review* 104/2 (1999), 427–45

——, *The Ideological Origins of the British Empire* (Cambridge: Cambridge University Press, 2000)

——, and Michael J. Braddick, eds, *The British Atlantic World, 1500–1800* (Basingstoke: Palgrave Macmillan, 2002)

——, 'Three Concepts of Atlantic History', in David Armitage and Michael J. Braddick, eds, *The British Atlantic World, 1500–1800* (Basingstoke: Palgrave Macmillan, 2002), 13–29

——, *Greater Britain, 1516–1776: Essays in Atlantic History* (Aldershot: Ashgate/Variorum, 2004)

——, ed., *British Political Thought in History, Literature and Theory 1500–1800* (Cambridge: Cambridge University Press, 2006)

Ash, M., *The Strange Death of Scottish History* (Edinburgh: Ramsay Head Press, 1980)

Bagwell, Richard, *Ireland Under the Tudors: With a Succinct Account of Earlier History*, 3 vols (London: Longmans, Green, 1885–90; reprinted 1963)

Baldwin, Robert C. H., 'John Dee's Interest in the Application of Nautical Science, Mathematics and Law to English Naval Affairs', *International Archives of the History of Ideas* 193 (2006), 97–130

Bailyn, Bernard, and Philip D. Morgan, eds, *Strangers within the Realm. Cultural Margins of the First British Empire* (Chapel Hill: University of North Carolina Press, 1991)

Bannerman, J. W. M., 'The Lordship of the Isles', in J. M. Brown, ed., *Scottish Society in the Fifteenth Century* (London: Edward Arnold, 1977), 209–40

——, *The Beatons: A Medical Kindred in the Classical Gaelic Tradition* (Edinburgh: John Donald, 1986)

Barber, J. W., and B. A. Crone, 'Crannogs: A Diminishing Resource? A Survey of the Crannogs of Southwest Scotland and Excavations at Buiston Crannog', *Antiquity* 67/256 (1993), 520–33

Bardon, Jonathan, *A History of Ulster* (Belfast: Blackstaff Press, 1996)

——, *The Plantation of Ulster: The British Colonisation of the North of Ireland in the Seventeenth Century* (Dublin: Gill & Macmillan, 2011)

Barnby, H., 'The Sack of Baltimore', *Journal of the Cork Historical and Archaeological Society* 74 (1969), 101–29

Barrowman, Rachael, ed., *Dùn Èistean, Ness, Isle of Lewis: The Excavation of a Late Medieval Clan Stronghold* (Stornoway: Acair Ltd, 2015)

Bartlett, Robert, *Gerald of Wales, 1146–1223* (Oxford: Clarendon, 1982)

Behringer, Wolfgang, *A Cultural History of Climate* (Munche, 2007; translated and reprinted Cambridge: Polity, 2010)

Bennett, Martyn, *The Civil Wars in Britain and Ireland, 1638–51* (Oxford, 1997)

Bhreathnach, Edel, and Bernadette Cunningham, *Writing Irish History: The Four Masters and Their World* (Dublin: Wordwell, 2007)

Black, Jeremy, *Maps and History: Constructing Images of the Past* (London and New Haven, CT: Yale University Press, 1997)

Blakeway, Amy L., 'The Privy Council of James V of Scotland, 1528–1542', *The Historical Journal* 59/1 (2016), 23–44

——, 'The Anglo-Scottish war of 1558 and the Scottish Reformation', *History: The Journal of the Historical Association* 120/350 (2017), 201–24

Boardman, Steve, 'The Campbells and Charter Lordship in Medieval Argyll', in Steve Boardman and Alasdair Ross, eds, *The Exercise of Power in Medieval Scotland, c.1200–1500* (Dublin: Four Courts Press, 2003), 95–117

Boardman, Stephen, '"Pillars of the community": Campbell Lordship and Architectural Patronage in the Fifteenth Century', in R. D. Oram and Geoffrey Stell, eds, *Lordship and Architecture in Medieval and Renaissance Scotland* (Edinburgh: John Donald, 2005), 123–59

——, *The Campbells, 1250–1513* (Edinburgh: John Donald, 2006)

——, 'Stewart, Robert, First Duke of Albany (c. 1340–1420), Prince and Governor of Scotland', in *Oxford Dictionary of National Biography* (Oxford: Oxford University Press, 2004; online edition 2008–14), <www.oxforddnb.com/>

Boulind, Richard, 'Ships of Private Origin in the Mid-Tudor Navy: The *Lartigue*, the *Salamander*, the *Mary Willoughby*, the *Bark Aucher* and the *Galley Blanchard*', *The Mariner's Mirror* 59/4 (1973), 385–408

Bowen, E. G., 'Britain and the British Seas', in D. Moore, ed., *The Irish Sea Province in Archaeology and History* (Cardiff: Cambrian Archaeological Association, 1970)

——, *Saints Seaways and Settlements in the Celtic Lands* (Cardiff: University of Wales Press, 1977)

Braddick, Michael J., *State Formation in Early Modern England, c.1550–1700* (Cambridge: Cambridge University Press, 2000).

——, and David L. Smith, eds, *The Experience of Revolution in Stuart Britain and Ireland: Essays for John Morrill* (Cambridge and New York: Cambridge University Press, 2011)

Bradshaw, Brendan, *The Irish Constitutional Revolution of the Sixteenth Century* (Cambridge: Cambridge University Press, 1979)

——, 'Manus 'The Magnificent': O'Donnell as Renaissance Prince', in Art Cosgrove and Donal McCartney, eds, *Studies in Irish History presented to R. Dudley Edwards* (Dublin: University College Dublin, 1979), 15–36

——, and John Morrill, eds, *The British Problem, c.1534–1707. State Formation in the Atlantic Archipelago* (Basingstoke, 1996)

——, 'The Tudor Reformation and the Revolution in Wales and Ireland: the Origins of the British Problem', in Brendan Bradshaw and John Morrill, eds, *The British Problem, c.1534–1707. State Formation in the Atlantic Archipelago* (Basingstoke: Macmillan, 1996), 39–66

——, and Peter Roberts, eds, *British Consciousness and Identity: The Making of Britain, 1533–1707* (Cambridge: Cambridge University Press, 1998)

——, 'The English Reformation and Identity Formation in Ireland and Wales', in Brendan Bradshaw and Peter Roberts, eds, *British Consciousness and Identity: The Making of Britain, 1533–1707* (Cambridge: Cambridge University Press, 1998), 43–111

Brady, Ciaran, 'Spenser's Irish Crisis: Humanism and Experience in the 1590s', *Past and Present* 111 (1986), 17–49

——, *The Chief Governors. The Rise and Fall of Reform Government in Tudor Ireland 1536–1588* (Cambridge: Cambridge University Press, 1994)

——,'Comparable Histories?: Tudor Reform in Wales and Ireland', in Steven G. Ellis and Sarah Barber, eds, *Conquest and Union: Fashioning a British State, 1485–1725* (London: Longman, 1995), 64–86

——, *Shane O'Neill* (Dundalk: Historical Association of Ireland by Dundalgan Press, 1996; reprinted Dublin: University College Dublin Press on behalf of the Historical Association of Ireland, 2015)

——, 'The Attainder of Shane O'Neill, Sir Henry Sidney and the Problems of Tudor State-Building in Ireland', in Ciaran Brady and Jane Ohlmeyer, eds, *British Interventions in Early Modern Ireland* (Cambridge: Cambridge University Press, 2005), 28–48

——, 'East Ulster, the MacDonalds and the Provincial Strategies of Hugh O'Neill, earl of Tyrone, 1585–1603', in William P. Kelly and John R. Young, eds, *Scotland and the Ulster Plantations. Explorations in the British Settlements of Stuart Ireland* (Dublin: Four Courts Press, 2009), 41–61

——, and Raymond Gillespie, eds, *Natives & Newcomers: The Making of Irish Colonial Society* (Dublin: Dublin Irish Academic, 1986)

——, and James Murray, 'Sir Henry Sidney and the Reformation in Ireland', in Elizabethanne Boran and Crawford Gribben, eds, *Enforcing Reformation in Ireland and Scotland, 1550–1700* (Aldershot: Ashgate, 2006), 14–39

Braudel, Fernand, *The Mediterranean and the Mediterranean World in the Age of Philip II*, trans. Siân Reynolds, 2 vols (Berkeley and Los Angeles, CA, and London: University of California Press, 1995)

Breen, Colin, *Dunluce Castle: History and Archaeology* (Dublin: Four Courts Press, 2012)

——, 'Randal MacDonnell and Early Seventeenth-Century Settlement in Northeast Ulster, 1603–30', in Éamonn Ó Ciardha and Micheál Ó Siochrú, eds, *The Plantation of Ulster. Ideology and Practice* (Manchester: Manchester University Press, 2012), 143–57

——,'Marine Fisheries and Society in Medieval Ireland', in J. H. Barrett and D. C. Oton, eds, *Cod and Herring. The Archaeology and History of Medieval Sea Fishing* (Oxford and Philadelphia: Oxbow Books, 2016), 91–98

——, and John Raven, 'Maritime Lordship in Late-Medieval Gaelic Ireland', *Medieval Archaeology* 61/1 (2017), 149–82

——, 'Maritime Connections: Landscape and Lordship along the Gaelic Atlantic Seaboard of Scotland and the North of Ireland during the Middle Ages', *Maritime Communities of the North Atlantic Arc in the Early Modern Period: Journal of the North Atlantic,* ed., Alison Cathcart, special volume 12 (2019), 3–15

Brochard, Thomas, 'Plantation: Its Process in Relation to Scotland's Atlantic Communities, 1590s–1630s', *Maritime Communities of the North Atlantic Arc in the Early Modern Period: Journal of the North Atlantic,* ed., Alison Cathcart, special volume 12 (2019), 73–94

Broun, Dauvit, 'Attitudes of *Gall* to *Gaedhel* in Scotland before John of Fordun', in Dauvit Broun and Martin MacGregor, eds, *Mìorun Mòr nan Gall, 'The Great Ill-Will of the Lowlander'? Lowland Perceptions of the Highlands Medieval and Modern* (Glasgow: University of Glasgow, 2009), 49–82

——, 'Statehood and Lordship in 'Scotland' before the Mid-twelfth Century', *The Innes Review*, 66/1 (2015), 1–71

Brown, Keith M., *Bloodfeud in Scotland, 1573–1625: Violence, Justice, and Politics in an Early Modern Society* (Edinburgh: John Donald, 1986)

——, 'A House Divided: Family and Feud in Carrick under John Kennedy, Fifth earl of Cassillis', *Scottish Historical Review* 75 (1996), 168–96

——, 'Seducing the Scottish Clio: Has Scottish History Anything to Fear from the New British History', in Glenn Burgess, ed., *The New British History: Founding a Modern State, 1603–1715* (London: I. B. Tauris & Co. Ltd, 1999), 238–65

——, *Noble Power in Scotland from the Reformation to the Revolution* (Edinburgh: Edinburgh University Press, 2011)

Brown, Michael, *James I* (Edinburgh: Canongate Academic, 1994)

——, *The Wars of Scotland, 1214–1371* (Edinburgh: Edinburgh University Press, 2004)

——, 'Stewart, Murdoch [Murdac], Second Duke of Albany (c. 1362–1425), Magnate', in *Oxford Dictionary of National Biography* (Oxford: Oxford University Press, 2004; online edition 2008–14), <www.oxforddnb.com/>

——, *Disunited Kingdoms. Peoples and Politics in the British Isles 1280–1460* (Harlow: Pearson, 2013)

Bruce, Susan, ed., *Three Early Modern Utopias: Utopia, New Atlantis and The Isle of Pines* (Oxford: Oxford University Press, 1996)

Buchanan, R. H., 'The Irish Sea: The Geographical Framework', in Michael McCaughan and John Appleby, eds, *The Irish Sea: Aspects of Maritime History* (Antrim: Queen's University Belfast, 1989), 1–11

Buisseret, David, ed., *Monarchs, Ministers and Maps: The Emergence of Cartography as a Tool of Government in Early Modern Europe* (Chicago and London: University of Chicago Press, 1992)

Burgess, Glenn, ed., *The New British History: Founding a Modern State, 1603–1715* (London: I. B. Tauris & Co. Ltd, 1999)

Bushnell, Amy Turner, and Jack P. Greene, 'Peripheries, Centers, and the Construction of Early Modern American Empires', in Christine Daniels and Michael V. Kennedy, eds, *Negotiated Empire. Centers and Peripheries in the Americas, 1500–1820* (New York and London: Routledge, 2002), 1–14

Caball, Marc, 'Responses to Transformation: Gaelic Poets and the Plantation of Ulster', in Éamonn Ó Ciardha and Micheál Ó Siochrú, eds, *The Plantation of Ulster: Ideology and Practice* (Manchester: Manchester University Press, 2012), 176–97

Cage, A. G., and W. E. N. Austin, 'Marine Climate Variability during the Last Millennium: The Loch Sunart Record, Scotland, UK', *Quarternary Science Reviews* 29 (2010), 1633–47

Calder, A., *Revolutionary Empire: The Rise of the English-Speaking Empires from the Fifteenth Century to the 1780s* (London: London Cape, 1981)

Caldwell, David H., 'Having the Right Kit: West Highlanders Fighting in Ireland', in Seán Duffy, ed., *The World of the Galloglass. Kings, Warlords and Warriors in Ireland and Scotland, 1200–1600* (Dublin: Four Courts Press, 2007), 144–68

——, *Islay: The Land of the Lordship* (Edinburgh: Birlinn, 2008)

Callow, J., 'Campbell, Archibald, Seventh Earl of Argyll (1575/6–1638), Magnate and Politician', *Oxford Dictionary of National Biography* (Oxford: Oxford University Press, 2004; online edition 2008–14), <www.oxforddnb.com/>

Cameron, Jamie, *James V: The Personal Rule, 1528–1542* (East Linton: John Donald, 1998)

Campbell, B., *The Great Transition: Climate, Disease and Society in the Late-Medieval World* (Cambridge: Cambridge University Press, 2016)

Campbell of Airds, Alastair, *A History of Clan Campbell, Volume II: From Flodden to the Restoration* (Edinburgh: Edinburgh University Press, 2002)

Canny, N. P., 'The Flight of the Earls, 1607', *Irish Historical Studies* XVI (1971), 380–99

Canny, Nicholas, 'The Ideology of English Colonisation: From Ireland to America', *William and Mary Quarterly*, third series 30 (1973), 575–98

——, 'Rowland White's *Discors touching Ireland*, c.1569', *Irish Historical Studies* XXIV (1977), 439–63

——, 'The Permissive Frontier: Social Control in English Settlements in Ireland and Virginia, 155–1650', in K. R. Andrews, N. P. Canny, and P. E. H. Hair, eds, *The Westward Enterprise. English Activities in Ireland, the Atlantic and America, 1480–1650* (Liverpool: Liverpool University Press, 1978), 17–44

Canny, Nicholas P., *The Elizabethan Conquest of Ireland: A Pattern Established 1565–76* (Hassocks: Harvester Press, 1976)

——, 'Edmund Spenser and the Development of an Anglo-Irish Identity', *Yearbook of English Studies: Colonial and Imperial Themes* 13 (1985), 1–19

——, "Spenser's Irish Crisis': A Comment', *Past and Present*, 120 (1988), 201–09

——, *Kingdom and Colony: Ireland in the Atlantic World 1500–1800* (Baltimore and London: John Hopkins University Press, 1988)

——, 'The Origins of Empire: An Introduction', in Nicholas Canny, ed., *The Origins of Empire. British Overseas Enterprise to the Close of the Seventeenth Century: The Oxford History of the British Empire I* (Oxford: Oxford University Press, 1998), 1–33

——, *Making Ireland British, 1580–1630* (Oxford: Oxford University Press, 2003)

Canny, Nicholas, and Anthony Pagden, eds., *Colonial Identity in the Atlantic World, 1500–1800* (Princeton, NJ: Princeton University Press, 1987)

Carey, Vincent P., 'Atrocity and History: Grey, Spenser and the Slaughter at Smerwick (1580)', in David Edwards, Pádraig Lenihan and Clodagh Tait, eds, *Age of Atrocity. Violence and Political Conflict in Early Modern Ireland* (Dublin: Four Courts Press, 2007), 79–94

Casada Soto, José Luis, 'Atlantic Shipping in Sixteenth-Century Spain and the 1588 Armada', in M. J. Rodríguez-Salgado and Simon Adams, eds, *England, Spain and the Gran Armada, 1585–1604* (Edinburgh: John Donald, 1991), 95–132

Cathcart, Alison, *Kinship and Clientage: Highland Clanship 1451–1609* (Leiden: Brill, 2006)

——, 'James V, King of Scotland - and Ireland?', in Seán Duffy, ed., *The World of the Galloglass. Kings, Warlords and Warriors in Ireland and Scotland, 1200–1600* (Dublin: Four Courts Press, 2007), 124–43

——, 'Scots and Ulster: The Late Medieval Context', in W. P. Kelly and J. R. Young, eds, *Scotland and the Ulster Plantations. Explorations in the British Settlements of Stuart Ireland* (Dublin: Four Courts Press, 2009), 62–83

——, 'The Statutes of Iona: The Archipelagic Context', *Journal of British Studies* 49/1 (2010), 4–27

——, 'The View from Scotland: The Scottish Context to the Flight of the Earls', in David Finnegan, Éamonn Ó Ciardha and Marie-Claire Peters, eds, *The Flight of the Earls: Imeacht na nIarlaí* (Derry: Guildhall Press, 2010), 132–39

——, 'The Forgotten '45: Donald Dubh's Rebellion in an Archipelagic Context', *Scottish Historical Review* XCI:2/232 (2012), 239–64

——, 'A Spent Force? The Clan Donald in the Aftermath of 1493', in Richard D. Oram, ed., *The Lordship of the Isles* (Leiden: Brill, 2014), 254–70

——, 'The Maritime Dimension to Plantation in Ulster, *c.*1550–*c.*1600', *Maritime Communities of the North Atlantic Arc in the Early Modern Period: Journal of the North Atlantic,* ed., Alison Cathcart, special vol. 12 (2019), 95–111

——, 'Island Empire: James VI and I and the Isle of Man', in Neil McIntyre and Alison Cathcart, eds, *Scotland and the Wider World* (Woodbridge: Boydell & Brewer, forthcoming 2022)

Clarke, Aidan, 'The Irish Economy, 1600–60', in T. W. Moody, F. X. Martin, and F. J. Byrne, eds, *A New History of Ireland Volume III: Early Modern Ireland 1534–1691* (Oxford: Clarendon Press, 1979; Oxford: Oxford Univerity Press, online 2011), 168–86

Clark, Wallace, 'Tides in the Waters of the Moyle', *The Glynns: Journal of the Glens of Antrim Historical Society* 6 (1978), accessed via <http://antrimhistory.net/tides-in-the-waters-of-moyle-by-wallace-clark/>

Clavin, Terry, 'MacDonnell, Sir Randal mac Sorley', *Dictionary of Irish Biography* (Cambridge University Press for the Royal Irish Academy, online 2009–), <dib.ie>

Collinson, Patrick, 'Elizabeth I (1533–1603)', *Oxford Dictionary of National Biography* (Oxford: Oxford University Press, 2004; online edition 2008–14), <www.oxforddnb.com/>

Connolly, S. J., ed., *Kingdoms United? Great Britain and Ireland since 1500: Integration and Diversity* (Dublin: Four Courts Press, 1999)

——, *Contested Island. Ireland 1460–1630* (Oxford: Oxford University Press, 2007)

Cosgrove, Art, 'Ireland beyond the Pale, 1399–1460', in Art Cosgrove, ed., *A New History of Ireland II: Medieval Ireland, 1169–1534* (Oxford: Clarendon Press, 1987; Oxford: Oxford University Press, online 2012), 569–90

Costello, Eugene, 'Seasonal Management of Cattle in the Booleying System: New Insights from Connemara, Western Ireland', in Michael O'Connell, Fergus Kelly, and James H. McAdam, eds, *Cattle in Ancient and Modern Ireland: Farming Practices, Environment and Economy* (Newcastle upon Tyne: Cambridge Scholars Publishing, 2016), 66–74

Costello, Kevin, *The Court of Admiralty of Ireland, 1575–1893* (Dublin: Four Courts Press, 2011)

Cowan, E. J., 'Kinship, Clanship and the Campbell Acquisition of Islay', *Scottish Historical Review*, LVIII:2 (1979), 132–57

——, 'Fishers in Drumlie Waters: Clanship and Campbell Expansion in the Time of Gilleasbuig Gruamach', *Transactions of the Gaelic Society of Inverness* 54 (1984–86), 269–312

——, 'The Discovery of the Gàidhealtachd in Sixteenth Century Scotland', *Transactions of the Gaelic Society of Inverness*, lx (1997–98), 259–84

Crawford, Ross, 'The Life of Sir James MacDonald of Knockrinsay', *The Innes Review*, 67/2 (2016), 107–37

——, 'Noble Power in the West Highlands and Isles. James VI and the End of the Mercenary Trade with Ireland, 1594–96', in Miles Kerr-Peterson and Steven J. Reid, eds, *James VI and Noble Power in Scotland, 1578–1603* (Abingdon: Routledge, 2017), 117–35

Cressy, David, *Coming Over: Migration and Communication between England and New England in the Sixteenth Century* (Cambridge: Cambridge University Press, 1987)

Croft, Pauline, *King James* (Basingstoke: Palgrave Macmillan, 2003)

Crone, B. A., 'Crannogs and Chronologies', *Proceedings of the Society of Antiquaries of Scotland*, 123 (1993), 245–54

Crone, A., *The History of a Scottish Lowland Crannog: Excavations at Buiston, Ayrshire, 1989–90* (Edinburgh: Scottish Trust for Archaeological Research, 2000)

Crone, Anne, and Ewan Campbell, with Colleen Batey et al., *A Crannog of the First Millennium AD: Excavations by Jack Scott at Loch Glashan, Argyll, 1960* (Edinburgh: Society of Antiquaries of Scotland, 2005)

Crone, A., and F. Watson, 'Sufficiency to Scarcity: Medieval Scotland 500–1600', in T. C. Smout, ed., *People and Woods in Scotland: A History* (Edinburgh: Edinburgh University Press, 2003), 60–81

Cronon, William, *Changes in the Land. Indians, Colonists, and the Ecology of New England* (New York: Hill and Wang, rev. edn 2003)

Crooks, Peter, David Green, and W. Mark Ormrod, eds, *The Plantagenet Empire, 1259–1453: Proceedings of the 2014 Harlaxton Symposium* (Donington: Shaun Tyas Publishing, 2016)

Crosby, Alfred W., *Ecological Imperialism: The Biological Expansion of Europe, 900–1900* (Cambridge and New York: Cambridge University Press, 1986, 2nd edn 2004)

Cullen, Karen J., *Famine in Scotland: The 'ill years' of the 1690s* (Edinburgh: Edinburgh University Press, 2010)

Cunningham, Bernadette, 'Bingham, Sir Richard (1527/8–1599), *Soldier and President of Connacht*', in *Oxford Dictionary of National Biography* (Oxford: Oxford University Press, 2004; online edition 2008–14), <www.oxforddnb.com/>

Davies, R. R., ed., *The British Isles, 1100–1500: Comparisons, Contrasts, Connections* (Edinburgh: John Donald, 1988)

——, *Domination and Conquest: The Experience of Ireland, Scotland, and Wales, 1100–1300* (Cambridge: Cambridge University Press, 1990)

——, *The First English Empire: Power and Identities in the British Isles 1093–1343* (Oxford: Oxford University Press, 2002)

Dawson, A. G., *So Foul and Fair a Day: A History of Scotland's Weather and Climate* (Edinburgh: Birlinn, 2009)

Dawson, A. G., K. Hickey, T. Holt, L. Elliot, S. Dawson, I. D. L. Foster, P. Wadhams, I. Jonsdottir, J. Wilkjinson, J. McKenna, N. R. Davis, and D. E. Smith, 'Complex North Atlantic Oscillation (NAO) Index Signal of Historic North Atlantic Storm-Track Changes', *The Holocene* 12/3 (2002), 363–69

——, L. Elliot, P. Mayewski, P. Locket, S. Noone, K. Hickey, T. Holt, P. Wadhams, and I. Foster, 'Late-Holocene North Atlantic Climate 'seesaws', Storminess Changes and Greenland Ice Sheet (GISP2) Palaeoclimates', *The Holocene* 13/3 (2003), 381–92

——, L. Elliot, S. Noone, K. Hickey, T. Holt, P. Wadhams, and I. Foster, 'Historical Storminess and Climate 'see-saws' in the North Atlantic Region', *Marine Geology* 201 (2004), 247–59

Dawson, Jane, E. A., 'William Cecil and the British Dimension of Early Elizabeth Foreign Policy', *History* 74 (1989), 196–216

——, 'The Gaidhealtachd and the Emergence of the Scottish Highlands', in Brendan Bradshaw and Peter Roberts, eds, *British Consciousness and Identity: The Making of Britain, 1533–1707* (Cambridge: Cambridge University Press, 1998), 259–300

——, *The Politics of Religion in the Age of Mary, Queen of Scots. The Earl of Argyll and the Struggle for Britain and Ireland* (Cambridge: Cambridge University Press, 2002)

——, *Scotland Re-formed, 1488–1587* (Edinburgh: Edinburgh University Press, 2007)

DeJohn Anderson, Virginia, *Creatures of Empire. How Domestic Animals Transformed Early America* (Oxford: Oxford University Press, 2004)

De Vries, Jan and Ad Van Der Woude, *The First Modern Economy: Success, Failure, and Perseverance of the Dutch Economy, 1500–1815* (Cambridge: Cambridge University Press, 1997)

Devine, T. M., *Scotland's Empire, 1600–1815* (London: Allan Lane, 2003)

——, ed., *Recovering Scotland's Slavery Past: The Caribbean Connection* (Edinburgh: Edinburgh University Press, 2015)

Ditchburn, David, 'Piracy and War at Sea in Late Medieval Scotland', in T. C. Smout, ed., *Scotland and the Sea* (Edinburgh: John Donald, 1992), 35–58

Dodgshon, Robert A., 'West Highland Chiefdoms, 1500–1745: A Study in Redistributive Exchange', in Rosalind Mitchison and Peter Roebuck, eds, *Economy and Society in Scotland and Ireland, 1500–1939* (Edinburgh: John Donald, 1988), 27–37

——, *From Chiefs to Landlords. Social and Economic Change in the Western Highlands and Islands, c.1493–1820* (Edinburgh: Edinburgh University Press, 1998)

——, 'The Little Ice Age in the Scottish Highlands and Islands: Documenting its Human Impact', *Scottish Geographical Journal* 121/4 (2005), 321–37

Donaldson, Dixon, *Historical, Traditional and Descriptive Account of Islandmagee* (Islandmagee: privately published, 1927)

Donaldson, Gordon, *Scotland: James V – James VII* (Edinburgh: Oliver & Boyd, 1965)

Duffy, Seán, 'The Bruce Brothers and the Irish Sea World, 1306–29', *Cambridge Medieval Celtic Studies* 21 (1991), 55–86

——, 'The Lords of Galloway, Earls of Carrick, and the Bissets of the Glens: Scottish Settlement in Thirteenth-Century Ulster', in David Edwards, ed., *Regions and Rulers in Ireland, 1100–1650. Essays for Kenneth Nicholls* (Dublin: Four Courts Press, 2004), 37–50

——, 'The Prehistory of the Galloglass', in Seán Duffy, ed., *The World of the Galloglass. Kings, Warlords and Warriors in Ireland and Scotland, 1200–1600* (Dublin: Four Courts Press, 2007), 1–23

Dunlop, Robert, 'The Plantation of Munster, 1584–89', *English Historical Review* 3/10 (1888), 250–69

——, 'Sixteenth-Century Maps of Ireland', *English Historical Review* 20/78 (1905), 309–37

Dunshea, Philip M., '*Druim Alban, Dorsun Britanniae* – 'the Spine of Britain'', *Scottish Historical Review* XCII:2/235 (2013), 275–89

Edwards, David, 'Ideology and Experience: Spenser's *View* and Martial Law in Ireland', in Hiram Morgan, ed., *Political Ideology in Ireland, 1541–1641* (Dublin: Four Courts Press, 1991), 127–57

——, 'Beyond Reform: Martial Law and the Tudor Reconquest of Ireland', *History Ireland* 5/2 (1997), 16–21

——, 'Securing the Jacobean Succession: The Secret Career of James Fullerton of Trinity College, Dublin', in Seán Duffy, ed., *The World of the Galloglass. Kings, Warlords and Warriors in Ireland and Scotland, 1200–1600* (Dublin: Four Courts Press, 2007), 188–219

——, 'Questioning the Viceroys: Towards a New Module of English Government in Tudor Ireland, 1536–1594', in Sarah Covington, Vincent P. Carey, and Valerie McGowan-Doyle, eds, *Early Modern Ireland. New Sources, Methods and Perspectives* (London: Routledge, 2019), 147–65

——, with Egan, Simon, eds, *The Scots in Early Stuart Ireland. Union and Separation in Two Kingdoms* (Manchester: Manchester University Press, 2016)

——, Tait, Clodagh, and Carey, Vincent, eds, *Age of Atrocity: Violence and Political Conflict in Early Modern Ireland* (Dublin: Four Courts Press, 2007)

Elliot, J. H., 'A Europe of Composite Monarchies', *Past and Present* 137 (1992), 48–71

——, *Empires of the Atlantic World. Britain and Spain in America 1492–1850* (New Haven and London: Yale University Press, 2006)

——, 'Atlantic History: A Circumnavigation', in David Armitage and Michael J. Braddick, eds, *The British Atlantic World, 1500–1800* (Basingstoke: Palgrave Macmillan, 2009), 253–70

Ellis, Steven G., 'The Kildare Rebellion and the Early Henrician Reformation', *Historical Journal* 19/4 (1976), 807–30

——, *Tudor Ireland: Crown, Community and the Conflict of Cultures, 1470–1603* (London : Longman, 1985)

——, *Tudor Frontiers and Noble Power: The Making of the British State* (Oxford: Clarendon Press, 1995)

——, *Ireland in the Age of the Tudors, 1447–1603: English Expansion and the End of Gaelic Rule* (London and New York: Longman, Addison Wesley Longman, 1998)

——, 'Fitzgerald, Gerald, Eighth Earl of Kildare (1456?–1513), Magnate and Administrator', *Oxford Dictionary of National Biography* (Oxford: Oxford University Press, 2004; online edition 2008–14), <www.oxforddnb.com/>

——, '"Reducing their wildness … unto civility': England and the 'Celtic fringe', 1415–1625', in Brendan Smith, ed., *Ireland and the English World in the Late Middle Ages: Essays in Honour of Robin Frame* (Houndmills, England and New York: Palgrave Macmillan, 2009), 176–92

——, with Maginn, Christopher, *The Making of the British Isles: The State of Britain and Ireland, 1450–1660* (Harlow: Pearson/Longman, 2007)

——, and Barber, Sarah, eds, *Conquest and Union: Fashioning a British State, 1485–1725* (London: Longman, 1995)

Fagan, Brian, *The Little Ice Age. How Climate Made History 1300–1850* (New York: Basic Books, 2000)

Farrell, Gerard, *The 'Mere Irish' and the Colonisation of Ulster, 1570–1641* (Cham: Palgrave Macmillan, 2017)

Finnegan, David, 'Why Did the Earl of Tyrone Join the Flight?', in David Finnegan, Éamonn Ó Ciardha and Marie-Claire Peters, eds, *The Flight of the Earls: Imeacht na nIarlaí* (Derry: Guildhall Press, 2010), 2–12

Fitzpatrick, Elizabeth, *Royal Inauguration in Gaelic Ireland, c.1100–1600: A Cultural Landscape Study* (Woodbridge: Boydell Press, 2004)

Fitzgerald, Patrick, 'Scottish Migration to Ireland in the Seventeenth Century', in Alexia Grosjean and Steve Murdoch, eds, *Scottish Communities Abroad in the Early Modern Period* (Leiden: Brill, 2005), 27–52

Fitzsimmons, Fiona, 'Fosterage and Gossiprid in Late Medieval Ireland. Some New Evidence', in Patrick J. Duffy, David Edwards and Elizabeth FitzPatrick, eds, *Gaelic Ireland c.1250–c.1650: Land, Lordship & Settlement* (Dublin: Four Courts Press, 2004), 138–52

Flavin, Susan and Jones, Evan T., *Bristol's Trade with Ireland and the Continent 1503–1601: The Evidence of the Exchequer Customs Accounts* (Dublin: Four Courts Press/Bristol Record Society, 2009)

Forte, A. D. M., 'The Identification of Fifteenth-Century Ship Types in Scottish Legal Records', *The Mariner's Mirror* 84/1 (1998), 3–12

——, '"Kenning be Kenning and Course be Course', Alexander Linsday's Rutter and the Problematics of Navigation in Fifteenth and Sixteenth Century Scotland', *Review of Scottish Culture* 11 (1998–99), 32–45

——, Richard D. Oram, and Frederik Pedersen, *Viking Empires* (Cambridge: Cambridge University Press, 2005)

Frame, Robin, *The Political Development of the British Isles, 1100–1400* (Oxford: Oxford University Press, 1995)

——, *Ireland and Britain, 1170–1450* (London: Hambledon Press, 1998)

Frost, Robert, *The Oxford History of Poland-Lithuania Volume I: The Making of the Polish-Lithuanian Union, 1385–1569* (Oxford: Oxford University Press, 2015)

Fulton, T. W., *The Sovereignty of the Sea. An Historical Account of the Claims of England to the Dominions of the British Seas, and of the Evolution of the Territorial Waters: with Special Reference to the Rights of Fishing and the Naval Salute* (London and Edinburgh: Blackwood, 1911)

Games, Alison, *Migration and the Origins of the English Atlantic World* (Cambridge, MA and London: Harvard University Press, 1999)

Gardiner, Mark, and T. E. McNeill, 'Seaborne Trade and the Commercialisation of Fifteenth- and Sixteenth-Century Gaelic Ulster', *Proceedings of the Royal Irish Academy. Section C: Archaeology, Celtic Studies, History, Linguistics, Literature* (2016), 1–34

Gillespie, Raymond, *Colonial Ulster: The Settlement of East Ulster 1600–1641* (Cork: Cork University Press, 1985)

——, 'Success and Failure in the Ulster Plantation', in Éamonn Ó Ciardha and Micheál Ó Siochrú, eds, *The Plantation of Ulster: Ideology and Practice* (Manchester: Manchester University Press, 2012), 98–115

Glasgow Jr, Tom, 'The Shape of the Ships That Defeated the Spanish Armada', *The Mariner's Mirror* 50/3 (1964), 177–87

Goodare, Julian, 'The Statutes of Iona in Context', *Scottish Historical Review* LXXVII: 203 (1998), 31–57

——, *State and Society in Early Modern Scotland* (Oxford: Oxford University Press, 1999)

——, *The Government of Scotland 1560–1625* (Oxford: Oxford University Press, 2005)

——, 'Mary (1542–1587)', *Oxford Dictionary of National Biography* (Oxford: Oxford University Press, 2004; online edition 2008–14), <www.oxforddnb.com/>

——, and Michael Lynch, 'James VI: Universal King?', in Julian Goodare and Michael Lynch, eds, *The Reign of James VI* (East Linton: John Donald, 2000), 1–31

Gorski, Philip S., 'Beyond Marx and Hintze? Third-Wave Theories of Early Modern State Formation', *Society for the Comparative Study of Society and History* (2001), 851–61

Graham, B. J., and L. J. Proudfoot, eds, *An Historical Geography of Ireland* (London: Academic Press, 1993)

Grant, Ruth, 'Brig o'Dee Affair, the Sixth Earl of Huntly and the Politics of the Counter-Reformation', in Julian Goodare and Michael Lynch, eds, *The Reign of James VI* (East Linton: John Donald, 2000), 93–109

——, 'Friendship, Politics and Religion: George Gordon, Sixth Earl of Huntly and King James VI, 1581–1595', in Miles Kerr-Peterson and Steven J. Reid, eds, *James VI and Noble Power in Scotland 1578–1603* (Abingdon: Routledge, 2017), 57–80

Gregory, Donald, *History of the Western Highlands and Isles of Scotland, from AD 1493 to AD 1625: With a Brief Introductory Sketch, from AD 80 to AD 1493* (Edinburgh: W. Tait, 1836; reprinted Edinburgh: John Donald, 2008 with an introduction by Martin MacGregor)

Groundwater, Anna, *The Scottish Middle March 1573–1612. Power, Kinship, Allegiance* (London: Royal Historical Society, 2010)

Gunn, S. J., 'Henry VII (1457–1509)', *Oxford Dictionary of National Biography* (Oxford: Oxford University Press, 2004; online edition 2008–14), <www.oxforddnb.com/>

Hadfield, Andrew, 'Rocking the Boat: A Response to Hiram Morgan', *Irish Review*, 14 (1993), 15–19

——, 'Educating the Colonial Mind: Spenser and the Plantation', in Éamonn Ó Ciardha and Micheál Ó Siochrú, eds, *The Plantation of Ulster. Ideology and Practice* (Manchester: Manchester University Press, 2012), 158–75

Hadfield, Andrew, *Edmund Spenser: A Life* (Oxford: Oxford University Press, 2012)

——, and Willy Maley, eds, *Edmund Spenser. A View of the State of Ireland* (Oxford: Blackwell, 1997)

Harris, Tim, 'Critical Perspectives: The Autonomy of English History?', in Glenn Burgess, ed., *The New British History: Founding a Modern State, 1603–1715* (London: I. B. Tauris & Co. Ltd, 1999), 266–86

——, *Revolution: The Great Crisis of the British Monarchy, 1685–1720* (London: Allen Lane, 2006)

——, *The Final Crisis of the Stuart Monarchy: The Revolutions of 1688–91 in the British Atlantic and European Contexts* (Woodbridge: Boydell & Brewer, 2015)

Hayes-McCoy, Gerald A., *Scots Mercenary Forces in Ireland (1565–1603): An Account of Their Service during That Period and of the Reaction of Their Activities on Scottish Affairs, and of the Effect of Their Presence in Ireland, together with an Examination of the Gallóglaigh or Galloglass* (Dublin: Edmund Burke Publisher, 1937; reprinted 1996)

——, 'Conciliation, Coercion and the Protestant Reformation, 1547–71', in T. W. Moody, F. X. Martin, and F. J. Byrne, eds, *A New History of Ireland Volume III: Early Modern Ireland 1534–1691* (Oxford: Clarendon Press, 1979; Oxford: Oxford University Press, online 2011), 69–93

Hechter, Michael, *Internal Colonialism: The Celtic Fringe in British National Development, 1536–1966* (London: Routledge and Kegan Paul, 1975)

Heffernan, David, *Debating Tudor Policy in Sixteenth-Century Ireland: 'Reform' Treatises and Political Discourse* (Manchester: Manchester University Press, 2018)

Henderson, Jon C., 'Islets Through Time: The Definition, Dating and Distribution of Scottish Crannogs', *Oxford Journal of Archaeology* 17/2 (1998), 227–44

Hendry, Frederic, 'James IV and the Scottish Navy', *Aberdeen University Review* (1920), 46–48

Herron, Thomas, 'Orpheus in Ulster: Richard Bartlett's Colonial Art', in Thomas Herron and Michael Potterton, eds, *Ireland in the Renaissance, c.1540–1660* (Dublin: Four Courts Press, 2007), 289–308

Hill, George, *An Historical Account of the Macdonnells of Antrim: Including Notices of Some Other Septs, Irish and Scottish* (Belfast: Archer, 1873)

Hill, J. Michael, 'The Origins of the Scottish Plantations in Ulster to 1625: A Reinterpretation', *Journal of British Studies* 32/1 (1993), 24–43

Hindle, Steve, *The State and Social Change in Early Modern England, 1550–1640* (Basingstoke: Palgrave, 2002)

Hoffman, Richard C., *An Environmental History of Medieval Europe* (Cambridge: Cambridge University Press, 2014)

Holloway, Ernest R., *Andrew Melville and humanism in Renaissance Scotland, 1545–1622* (Leiden: Brill, 2011)

Holmes, Peter, 'Hamilton, Claud, First Lord Paisley (1546?–1621)', in *Oxford Dictionary of National Biography* (Oxford: Oxford University Press, 2004; online edition 2008–14), <www.oxforddnb.com/>

Hore, Herbert F., 'The Earl of Essex's Enterprise for the Recovery of Ulster', *Ulster Journal of Archaeology*, first series 9 (1861/2), 245–55

Horning, Audrey J., 'Archaeological Explorations of Cultural Identity and Rural Economy in the North of Ireland: Goodland, County Antrim', *International Journal of Historical Archaeology* 8 (2004), 199–215

——, '"Dwelling houses in the old Irish barbarous manner": Archaeological Evidence for Gaelic Architecture in an Ulster Plantation Village', in Patrick J. Duffy, David Edwards, and Elizabeth FitzPatrick, eds, *Gaelic Ireland c.1250–c.1650: Land, Lordship & Settlement* (Dublin: Four Courts Press, 2004), 375–96

——, 'On the Banks of the Bann: The Riverine Economy of an Ulster Plantation Village', *Historical Archaeology* 41/3 (2007), 94–114

——, *Ireland in the Virginian Sea. Colonisation in the British Atlantic* (Chapel Hill: University of North Carolina Press, 2013)

Hunter, Robert J., ed., *Strabane Barony during the Ulster Plantation 1607–1641* (Belfast: Ulster Historical Foundation, 2011)

——, *The Ulster Port Books 1612–15* (Belfast: Ulster Historical Foundation, 2012)

Insh, G. P., *Scottish Colonial Schemes 1620–1686* (Glasgow: Maclehose, Jackson & Co., 1922)

Ives, E., 'Henry VIII (1491–1547), King of England and Ireland', in *Oxford Dictionary of National Biography* (Oxford: Oxford University Press, 2004; online edition 2008–14), <www.oxforddnb.com/>

Jefferies, Henry A., 'George Montgomery, First Protestant Bishop of Clogher (1605–1621)' *Clogher Record* 16/3 (1999), 127–29

——, 'George Montgomery, First Protestant Bishop of Derry, Raphoe and Clogher (1605–1610)', in H. A. Jefferies and Ciaran Devlin, eds, *History of the Diocese of Derry* (Dublin: Four Courts Press, 2000), 140–66

——, 'Montgomery, George (1569–70–1621), Church of Ireland Bishop of Meath and Clogher', in *Oxford Dictionary of National Biography* (Oxford: Oxford University Press, 2004; online edition 2008–14), <www.oxforddnb.com/>

——, 'O'Neill, Sir Turlough Luineach (*c.*1530–1595)', in *Oxford Dictionary of National Biography* (Oxford: Oxford University Press, 2004; online edition 2008–14), <www.oxforddnb.com/>

——, 'Why the Reformation Failed in Ireland', *Irish Historical Studies* 40/158 (2016), 151–70

Jope, E. M., 'Scottish Influences in the North of Ireland: Castles with Scottish Features, 1580–1640', *Ulster Journal of Archaeology* third series 14 (1951), 31–47

Kane, Brendan, 'Ordinary Violence? Ireland as Emergency in the Tudor State', *History* 99/3 (2014), 444–67

Kelleher, Connie, *The Alliance of Pirates. Ireland and Atlantic Piracy in the Early Seventeenth Century* (Cork: Cork University Press, 2020)

Kennedy, Allan, *Governing Gaeldom: The Scottish Highlands and the Restoration State, 1660–1688* (Leiden: Brill, 2014)

Kenyon, J. P., and Jane Ohlmeyer, eds, *The Civil Wars: A Military History of England, Scotland and Ireland* (Oxford: Oxford University Press, 1998)

Kerney Walsh, M., *'Destruction by peace': Hugh O'Neill after Kinsale* (Armagh: Armagh Diocesan Historical Society, 1986)

Kidd, Colin, *British Identities before Nationalism: Ethnicity and Nationhood in the Atlantic World, 1600–1800* (Cambridge: Cambridge University Press, 1999)

Kingston, Simon, *Ulster and the Isles in the Fifteenth Century: The Lordship of the Clann Domhnaill of Antrim* (Dublin: Four Courts Press, 2004)

Klein, Bernhard, 'English Cartographers and the Mapping of Ireland in the Early Modern Period', *Journal for the Study of British Cultures* II (1995), 115–39

Kupperman, Karen O., *The Jamestown Project* (Cambridge, MA and London: Harvard University Press, 2007)

Landsman, Ned C., *Nation and Province in the First British Empire: Scotland and the Americas 1600–1800* (Lewisburg, PA and London: Bucknell University Press and Associated University Press, 2001)

Lee, Maurice, 'The Government of Scotland after 1603', *Scottish Historical Review* LV:159 (1976), 41–53

——, *Government by Pen: Scotland under James VI and I* (Urbana, IL: University of Illinois Press, 1980)

Lee Jnr, Maurice, *Great Britain's Solomon: James VI and I in His Three Kingdoms* (Urbana, IL: University of Illinois Press, 1990)

Leersen, J., 'Wildness, Wilderness and Ireland: Medieval and Early-Modern Patterns in the Demarcation of Civility', *Journal of the History of Ideas* 56 (1995), 25–39

Lennon, Colm, *Sixteenth-Century Ireland: The Incomplete Conquest* (Dublin: Gill & Macmillan, 2005)

Levack, Brian P., *The Formation of the British State. England, Scotland and the Union 1603–1707* (Oxford: Clarendon Press, 1987)

Loades, David, *The Tudor Navy: An Administrative, Political and Military History* (Aldershot: Scolar, 1992)

——, 'Dudley, John, Duke of Northumberland (1504–1553), *Royal Servant*', in *Oxford Dictionary of National Biography* (Oxford: Oxford University Press, 2004; online edition 2008–14), <www.oxforddnb.com/>

——, *The Making of the Elizabethan Navy 1540–1590. From the Solent to the Armada* (Woodbridge: Boydell & Brewer, 2009)

Loeber, Rolf, 'English and Irish Sources for the History of Dutch Economic Activity in Ireland, 1600–89', *Irish Economic and Social History* 8 (1981), 70–85

——, 'Settlers' Utilisation of the Natural Resources', in Ken Hannigan and William Nolan, eds, *Wicklow, History and Society: Interdisciplinary Essays on the History of an Irish County* (Dublin: Geography Publications, 1994), 267–304

——, 'An Architectural History of Gaelic Castles and Settlements, 1370–1600', in Patrick J. Duffy, David Edwards, and Elizabeth FitzPatrick, eds, *Gaelic Ireland c.1250–c.1650: Land, Lordship & Settlement* (Dublin: Four Courts Press, 2004), 271–314

——, '"Certyn notes': Biblical and Foreign Signposts to the Ulster Plantation', in J. Lyttleton and C. Rynnes, eds, *Plantation Ireland. Settlement and Material Culture, c.1550–c.1700* (Dublin: Four Courts Press, 2009), 23–42

Logan, George M., and Robert M. Adams, eds, *More: Utopia* (Cambridge: Cambridge University Press, rev. edn 2002)

Lyall, Andrew, 'Waterhouse, Sir Edward (1535–1591)', in *Oxford Dictionary of National Biography* (Oxford: Oxford University Press, 2004; online edition 2008–14), <www.oxforddnb.com/>

Lydon, James, 'The Impact of the Bruce Invasion, 1315–27', in Art Cosgrove, ed., *A New History of Ireland, Volume II: Medieval Ireland 1169–1534* (Oxford: Clarendon Press, 1987), chapter 10 reprinted in Seán Duffy, ed., *Robert the Bruce's Irish Wars. The Invasions of Ireland, 1360–1329* (Tempus: Stroud, 2002), 119–52

——, 'The Scottish Soldier in Medieval Ireland: The Bruce Invasion and the Galloglass', in G. G. Simpson, ed., *The Scottish Soldier Abroad 1247–1967* (Edinburgh: John Donald, 1992), 1–15

Lynch, Michael, 'James VI and the 'Highland Problem'', in Julian Goodare and Michael Lynch, eds, *The Reign of James VI* (East Linton: John Donald, 2000), 208–27

Lyons, Mary Ann, 'Fitzwilliam, Sir William (1526–1599)', in *Oxford Dictionary of National Biography* (Oxford: Oxford University Press, 2004; online edition 2008–2014), <www.oxforddnb.com/>

——, *Franco-Irish Relations, 1500–1601. Politics, Migration and Trade* (Woodbridge: Boydell & Brewer, 2003; reprinted 2015)

Macaulay, T. B., *The Works of Lord Macaulay: Complete,* ed., Lady Trevelyan, 8 vols (London, 1879)

MacCaffrey, Wallace T., 'Radcliffe, Thomas, Third Earl of Sussex (1526/7–1583)', in *Oxford Dictionary of National Biography* (Oxford: Oxford University Press, 2004; online edition 2008–14), <www.oxforddnb.com/>

——, 'Cecil, William, First Baron Burghley (15202/1–1598), *Royal Minister*', in *Oxford Dictionary of National Biography* (Oxford: Oxford University Press, 2004; online edition 2008–14), <www.oxforddnb.com/>

——, 'Sidney, Sir Henry (1529–1586)', *Oxford Dictionary of National Biography* (Oxford: Oxford University Press, 2004; online edition 2008–14), <www.oxforddnb.com/>

MacCarthy-Morrogh, Michael, *The Munster Plantation. English Migration to Southern Ireland, 1583–1641* (Oxford: Clarendon Press, 1986)

MacCoinnich, Aonghas, "'His spirit was given only to warre': Conflict and Identity in the Scottish *Gàidhealtachd* c.1580–c.1630', in Steve Murdoch and A. Mackillop, eds, *Fighting for Identity. Scottish Military Experience c.1550–1900* (Leiden: Brill, 2002), 147–53

——, "'Kingis rabellis' to 'Cuidich 'n Rìgh'? Clann Choinnich: The Emergence of a Kindred, *c.* 1475–*c.*1514', in Steve Boardman and Alasdair Ross, eds, *The Exercise of Power in Medieval Scotland, c.1200–1500* (Dublin: Four Courts Press, 2003), 175–200

——, *Plantation and Civility in the North Atlantic World: The Case of the Northern Hebrides, 1570–1639* (Leiden: Brill, 2015)

——, 'The Maritime Dimension to Scotland's 'Highland Problem', ca.1540–1630', *Maritime Communities of the North Atlantic Arc in the Early Modern Period: Journal of the North Atlantic,* ed., Alison Cathcart, special volume 12 (2019), 44–72

MacDonald, Alan R., 'James VI and the General Assembly, 1586–1618', in Julian Goodare and Michael Lynch, eds, *The Reign of James VI* (East Linton: John Donald, 2000), 170–85

——, 'Kennedy, John, fifth earl of Cassillis (1574/5–1615)', in *Oxford Dictionary of National Biography* (Oxford: Oxford University Press, 2004; online edition 2008–14), <www.oxforddnb.com/>

MacDonald, Fiona A., *Missions to the Gaels. Reformation and Counter Reformation in Ulster and the Highlands and Islands of Scotland, 1560–1760* (Edinburgh: John Donald, 2006)

——, 'MacDonald, Angus, of Dunyvaig and the Glens (*c.*1548–1613), Chief of Clan Iain Mhòr or Clan Donald South', in *Oxford Dictionary of National Biography* (Oxford: Oxford University Press, 2004; online edition 2008–14), <www.oxforddnb.com/>

MacDonald, Iain G., *Clerics and Clansmen: The Diocese of Argyll between the Twelfth and Sixteenth Centuries* (Leiden: Brill, 2013)

Macdougall, Norman, *James III: A Political Study* (Edinburgh: Donald, 1982)

——, *James IV* (Edinburgh: Tuckwell Press, 1997)

——, "'Achilles' Heel? The Earldom of Ross, the Lordship of the Isles, and the Stewart Kings, 1449–1507', in E. J. Cowan and R. A. McDonald, eds, *Alba. Celtic Scotland in the Medieval Era* (East Linton: Tuckwell Press, 2000), 248–75

Mac Ettagáin, Darren, 'The Renaissance and the Late Medieval Lordship of Tír Chonaill, 1461–1555', in William Nolan, Liam Ronayne, and Mairead Dunlevy, eds, *Donegal: History and Society. Interdisciplinary Essays on the History of an Irish County* (Dublin: Geography Publications, 1995), 203–38

MacGregor, Martin, 'The Genealogical Histories of Gaelic Scotland', in Adam Fox and Daniel Woolf, eds, *The Spoken Word. Oral Culture in Britain, 1500–1850* (Manchester: Manchester University Press, 2002), 196–239

——, 'The Statutes of Iona: Text and Context', *Innes Review* 57/2 (2006), 111–81

——, 'Gaelic Barbarity and Scottish Identity in the Later Middle Ages', in Dauvit Broun and Martin MacGregor, eds, *Mìorun Mòr nan Gall, 'The Great Ill-Will of the Lowlander'? Lowland Perceptions of the Highlands Medieval and Modern* (Glasgow: University of Glasgow, 2009), 7–48.

Macinnes, Allan I., 'Crown, Clan and Fine: The Civilising of Scottish Gaeldom, 1587–1603', *Northern Scotland* 13 (1993), 31–55

——, 'Social Mobility in Medieval and Early Modern Scottish Gaeldom: The Controvertible Evidence', *Transactions of the Gaelic Society of Inverness* 58 (1993–94), 371–405

——, *Clanship, Commerce and the House of Stuart, 1603–1788* (East Linton: Tuckwell Press, 1996)

——, *The British Revolution, 1629–1660* (Basingstoke: Palgrave Macmillan, 2005)

——, 'Making the Plantations British, 1603–38', in Steven G. Ellis and Raingard Esser, eds, *Frontiers and the Writing of History, 1500–1850* (Hannover-Laatzen: Wehrhahn, 2006), 95–125

——, *The British Confederate. Archibald Campbell, Marquess of Argyll, c.1607–1661* (Edinburgh: John Donald, 2011)

MacKenzie, Ross, *Ayr's Export Trade at the End of the 16th Century* (Ayrshire: Ayrshire Archaeological and Natural History Society, 1988)

MacKillop, Andrew, *More Fruitful than the Soil: Army, Empire and the Scottish Highlands, 1715–1815* (Edinburgh: Tuckwell Press, 2000)

Maclean-Bristol, Nicholas, *Murder Under Trust: The Crimes and Death of Sir Lachlan Mor Maclean of Duart, 1558–1598* (East Linton: Tuckwell Press, 1995)

——, 'MacDonald, James, of Dunyvaig and the Glens (d. 1565), Clan Chief', in *Oxford Dictionary of National Biography* (Oxford: Oxford University Press, 2004; online edition 2008–14), <www.oxforddnb.com/>

MacLeod, Wilson, *Divided Gaels. Gaelic Cultural Identities in Scotland and Ireland, c.1200–c.1650* (Oxford: Oxford University Press, 2004)

Macpherson, Rob, 'Stewart, Francis, First Earl of Bothwell (1562–1612)', in *Oxford Dictionary of National Biography* (Oxford: Oxford University Press, 2004; online edition 2008–14), <www.oxforddnb.com/>

MacQueen, Hector L., 'Montgomery Family (*per.* *c.*1350–*c.*1485)', in *Oxford Dictionary of National Biography* (Oxford: Oxford University Press, 2004; online edition 2008–14), <www.oxforddnb.com/>

——, and John Simmons, 'Cunningham Family (*per. c.*1340–1631)', in *Oxford Dictionary of National Biography* (Oxford: Oxford University Press, 2004; online edition 2008–14), <www.oxforddnb.com/>

Maginn, Christopher, 'O'Neill, Conn Bacach, First Earl of Tyrone (*c.*1482–1559)', in *Oxford Dictionary of National Biography* (Oxford: Oxford University Press, 2004; online edition 2008–14), <www.oxforddnb.com/>

——, '"Surrender and Regrant' in the Historiography of Sixteenth-Century Ireland', *Sixteenth Century Journal* 38/4 (2007), 955–74

——, 'Whose Island?: Sovereignty in Late Medieval and Early Modern Ireland', *Éire-Ireland* 44/3&4 (2009), 229–47

——, *William Cecil, Ireland, and the Tudor State* (Oxford: Oxford University Press, 2012)

Maley, Willy, '"Barbarisme and obdurate wilfulnesse'. Agricultural Materialism, Animal Welfare, and Irish Studies', in Sarah Covington, Vincent P. Carey, and Valerie McGowan-Doyle, eds, *Early Modern Ireland. New Sources, Methods and Perspectives* (London: Routledge, 2019), 233–53

Mancall, Peter C., *Hakluyt's Promise. An Elizabethan's Obsession for an English America* (New Haven, CT and London: Yale University Press, 2007)

Margey, Annaleigh, 'Representing Plantation Landscapes: The Case of Ulster, c.1560–1640', in James Lyttleton and Colin Rynne, eds, *Plantation Ireland: Settlement and Material Culture, c.1550–1700* (Dublin: Four Courts Press, 2009), 140–64

——, 'After the Flight: The Impact of Plantation on the Ulster Landscape', in David Finnegan, Éamonn Ó Ciardha, and Marie-Claire Harrigan, eds, *The Flight of the Earls: Imeacht na nIarlaí* (Derry: Guildhall Press, 2010), 247–58

——, 'Representing Colonial Landscapes: Early English Maps of Ulster and Virginia, 1580–1612', in B. MacCuartha, ed., *Reshaping Ireland: Colonization and Its Consequences 1550–1700 (essays presented to Nicholas Canny)* (Dublin: Four Courts Press, 2011), 61–81

Marshall, Rosalind K., 'Hamilton, James, Third Earl of Arran (1537/8?–1609)', in *Oxford Dictionary of National Biography* (Oxford: Oxford University Press, 2004; online edition 2008–14), <www.oxforddnb.com/>

Martin, Colin, and Geoffrey Parker, *The Spanish Armada* (London: Penguin, 1988)

——, 'A Maritime Dominion – Sea-Power and the Lordship', in Richard D. Oram, ed., *The Lordship of the Isles* (Leiden: Brill, 2014), 176–99

Martin, F. X., 'John, Lord of Ireland, 1185–1216', in Art Cosgrove, ed., *A New History of Ireland II: Medieval Ireland, 1169–1534* (Oxford: Clarendon Press, 1987; Oxford University Press, online 2012), 127–55

Mason, Roger A., 'Scotching the Brut', in Roger A. Mason, ed., *Scotland and England, 1286-1815* (Edinburgh: John Donald, 1987), 60–84

——, 'This Realm of Scotland Is an Empire? Imperial Ideas and Iconography in Early Renaissance Scotland', in B. E. Crawford, ed., *Church, Chronicle and Learning in Medieval and Early Renaissance Scotland* (Edinburgh: Mercat Press, 1999), 73–91

——, 'Civil Society and the Celts', in Edward J. Cowan and Richard J. Finlay, eds, *Scottish History. The Power of the Past* (Edinburgh: Edinburgh University Press, 2002), 95–120

——, 'Renaissance and Reformation: The Sixteenth Century' in, Jenny Wormald, ed., *Scotland: A History* (Oxford: Oxford University Press, 2005), 107–42

——, 'Beyond the Declaration of Arbroath: Kingship, Counsel and Consent in Late Medieval and Early Modern Scotland', in Steve Boardman and Julian Goodare, eds, *Kings, Lords and Men in Scotland and Britain, 1300–1625. Essays in Honour of Jenny Wormald* (Edinburgh: Edinburgh University Press, 2014), 265–82

——, 'Debating Britain in Seventeenth-Century Scotland: Multiple Monarchy and Scottish Sovereignty', *Journal of Scottish Historical Studies* 35/1 (2015), 1–24

Maxwell, C., ed., *Irish History from Contemporary Sources, 1509–1610* (London: G. Allen & Unwin, 1923)

McBride, Ian, *Protestantism and National Identity: Britain and Ireland, c.1650–c.1850* (Cambridge: Cambridge University Press, 1998)

McCavitt, J., 'The Flight of the Earls', *Irish Historical Studies* XXIX (1994), 159–73

——, *The Flight of the Earls* (Dublin: Gill & Macmillan, 2002)

McCorristine, Laurence, *The Revolt of Silken Thomas: A Challenge to Henry VIII* (Dublin: Wolfhound Press, 1987)

McDonald, R. Andrew, 'Matrimonial Politics and Core-Periphery Interactions in the Twelfth- and Early Thirteenth-Century Scotland', *Journal of Medieval History* 21/3 (1995), 227–47

——, 'The Manx Sea Kings and the Western Ocean: The Late Norse Isle of Man in Its North Atlantic Context, 1079–1265', in Benjamin Hudson, ed., *Studies in the Medieval Atlantic* (New York: Palgrave Macmillan, 2012)

McDonald, Theresa, 'The 'Ups and Downs' of Booleying in Achill, Co. Mayo, Ireland', in Michael O'Connell, Fergus Kelly, and James H. McAdam, eds, *Cattle in Ancient and Modern Ireland: Farming Practices, Environment and Economy* (Newcastle upon Tyne: Cambridge Scholars Publishing, 2016), 56–66

McDonnell, Hector, 'MacDonnell, Randal, First Earl of Antrim (*d.* 1636)', in *Oxford Dictionary of National Biography* (Oxford: Oxford University Press, 2004; online edition 2008–14), <www.oxforddnb.com/>

McGettigan, Darren, *Red Hugh O'Donnell and the Nine Years War in Ireland, 1594–1603* (Dublin: Four Courts Press, 2005)

McGladdery, C. A., *James II* (Edinburgh: John Donald, 1990)

McGurk, John, *The Elizabethan Conquest of Ireland. The 1590s Crisis* (Manchester: Manchester University Press, 1997)

——, *Sir Henry Docwra, 1564–1631. Derry's Second Founder* (Dublin: Four Courts Press, 2006)

McGurk, J. J. N., 'Devereux, Walter, First Earl of Essex (1539–1576)', in *Oxford Dictionary of National Biography* (Oxford: Oxford University Press, 2004; online edition 2008–14), <www.oxforddnb.com/>

McIlvaney, Liam, and Ray Ryan, eds, *Ireland and Scotland: Culture and Society, 1700–2000* (Dublin: Four Courts Press, 2005)

McLaughlin, Joseph, and Richard Hadsor, 'Select Documents XLVII: Richard Hadsor's 'Discourse' on the Irish State, 1604', *Irish Historical Studies* 30/119 (1997), 337–53

McLaughlin, Rowan, and James Lyttleton, eds, *An Archaeology of Northern Ireland 1600–1650* (Antrim: Department for the Communities, 2017)

McWhannell, Donald C., 'Ship Service and Indigenous Sea Power in the West of Scotland', *West Highland Notes & Queries: Special Maritime Issue* series 3: 1 (2000), 3–18

——, 'The Galleys of Argyll', *The Mariner's Mirror* 88/1 (2002), 14–32

——, 'Campbell of Breadalbane and Campbell of Argyll Boatbuilding Accounts 1600 to 1700', *The Mariner's Mirror* 89/4 (2003), 405–24

Merriman, Marcus, 'The Assured Scots: Scottish Collaborators with England during the Rough Wooing', *Scottish Historical Review* XLVII:1/147 (1968), 10–34

——, *The Rough Wooings: Mary Queen of Scots, 1542–1551* (East Linton: Tuckwell Press, 2000)

——, 'Hamilton, James, Second Earl of Arran, and Duke of Châtelherault in the French Nobility (*c.*1519–1575)', in *Oxford Dictionary of National Biography* (Oxford: Oxford University Press, 2004; online edition 2008–14), <www.oxforddnb.com/>

Mijers, Esther, *'News from the Republick of Letters': Scottish Students, Charles Mackie, and the United Provinces, 1650–1750* (Leiden: Brill, 2012)

Montaño, John, *The Roots of English Colonialism in Ireland* (Cambridge: Cambridge University Press, 2011)

——, 'Cultural Conflict and the Landscape of Conquest in Early Modern Ireland', *The Canadian Journal of Irish Studies* 40, special issue: Irish Environmental Humanities (2017), 120–41

Moody, T. W., 'The Revised Articles of the Ulster Plantation, 1610', *Bulletin of the Institute of Historical Research* 12 (1934–35), 178–83

——, *The Londonderry Plantation, 1609–41. The City of London and the Plantation in Ulster* (Belfast: W. Mullen and son, 1939)

——, 'Sir Thomas Phillips of Limavady, Servitor', *Irish Historical Studies* I/3 (1939), 251–72

Morgan, Hiram, 'The Colonial Venture of Sir Thomas Smith in Ulster, 1571–1575', *The Historical Journal* 28 (1985), 261–78

——, 'The End of Gaelic Ulster: A Thematic Interpretation of Events between 1534 and 1610', *Irish Historical Studies* 26/101 (1988), 8–32

——, 'Mid-Atlantic Blues', *Irish Review* 11 (1991/2), 50–5

——, *Tyrone's Rebellion. The Outbreak of the Nine Years War in Tudor Ireland* (Woodbridge: Boydell & Brewer, 1993, reprinted 1999)

——, 'Hugh O'Neill and the Nine Years' War in Tudor Ireland', *The Historical Journal* 36/1 (1993), 21–37

——, 'The Fall of Sir John Perrot', in John Guy, ed., *The Reign of Elizabeth: Court and Culture in the Last Decade* (Cambridge: Cambridge University Press, 1995), 109–25

——, 'Overmighty Officers: The Irish Lord Deputyship in the Early Modern British State', *History Ireland* 7/4 (1999), 17–21

——, 'Giraldus Cambrensis and the Tudor Conquest of Ireland', in Hiram Morgan, ed., *Political Ideology in Ireland, 1541–1641* (Dublin: Four Courts Press, 1999), 22–44

——, '"Never any realm worse governed': Queen Elizabeth and Ireland', *Transactions of the Royal Historical Society* 14 (2004), 295–308

——, 'The Deputy's Defence: Sir William Fitzwilliam's Apology on the Outbreak of the Nine Years War in Ireland', *Proceedings of the Royal Irish Academy Section C: Archaeology, Celtic Studies, History, Linguistics, Literature* 114 (2014), 181–214

Morrill, John, 'The British Problem, c.1534–1707', in Brendan Bradshaw and John Morrill, eds, *The British Problem, c.1534–1707. State Formation in the Atlantic Archipelago* (Basingstoke: Macmillan, 1996), 1–38

——, 'The War(s) of the Three Kingdoms', in G. Burgess, ed., *The New British History: Founding a Modern State, 1603–1720* (London: I. B. Tauris & co. Ltd, 1999), 65–91

Morrill, J. S., '*Uneasy Lies the Head that Wears a Crown': Dynastic Crises in Tudor and Stewart Britain, 1504–1746*, Stenton Lecture, University of Reading (Reading: University of Reading, 2005)

Morton, R. C., 'The Enterprise of Ulster', *History Today* 17/2 (1967), 114–21

Mullen, Stephen, *The Glasgow Sugar Aristocracy: Scotland and Carribean Slavery, 1775–1838* (London: University of London Press, forthcoming 2022)

Mumford Jones, Howard, 'Origins of the Colonial Idea in England', *Proceedings of the American Philosophical Society* 85/5 (1942), 448–65

Munro, Jean, 'The Lordship of the Isles', in L. Maclean, ed., *The Middle Ages in the Highlands* (Inverness: Inverness Field Club, 1981), 23–37

——, 'When Island Chiefs Came to Town', *Notes & Queries of the Society of the West Highlands and Island Historical Research* XIX (1982), 11–19

Murdoch, Steve, *Terror of the Seas?: Scottish Maritime Warfare, 1513–1713* (Leiden: Brill, 2010)

Nenadic, Stana, *Lairds and Luxury. The Highland Gentry in Eighteenth Century Scotland* (Edinburgh: John Donald, 2007)

Newfield, Timothy P., 'A Cattle Panzootic in Early Fourteenth-Century Europe', *Agricultural History Review* 57 (2009), 155–90

Nicholls, Kenneth, *Gaelic and Gaelicized Ireland in the Middle Ages* (Dublin: Gill and Macmillan, 2003)

——, 'Woodland Cover in Pre-modern Ireland', in Patrick J. Duffy, David Edwards, and Elizabeth FitzPatrick, eds, *Gaelic Ireland, c.1250–c.1650: Land, Lordship and Settlement* (Dublin: Four Courts Press, 2004), 181–206

——, 'Scottish Mercenary Kindreds in Ireland, 1250–1600', in Seán Duffy, ed., *The World of the Galloglass. Kings, Warlords and Warriors in Ireland and Scotland, 1200–1600* (Dublin: Four Courts Press, 2007), 86–105

O Buachalla, Breandán, 'James Our True King: The Ideology of Irish Royalism in the Seventeenth Century', in D. G. Boyce, ed., *Political Thought in Ireland since the Seventeenth Century* (London: Routledge, 1993), 7–35

Ó Ciardha, Éamonn, and Ó Sìochrú, Micheál, eds, *The Plantation of Ulster: Ideology and Practice* (Manchester: Manchester University Press, 2012)

Ó Doibhlin, Diarmaid, 'The Plantation of Ulster: Aspects of Gaelic Letters', in Éamonn Ó Ciardha and Micheál Ó Siochrú, eds, *The Plantation of Ulster: Ideology and Practice* (Manchester: Manchester University Press, 2012), 198–217

Ó Siochrú, Micheál, 'Foreign Involvement in the Revolt of Silken Thomas, 1534–5', *Proceedings of the Royal Irish Academy* 96 C/2 (1996), 2–66

O'Connell, Michael, Fergus Kelly, and McAdam, James H., eds, *Cattle in Ancient and Modern Ireland. Farming Practices, Environment and Economy* (Newcastle-upon-Tyne: Cambridge Scholars Publishing, 2018)

O'Connor, Thomas, and Mary Ann Lyons, *Irish migrants in Europe after Kinsale, 1602–1820* (Dublin: Four Courts Press, 2003)

——, and Mary Ann Lyons, eds, *Irish Communities in Early Modern Europe* (Dublin: Four Courts Press, 2006)

O'Neill, James, *The Nine Years War 1593–1603* (Dublin: Four Courts Press, 2017)

O'Neill, Timothy, *Merchants and Mariners in Medieval Ireland* (Dublin: Irish Academic, 1987)

O'Sullivan, Aidan, 'Crannogs in Late Medieval Gaelic Ireland, *c.*1350–*c.*1650', in Patrick J. Duffy, David Edwards, and Elizabeth FitzPatrick, eds, *Gaelic Ireland, c.1250–c.1650: Land, Lordship and Settlement* (Dublin: Four Courts Press, 2004), 397–417

——, and Breen, Colin, *Maritime Ireland: An Archaeology of Coastal Communities* (Stroud: History Press, 2007)

Ohlmeyer, Jane H., *Civil War and Restoration in the Three Stuart Kingdoms. The Career of Randal MacDonnell, Marquis of Antrim* (Cambridge: Cambridge University Press, 1993; reprinted Dublin, 2001)

——, '"Civilizinge of those rude partes': Colonisation within Britain and Ireland, 1580s–1640s', in Nicholas Canny, ed., *The Origins of Empire. British Overseas Enterprise to the Close of the Seventeenth Century: The Oxford History of the British Empire I* (Oxford: Oxford University Press, 1998), 124–47

——, 'Seventeenth-Century Ireland and the New British and Atlantic Histories', *American Historical Review* 104/2 (April 1999), 446–62

——, 'A Laboratory for Empire?: Early Modern Ireland and England Imperialism', in Kevin Kenny, ed., *Ireland and the British Empire* (Oxford: Oxford University Press, 2005), 26–60

Oram, Richard D., *Domination and Lordship: Scotland 1070–1230* (Edinburgh: Edinburgh University Press, 2011)

——, 'A Celtic Dirk at Scotland's Back? The Lordship of the Isles in Mainstream Scottish Historiography since 1828', in Richard D. Oram, ed., *The Lordship of the Isles* (Leiden: Brill, 2014), 1–39

——, 'Between a Rock and a Hard Place: Climate, Weather and the Rise of the Lordship of the Isles', in Richard D. Oram, ed., *The Lordship of the Isles* (Leiden: Brill, 2014), 40–61

——, and P. Adderley, 'Lordship and Environmental Change in Central Highland Scotland, c.1300–c.1450', *Journal of the North Atlantic* 1 (2008), 78–84

——, and W. Paul Adderley, 'Innse Gall: Culture and Environment on a Norse Frontier in the Scottish Western Isles', in Steinar Imsen, ed., *The Norwegian Domination and the Norse World,* c.*1100*–c.*1400* (Trondheim: Tapir Academic Press, 2010), 125–49

Overton, Mark, *Agricultural Revolution in England. The Transformation of the Agrarian Economy 1500–1850* (Cambridge: Cambridge University Press, 1996)

Pagden, Anthony, *The Fall of Natural Man: The American Indian and the Origins of Comparative Ethnology* (Cambridge: Cambridge University Press, 1982)

——, *Lords of All the World. Ideologies of Empire in Spain, Britain and France c.1500–c.1800* (New Haven and London: Yale University Press, 1995)

Parker, Geoffrey, 'The *Dreadnought* Revolution of Tudor England', *The Mariner's Mirror* 82/3 (1996), 269–300

Patterson, Nerys, *Cattle, Lords and Clansmen. The Social Structure of Early Ireland* (Notre Dame and London: University of Notre Dame Press, 1994)

Payne, Anthony, 'Hakluyt, Richard (1552?–1616)', in *Oxford Dictionary of National Biography* (Oxford: Oxford University Press, 2004; online edition 2008–14), <www.oxforddnb.com/>

Penman, Michael A., 'The MacDonald Lordship and the Bruce Dynasty, *c.*1306–*c.*1371', in Richard D. Oram, ed., *The Lordship of the Isles* (Leiden: Brill, 2014), 62–87

Perceval-Maxwell, Michael, *Scottish Migration to Ulster in the Reign of James I* (London: Routledge & K. Paul, 1973)

Pincus, Steven C. A., *1688: The First Modern Revolution* (New Haven and London: Yale University Press, 2009)

Pluymers, Keith, 'Taming the Wilderness in Sixteenth and Seventeenth Century Ireland and Virginia', *Environmental History* 16 (2011), 610–32

——, "Pirates' and the Problems of Plantation in Seventeenth-Century Ireland', in Peter C. Mancall and Carole Shammas, eds, *Governing the Sea in the Early Modern Era: Essays in Honor of Robert C. Ritchie* (San Marino: The Huntington Library, 2015), 79–108

Pocock, John G. A., 'British History: A Plea for a New Subject', *New Zealand Historical Journal* 8 (1974), 3–12

——, 'British History: A Plea for a New Subject', *Journal of Modern History* 74/4 (1975), 601–21

——, 'The Limits and Divisions of British History: In Search of the Unknown Subject', *American Historical Review* 87/2 (1982), 311–26

——, 'The New British History in Atlantic Perspective: An Antipodean Commentary', *American Historical Review* 104/2 (1999), 490–500

Pope, Peter, *Fish into Wine. The Newfoundland Plantation of the Seventeenth Century* (Chapel Hill: University of North Carolina Press, 2004)

Quinn, David B., 'Sir Thomas Smith (1513–1577) and the Beginnings of English Colonial Theory', *Proceedings of the American Historical Society* 89/4 (1945), 543–60

——, 'Ireland and Sixteenth Century European Expansion', in T. Desmond Williams, ed., *Historical Studies* I (London: Bowes & Bowes, 1958), 21–32

——, 'The Munster Plantation: Problems and Opportunities', *Journal of Cork Historical & Archaeological Society* 71 (1966), 19–40

——, 'Renaissance Influences in English Colonisation: The Prothero Lecture', *Transactions of the Royal Historical Society* fifth series 26 (1976), 73–92

——, 'A Vewe of the Present State of Ireland', in A. C. Hamilton et al., ed., *The Spenser Encyclopaedia* (London: Routledge, 1990), 713–15

——, and K. W. Nicholls, 'Ireland in 1534', in T. W. Moody, F. X. Martin, and F. J. Byrne, eds, *A New History of Ireland Volume III: Early Modern Ireland 1534–1691* (Oxford: Clarendon Press, 1979; Oxford University Press, online 2011), 1–38

——, and A. N. Ryan, *England's Sea Empire, 1550–1642* (London, 1983)

Rapple, Rory, 'Gilbert, Sir Humphrey (1537–1583)', in *Oxford Dictionary of National Biography* (Oxford: Oxford University Press, 2004; online edition 2008–14), <www.oxforddnb.com/>

——, *Martial Power and Elizabethan Political Culture: Military Men in England and Ireland, 1558–1594* (Cambridge: Cambridge University Press, 2009)

——, 'Writing about Violence in the Tudor Kingdoms', *The Historical Journal* 54/3 (2011), 829–54

——, 'Brinkmanship and Bad Luck: Ireland, the Nine Years' War and the Succession', in Susan Doran and Paulina Kewes, eds, *Doubtful and Dangerous. The Question of Succession in Late Elizabeth England* (Manchester: Manchester University Press, 2014), 236–56

Reeve, John, 'Britain or Europe? The Context of Early Modern English History: Political and Cultural, Economic and Social, Naval and Military', in Glenn Burgess, ed., *The New British History: Founding a Modern State, 1603–1715* (London: I. B Tauris & Co. Ltd, 1999), 287–312

Ridel, Élisabeth, 'From Scotland to Normandy: The Celtic Sea Route of the Vikings', in Beverley Ballin Smith, Simon Taylor, and Gareth Williams, eds, *West over Sea: Studies in Scandinavian Sea-Borne Expansion and Settlement before 1300: A Festschrift in Honour of Dr Barbara E. Crawford* (Leiden: Brill, 2007), 81–94

Ritchie, Pamela E., *Mary of Guise in Scotland, 1548–1560: A Political Career* (East Linton: Tuckwell Press, 2002)

Rixon, Denis, *The West Highland Galley* (Edinburgh: Birlinn, 1998)

Roberts, R. Julian, 'Dee, John (1527–1609), *Mathematician, Astrologer, and Antiquary*', *Oxford Dictionary of National Biography* (Oxford: Oxford University Press, 2004; online edition 2008–14), <www.oxforddnb.com>

Robertson, Barry, *Lordship and Power in the North of Scotland. The Noble House of Huntly, 1603–1690* (Edinburgh: John Donald, 2011)

Robinson, A. H. W., *Marine Cartography in Britain* (Leicester: Leicester University Press, 1962)

Robinson, Philip, *The Plantation of Ulster: British Settlement in an Irish Landscape, 1600–1670* (Belfast: Ulster Historical Foundation, 1984; reprinted 2000)

Roddie, Alan, 'Jacob, the Diver', *The Mariner's Mirror* 62/3 (1976), 253–69

Rodger, N. A. M., *The Safeguard of the Sea. A Naval History of Britain, 660–1649* (London: Penguin, 2004)

——, 'Queen Elizabeth and the Myth of Sea-Power in English History', *Transactions of the Royal Historical Society* 14 (2004), 153–74

Roebuck, P., 'The Making of an Ulster Great Estate: The Chichesters, Barons of Belfast and Viscounts of Carrickfergus, 1599–1648', *Proceedings of the Royal Irish Academy. Section C: Archaeology, Celtic Studies, History, Linguistics, Literature* 79 (1970), 1–25

Rorke, Martin, 'The Scottish Herring Trade, 1470–1600', *Scottish Historical Review* LXXXIV/2 (2005), 149–65

——, 'Trade and Traders: Edinburgh's Sixteenth-Century Exporting Community', *Historical Research* 81/213 (2007), 447–62

Rose, Susan, 'Mathematics and the Art of Navigation: The Advance of Scientific Seamanship in Elizabethan England', *Transactions of the Royal Historical Society* sixth series 14 (2004), 175–84

Roulston, William, 'Scottish Settlement and Society in Plantation Ulster, 1610–40', in David Edwards with Simon Egan, eds, *The Scots in Early Stuart Ireland. Union and Separation in Two Kingdoms* (Manchester: Manchester University Press, 2016), 95–115

Royle, S. A., 'Island Life Off Co. Down: The Copeland Islands', *Ulster Journal of Archaeology* third series 57 (1994), 177–82

Sacks, David Harris, 'Discourses of Western Planting: Richard Hakluyt and the Marking of the Atlantic World', in Peter C. Mancall, ed., *The Atlantic World and Virginia, 1550–1624* (Chapel Hill: University of North Carolina Press, 2007), 410–53

Scarisbrick, J. J., *Henry VIII* (New Haven and London: Yale University Press, 1987)

Scott Pearson, A. F., 'Alumni of St Andrews and the Settlement of Ulster', *Ulster Journal of Archaeology* third series 14 (1951), 7–14

Sellar, W. D. H., 'The Earliest Campbells – Norman, Briton or Gael?', *Scottish Studies* XVII (1977), 109–25

Senior, W., 'The Rutter of the Sea', *The Mariner's Mirror* 6/8 (1920), 243–46

Sheehy, Maurice P., 'The Bull *Laudabiliter*: A Problem in Medieval Diplomatique and History', *Journal of the Galway Archaeological and Historical Society* 29:3/4 (1961), 45–70

Shuger, Debora, 'Irishmen, Aristocrats, and Other White Barbarians', *Renaissance Quarterly* 50/1 (1997), 494–525

Simmons, John, 'Kennedy, Gilbert, Fourth Earl of Cassillis (*c.*1541–1576)', in *Oxford Dictionary of National Biography* (Oxford: Oxford University Press, 2004; online edition 2008–14), <www.oxforddnb.com/>

Simms, Katharine, 'Guesting and Feasting in Gaelic Ireland', *The Journal of the Royal Society of Antiquaries of Ireland* 108 (1978), 67–100

——, *From Kings to Warlords* (Woodbridge: Boydell & Brewer, 1987, reprinted 2000)

——, *Gaelic Ulster in the Middle Ages. History, Culture and Society* (Dublin: Four Courts Press, 2020)

Skinner, Quentin, 'Sir Thomas More's *Utopia* and the Language of Renaissance Humanism', in Anthony Pagden, ed., *The Languages of Political Theory in Early Modern Europe* (Cambridge: Cambridge University Press, 1987), 123–57

Slavin, Philip, 'The Great Bovine Pestilence and Its Economic and Environmental Consequences in England and Wales, 1318–50', *Economic History Review* 65/4 (2012), 1239–66

Smith, Brendan, *Crisis and Survival in Late Medieval Ireland: The English of Louth and Their Neighbours, 1330–1450* (Oxford: Oxford University Press, 2013)

Smout, T. C., ed., *Exploring Environmental History: Selected Essays* (Edinburgh: Edinburgh University Press, 2009)

——, ed., *Scottish Woodland History* (Edinburgh: Scottish Cultural Press, 1997)

——, MacDonald, Alan, R., and Watson, Fiona, eds, *A History of the Native Woodland of Scotland, 1500–1920* (Edinburgh: Edinburgh University Press, 2005)

Smuts, R. Malcolm, 'States, Monarchs and Dynastic Transitions: The Political Thought of John Hayward', in Susan Doran and Paulina Kewes, eds, *Doubtful and Dangerous. The Question of Succession in Late Elizabeth England* (Manchester: Manchester University Press, 2014), 276–94

Smyth, William J., *Map-Making, Landscapes and Memory; A Geography of Colonial and Early Modern Ireland, c.1530–1750* (Cork: Cork University Press, 2006)

Steer, K. A., and J. W. M. Bannerman, *Late Medieval Monumental Sculpture in the West Highlands* (Edinburgh: Royal Commission on the Ancient and Historical Monuments of Scotland, 1977)

Stevenson, David, *Highland Warrior. Alasdair MacColla and the Civil Wars* (Edinburgh: John Donald, 1980; reprinted 2003)

——, 'Campbell, Archibald, Marquess of Argyll (1605x7–1661), Nobleman and Politician', in *Oxford Dictionary of National Biography* (Oxford: Oxford University Press, 2004; online edition 2008–14), <www.oxforddnb.com/>

Stevenson, Katie, *Power and Propaganda: Scotland 1306–1488* (Edinburgh: Edinburgh University Press, 2014)

Taylor, E. G. R., *Tudor Geography, 1485–1583* (London: Methuen and Co., 1930)

——, *Late Tudor and Early Stuart Geography 1583–1650. A Sequel to Tudor Geography, 1485–1583* (London: Methuen and Co., 1934)

Thirsk, Joan, *England's Agricultural Regions and Agrarian History, 1500–1750* (Basingstoke: Macmillan, 1987)

Thomas, Andrea, *Princelie Majestie: The Court of James V of Scotland, 1528–1542* (Edinburgh: John Donald, 2005)

Thomas, Keith, *Man and the Natural World. Changing Attitudes in England 1500–1800* (London: Allen Lane, 1984)

——, *In Pursuit of Civility: Manners and Civilisation in Early Modern England* (New Haven: Yale University Press, 2018)

Thornton, Helen, 'Hugo Grotius and the Freedom of the Seas', *International Journal of Maritime History* 16/2 (2004), 17–38

Treadwell, Victor, 'The Survey of Armagh and Tyrone, 1622', *Ulster Journal of Archaeology* third series XXIII (1960), 126–37

——, 'The Survey of Armagh and Tyrone, 1622 (continued)', *Ulster Journal of Archaeology* third series XXVII (1964), 140–54

——, 'Sir John Perrot and the Irish Parliament of 1585–6', *Proceedings of the Royal Irish Academy Section C: Archaeology, Celtic Studies, History, Linguistics, Literature* 85 (1985), 259–308

——, 'Richard Hadsor and the Authorship of 'Advertisements for Ireland', 1622/3', *Irish Historical Studies* 30/119 (1997), 305–36

Trim, D. J. B., 'Medieval and Early-Modern Inshore, Estuarine, Riverine and Lacustrine Warfare', in D. J. B. Trim and Mark Charles Fissel, eds, *Amphibious Warfare 1000–1750. Commerce, State Formation and European Expansion* (Leiden: Brill, 2006), 357–419

Turgeon, L., 'Codfish, Consumption and Colonisation. The Creation of the French Atlantic World during the Sixteenth Century', in C. A. Williams, ed., *Bridging the Early Modern Atlantic World. People, Products and Practices on the Move* (Farnham: Ashgate, 2009), 33–56

Turnock, David, *The Making of the Scottish Rural Landscape* (Aldershot: Scolar Press, 1995)

Turvey, Roger, 'Perrot, Sir John (1528–1592)', in *Oxford Dictionary of National Biography* (Oxford: Oxford University Press, 2004; online edition 2008–14), <www.oxforddnb.com/>

Tytler, P. F., *History of Scotland*, 9 vols (Edinburgh: W. Tait, 1828)

Ullman, Walter, 'This Realm of England is an Empire', *Journal of Ecclesiastical History* 30/2 (1979), 175–203

Van Ittersum, M. J., 'Mare Liberum versus the Propriety of the Seas? The Debate between Hugo Grotius (1583–1645) and William Welwood (1552–1624) and Its Impact on Anglo-Scottish-Dutch Fishery Disputes in the Second Decade of the Seventeenth Century', *Edinburgh Law Review* 10 (2006), 239–76

Wallerstein, Immanuel, *The Modern World-System: Capitalist Agriculture and the Origins of the European World-Economy in the Sixteenth Century* (New York: Academic Press, 1974)

——, *The Modern World System II: Mercantilism and the Consolidation of the European World-Economy, 1600–1750* (New York: Academic Press, 1980)

——, *The Modern World-System III: The Second Era of Great Expansion of the Capitalist World-Economy, 1730–1840* (San Diego: Academic Press, 1989)

Warner, R., 'On Crannogs and Kings (Part I)', *Ulster Journal of Archaeology* third series 57 (1994), 61–69

Watson, Fiona and Dixon, Piers W., *A History of Scotland's Landscapes* (Edinburgh: Historic Environment Scotland, 2018)

Weikel, Ann, 'Mary I (1516–1558)', in *Oxford Dictionary of National Biography* (Oxford: Oxford University Press, 2004; online edition 2008–2014), <www.oxforddnb.com/>

Williamson, Arthur, 'Scots, Indians and Empire: The Scottish Politics of Civilization, 1519–1609', *Past and Present* 150 (February, 1996), 46–83

Withington, Phil, *Society in Early Modern England. The Vernacular Origins of Some Powerful Ideas* (Cambridge: Polity, 2010)

——, 'Plantation and Civil Society', in Éamonn Ó Ciardha and Micheál Ó Siochrú, eds, *The Plantation of Ulster. Ideology and Practice* (Manchester: Manchester University Press, 2012), 55–77

Wormald, Jenny, *Court, Kirk and Community: Scotland, 1470–1625* (Edinburgh: Edward Arnold, 1981)

——, 'James VI and I, *Basilikon Doron* and the *Trew Law of Free Monarchies*: the Scottish Context and the English Translation', in Linda Levy Peck, ed., *The Mental World of the Jacobean Court* (Cambridge: Cambridge University Press, 1991), 36–54

——, 'The Creation of Britain: Multiple Kingdoms or Core and Colonies?', *Transactions of the Royal Historical Society* sixth series 2 (1992), 175–94

——, 'James VI, James I and the Identity of Britain', in Brendan Bradshaw and John Morrill, eds, *The British Problem, c.1534–1707. State Formation in the Atlantic Archipelago* (Basingstoke: Macmillan, 1996), 148–71

——, 'Confidence and Perplexity: The Seventeenth Century', in Jenny Wormald, ed., *Scotland, A History* (Oxford: Oxford University Press, 2005), 143–76

——, 'The Headaches of Monarchy: Kingship and the Kirk in the Early Seventeenth Century', in Julian Goodare and Alasdair A. MacDonald, eds, *Sixteenth-Century Scotland. Essays in Honour of Michael Lynch* (Leiden: Brill, 2008), 365–94

——, 'James VI and I (1566–1625), King of Scotland, England and Ireland', in *Oxford Dictionary of National Biography* (Oxford: Oxford University Press, 2004; online edition 2008–14), <www.oxforddnb.com/>

——, 'The 'British' Crown, the Earls and the Planation of Ulster', in Éamonn Ó Ciardha and Micheál Ó Siochrú, eds, *The Plantation of Ulster: Ideology and Practice* (Manchester: Manchester University Press, 2012), 18–32

Worthington, David, *Scots in the Habsburg Service, 1618–1648* (Leiden: Brill, 2004)

——, *British and Irish Experiences and Impressions of Central Europe, c.1560–1688* (Farnham: Ashgate, 2012)

Young, G. V. C., *The Hebridean Birlinn, Nyvaig and Lymphad* (Peel: The Mansk Svenska Publishing Co. Ltd, 1997)

Unpublished theses

Crawford, Ross, 'Warfare in the West Highlands and Isles of Scotland, *c.* 1544–1615' (University of Glasgow, PhD, 2016)

Egan, Simon, 'The Resurgence of Gaelic Power in Ireland and Scotland and Its Wider Impact, *c.*1350–1513' (University College Cork, PhD, 2016)

Haggerty, Charles, "Unredeemed by any one single virtue'?: Esmé Stuart's Political Career in Scotland, 1579–1583' (University of Strathclyde, MRes, 2011)

Mitchell, James A., 'The O'Donnell Lords of Tyrconnell, 1537–1603: A Study of Their Efforts to Maintain Their Local Power in Sixteenth-Century Tudor Ireland' (University of Strathclyde, PhD, 2015)

Pluymers, Keith, 'Colonizing Lands and Landscapes in the English Atlantic, c.1580–c.1640' (University of Southern California, PhD, 2015)

Raven, John, 'Medieval Landscapes and Lordship in South Uist' (University of Glasgow, PhD, 2005)

Archaeological reports

Horning, A., and Brannon, N., 'Summary report on excavations at Goodland, Co. Antrim', Unpublished excavation report for Department of Communities: Historical Environment Division Lic. AE/07/67 (2007), 13–17

Northern Ireland Sites and Monument Record Ref: Ant 041:003 at <http://www.bnfc.org.uk/BNFC/Islandmagee.html>

Index

Archipelagic Studies

Series Editors

Abstract
This series focuses on the islands of the North Atlantic archipelago and on the water that surrounds those islands from pre-history through to the eighteenth century. Moving beyond traditional national histories, the series highlights research that examines localities or regions bounded by geography and transnational studies of the insular world, and connections between peoples and societies within the archipelago and their neighbours to the south (Brittany) and the north (Norway and beyond). Archipelagic Studies explores a range of themes (landscape, society, culture, language, religion, trade networks) and incorporates a number of disciplines and approaches (archaeology, heritage, history, literature, historical ecology, environmental, marine, political, social).

Vol. 1 Alison Cathcart
Plantations by Land and Sea: North Channel Communities of the Atlantic Archipelago c.1550-1625
2022. ISBN 978-1-78997-378-5

www.ingramcontent.com/pod-product-compliance
Ingram Content Group UK Ltd.
Pitfield, Milton Keynes, MK11 3LW, UK
UKHW021008120926
8556IPUK00028B/193

9 781789 973785